HP

MW01264423

The McGraw-Hill Series on Computer Communications (Selected Titles)

In order to receive additional information on these or any other McGraw-Hill titles, in the United States please call 1-800-822-8158. In other countries, contact your local McGraw-Hill representative.

HP OpenView:
A Manager's Guide

Jill Huntington-Lee
Kornel Terplan
Jeffrey A. Gibson

0 8 JUN 1998

McGraw-Hill
New York San Francisco Washington, D.C. Auckland Bogotá
Caracas Lisbon London Madrid Mexico City Milan
Montreal New Delhi San Juan Singapore
Sydney Tokyo Toronto

Library of Congress Cataloging-in-Publication Data
Huntington-Lee, Jill.
    HP's OpenView : a manager's guide / Jill Huntington-Lee, Kornel
Terplan, Jeffrey A. Gibson
        p.   cm. — (McGraw-Hill series on computer communications)
    Includes index.
    ISBN 0-07-031382-2
    1. Computer networks—Management. 2. OpenView. 3. TCP/IP
(Computer network protocol) 4. Client/server computing.
I. Terplan, Kornel.   II. Gibson, Jeffrey A.   III. Title.
IV. Series.
TK5105.5.H86   1996
005.7'13—dc21   96-39021
                                              CIP

McGraw-Hill

A Division of The McGraw·Hill Companies

Copyright © 1997 by The McGraw-Hill Companies, Inc. All rights reserved. Printed in
the United States of America. Except as permitted under the United States Copyright
Act of 1976, no part of this publication may be reproduced or distributed in any form or
by any means, or stored in a data base or retrieval system, without the prior written
permission of the publisher.

    3 4 5 6 7 8 9 DOC/DOC 9 0 0 9 8 7

ISBN 0-07-031382-2

*The sponsoring editor for this book was Steve Elliot, the editing supervisor was Sally
Glover, and the production supervisor was Pamela Pelton. This book was set in New
Century Schoolbook. It was composed in Hightstown, N.J.*

Printed and bound by R. R. Donnelly & Sons Company.

McGraw-Hill books are available at special quantity discounts to use as premiums
and sales promotions, or for use in corporate training programs. For more information,
please write to the Director of Special Sales, McGraw-Hill, 11 West 19th Street,
New York, NY 10011. Or contact your local bookstore.

Product or brand names used in this book may be trade names or trademarks. Where
we believe that there may be proprietary claims to such trade names or trademarks,
the name has been used with an initial capital or it has been capitalized in the style
used by the name claimant. Regardless of the capitalization used, all such names have
been used in an editorial manner without any intent to convey endorsement of or other
affiliation with the name claimant. Neither the author nor the publisher intends to
express any judgment as to the validity or legal status of any such proprietary claims.

Information contained in this work has been obtained by McGraw-Hill from
sources believed to be reliable. However, neither McGraw-Hill nor its authors
guarantee the accuracy or completeness of any information published herein
and neither McGraw-Hill nor its authors shall be responsible for any errors,
omissions, or damages arising out of use of this information. This work is published with the understanding that McGraw-Hill and its authors are supply-
ing information but are not attempting to render engineering or other
professional services. If such services are required, the assistance of an appropriate professional should be sought.

Contents

Foreword

I first heard of OpenView in 1990. At that time, it was a pretty well kept secret. It was an unknown in the network management marketplace. Certainly it was a good idea, but everyone knew that other companies already had the market pretty well locked up. Who did Hewlett-Packard think it was—trying to take on some of the giants of the industry?

Time has clearly shown the world of network and systems management who HP is and what its OpenView product can do. Very simply, OpenView came out of nowhere and succeeded in challenging and defeating one competitor after another. Today, OpenView is the leading platform for network and systems management throughout the world. It is no longer a single product focused merely on network management. OpenView has grown and expanded to the point that it represents an entire suite of products, addressing a broad spectrum of the management equation. Becoming familiar with OpenView's capabilities is no longer a matter of merely sitting down with an account representative for an hour or so over a cup of coffee. Even within Hewlett-Packard itself, there are relatively few people who can explain the functionality of each part of the product set.

The name OpenView is known throughout the network and systems management community. Unfortunately, too many people know little more than the name, or what they may have read about it in the trade press. In many cases, even managers in companies that already have OpenView know very little about it or the capabilities of its various components. Until now there has not been a source that managers could turn to for an honest, objective, comprehensive review of the capabilities of OpenView. Certainly HP (or any of its competitors) could not be considered an objective source for this information.

When I learned of the plans that Jill Huntington-Lee, Kornel Terplan, and Jeffrey Gibson had to develop this book, I was pleased. I was glad that finally someone was willing to take up the rather daunting task of providing the industry with an objective perspective on the OpenView suite of products. I felt that this could help people to better understand this piece of the technology puzzle. While I was pleased at the prospect of the production of this book, at the same time I was somewhat guarded in my enthusiasm. Writing any book is challenging. Writing a book that would adequately address the various facets of OpenView would be particularly so. The authors would have to guard against dealing with the subject too lightly, or else the book would become superficial. Similarly, they needed to avoid taking the reader down into the bowels of the software, in arcane discussions of its inner workings. Only time would tell whether they could succeed.

After many months of hard work, writing, and rewriting several chapters at a time, this book has finally become a reality. I have to say that the authors have done an excellent job of meeting the challenge of striking a balance in the level of detail covered in the material. The result is an excellent work that provides the reader with a balanced, objective description of OpenView and its capabilities. I am not aware of any other place where a manager can find such a thorough and objective perspective on the capabilities of OpenView. This book should prove to be a valuable resource for anyone needing to become familiar with OpenView and its strengths and weaknesses relative to its competitors.

I frequently encourage managers to stop reinventing the wheel. In today's business environment, it is essential that we try not to make things any harder for ourselves than need be. Things are hard enough without us making them worse. In that vein, one particular point that I try to impress upon people is that whenever possible they should leverage the work of others. This book provides managers with an excellent opportunity for that kind of leverage. This book is the result of hundreds of hours of research. Any manager needing to learn about OpenView (and its competitors) can save a tremendous amount of time with this book. That need might arise as part of a product selection process, or simply the need to know more about a product that a company already has in-house.

Another important message that I try to communicate to audiences and clients is that implementing a management platform like OpenView is a major undertaking. The product itself is cheap. However, to take full advantage of it, and to realize its benefits, it requires a company to commit to a major systems integration effort. Total expenditures may range from several hundred thousand dollars to a few million dollars. Decisions of this type are not to be made lightly. This book will make readers much more qualified to face these decisions.

> Rick Sturm, OpenView Forum cofounder,
> former president, and currently a member of
> the board of directors of the OpenView users'
> group, writes monthly columns on network
> and systems management for
> *Communications Week*. In addition,
> he is a consultant on network
> and systems management.

Introduction

Organizations are downsizing their information systems. While most of these organizations spend considerable effort selecting operating systems and client/server applications, relatively few have given the same amount of serious consideration to how those systems can be managed effectively. Many of the same organizations have experienced dramatic growth in the number of local area networks (LANs) and interconnected LANs, or internetworks, built upon the Transmission Control Protocol/Internet Protocol (TCP/IP). Now that the Unix operating system, client/server computing, and TCP/IP internetworking are becoming mainstream, organizations are being forced to confront the open systems and network management problem.

Hewlett-Packard's HP OpenView product family is the commercial platform of choice for managing TCP/IP networks and heterogeneous client/server systems, and its popularity is expected to increase. Many organizations, however, misunderstand HP OpenView's capabilities and limitations, and underestimate the implementation effort involved in creating a comprehensive systems and network management solution. Hence, the need for this book. The goal of this book is to clarify HP OpenView's capabilities and to provide guidance to help network managers effectively deploy the product. It is our hope that readers will keep and use this book as they expand HP OpenView's role in managing their growing TCP/IP networks and heterogeneous client/server systems.

This book was written with two general audiences in mind:

- Organizations that have not yet invested in an open management platform.
- Organizations that have already purchased one of the HP OpenView products.

This book can help guide the product selection process by explaining what customers can expect from HP OpenView, what the product can and cannot do, the implementation effort involved, and how to justify the cost of purchasing HP OpenView. Readers will find comparisons between HP OpenView and alternative products to be particularly useful.

This book provides implementation advice and examples of how to integrate HP OpenView with HP value-added and third-party applications. The book also will help current HP OpenView customers plan for the future, as Hewlett-Packard unveils more of its network and systems management strategy.

The following paragraphs provide a chapter-by-chapter summary of the contents and benefits of this book.

Part I: Introduction

Why HP OpenView? Chapter 1 describes HP OpenView's purpose—managing internet protocol (IP) data networks—and positions OpenView among its chief competitors. The goal of this chapter is to help organizations decide whether HP OpenView is an appropriate product to deploy in their networks.

HP OpenView and Standards. Chapter 2 outlines HP OpenView's chief advantages: openness, flexibility, and adherence to standards. This chapter is particularly helpful to novice administrators or upper-level managers seeking to understand the greater context of standards-based network management within which HP OpenView operates.

Part II: Network Management

An Open Framework. Chapter 3 highlights integration with value-added products as fundamental to fashioning OpenView into a total solution. The HP OpenView Solution Framework, Tornado, and other milestones in OpenView product evolution are discussed. The chapter closes with an explanation of OpenView NNM's evolution toward distributed management.

Using HP OpenView Network Node Manager. Chapter 4 focuses on the basic features of HP OpenView NNM, the most widely used product in the OpenView suite. Chapter 4 is of particular interest to customers who already have invested in OpenView. Key NNM processes are described, including processes and filters supporting distributed management.

Data Collection using HP OpenView. Chapter 5 provides a hands-on guide for beginners seeking to exploit OpenView's outstanding data collection capabilities, as well as information on how to combine OpenView with other HP data collection tools, including HP NetMetrix, HP LanProbe, and HP EASE.

Diagnosing Faults. Chapter 6 assists network administrators in diagnosing faults using third-party applications that supplement HP OpenView. The emphasis in this chapter is on automating the fault diagnostic and fault resolution process.

Fine-Tuning the Fault Management Process. Chapter 7 builds upon the previous chapters and describes how to fine-tune the fault management process. The emphasis in this chapter is on using NerveCenter to better support more efficient "management by exception" techniques. Integration of trouble ticketing systems with HP OpenView NNM is briefly discussed.

Analyzing Data. Chapter 8 assists network administrators in leveraging OpenView technology further by combining it with third-party applications. The chapter describes automated performance reporting tools and services for measuring overall network health using baselining techniques. Baselining and capacity planning using NetSys for Cisco-routed networks is discussed. A comparison to out-tasking services is provided.

Maintaining the Network. Chapter 9 highlights third-party applications that can be launched from OpenView to support configuration of network devices. This chapter also describes how third-party applications can be used to extend the reach of HP OpenView beyond Internet Protocol (IP) networks into IBM SNA and other non-IP protocols.

Telecommunications Management. Chapter 10 describes HP OpenView DM product and its applicability for managing large, global networks such as those maintained by telecommunications companies. The chapter also includes example implementations of HP OpenView DM managing PBXs and wireless networks.

Part III: Unix Systems Administration

Unix and NT Fault and Performance Management. Chapter 11 describes the critical, complex problem of automating Unix fault and performance monitoring across the enterprise. The chapter describes several important HP OpenView offerings that address Unix systems management, and compares those products with competing offerings.

HP IT/Administration. Chapter 12 describes the emerging technologies for automating Unix data center operations, and how HP's OpenView IT/Administration fits into this area. Competing products are compared to HP's offerings.

Part IV: Interconnected Workgroup Management

OpenView Workgroup Node Manager and Other HP Workgroup Products. Chapter 13 helps network administrators understand the relationship between OpenView Workgroup Manager (HP's Windows-based management product) and the more widely known Unix-based OpenView Network Node Manager. Similarities as well as differences between the two OpenView products are described, as well as third-party applications for the Windows environment. HP IT/Administration for Workgroups and other HP workgroup-related products are described, including HP's directions for supporting management of Windows NT environments.

HP OpenView and Internet and Intranet Management. Chapter 14 describes the current capabilities of the HP OpenView product suite for managing Internet/Web Servers. Competing alternatives also are discussed. A brief tutorial on Web technology is included.

Part V: HP OpenView Derivatives

IBM NetView for AIX (SystemView AIX). Chapter 15 describes how IBM initially based its NetView for AIX on HP OpenView code, but is now departing from that code base. The chapter points out both the similarities and differences between HP and IBM's product strategies.

Digital PolyCenter on NetView. Chapter 16 describes how Digital Equipment Corporation (DEC) is using IBM NetView for AIX as the basis for its network management offering, and points out the similarities and differences between HP and Digital product suites.

NCR OneVision and OperationsAdvantage; AT&T OneVision. Chapter 17 describes how NCR is using HP OpenView as the basis for its OneVision network management offering, and IT/Operations for the NCR systems management offering, OperationsAdvantage. A discussion of AT&T OneVision is provided.

Part VI: Looking Ahead

Distributed Management and Data Integration. Chapter 18 describes HP OpenView's evolution toward distributed management. This chapter points out a longstanding weakness of HP OpenView: its inability to integrate management data from multiple applications into a single repository. Enhancements in NNM 4.1 that address this problem are described. Third-party products from Micromuse and Bridgeway are discussed as alternatives for overcoming remaining OpenView limitations. HP OpenView Event Correlation Services (ECS) technology for distributed event correlation is described, as is the HP MetaSchema for Data Integration.

Cost-Justifying HP OpenView. Chapter 19 provides general cost-justification ideas, along with guidelines for estimating the costs associated with deploying an OpenView-based solution.

The HP OpenView User's Forum. Chapter 20 discusses the role of the HP OpenView User's Forum in supporting OpenView customers and influencing HP OpenView product enhancement plans. This chapter provides information on Forum conferences and Forum-sponsored surveys.

To help show how HP OpenView fits into the real world of network management, four case studies are presented, each describing how HP OpenView is used to manage a different network topology.

Finally, there is a comprehensive list of acronyms (spelled out) used throughout the book, and a list of names and addresses of vendors cited in this book.

Introduction

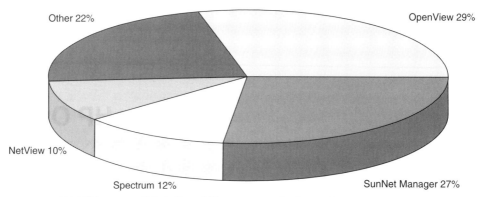

Figure 1.1 1994 Shipments of Unix-Based Management Platforms. Source: IDC.

- Open application programming interfaces (APIs), allowing for the addition of third-party and customer-written software to extend HP OpenView's capabilities and to ensure flexibility in the face of uncertain future requirements.

- A friendly graphical user interface (GUI) supporting point-and-click manipulation of management data.

All products in the HP OpenView family share these traits to some degree. But these traits are not unique to HP OpenView. Many competing products overlap with OpenView in both functionality and approach. As a result, organizations must give careful thought to deciding whether HP OpenView is an appropriate management solution—indeed, the best solution—for managing critical networked systems.

The first step toward making the right choice is to understand what HP OpenView is and how it compares with the competition.

The HP OpenView Product Set

Many in the network management industry use the term "HP OpenView" when referring to HP OpenView Network Node Manager (NNM), HP's Unix-based offering for managing IP networks. But NNM is only one of many products carrying the OpenView family name.

HP OpenView includes more than a dozen packages, as listed in Table 1.1. Products in the HP OpenView family span the two broad areas of network management and systems management. Integration of third-party applications into the OpenView framework extend this reach into the areas of database management and applications management.

Table 1.2 provides general comparative definitions of network and systems management according to managed objects, functions, and processes. For a more detailed discussion of the demarcation line between network and systems management, see (Terplan 1995).

Core HP OpenView products that address network management include the following:

- HP OpenView for Windows—Workgroup Node Manager (WNM)

- HP OpenView Network Node Manager (NNM)
- HP OpenView Distributed Management (DM) Platform

Core HP OpenView products that address systems management include:

- HP IT/Operations
- HP MeasureWare/PerfView
- HP IT/Administration

These core products are designed to support value-added HP and third-party provided applications. As such, they are *platforms* upon which customers can build more complete management solutions. Note that Table 1.1 lists HP management applications that work in conjunction with these six core HP OpenView products.

Each of these core products is described in detail in subsequent chapters. The following paragraphs provide brief overviews of these core products and describe their positions among the competition.

HP OpenView for Windows—Workgroup Node Manager

At the LAN level, HP offers HP OpenView for Windows—Workgroup Node Manager (WNM). HP targets WNM sales at networks with 250 nodes or fewer. In practice, WNM typically is used to manage between 50 and 100 (IP/IPX) nodes, including servers, critical workstations, bridges, hubs, and perhaps several routers.

WNM is referred to as a network management platform because it provides application programming interfaces (APIs) for adding third-party or user-written software to the WNM core. Like Network Node Manager, WNM supports IP network node discovery and mapping, as well as SNMP MIB browsing and trap handling. (Chapter 2 provides a detailed discussion of SNMP, SNMP MIBs, and traps.) Unlike Network Node Manager, WNM supports Novell/IPX node

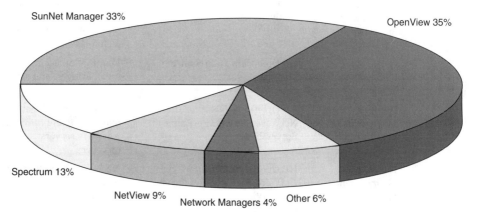

Figure 1.2 1H95 Shipments of Unix-based Management Platforms. Source: IDC.

Table 1.1. HP OpenView Product Family

Product type	Product name	Area of focus
Network management platform and core product	HP OpenView for Windows— Workgroup Node Manager	Single-segment IP LANs, several interconnected LANs on a single campus; runs on DOS/Windows-based PCs
Network management platform and core product	HP OpenView Network Node Manager (includes SNMP Platform)	Large sites with interconnected LANs (TCP/IP Internetworks) on one or more campuses; includes SNMP Platform; runs on HP-UX or SunOS/Solaris workstations
Network management developer's kit	HP OpenView SNMP Developer's Kit	Development environment for creating applications to manage SNMP-TCP/IP devices
Network management platform	HP OpenView SNMP Platform	IP network node discovery and mapping, SNMP MIB browsing, and SNMP trap handling, GUI.
Network management platform and core product	HP OpenView Distributed Management Platform (DM)	Globas, multiprotocol networks (TCP/IP, OSI, legacy); runs on HP-UX
Network management developer's kit	HP OpenView Distributed Management Developer's Kit	Development environment for creating applications to manage SNMP-TCP/IP, CMIP-OSI, and other heterogeneous networks
Network management developer's kit	HP OpenView HARMONi	Development environment for writing service inventory, management, billing & service order management, and other telco-oriented customer network management applications
Network management application	HP NetMetrix	Software-based performance monitor for internetworks; supports RMON
Network management application	HP OpenView History Analyzer/UX	Network capacity planning tool for analyzing historical data; based on HP's EASE sampling technology
Network management application	HP OpenView Interconnect Manager/UX	Monitors and controls HP hubs, bridges, and routers
Network management application	HP OpenView NNM for NetWare Servers (Peregrine ServerView)	NNM-based application for monitoring and configuring NetWare servers; supports IPX discovery
Network management application	HP OpenView NNM for NetWare Stations (Peregrine StationView)	NNM-based application for monitoring and configuring NetWare-based PC clients

Product type	Product name	Area of focus
Network management application	HP OpenView Probe Manager	Probe-based traffic monitor for Ethernet and Token-Ring networks; supports RMON
Network management application	HP OpenView Resource Manager/UX	Real-time traffic monitoring application using HP's EASE sampling technology embedded in HP hubs, bridges, and routers
Network management application	HP OpenView SNA Node Manager (Peregrine OpenSNA)	NNM-based application for displaying topology and status of IBM SNA networks
Network management application	HP OpenView Traffic Expert/UX	Network tuning and capacity planning tool utilizing EASE sampling technology embedded in HP hubs, bridges, and routers
Systems management platform and core product	HP IT/Operations	Distributed Unix servers and critical workstations—message translation, consolidation, and automated response
Systems management core product	HP PerfView/PCS/GlancePlus	Distributed Unix servers—in-depth performance analysis
Systems management core product	HP IT/Administration	Distributed Unix servers and workstations—user administration and change control
Systems management application	HP OpenView OmniBack II	Enterprise-wide backup and restore application
Systems management application	HP OpenView OmniStorage	Hierarchical Storage Management (HSM) for centralized, unattended tape, disk, and optical disk storage management
Systems management application	HP OpenView OpenSpool	Print management application for enterprise-wide monitoring and control of print services
Systems management application	HP OpenView Software Distributor	Electronic software distribution application
Systems management application	HP OpenView X.400 Manager	Centralized monitoring and administration of HP X.400 nodes

Table 1.2. Comparative Definitions of Network and Systems Management in the Open Systems Environment

Area	Managed objects	Tasks	Processes and protocols used
Network Management	routers bridges hubs repeaters cabling modems terminal servers multiplexers CSU/DSUs T-1 lines frame relay links ATM connections	device configuration, IP address administration, directory services, traffic monitoring, fault isolation, alarm handling, service restoral, data analysis and reporting, trouble ticketing, service provisioning, network security	For IP networks: SNMP, ICMP, ping, telnet; for all networks: protocol analysis--packet capture and decode; network node discovery; network mapping;
Systems Management	file servers print servers databases workstations operating systems e-mail applications: shrink-wrapped in-house apps financial apps other apps	console automation, performance monitoring, fault isolation, inventory, software distribution, user administration, trouble-ticketing, backup storage management, spool management, system security	console message management, terminal emulation, RPC-based applications, Unix command schedulers, Unix processes and statistics; RDBMS SQL table statistics; DMTF/DMI

discovery out of the box. Network Node Manager requires an add-on third-party application for Novell/IPX management.

WNM is similar to Network Node Manager in look and feel, but the two products differ in many respects. Network Node Manager runs on HP-UX and SunOS/Solaris, and with a new version for Windows NT forthcoming. WNM is strictly a DOS/Windows product. Network Node Manager supports an embedded Ingres or Oracle SQL RDBMS, while WNM stores alarm data in Paradox.

Network Node Manager is capable of auto-adjusting poll rates to compensate for WAN response time delays, while WNM is not. WNM can be extended by customer-written Visual Basic routines; most NNM customers choose Unix shell scripts or C code to extend Network Node Manager. Table 1.3 summarizes key differences between Network Node Manager and WNM.

In practice, interoperability between Network Node Manager and WNM is limited to alert forwarding. This feature may be useful in the following scenario: After business hours and on weekends, alerts normally displayed at the local WNM console can be forwarded to a central-site network operations center (NOC) running Network Node Manager in 24 × 7 operation.

Because of the differences in databases and underlying storage routines, NNM and WNM cannot share topology data or stored event information. In other words, HP OpenView for Windows is *not* NNM running under Windows. The two products are different programs with different APIs.

HP OpenView WNM directly competes with products from Digital, Novell, IBM/Network Managers, CastleRock, and Unisys/VisiSoft (Table 1.4). WNM also faces an indirect but strong threat from Microsoft Systems Management Server (SMS).

HP OpenView Network Node Manager (NNM)

NNM is HP's flagship network management offering. NNM's primary function is the collection of management data across interconnected TCP/IP LANs. In other words, NNM collects information that can be used to manage IP internetworks. NNM's secondary function is to act as a launching pad or integration point for additional HP, third-party, or user-written management applications.

NNM includes built-in support for SNMP MIB II, and provides an excellent MIB compiler for adding support for third-party private MIB extensions. (For more information about SNMP and MIBs, see Chap. 2.)

NNM supports a fairly good discovery capability for automating the process of detecting and then mapping IP network nodes. The discovery feature allows

**Table 1.3. HP OpenView Network Node Manager (NNM)
Compared to HP OpenView Workgroup Node Manager (WNM)**

Feature/function	Network Node Manager (NNM)	Workgroup Node Manager (WNM)
Base list price	$15,975	$1495 and up
Number of managed nodes (typical)	250 to 500	50 to 250
Type of data collected (out of the box)	TCP/IP	TCP/IP, IPX
Automatic node discovery	Supported	Supported
Poll rate adjustment	auto-adjusting or manual	Manual only
Embedded database	Flat file, Ingres, Oracle	Paradox
MIB Application Builder	Via dialog box menus, scripts	Visual basic
Typical sales channel	Direct sale	VAR

**Table 1.4. HP OpenView Workgroup Node
Manager and Competitors**

Product	Traffic monitoring capability	Extensibility	Comments
HP OpenView WNM	RMON; HP ProbeView ($5000 plus cost of probes)	Very good; strong MIB compiler; many third-party applications available	Sold and supported through VARs; alert forwarding to HP OpenView NNM
Novell ManageWise	$2500 for LANalyzer application plus cost of agents	Good; many third-party applications available	Sold and supported through VARs; many extras (Intel virus scan, NetWare server configuration) scalable architecture; forwards traps to any SNMP station
IBM NetView for Windows (Network Managers)	RMON provided by AXON ($1500 for application plus probes)	Excellent; integrator kit allows add-on "product-specific modules"; many PMCs available; protocol-independent architecture	Sold and supported by IBM and NMC; APIs consistent throughout IBM NetView product line
CastleRock SNMPc	Not supported	Fair; MIB compiler included	Sold via telemarketing; phone support from vendor

administrators to better understand the topology of the network. Such an understanding is crucial to maximizing the effectiveness of fault isolation procedures, for example. NNM's discovery function must be initiated by knowledgeable administrators, however, as the process can spin out of control if parameters are not carefully set. Chap. 4 provides some advice for administering the discovery process.

NNM also provides a nice graphical user interface (GUI) and a convenient MIB application builder, making it easy for anyone familiar with SNMP to write scripts and graph MIB values. For this reason alone, NNM is worth the price to many customers. NNM can be used to organize and store the many scripts and routines that technicians write to solve a management crisis. Without a "holding tank" like NNM, six months later those same scripts may easily be lost or forgotten.

In short, HP OpenView NNM provides good support for SNMP, is extensible, and provides a friendly GUI. As explained in the following chapters, however, NNM is not a complete turnkey solution. It is a platform, a foundation upon which to build. It takes weeks, months, even years, of time and effort to transform a platform such as NNM into a useful, customized management tool that does what a customer's organization needs it to do.

To use NNM effectively, an administrator must know which SNMP MIB variables to poll, how often to poll, and what the polling results mean. This alone takes months of experience to learn. Also, an administrator must add the right mix of value-added applications, taking into consideration how many extra applications NNM can sustain without exhibiting performance problems. Administrators must focus on managing the most critical elements and processes of the network, and build complete solutions around those aspects. Polling extravagantly or adding frivolous applications can bring NNM to its knees. On the other hand, limiting NNM to a barebones implementation might not solve the network management problem at hand. Deploying NNM effectively is truly a balancing act—one that can succeed only if the administrator is armed with enough information to plan carefully and to execute wisely.

NNM Competitors

NNM has become so enormously popular that few, if any, vendors offering similar products dare to position themselves as competitors. Perhaps the greatest testimony to NNM's popularity is that IBM, Digital, and NCR, three of HP's primary competitors in the workstation marketplace, chose to license HP OpenView source code rather than to develop competing products from a totally different code base.

The products offered by IBM, NCR, and Digital are considered OpenView *derivatives*. While they share some core code (less and less as time goes on and vendor-specific enhancements are made to this code base), each of these derivative products is different in terms of price/performance and value-added features such as ease of use and alarm handling. Each OpenView derivative supports a different set of third-party applications.

HP OpenView NNM derivatives include the following:

- IBM SystemView/NetView for AIX
- Digital Polycenter NetView
- NCR OneVision

IBM SystemView/NetView for AIX is described in detail in Chap. 15. Digital Polycenter NetView is described in detail in Chap. 16. NCR OneVision is described in detail in Chap. 17.

HP OpenView NNM also faces direct competition from products that do not share the OpenView code base. These products include:

- Sun Solstice Site Manager and Domain Manager (formerly SunNet Manager)
- Cabletron Spectrum
- Network Managers NMC Vision

HP OpenView NNM sometimes is viewed as competing with the following products that may, in fact, be used in combination with HP OpenView to extend its capabilities:

- Boole & Babbage Command/Post
- MAXM MAX/Enterprise
- OSI NetExpert

Following are descriptions of the top five competing products in these two categories: Sun Solstice Site Manager, Cabletron Spectrum, Boole & Babbage Command/Post, MAXM MAX/Enterprise, and OSI NetExpert.

SunSoft Solstice Site Manager

When Site Manager was first introduced as SunNet Manager in 1989, it became the first open management platform on the market to gain a critical mass of third-party support. Site Manager is based on a protocol-independent architecture that uses Sun's Open Network Computing Remote Procedure Call (ONC RPC) messaging services. The product supports SNMP via proxy agents. Site Manager can communicate with any proprietary management proctocol through a proxy written to its agent services API. Site Manager's popularity is due to its affordable price ($3995) and Sun's vast installed base of Unix workstations, as well as to its early entrance into the market (Terplan 95).

SunSoft is positioning Site Manager as a departmental solution within the Solstice framework. Using an optional application called Cooperative Consoles, multiple copies of Site Manager can communicate with each other. Communication with SunSoft's high-end distributed system, Solstice Enterprise Manager (EM) is only loosely supported and has not been widely tested in the field.

Site Manager's strengths include protocol-independent architecture, affordable price point, and wealth of third-party support (at least 100 different third-party applications are available to customers). However, Site Manager's map-editing capabilities are awkward and inflexible, and the GUI overall is not as user-friendly as is OpenView NNM's.

On the other hand, Solstice EM is a sophisticated, object-oriented program that uses CMIP and an object request broker modeled after the OSI Guidelines for the Definition of Managed Objects (GDMO) specifications. (Chapter 2 provides more information on GDMO.) Solstice EM is much more scalable than HP NNM; it is actually more similar to HP OpenView DM. Its sophistication may put off some commercial end-user organizations; and the lack of seamless integration between Site Manager and Solstice EM might confuse this same segment of the market. Future enhancements to both platforms will likely be JAVA-based.

Cabletron Spectrum

Spectrum Version 3.0 provides critical capabilities that HP OpenView NNM still lacks, including advanced alarm handling, efficient multiuser support, and distributed client/server architecture (Fig. 1.3). The end-user interface is embodied in processes running in the SpectroGraph component. Spectrum's object-oriented database of events, statistics, and device configurations reside in the SpectroServer component. SpectroServer is a virtual network machine that contains more than 50 device models (model types and relations) that represent network elements and their behaviors.

Starting with Release 2.0, Spectrum supported the ability for multiple SpectroGraphs to access a single SpectroServer, a capability that is not supported by HP OpenView NNM Manager or SunNet Manager.

In Release 3.0, Spectrum supports multiple SpectroServers (virtual network machines) communicating with multiple SpectroGraphs. This feature officially is called the Distributed SpectroServer (DSS). Using DSS, users can divide the network model among several *landscapes*, each of which is uniquely identified.

The DSS capability provides two important benefits: simultaneous access from multiple locations, and simultaneous access from multiple perspectives.

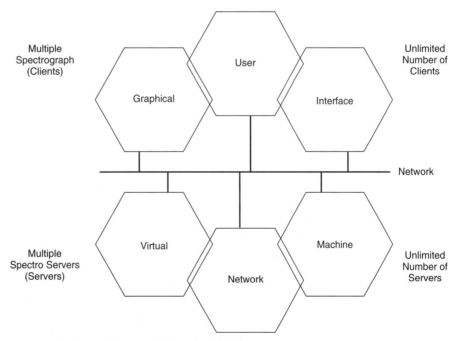

Figure 1.3 Cabletron Spectrum's Distributed Architecture

An operator in New York can access Spectrum via a local SpectroGraph process and see views consistent with what is displayed by a SpectroGraph station in Los Angeles. Both SpectroGraphs can tap into management data, the consistency of which is maintained by the SpectroServer. At the same time, because SpectroServer can partition the network into customized operator views, administrators can limit operators to only the portion of the network they need to see. One operator can monitor routers, while another operator sees only e-mail processes, etc.

Scalability is another benefit of the DSS architecture. By geographically distributing SpectroServer components, polling and threshold monitoring can occur locally rather than over the wide area.

The SpectroServer component is called a "virtual network machine" because it operates on information stored in models, not just on raw event data. Spectrum's modeling capability can infer the behavior of one device by looking at the behavior of other devices connected to it. Improved fault isolation is a primary benefit of this modeling technology. Cabletron's built-in device models (numbering about 50), which describe connectivity relationships as well as individual device behavior, allow Spectrum to more quickly identify the source of failure. In many instances, this can reduce the time it takes to isolate failures from hours or minutes to a few seconds.

Spectrum's Configuration Manager helps to automate portions of the network configuration process. Spectrum provides user-definable configuration templates that allow configurations to be replicated across multiple devices. Spectrum's Configuration Manager supports not only Cabletron hubs, but several other major vendors' products, including Cisco routers, 3Com hubs, SynOptics hubs, and Xyplex terminal servers. The Configuration Manager also is capable of comparing actual device configurations to authorized configurations stored in the Spectrum database, and can detect and report unauthorized configuration changes (Huntington-Lee 1995a).

Table 1.5 compares salient features of HP OpenView NNM to SunSite Manager and Cabletron Spectrum.

Fault and Legacy System Managers

As mentioned previously, HP OpenView NNM out of the box is incapable of collecting data from non-IP network nodes, also called *legacy systems*. NNM supports only rudimentary alarm processing. Although this can be supplemented by NetLabs/Seagate's NerveCenter, integration is anything but seamless (See Chap. 7). Several products on the market support sophisticated alert processing and automation for all types of environments, including non-IP networks. These high-end fault management applications include Boole & Babbage Command/Post, MAXM Systems MAX/Enterprise, and Objective Systems Integrator's NetExpert.

The fault management platforms can obtain messages from virtually any device or system that emits an electronic status or sends ASCII status messages to a console or RS-232 port. Parsing routines are used to identify incoming

Table 1.5. HP OpenView Network Node Manager, (NNM), Cabletron Spectrum, and SunSite Manager

Product	Scalability	Extensibility	Database	Third-party support	Price
HP OpenView	Fair; each NNM can manage 250-500 nodes in practice; supports multiple users via X-Windows only; no manager-to-manager communications	Very good; nice GUI and MIB application builder; developer's toolkit supports multiple levels of integration	Good; supports links to Ingres, Oracle RDBMSs; support for distributed database not yet announced	Excellent; large and growing number of third-party developers	Moderate; approx. $20,000; however, value-added applications cost extra and require more processing power
SunSite Manager	Fair to poor; each copy manages up to 250 nodes; can't support multiple operators; lacks manager-to-manager communications	Fair to good; straight-forward, although laborious; GUI can be awkward	Good; SQL links support by third-party applications	Excellent; large, a growing number of third-party developers	Very affordable; $3995 base price; value-added applications cost extra and require more processing power
Cabletron Spectrum	Excellent; supports multiple clients multiple server; distributes processing across multiple servers; supports manager-to-manager comm	Integration can be complex, however, very tight integration is supported	Very good; allows data-base to be distributed; databases can com-municate	Fair; small number of third-party developers, however, this is expected to improve in 1996	Moderate to expensive ($20,000 and up for base system with device management modules); requires high-powered workstation

messages, translation routines reformat messages into a common format, and filtering rules suppress unnecessary alerts and categorize the remaining alerts according to priority and status.

In years past, these fault management platforms were referred to as manager of managers or *MOMs* (Terplan 95). Today, however, the popularity of HP OpenView has prompted MOM vendors to reposition their products as complementary to HP OpenView et al—and indeed, they are. They can monitor and control the vast world of non-IP devices and systems, whereas HP OpenView NNM cannot. They can efficiently and automatically process high volumes of incoming messages, filtering out extraneous information and bringing only the most critical messages to the operator's attention. They even can automate responses to critical problems for split-second resolution.

While these products have some overlapping functionality with OpenView, customers can, and are, using them in conjunction with OpenView NNM to provide a more complete solution.

Following are brief descriptions of three important fault/legacy management products.

Boole & Babbage Command/Post

Command/Post accepts unsolicited messages (typically ASCII text) supplied to an outside device by equipment or computer hosts. Command/Post can be used in conjunction with Boole's Ensign application. Ensign is somewhat equivalent to HP IT/Operations, in that both products rely on agent technology to obtain performance statistics and status information from Unix operating systems. Ensign agents are available for SunOS, Solaris, HP-UX, IBM AIX, Sequent, SCO UNIX, NCR SVR4, SG IRIX, NetWare, and NT. These agents can query Unix periodically by issuing kernel commands such as iostat, lpstat, etc., to obtain information on operating system activity, disk space, swap space, etc.

Boole's Ensign supports threshold monitoring at the agent level for detecting various Unix system problems. Boole has established relationships with other companies that supply agents running on IBM AS/400, Digital systems, and other non-IP systems. Boole has built interfaces with those agents to support a more intelligent dialogue and to allow interaction with Command/Post if failures can't be recovered at the agent level.

Each incoming message received by Command/Post passes through a filter comprised of rules. Command/Post's Alert Logic Filter Editor (ALFE) defines the message-processing rules to be applied to incoming message streams as they are parsed. To make a filter, the user must create a set of rules describing how each alert should be categorized and displayed. ALFE contains a *like* function that allows users to duplicate rules for similar alerts, making it easier to configure new alerts.

ALFE is not an expert system; conditions can be applied only to individual incoming messages. ALFE cannot perform comparisons on multiple incoming messages before deciding whether to generate an alert. Alerts that are not recognized as being defined by ALFE still can be presented as an alert to the operator.

ALFE suppresses unnecessary alerts and unnecessary portions of meaningful alerts. Less important events can be removed completely or assigned status of *informational*. ALFE prioritizes the remaining alerts according to one of six severity levels, and categorizes the alert into one of seven groups (circuit, equipment, facility, LAN, multipoint circuit, service, or software).

Messages can be logged, filtered, or processed automatically. The message follows a *path* of filters, sessions, and operator response or automation. Automation is supported by an optional AutoCOMMAND application that allows activation of user-written scripts (EXECs) to automate operator responses to alerts. These scripts are written in UniREXX. Once the EXECs are installed, the user must develop a trigger describing the conditions that will initiate the EXEC. An AutoCOMMAND EXEC can be initiated by a particular alert state. An EXEC also can be initiated by another currently executing EXEC.

In either case, the EXEC may use a terminal emulator, extended by programmatic interfaces/API, to utilize existing screen formats for a given device or system and issue commands back to that system. For example, an AS/400 gives a message that major task has failed; the EXEC uses the emulation API to issue the command back to the AS/400.

Command/Post supports a variety of terminal emulators. Boole also offers a voice paging application called PhonePoint, with call-out, call-in and escalation capabilities from any tone-dial phone. PhonePoint is a paging system that allows authorized administrators to issue commands from a tone-dial phone. The customer must purchase a PC with voice cards to support PhonePoint, which was developed for Boole by Single Point Systems.

Another Command/Post option is Connect/MVS, which provides predefined filters for critical MVS and JES messages. It automates IML and IPL processes, and consolidates multiple MVS consoles into a single display.

Command/Post supports integration with HP OpenView on multiple levels, including OSF/Motif compliance, menu bar integration, loadable MIB support, event integration, tracing/logging, and file placement. Command/Post's integration with OpenView also complies with HP's guidelines for product installation and process management.

Command/Post utilizes HP's OVwDB application programming interface (API) routines, enabling the OpenView database to manage the object and field information in Command/Post's displays. As a result, Command/Post objects can be represented on an HP OpenView map—seamless drill-down is supported. Similarly, HP OpenView objects can appear on Command/Post maps, with each object representing either an entire HP OpenView management system, or a group of tools managed by OpenView (Huntington-Lee 1996a).

Command/Post has been connected to approximately 300 types of systems and devices.

OSI NetExpert

NetExpert can collect data from any device, application, or subsystem that emits electronic status information. This includes telephone company switches, host computers, televisions, satellites, testing equipment, and environmental controls.

Device messages are fed into *Generic Gateways* for processing. The Generic Gateways feature of NetExpert accepts raw messages from managed objects, filters them, and reformats the returned message into a CMIP event message. There is an instance of Generic Gateway for each managed object; Generic Gateways collect and filter raw data to form an event.

Generic Gateways communicate with managed objects in two ways:

- Dial-in/dial-out (asychronous ASCII)—unsolicited messages
- Direct connection (X.25, 3270, Ethernet/Internet)—solicited messages

Generic Gateway's runtime analysis is governed by user-defined rules that are downloaded from the NetExpert Database when a Generic Gateway is started. There are four types of rules:

- Message Identification rule
- Message Parse rules
- Dialog Command State rules
- Dialog Response rules

Generic Gateways accept unsolicited messages which a device supplies to an output device, usually in the form of ASCII text. NetExpert also can accept input from both SNMP and CMIP agents, although OSI does not sell agents. Systems integrators have successfully used intelligent SNMP/CMIP agents from Legent (formerly Digital Analysis Corp.) to obtain from remote Unix servers information that is fed into NetExpert. OSI has a MIB loader module that can read MIBs from any SNMP device and automatically populate the embedded NetExpert MIB.

NetExpert can generate events internally based on information stored in the embedded expert system.

NetExpert parses incoming messages and translates them into CMIP events (M-EVENT-REPORTS). These events are passed on to the Intelligent Dynamic Event Analysis System (IDEAS) for further analysis. The IDEAS expert system filters messages according to user-defined rules. Rules can be created using arithmetic and boolean operations, conditional logic, event correlation, timers, thresholds, and dialoging between NetExpert and the managed object.

IDEAS correlates events across multiple managed objects, tests thresholds, adds descriptive data, and determines priorities based on user-configurable security levels. IDEAS highlights primary events (such as alerts) at the operator workstation and suppresses the sympathetic events by writing them to a log file. IDEAS maintains complete real-time network status in shared memory.

NetExpert supports an embedded trouble-ticketing capability allowing the operator to create, update, search, and view tickets. Tickets are date/time stamped and logged. Trouble tickets can be created manually or automatically based on device input.

An optional application called NetImpact, developed by Strategic Solutions International, supports IBM MVS automation. NetImpact enables operators and automation scripts (running under OS/2 and UNIX) to identify and manage problems with resources and MVS IBM Systems Network Architecture (SNA) applications. NetImpact monitors MVS console messages and enables NetExpert to correlate problems across mainframe computers, VTAM applications, and attached equipment. NetImpact tracks service-level objectives for the reliability and availability of SNA resources and MVS applications. Using NetImpact, operators immediately can assess the number of network users affected by a problem and can reallocate resources to alleviate the problem. Because NetImpact uses LU6.2 links between mainframe-resident SNA agents, instead of relying on 3270 HLLAPI or IBM NetView, it is not resource-intensive.

NetExpert can receive SNMP traps from any SNMP-based management system such as HP OpenView, IBM NetView for AIX, SunNet Manager. NetExpert typically views these management systems as element management systems (EMSs). NetExpert is capable of communicating with other management systems using CMIP.

MAX/Enterprise

MAXM Systems MAX/Enterprise is a suite of applications for integrating, consolidating, processing, and automating responses to network and system events from both legacy- and standards-based devices. MAX/Enterprise processes event data, generating automatic responses and distributing derived information to operator workstations.

MAX/Enterprise acquires unsolicited messages from RS-232 or other communications interfaces, and can solicit and gather messages from host console ports by using REXX automation scripts. MAX/Enterprise can obtain raw event data by issuing queries such as iostat, diskpace, and similar commands to remote Unix hosts.

Once event data is obtained, MAX/Enterprise identifies significant events using a rules-based mechanism. MAXM rulesets can be defined to identify events based on ASCII strings, or on the logical comparison of data values contained within the raw event. MAX/Enterprise can identify significant events based on the failure to receive a particular raw event within a given period of time. For example, if MAX/Enterprise did not receive a "heartbeat" message from a critical host system within 10 minutes, a derived event would be created.

MAX/Enterprise rulesets are defined to parse significant data values within the event, such as the affected resource, event text, timestamp, and performance data values. Rulesets can be defined to suppress sympathetic or otherwise insignificant events, to compress events to distill verbose event streams to essential message content (helping operators focus on what's important), and to translate events into a common format. Multiple instances of the same event can be condensed into one alert with a counter indicating the number of instances.

MAX/Enterprise also supports thresholding to distinguish between significant derived events and insignificant events.

In addition to alert processing functions, MAX/Enterprise supports the creation of automation scripts in REXX language. Scheduled automation is triggered by a scheduler running on the MAX/Enterprise server platform. Automation scripts also can be triggered by the reception of specific events, typically to support further diagnosis or corrective action such as rebooting the system. Operators can be alerted to use terminal emulation to perform additional diagnostic and control functions when specific events are detected.

MAXM's rulesets are easily programmed by users familiar with REXX.

MAXM Systems has ported MAX/Enterprise to the NCR OneVision management platform, providing OneVision customers with sophisticated event management and automation capabilities with the same look and feel as OneVision's SNMP-based management functions. (For more information on OneVision, see Chap. 17.)

Table 1.6 compares salient features of HP OpenView NNM with the aforementioned fault/legacy system managers.

HP OpenView Distributed Manager (DM)

OpenView DM is designed to manage large, complex networks comprising tens of thousands of nodes or more. DM has been purchased by telcos, including interexchange carriers (IXCs), and postal telephone telegraph (PTT) agencies. DM also is of interest to systems integrators contracted to manage global commercial or government networks.

DM, a superset of NNM, includes the SNMP platform capability resident in NNM. DM, however, supports several features lacking in NNM, such as the ability to support the Open System Interconnect (OSI) Common Management Information Protocol (CMIP), the X/Open Management API (XMAPI), and an Event Sieve Manager for more complex alarm processing.

While NNM is capable of processing scores of traps per minute, DM can handle hundreds. In practice, NNM can manage no more than several thousand objects, while DM is designed to manage tens of thousands.

The primary reason for this difference is DM's Event Sieve, an object request broker (ORB) that routes incoming traps indicating network problems to the appropriate management application. (The management application may be provided by HP, a third party, or written in-house.) In DM, each application registers to see only that traps it needs to see.

The products competing most directly with HP OpenView DM are Sun's Solstice Enterprise Manager, Digital's TeMIP, and IBM's NetView TMN Support Facility for AIX. Other products frequently found in the telco/systems integrator space include Objective Systems Integrators NetExpert and MAXM Systems MAX/Enterprise (described previously). HP OpenView DM lists for approximately $19,000. A full OSI stack with CMIP support costs an additional $3000, approximately. A single-user configuration of Sun Solstice Enterprise Manager is $19,500, or $32,000 for a two-user configuration.

Table 1.6. HP OpenView Network Node Manager and Fault/Legacy Management Systems

Feature/ function	HP OpenView NNM	Boole Command/ Post	MAXM MAX/ Enterprise	OSINetExpert
Alarm processing	Limited criteria for filtering alarms; no automation capabilities without third-party add-ons	Customer-defined rulesets filter incoming messages; automation supported by customer-written UniREXX scripts	Customer-defined rulesets filter incoming messages; automation supported by customer-written REXX scripts	IDEAS expert system filters messages; automation supported by customer-written scripts
Extensibility	Very good wrt. adding new MIBs, building MIB applications, and adding third-party applications	Support for new device types typically requires vendor assistance	Support for new device types can be developed by customers in some instances	Support for new device types typically requires vendor assistance
Support for other management platforms	No	Links to HP OpenView; will be more seamlessly integrated in next release	Links to AT&T OneVision forthcoming	Accepts SNMP alerts from any SNMP management station
Strengths	Large installed base; third-party support	Legacy system support; supports help-desk initiatives	Efficient, scalable fault management	Expert system supports sophisticated alarm processing, automation
Limitations	No support for non-IP environments; weak alarm processing	Lack of PC-based client; small installed base	Small, one-product vendor	Expert system requires constant maintenance

HP OpenView Systems Management Products

HP is increasing its emphasis on systems management products, primarily IT/Operations, MeasureWare/PerfView, and IT/Administration. While OpenView network management products currently sustain a much larger installed base, HP is expending considerable effort to expand the installed base of the systems management products to at least comparable levels. Judging from its past success with OpenView NNM, HP probably will succeed in making IT/Operations a de facto standard for systems management.

The systems management products are described in detail in later chapters. Below are brief descriptions of these products for purpose of comparison with the competition:

HP IT/Operations. HP IT/Operations is a high-end message consolidation console application. It is typically used in a data center for supporting network-wide Unix event processing and correlation. IT/Operations agents monitor log files, looking for specified ASCII text strings. Captured messages are date/time stamped, converted to a common message format, and forwarded to the central IT/Operations console. IT/Operations can intercept SNMP traps and MPE console messages, as well as encapsulate and extract Unix application and logfile messages.

IT/Operations includes an embedded version of HP OpenView NNM. Products competing with IT/Operations are described in Table 1.7. IT/Operations is described in detail in Chap. 11.

HP MeasureWare/PerfView. HP PerfView collects and analyzes performance data from individual Unix machines. By itself, HP PerfView is not a high-end solution. When used in conjunction with HP PerfView RX/Performance

Table 1.7. HT IT/ Operations and Competitors

Vendor	NCR Computer Manager	HP IT/Operations	Tivoli/Enterprise Console
Product name	Exception Reporting Agent with Distributed Scheduler & Message Collector	IT/Operations Agents	Event adapters
Primary technology	Unix scheduler with added asynchronous message capabilities; some filtering	Asynchronous message collection, translation, local filtering	Asynchronous message collection, translation, centralized rules-based filtering plus local filtering
Strengths	Unix fault mgt, user admin, security, flexible agent configurations, multiplatform support		Object-oriented, flexible, user admin security, rules-based message filtering; integration with Sentry
Limitations	UUCP-based, lack of network-wide event correlation and rules-base filtering, limited datastore; lack of ORB	High price; currently no integration with PerfView; lacks ORB	Lack of performance trending, not user-friendly

Collection Software and HP GlancePlus, however, the product forms the cornerstone of a very high-end, in-depth performance management solution. One current weakness of the OperationsCenter/PerfView product suite is the lack of integration between the two applications. HP will address this limitation in future releases.

Products competing with PerfView/PCS include Tivoli/Sentry, Landmark TMON for Unix, IBM Systems Monitor for AIX, CA Legent AgentWorks, and Digital Equipment's Polycenter System Watchdog.

In June 1995, HP introduced an enhanced product suite called MeasureWare, which includes PerfView agents. MeasureWare supports collection and display of data from four perspectives:

- Network traffic, collected by HP NetMetrix systems.

- Database, collected by BMC Patrol agents.

- Servers, collected by IT/Operations.

- Application, collected by MeasureWare agents from applications that have been instrumented with MeasureWare "hooks" for capturing application performance and status data.

Plots of statistics from all four views can be displayed concurrently on the MeasureWare screen, enabling operators to visually correlate changes in behavior occurring in these four critical areas. MeasureWare is described in detail in Chap. 11.

HP IT/Administration. IT/Administration centralizes and automates the configuration of Unix systems and servers, users/passwords, filesystems, and software. IT/Administration maintains an inventory of the configured objects. The product also supports administrator privilege policy setting, allowing a company to assign different responsibilities to different systems administrators as they see fit by creating customized management domains.

IT/Administration includes an embedded version of HP OpenView NNM. Products competing with IT/Administration include Computer Associates CA-Unicenter, Sun Solstice AdminTools, and Tivoli/Admin. The list price of HP IT/Administration is approximately $15,000. IT/Administration is described in detail in Chap. 12.

The Growing Importance of Systems Management

Figure 1.4 shows the relationship of network and systems management to the business processes that drive an organization. Applications management, followed by database management and systems management, enjoy a much closer proximity to strategic business processes than does network management.

By emphasizing its strategic systems management products—IT/Operations, IT/Administration, and MeasureWare/Perfview—HP is pursuing a product direction intended to enhance its position as a solutions provider, thereby cementing closer ties with its largest customers. To accomplish this goal, HP introduced the HP OpenView Solution Framework, described in Chap. 13. In this new framework, Network Node Manager provides "common services" rather than value-added capabilities. To avoid misconceptions about Network Node Manager, and to build a realistic network management architecture around NNM, it is critical to have a clear understanding of HP's overall direction. Chapter 3 discusses HP's strategic direction in detail.

Summary

HP OpenView has emerged as the most influential network and systems management platform of its kind. The primary reason for HP OpenView's popularity is that the product addresses the complex challenges of network and systems management with an open, flexible approach. HP OpenView includes more than a dozen packages that address many areas of network and systems management. By emphasizing its strategic systems management products— IT/Operations, IT/Administration, and MeasureWare/Perfview—HP is pursuing a product direction intended to enhance its position as a solutions provider, thereby cementing closer ties with its largest customers.

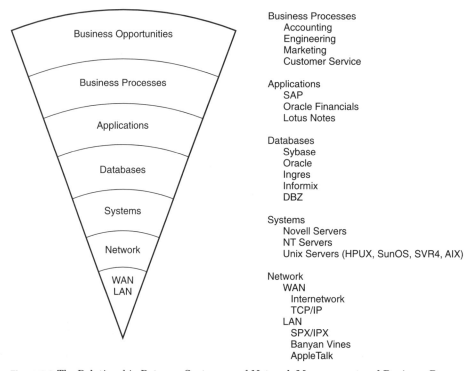

Figure 1.4 The Relationship Between Systems, and Network Management and Business Processes and Business Opportunities

Chapter

2

HP OpenView and Standards

Today's computing and networking environments are complex and geographically distributed; in the future, they will be even more so. If organizations are to maximize their investments in networking technology, they need a powerful, complete, long-term approach for managing multivendor systems and networks.

HP OpenView is a leading alternative to the solution of providing an integrated system and network management for enterprise-wide computing environments. The solution consists of a broad portfolio of management applications built on standards-based management platforms and a wide range of services.

HP OpenView's goal is to provide universal management processes that address the areas of configuration, change, problem, performance, security, and accounting management. At the heart of the HP OpenView solution are enabling management services that provide standards-based platforms and applications from Hewlett-Packard, or from HP's solution partners. The applications address business needs related to managing databases, applications, networks, systems, and services. Figure 2.1 shows the layers of this solution portfolio.

This solution structure may be broken down into four basic layers, addressing process management, task management, management technologies, and the management platform (Fig. 2.2). As can be seen, the managed environment includes all elements of the information technology (IT) infrastructure, not just systems, networks, and peripheral devices. OpenView addresses all applications and middleware that deliver the IT infrastructure value to users.

TCP/IP

It is obvious that TCP/IP will continue to play a significant role as a common denominator in interconnecting devices and networks. Most management solutions offered today require TCP/IP as an information source and information carrier. The TCP/IP architecture, like the OSI model, is layered. In the case of TCP/IP, four layers are involved: network access, internet, host-to-host, and process. Figure 2.3 compares these layers with those of OSI (Stallings 1993).

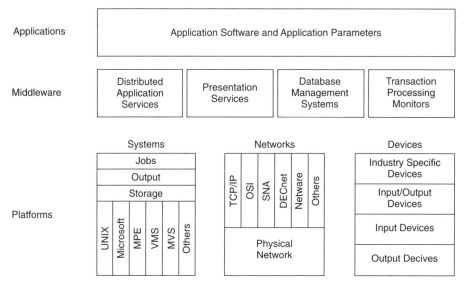

Applications

Middleware

Platforms

Figure 2.1 Managed Elements Addressed by OpenView Solutions

The network access layer contains the protocols that provide access to a communication network, such as local or wide area networks. Protocols at this layer are between a communication node and an attached host. The TCP/IP suite does not include unique protocols at this layer. Rather, the protocol appropriate for a particular network is used.

The internet layer consists of the procedures required to allow data to traverse multiple networks between hosts, and therefore must provide a routing function. This protocol is implemented within hosts and routers. A router relays data between networks using an internetwork protocol. The protocol at the layer is the Internet Protocol. IP typically is used to connect multiple LANs within the same building or to connect LANs at different sites through a wide area network.

The host-to-host layer provides the logic for assuring that data exchanged between hosts is reliably delivered, and is responsible for directing incoming data to the intended application. The protocol at this layer is the Transmission Control Protocol.

Finally, the process layer contains protocols for specific user applications. For each different type of application, such as file transfer, a protocol is needed to support that application. Three such protocols are included in the TCP/IP protocol suite: SMTP, FTP, and TELNET.

The Simple Mail Transfer Protocol (SMTP) provides a basic electronic mail facility. It offers a way of transferring messages among separate hosts. Features of SMTP include mailing lists, return receipts, and forwarding. However, SMTP does not specify how messages are to be created, which means an additional local editing or native electronic mail facility is required. Once messages are created, SMTP accepts the message and makes use of TCP to send it to an SMTP module on another host. The target SMTP module will make use of a local electronic mail package to store the incoming message in a user's mailbox.

The File Transfer Protocol (FTP) is used to send files from one system to another under user command. Both text and binary files are accommodated, and the protocol provides features for controlling user access. When a user wishes to engage in file transfer, FTP sets up a TCP connection to the target system for the exchange of control messages. Once a file transfer is approved, a second TCP connection is set up for the data transfer. The file is transferred over the data connection, without the overhead of any headers or control information at the application level. When the transfer is complete, the control connection is used to signal the completion.

TELNET provides a remote logon capability that enables a user at a terminal or personal computer to log into a remote computer and function as if directly connected to that computer. TELNET is implemented in two modules: User TELNET interacts with a local terminal, and server TELNET interacts with the application. Traffic between user and server TELNET is carried on a TCP connection. The benefits of using TCP/IP can be summarized as follows:

- Every major computer vendor supports TCP/IP.

- The TCP and IP specifications, along with many source-code implementations, are publicly available.

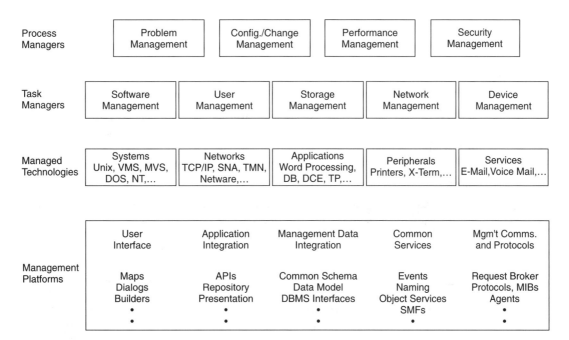

Figure 2.2 Management Solution Portfolio

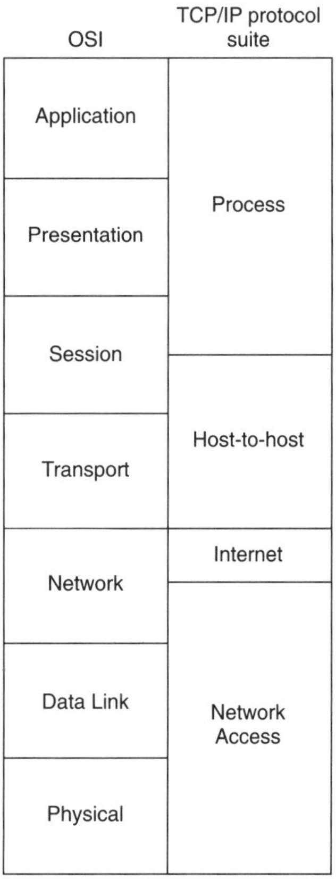

OSI	TCP/IP protocol suite
Application	Process
Presentation	
Session	
Transport	Host-to-host
Network	Internet
Data Link	Network Access
Physical	

Figure 2.3 A Comparison of the OSI and TCP/IP Communications Architectures

- There are no licensing fees.

- TCP/IP implementations require relatively little system memory and, in most cases, require far fewer processor resources than do most proprietary protocol alternatives.

- This protocol has been analyzed, refined, and debugged for more than two decades.

- Many of today's most popular applications can run TCP/IP because many platforms, operating systems, and network operating systems are integrating TCP/IP support.

There are some risks involved when TCP/IP is the strategic choice for users seeking broad multivendor connectivity and a single network transport:

- IP addresses are in short supply. This mainly affects organizations planning widespread, direct connectivity to many users.

- Its limited security may prohibit its use for sensitive applications, unless firewalls are implemented between the internetwork and user nodes.

- TCP/IP represents an old technology that may not be efficient with state-of-the-art networking technologies.

Protocol and application dependencies are shown in Fig. 2.4 (Stallings 1993). The Simple Network Management Protocol (SNMP) resides at the process layer. SNMP takes advantage of transport services by TCP/IP or User Datagram Protocol (UDP)/IP. SNMP Version 2 (SNMPv2) has been enhanced to use additional transport services, including OSI, AppleTalk, and Novell IPX, as well as TCP and UDP.

Network and systems management product solutions are greatly affected by emerging standards. These include proprietary solutions, such as IBM's Network Management Vector Transport (NMVT); de facto standards for TCP/IP-based networks, including SNMP versions; and open solutions, based on OSI and International Telecommunications Union (ITU) recommendations, including the Common Management Information Protocol (CMIP) and Telecommunication Management Protocol (TMN). In addition, various organizations are promoting

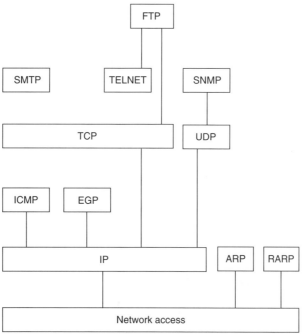

ICMP = internet-control message protocol
EGP   = external gateway protocol
ARP   = address resolution protocol
RARP = reverse address resolution protocol

Figure 2.4 Protocol Dependencies of TCP/IP

application programming interfaces (APIs) between standards and frameworks that include standards.

The use of standards will help accelerate widespread acceptance of management applications, providing some measure of future-proofing. The International Standards Organization (ISO), in documents concerning Open Systems Interconnect (OSI), has defined specific management functional areas and services. OSI management encompasses both WAN and LAN management, but the estimated overhead scares away vendors and users, with the exception of the telecommunications industry.

The Internet Engineering Task Force (IETF) in the United States also has defined standards for the management dialog in networks using TCP/IP. Among these standards is SNMP. The market rapidly embraced SNMP after its introduction in 1988, and the protocol is now a common denominator for management. It will continue to be so for the rest of this decade.

Figure 2.5 shows an overview of processes and communication links between managers, agents, subagents, and managed objects (Terplan 1995). These processes are similar for all types of protocols; differences occur in respect to the initiator of the communication exchange, contrasting polling- and event-based techniques. Both CMIP and SNMP are defined as application-layer protocols that use the underlying transport services of the protocol stack. Both protocols use the manager-agent paradigm, whereby an agent, a passive software process residing on a managed device or system, collects data and reports it to the manager, an active software application that typically supports a graphical user interface. The manager process is user initiated. Protocol alternatives which impact OpenView implementations will be covered in the next segments.

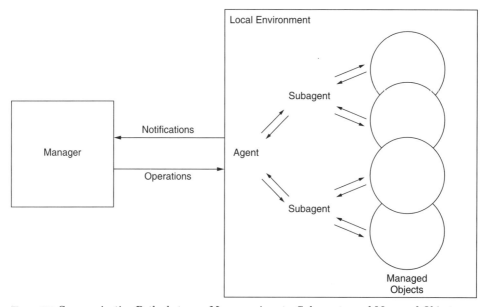

Figure 2.5 Communication Paths between Manager, Agents, Subagents, and Managed Objects

In terms of standardizing the manager-agent dialogue of enterprise network management, answers must be found to the following questions:

■ How will management information be formatted and how will the information exchange be regulated? This is actually the protocol definition problem.

■ How will the management information be transported between manager and agent? OSI standards employ the OSI protocol stack, and TCP/IP standards use the TCP/IP protocol stack. This is no longer the only solution. Several protocols demonstrate the emerging independence of management protocols from underlying protocol layers.

Both CMIP and SNMP employ the concept of managed objects. Managed objects are defined by their attributes, the operations that may be performed upon them, and the notification that may result. The set of managed objects in a system, together with their attributes, constitute that system's management information base (MIB). In addition to MIBs, the structure of management information (SMI) defines the logical structure of OSI or SNMP information. The MIB can be extended to include private variables for describing devices or components offered by vendors or developed by users.

SNMPv1 and SNMPv2

In the SNMP environment, the manager can obtain information from the agent by periodically polling managed objects. Agents can transmit unsolicited event messages, called *traps*, to the manager. The management data exchanged between managers and agents is called the management information base (MIB). Data definitions outlined in SMI must be understood by both managers and agents.

The manager, a software program housed within the management station, has the ability to query agents using various SNMP commands. The management station is in charge of interpreting MIB data, constructing views of the systems and networks, compressing data, and maintaining data in relational or object-oriented databases. Figure 2.6 shows a generic SNMP-management structure (Terplan 1995).

New MIBs are being defined constantly. In addition to standard MIBs, such as MIB I and II (Table 2.1), the IETF has defined a number of adjunct MIBs covering hosts, bridges, hubs, repeaters, FDDI networks, AppleTalk networks, and frame relay networks. Selected MIB variables are listed in Table 2.2 (Waldbusser, Nair, and Hoerth 1992).

In terms of SNMP, the following trends are expected:

■ A greater number of vendors will provide SNMP agent-level support.

■ Only a few leading vendors will provide SNMP manager-level support, in the form of several widely accepted platforms, such as HP OpenView.

■ Management platforms will provide basic services, leaving customization to vendors and users.

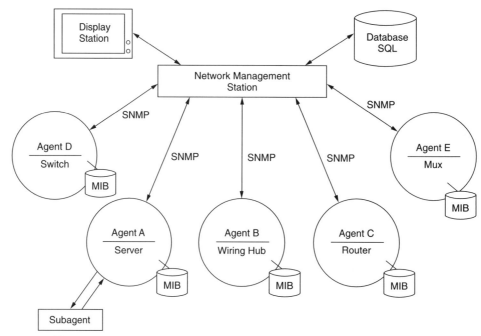

MIB   = Management Information Base
SNMP = Simple Network Management Protocol

Figure 2.6 Structure of SNMP-Based Management Solutions

Wider use of intelligent agents also is expected. Intelligent agents are capable of responding to a manager's request for information and of performing certain manager-like functions, including testing for thresholds, filtering, and processing management data. Intelligent agents enable localized polling and filtering on servers, workstations, and hubs, for example. Thus, these agents reduce polling overhead and management data traffic, forwarding only the most critical alerts and processed data to the SNMP manager.

The Remote Monitoring (RMON) MIB will help to bridge the gap between the limited services provided by management platforms and the rich sets of data and statistics provided by traffic monitors and analyzers.

SNMP's strengths include the following:

- Agents are widely available.
- It is simple to implement.
- Agent-level overhead is minimal.
- Polling approach is good for LAN-based managed objects.
- It is robust and extensible.
- It offers the best direct manager-agent interface.

SNMP met a critical need; it was available and able to be implemented at the right time. But SNMP has weaknesses, which include include the following:

- It is too simple, and does not scale well.
- It has no object-oriented data view.
- Its unique semantics make integration with other approaches difficult.
- It has high communication overhead due to polling.
- It has many implementation-specific (private MIB) extensions.
- It has no standard control definition.
- Small agent (one agent per device) may be inappropriate for systems management.

SNMP is being improved and extended continuously. SNMPv2 addresses many of the shortcomings of version 1, and can support either a highly centralized management strategy or a distributed one. In the latter case, some systems operate both in the role of manager and agent. A system in an agent role will accept commands from a superior manager; these commands may deal with access of information stored locally at the intermediate manager, or may require the intermediate manager to provide summary information about subagents.

The principal enhancements to SNMPv1 provided by version 2 fall into the following categories (Stallings 1993):

- SMI enhancements
- Transport mappings
- Protocol operations
- MIB extensions

Table 2.1. MIB II Structure

11 Categories of mgmt (2) Subtree	Information in the category
system (1)	network device operating system
interfaces (2)	network interface specific
address translation (3)	address mappings
ip (4)	Internet Protocol specific
icmp (5)	Internet Control Message Protocol specific
tcp (6)	transmission protocol specific
udp (7)	user Datagram protocol specific
egp (8)	Exterior Gateway Protocol specific
cmot (9)	Common Management Information Services on TCP specific
transmission (10)	transmission protocol specific
snmp (11)	SNMP specific

■ Manager-to-manager communications

■ Security

The Structure of Management Information (SMI) is being expanded in several ways. The macro used to define object types has been expanded to include several new data types and to enhance the documentation associated with an object. Of note is a new convention for creating and deleting conceptual rows in a table. This capability originates with RMON.

Table 2.2. A Comparison of MIB Coverage

	MIB II	Host MIB	Bridge MIB	Hub MIB	RMON MIB
Interface statistics	X				
IP, TCP, UDP statistics	X				
SNMP statistics	X				
Host job counts		X			
Host file system information		X			
Spanning-tree performance			X		
Wide-area link performance			X		
Link testing			X	X	
Network traffic statistics			X	X	X
Host table of all addresses				X	X
Host statistics				X	X
Historical data					X
Alarm thresholds					
Configurable statistics					X
Traffic matrix with all nodes					X
"Host top N" tables					X
Packet capture/protocol analysis					X
Distributed logging of events					X

Reprinted from May 1992 *Data Communications Magazine*. Copyright (May 1992) McGraw-Hill, Inc. (Waldbusser, Nair, and Hoerth, 1992)

New transport mappings allow use of different protocol stacks to transport SNMP information other than user datagram protocol (UDP); the enhancements include support for OSI connectionless-mode protocol, Novell Internetwork Packet Exchange (IPX) protocol, and AppleTalk.

Protocol operations have been expanded to include two new protocol data units (PDUs). The GetBulkRequest PDU enables the manager to retrieve efficiently large blocks of data, providing a powerful mechanism for retrieving multiple rows in a table. The new InformRequest PDU enables one manager to send trap-type information to another.

MIB extensions contain basic traffic information about the operation of the SNMPv2 protocol; this is identical to SNMP MIB II. The SNMPv2 MIB contains other information related to the configuration of SNMPv2 manager-to-agent.

A manager-to-manager capability is specified in a special MIB, called M2M. It provides functionality similar to the RMON MIB. In this case, the M2M MIB may be used to allow an intermediate manager to function as a remote monitor of network media traffic. Reporting also is supported, as are two major groups, Alarm and Event.

The SNMPv2 security includes a wrapper containing authentication and privacy information as a header to PDUs.

The SNMPv2 framework is derived from the SNMP framework. The intent is that the evolution from SNMP to SNMP2 be seamless. The easiest way to accomplish that is to upgrade the manager to support SNMPv2 in a way that allows for the coexistence of SNMPv2 managers, SNMPv2 agents, and SNMP agents. Figure 2.7 demonstrates The role of a proxy agent in this coexistence (Stallings 1993).

Figure 2.7 also illustrates the mapping of protocol elements. The actual implementation of the proxy agent depends on the vendor; it could be implemented into the agent or into the manager.

RMON

The Remote MONitoring (RMON) MIB will help bridge the gap between the limited services provided by management platforms and the rich sets of data and statistics provided by traffic monitors and analyzers. RMON defines the next generation of network monitoring with more comprehensive network fault diagnosis, planning, and performance-tuning features than any current monitoring solution. The design goals for RMON are:

- Offline operation
- Preemptive monitoring
- Problem detection and reporting
- Value-added data

Offline operation. In order to reduce overhead related to communication links, it may be necessary to limit or halt polling of a monitor by the manager. In general, the monitor should collect fault, performance, and configuration information continuously, even if it is not being polled by a manager. The

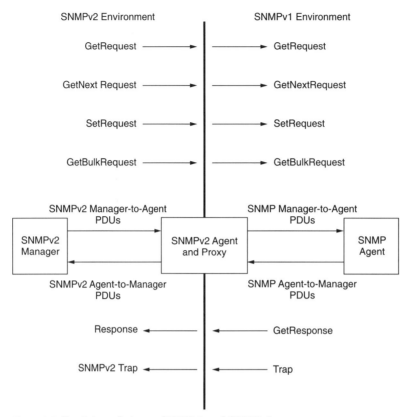

Figure 2.7 Coexistence between SNMPv1 and SNMPv2

monitor simply continues to accumulate statistics that may be retrieved by the manager at a later time. The monitor also may attempt to notify the manager if an exceptional event occurs.

Preemptive monitoring. If the monitor has sufficient resources, and the process is not disruptive, the monitor can continuously run diagnostics and log performance. In the event of a failure somewhere in the network, the monitor may be able to notify the manager and provide useful information for diagnosing the failure.

Problem detection and reporting. Preemptive monitoring involves an active probing of the network and the consumption of network resources to check for error and exception conditions. Alternatively, the monitor can passively—without polling—recognize certain error conditions and other conditions, such as congestions and collisions, on the basis of the traffic that it observes. The monitor can be configured to continuously check for such conditions. When one of these conditions occurs, the monitor can log the condition and notify the manager.

Value-added data. The network monitor can perform analyses specific to the data collected on its subnetworks, thus offloading the manager of this responsibility. The monitor, for instance, can observe which station generates the most traffic or errors in network segments. This type of information is not otherwise accessible to a manager that is not directly attached to the segment.

Multiple managers. An internetworking configuration may have more than one manager to achieve reliability, perform different functions, and provide management capability to different units within an organization. The monitor can be configured to deal with more than one manager concurrently.

Table 2.3 summarizes the RMON MIB groups for Ethernet segments (Mier 1993). Table 2.4 defines the RMON MIB groups for Token-Ring segments. Currently, only a few monitors can measure both types of segments using the same probe.

Because RMON is rich in features, there is a real risk of overloading the monitor, the communication links, and the manager when all the details are recorded, processed, and reported. The preferred solution is to do as much of the analysis as possible locally at the monitor, and send only the aggregated data to the manager. This architecture assumes powerful monitors. In other applications, monitors may be reprogrammed during operations by the managers. This is very useful when diagnosing problems.

Even if the manager can define specific RMON requests, it is necessary to be aware of the trade-offs involved. A complex filter will allow the monitor to capture and report a limited amount of data, thus avoiding overhead on the network. But complex filters consume processing power at the monitor; if too many filters are implemented, the monitor will become overloaded. This is particularly true if the network segments are busy, which is often the time when measurements are most valuable.

CMIP and TMN

Telecommunication Management Network (TMN), a special network in its own right, is implemented to help manage the service provider's telecommunication network. As such, TMN interfaces to one or more individual networks at several points in order to exchange information. It is logically separate from the networks it manages, and may be physically separate as well. However, TMN may use parts of the telecommunication networks for its own communications. Figure 2.8 shows the relationship between TMN and the telecommunication network.

TMN is an extension of the OSI standardization process. It attempts to standardize some of the functionality and many of the interfaces of the managed networks. When TMN is fully implemented, the result will be a higher level of integration. TMN usually is described by three architectures—functional, information, and physical.

The *functional architecture* describes the appropriate distribution of functionality within TMN, appropriate in the sense of allowing implementations to create function blocks from which a TMN of any complexity can be implemented. The definition of function blocks and the reference points between them leads to the requirements for the TMN-recommended interface specifications.

Table 2.3. RMON MIB Groups for Ethernet

Statistics Group	Features a table that tracks about 20 different characteristics of traffic on the Ethernet LAN segment, including total octets and packets, oversized packets, and errors.
History Group	Allows a manager to establish the frequency and duration of traffic — observation intervals, called *buckets*. The agent can then record the characteristics of traffic according to these bucket intervals.
Alarm Group	Permits the user to establish the criteria and thresholds that will prompt the agent to issue alarms.
Host Group	Organizes traffic statistics by each LAN node, based on time intervals set by the manager.
HostTopN Group	Allows the user to set up ordered lists and reports based on the highest statistics generated via the Host Group.
Matrix Group	Maintains two tables of traffic statistics based on pairs of communicating nodes: one is organized by sending node addresses, the other by receiving node addresses.
Filter Group	Allows a manager to define, by channel, particular characteristics of packets. A filter might instruct the agent, for example, to record packets with a value that indicates they contain DECnet messages.
Packet Capture Group	This group works with the Filter Group and lets the manager specify the memory resources to be used for recording packets that meet the filter criteria.
Event Group	Allows the manager to specify a set of parameters or conditions to be observed by the agent. Whenever these parameters or conditions occur, the agent win record an event into a log <MIER93>.

Table 2.4. RMON MIB Groups for Token-Ring

Statistics Group	This group includes packets, octets, broadcasts, dropped packets, soft errors, and packet distribution statistics. Statistics are at two levels: MAC for the protocol level, and LLC statistics to measure traffic flow.
History Group	Long-term historical data for segment trend analysis. Histories include both MAC and LLC statistics.
Host Group	Collects information on each host discovered on the segment.
HostTopN Group	Provides sorted statistics that allow reduction of network overhead by looking only at the most active hosts on each segment.
Matrix Group	Reports on traffic errors between any host pair for correlating conversations on the most active nodes.
Ring Station Group	Collects general ring information and specific information for each station. General information includes: ring state (normal, beacon, claim token, purge); active monitor; number of active stations. Ring Station information includes a variety of error counters, station status, insertion time, and last enter/exit time.
Ring Station Order	Maps station MAC addresses to their order in the ring.
Source Routing Statistics	In source-routing bridges, information is provided on the number of frames and octets transmitted to and from the local ring. Other data includes broadcasts per route and frame counter per hop.
Alarm Group	Reports changes in network characteristics based on thresholds for any or all MIBs. This allows RMON to be used as a proactive tool.
Event Group	Logging of events on the basis of thresholds. Events may be used to initiate functions such as data capture or instance counts to isolate specific segments of the network.
Filter Group	Definitions of packet matches for selective information capture. These include logical operations (AND, OR, NOT) so network events can be specified for data capture, alarms, and statistics.
Packet Capture Group	Stores packets that match filtering specifications.

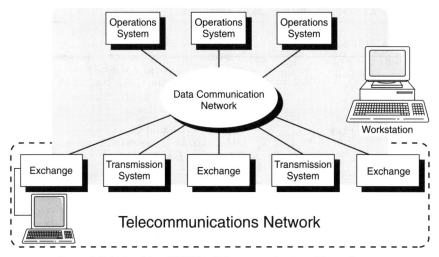

Figure 2.8 General Relationship of TMN to Telecommunications Network

The *information architecture*, based on an object-oriented approach, gives the rationale for applying OSI Systems Management Principles to the TMN Principles. OSI Systems Management Principles are mapped onto the TMN Principles, and where necessary are expanded to fit the TMN environment.

The *physical architecture* describes interfaces that can be implemented, together with examples of physical components that make up the TMN.

TMN management functions are grouped into the five functional areas identified as part of the OSI model. Examples are:

- Fault management (alarm surveillance, testing, trouble administration)

- Configuration management (provisioning, tariffing)

- Performance management (monitoring quality of service, traffic control)

- Security management (managing access and authentication)

- Accounting management (tariffing and billing)

TMN protocols include OSI protocols such as CMIP and FTMP, ISDN and Signalling System No. 7 protocols. They are organized into protocol suites or profiles for specific TMN interfaces. Functions and protocols support TMN services, including the following:

- Traffic management

- Customer management

- Switching

- Management of transport networks

- Management of intelligent networks

- Tariffing and changing

The primary protocol used within TMN is Common Management Information Protocol (CMIP). The estimated overhead scares away both vendors and users, with the exception of the telecommunication industry, where separate channels can be used for management. CMIP is event-driven, and assumes the availability of processing capabilities at the agent level. Once fault and performance thresholds are exceeded, the manager is alerted by the agent. This is similar to SNMP traps. The strengths of CMIP include:

- General and extensible object-oriented approach
- Support from the telecommunication industry
- Support for manager-to-manager communications
- Support for a framework for automation

Weaknesses of CMIP include:

- It is complex and multilayered.
- It incurs high overhead, because it supports many confirmations.
- Few CMIP-based management systems are shipping.
- Few CMIP-based agents are in use.

CMIP assumes the use of the OSI-stack for exchanging CMIP protocol data units. Layer 7 contains other applications that may be combined with CMIP.

Complete implementation of TMN will occur over 3 to 5 years. Practical help is expected from OMNIPoint and Spirit, two initiatives supported by the NM Forum. Chapter 10 includes further details on TMN architecture and implementations.

NM/Forum OMNIPoint and Spirit

OMNIPoint (Open Management Interoperability Point) provides a practical way to implement standards across management systems from multiple suppliers. OMNIPoint attempts to embrace both existing and emerging management standards and technologies. Consequently, it goes beyond TMN by including concepts from the Open Software Foundations' Distributed Communications Environment (OSF/DCE), OSF's Distributed Management Environment (DME), the Telecommunications Intelligent Network Architecture (TINA), and the Object Management Group's Common Object Request Broker Architecture (OMG CORBA). As these technologies mature, they will be more fully utilized by future OMNIPoint releases.

OMNIPoint brings together the many standards and specifications from all parts of the telecommunications and computing industries, turning divergent outputs into a coordinated set of tools that will work together to achieve a specific business goal. In addition to traditional management standards from ISO and the International Telecommunications Union, OMNIPoint takes into consideration service providers' need to interface with their customers' management systems. OMNIpoint can work in conjunction with Internet Engineering Task Force (IETF) standards including SNMP. Similarly, because OMNIPoint is focused on implementation, the work of X/Open and the Object Management Group (OMG) to advance computing platform technology is considered critical.

Through a series of controlled releases, OMNIPoint provides "freeze" points at which developers can build to a specific version of a standard with confidence that their investments will not be worthless in a couple of months. OMNIPoint releases typically are updated in 24- to 30-month cycles; migration strategies make the job of upgrading to the next release relatively easy.

The NM Forum provides two types of OMNIPoint documentation—functional specifications and ensembles. OMNIPoint 1 documentation includes the following functional specifications:

- Testing management, which allows a managing system to invoke, control, monitor, and obtain results of tests on a remote system through an interoperable interface.

- Scheduling management, which allows the scheduled triggering of a function within a managed resource via an interoperable interface.

- Path tracing, which identifies all managed resources involved in an end-to-end communications path.

- Trouble management, which provides for trouble reporting and tracking between systems cooperating toward the resolution of a problem via an interoperable interface. OMNIPoint provides cross-jurisdictional trouble management.

- Security management, which provides for the exchange of security information across an interoperable interface, such as authentication, access control, security alarm, and security audit trail.

The end product is the ensemble, a package of specifications intended to solve one specific management problem by addressing it from a functional point of view. This is the documentation form that can, in one place, provide all information needed to specify a new OMNIPoint-compliant service. It includes requirements, examples, scenarios, information model definitions, references to managed object classes in libraries, and references to all applicable standards. To ensure interoperability, it also references conformance documents. OMNIPoint 1 includes two ensembles relating to Reconfigurable Circuit Service.

In order to work with OMNIPoint recommendations, software portability is extremely important. OMNIPoint specifies the following APIs to isolate an application from particular implementations of underlying services:

- XMP (X/Open Management Protocol) API specifies the protocol interface between an application and a CMIP or SNMP manager, making the application portable from one manager implementation to another. It is used to access the service elements of CMIP and SNMP agents in the managed system.

- XOM (X/Open OSI-abstract-data Manipulation) API specifies the data interface between an application and a CMIP or SNMP manager, making the application portable from one manager implementation to another. It is used to generate the data arguments and parameters in conjunction with XMP to access attribute data in managed objects.

- CORBA (Common Object Request Broker Architecture) specifies the interface between an application object and an Object Request Broker (ORB), making the objects portable from one ORB implementation to another. An ORB allows one object to use another without regard to their remote physical locations in a distributed object environment.

A working team within the Network Management Forum called SPIRIT (Service Providers Integrated Requirements for Information Technology) is attempting to define general purpose software platform requirements to establish a broader basis for network management application portability, interoperability, and modularity. The focus of SPIRIT is displayed in Fig. 2.9.

In principle, for general computing requirements, SPIRIT will follow the work of X/Open guidelines. For application as either a Management Platform or as a Managed Agent, the OMNIPoint specifications will be followed.

DMTF

SNMP may be utilized to manage systems with components that accommodate SNMP agents. Few PC system component vendors have defined MIBs for their products, however, making it difficult to support SNMP-based management of PC systems.

The Desktop Management Interface (DMI) is an important emerging standard for desktop management. The Desktop Management Task Force (DMTF) had created the DMI to accomplish the following goals:

- Enable and facilitate desktop, local, and network management.

- Solve software overlap and storage problems.

- Create a standard method for management of hardware and software components using Management Information Files (MIFs).

- Provide a common interface for managing desktop computers and their components.

- Provide a simple method to describe, access, and manage desktop components.

The scope of management under DMTF includes CPUs, I/Os, mother boards, video cards, network interface cards, faxes, modems, mass storage devices, printers, and applications. The support from the important players is different; Hewlett-Packard is supporting it, Microsoft has left the group to pursue individual ways of managing desktops. IBM and Intel are still primary supporters of DMTF.

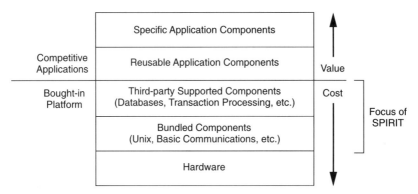

Figure 2.9 The Scope of the SPIRIT Activity

IEEE Posix 1387.2

IEEE Posix 1387.2 addresses the area of software distribution. Electronic software distribution evolved because of the need to automate and control the distribution of both shrink-wrapped and in-house applications to an increasingly diverse set of distributed computers—Unix, OS/2, and DOS/Windows. To address the complexities of this diverse environment, ESD products must possess complex and sophisticated technology while presenting a user interface that shields administrators from the underlying complexities of the task at hand.

The IEEE Posix 1387.2 standard describes how software distribution packages should be defined, and how they should be moved from one platform to another. By 1995, the only major vendor to support this standard was Hewlett-Packard. HP's Software Distributor product implements IEEE Posix 1387.2 as currently specified.

A software distribution package includes the software to be distributed (files, shrink-wrapped applications, in-house software, data, etc.) plus preinstallation scripts or programs, and postinstallation scripts or programs. Some users report that it is much easier to use a graphical user interface (GUI) to build packages, than a text-based command-line interface (CLI). Because different scripts may be needed for different computer configurations, and because desktop configurations vary remarkably from user to user in any organization, the package-building process can be time-consuming. Ease of use in package-building is becoming a key product differentiator.

HP is promoting compliance with this emerging standard. HP has been successful in the past at tying its products to standards such as DME, even though DME standards were not as influential as expected. IBM has promised compliance with this standard.

Summary

Enterprise management requires that all elements of the information technology be included in the management architecture. As a platform, HP

OpenView plays the role of an enabler of enterprise management. Vendors and users are expected to work with Hewlett-Packard to write and integrate applications. In terms of standards, SNMP will play an important role for the majority of commercial management applications. The role of CMIP involves specific applications for the telecommunications industry. HP OpenView in the role of a platform is able to work with all relevant standards. The depth of support is different and governed largely by user demand.

Network Management

An Open Framework

HP OpenView Network Node Manager (NNM) currently occupies a dominant position in the open systems network management market. Looking at NNM by itself, this may seem somewhat surprising, because from its introduction until late 1996, the product lacked distributed management capabilities. Even today, it includes few extras beyond basic Internet Protocol (IP) management functions such as IP node discovery/mapping, SNMP-based monitoring, and SNMP Management Information Base (MIB) application building. Indeed, there are many gaps in NNM's functionality, as this chapter will illustrate.

But the success enjoyed by HP OpenView is no fluke. The sum total of NNM's worth is actually much more than the shrink-wrapped software delivered to the customer. Organizations purchasing NNM are buying into an open systems and network management architecture. NNM acts as the foundation upon which customers layer third-party applications, custom-developed scripts, and even HP value-added software. Most customers purchased NNM anticipating future OpenView releases capable of supporting distributed management features and emerging protocols such as the Object Management Group's Common Object Request Broker Architecture (CORBA), SNMPv2, described in Chap. 2.

HP disappointed many customers in January 1995 by announcing a year's delay in delivering critical NNM enhancements. However, HP is committed to retaining and enlarging its installed base of OpenView customers. In 1996, HP introduced NNM 4.1, featuring distributed polling and topology data-collection features. Additionally, HP strengthened the reach of its existing HP OpenView Solution Framework by embedding NNM into both IT/Operations and IT/Administration, thereby strengthening the integration between the network and system management components of OpenView. Also in 1996, HP announced new event correlation technology that probably will support OpenView in the near term. In coming years, HP is expected to deliver object-oriented functionality based on CORBA.

As a result, customers must understand three strategic aspects of the OpenView family to leverage their investments in the NNM foundation most effectively. These three critical aspects include:

- Availability and viability of third-party add-on applications for NNM and IT/Operations
- Tighter integration between NNM and IT/Operations—operationally, architecturally, and strategically
- Future product directions for the OpenView product suite, including forthcoming releases of NNM

Armed with an understanding of these three concepts, customers will be better equipped to exploit OpenView's potential today and over the next few years.

Gaps in OpenView Functionality

Table 3.1 lists more than 20 areas of network and systems management, illustrating the areas supported by HP OpenView Network Node Manager, other HP products, and applications developed by third parties. In the area of network management, HP OpenView Network Node Manager lacks the following critical facilities:

- Trouble-ticketing
- Data analysis and reporting
- Non-IP fault monitoring and control
- PC administration and control

PC administration and control is handled by IT/Administration for Workgroups, as described in Chap. 13. IT/Administration is not integrated with Network Node Manager, however. Note that the broad areas of SNA, DECnet, NetWare, and legacy management must be addressed entirely by third-party solutions. In the spring of 1996, HP announced intentions to port Network Node Manager and IT/Administration to the Windows NT platform. While the NT environment will be manageable from the HP-UX version of IT/Operations, porting the server portion to NT is not expected until late 1997, as noted in Chap. 13.

In systems management and administration, IT/Operations and IT/Administration lack these important facilities:

- Trouble-ticketing/problem management
- Enhanced security
- Resource accounting and chargeback
- Database and applications management

Table 3.1. Areas of Network and Systems Management Addressed by HP OpenView, HP Applications, and Third-Party Applications

Functional area	HP OpenView Network Node Manager (NNM)	Other HP applications	Third-party applications
SNMP polling	Yes	Yes—HP NetMetrix, LanProbe	Yes—Axon LANServant Manager, NAT EtherMeter, others
SNMP trap handling	Yes	Yes—HP NetMetrix, LanProbe	Yes—Axon LANServant Manager, NAT EtherMeter, others
SNMP MIB application building	Yes	No (addressed by NNM)	Yes—Bridgeway EventIX, Legent ProxyFactory, others
Autodiscovery & topology	Yes	Yes—HP Interconnect Manager	Some monitors
Advanced event handling, filtering	No	Yes—HP IT/Operations	Yes—NetLabs NerveCenter, Boole Command/Post
Automation, rules-based engine, expert system	No	No	Yes—Boole AutoCommand, Gensym G2
Trouble ticket/ help desk	No	No	Remedy AR System, Legent Paradigm, Prolin HelpDesk, others
Network device configuration	No	Yes—HP Interconnect Manager, HP Switch/PAD Manager, others	Yes, many—CiscoWorks, Chipcom OnDemand, SynOptics Optivity, Wellfleet Site Manager, other
Traffic monitoring and analysis	No	Yes—HP NetMetrix, HP LanProbe, EASE	Yes—Axon LANServant Manager, Frontier NetScout, NAT EtherMeter, Wandel & Goltermann IDMS
Data analysis and reporting	No	Yes—PerfView (for Unix servers)	Yes—SAS CPE for Open Systems; some traffic monitors
Physical asset/cable management	No	Yes—HP AssetView	Yes—Accugraph MountainView, Isicad Command, others

Table 3.1. *(continued)*

Functional area	HP OpenView Network Node Manager (NNM)	Other HP applications	Third-party applications
Non-IP management	No	No	Yes—MicroMuse Legacy Watch, Peregrine OpenSNA, StationView/ServerView (OEM'd by HP); Ki DNM, NetTech EView, BridgeWay Eventix
Capacity planning, network design	No	HP Traffic Expert, Resource Manager	Yes—but not integrated
PC, NetWare management	No	Yes— IT/Administration for Workgroups	Yes—Peregrine StationView/ServerView, Network Computing LANAlert (OEM'd by HP)
Message Consolidation/ console automation	No	Yes— IT/Operations	Yes—CA-Unicenter
Database and applications management	No	No	Yes—BMC Patrol, CompuWare EcoTools, Legent, Platinum DB Vision
Change control and configuration management	No	Yes— IT/Administration	Yes—CA-Unicenter
Workload management	No	No	Yes—Unison Maestro
Storage management and backup	No	Yes—HP OmniStorage, HP OmniBack Link II	Yes—CA-Unicenter, Raxco Backup.uunet
Report, print, and spool management	No	Yes—HP OpenSpool	Yes—CA-Unicenter, Raxco Print.uunet
Software distribution	No	Yes—HP Software Distributor	Yes—Platinum Xfer
Resource accounting and chargeback	No	Yes—HP AssetView	Yes—CA-Unicenter
Enhanced security	No	No	Yes—CA Unicenter, Securix BoKS

These areas are addressed by important third-party partners, chiefly Remedy Corp., CA/Legent, Platinum, BMC, and CompuWare.

Using Third-Party Applications to Fill the Gaps

One of HP OpenView's greatest strengths is the breadth of third-party support. Table 3.2 lists more than 60 third-party vendors whose applications can be used in conjunction with Network Node Manager.

In many cases, the level of integration between NNM and third-party applications is limited to the user interface (OSF/Motif support and menu bar) and SNMP event passing. For customers, this means that there may be duplication of effort between NNM and add-on applications, including redundant polling, data collection, and storage of data in redundant topology or event databases. Also, the opportunities for automation are limited when integration stops at the menu bar. Since little or no context is passed between NNM and the application launched from the menu bar, it is impossible for the application to leverage fault diagnostic or topology information that NNM might possess.

There are a number of integration points supported by NNM, as shown in Table 3.3. These integration points include the following:

- OSF/Motif
- Menu bar (user interface)
- SNMP MIB (loadable MIB)
- Event integration
- Ingres usage
- OVwDB usage
- OV SNMP APIs
- OV Install Process
- OV Process management API
- Tracing/logging
- File placement

Table 3.4 categorizes third-party applications according to function, indicating the level of integration supported by each application. Almost all applications listed support integration at the user interface level, at minimum. The vehicle for integrating applications at the OpenView Windows (OVW) level is the Application Registration File.

Application Registration Files define many aspects of the application's interaction with NNM. The Application Registration File specifies how the application will fit into NNM's menu structure, how the application is invoked from selected menu items (for loose integration) or map symbols (for tighter integration), and where to locate application-specific help. The Application

Table 3.2. Third-Party Applications for Network Node Manager — by Vendor

Vendor	Product	Type
3Com	LinkBuilder, NetBuilder, LanPlex Manager	device-specific (hub)
Accugraph	MountainView	physical asset and cable management
Acsys	Paragon	device-specific (hub)
Answer Computer	A priori	help desk
Armon Networking	On-site	traffic monitoring and analysis
AT&T Paradyne	Acculink	device-specific (CSU/DSU)
Autotrol	Konfig	physical asset and cable management
Axon Networks	LANservant Manager	traffic monitoring and analysis
Bay/SynOptics	Optivity	device-specific (hub)
Boole & Babbage	Command/Post	fault management; legacy system management
Bridgeway	EventIX	MIB builder; legacy system management
Bytex	7700 NMS	device-specific (hub)
Cabletron	Spectrum for OpenView	device-specific (hub)
Chipcom	ONdemand NCS	device-specific (hub)
Cisco Systems	Crescendo Manager	device-specific (hub)
Cisco Systems	CiscoWorks	device-specific (router)
ComConsult	CCM	physical asset and cable management
Concord Communications	Trakker	traffic monitoring and analysis
ConWare	NEMA	device-specific (hub)
DCS Dialog	LANconnect Security Manager	device-specific (bridge/router)
Dornier	Cable and Configuration Manager	physical asset and cable management
FiberMux	LightWatch Open	device-specific (hub)
ForeSystems	ForeView	device-specific (ATM switch)
Frontier Software	NetScout Manager	traffic monitoring and analysis
Gandalf Systems	Passport	device-specific (multiplexers and routers)
General DataCom	ENmacs	device-specific (multiplexers and routers)
GenSym	G2	expert system
Hirschmann	StarCoupler Manager	device-specific (hub)
Independence Technologies	SNMP Agent	SNMP MIB builder; applications management
Isicad/Cambio	Command	physical asset and cable management
Ki Networks	DNM	DECnet management
Landmark	TMON for Unix	Unix systems management
LANNET	MultiMan OV	device-specific (hub)

Vendor	Product	Type
Legent	AgentWorks	Unix systems management, database monitoring, SNMP MIB builder
Legent	Paradigm	trouble ticket/help desk
Motorola Codex	9000-UX	device-specific (modem/mux)
Network Application Technology	EtherMeter	traffic monitoring
Network Computing, Inc.	LANAlert	LAN/PC monitoring
Network General	Distributed Sniffer	traffic monitoring and analysis
Network Partners	Trapper	Unix system, database monitoring
N.E.T.	Frame Express	device-specific (frame relay switch)
Onion Peel Software	Productivity Series	mapping, MIB tools, report writer
Open Network Enterprises	M.O.O.N.	applications, server monitoring
Optical Data Systems (ODS)	LANvision	device-specific (hub)
Peregrine Systems	PNMS/Cover	problem management, change control
Peregrine Systems	OpenSNA	SNA network monitoring
Peregrine Systems	StationView/ServerView	PC/NetWare monitoring and control
Perform	SAGE	X.25 network monitoring
Platinum	DB-Vision	database monitoring
Platinum	X-fer	software distribution
Prolin Automation	Pro/HelpDesk	help desk, trouble ticketing
Racal	CMS 6000	device-specific (modem/mux)
RAD Network Devices	MultiVu	device-specific (routers)
Raxco	Backup.unet	backup and restore
Raxco	Print.unet	print spooler
Raxco	Security Toolkit/Unix	security enhancement
Remedy	AR System	help desk/trouble-ticketing
SAS	SASCPE for Open Systems	statistical analysis, trending, reporting
Securix	BoKS	security enhancement
SNMP Research	MLM Configuration Tool	platform enhancement
Telco Systems	MVX	device-specific (Tl mux, CSU/DSUs)
Telemon	TelAlert	pager, alert forwarding system
UB-Networks	NetDirector, AccessEmpower	device-specific (hub)
Unison Software	Maestro	workload management, job scheduler
Wandel & Goltermann	IDMS Manager	traffic monitoring and analysis
Wellfleet/Synoptics	Site Manager	device-specific (router)
WilTel	WilView/ OpenView Link	frame relay/circuit connections
Xyplex	ControlPoint	device-specific (hub)

Registration File also defines which fields to display in OVW dialog boxes, and how the application itself will be managed by NNM.

HP provides a MIB Application Builder GUI to help ease creation of Application Registration Files. For example, using point-and-click, the developer can choose whether an application should display data in the form of a graph, table, or form. The GUI also lets the developer key in the appropriate help text that should be linked with the application.

Table 3.3. HP OpenView Network Node Manager Integration Points

Integration Point	Description
OSF/Motif compliance	Application supports an OSF/Motif-compliant graphical user interface (GUI)
Menu bar integration	Application can be launched by selecting an item from the OpenView menu
SNMP MIB (loadable MIB)	The management information bases (MIBs) required by this application are loaded by the HP OpenView MIB Loader
Event Integration	Events generated by the application are handled by NNM's *trapd* process; events are registered with NNM
Ingres Usage	The application can store data in an Ingres RDBMS, allowing users to access using standard SQL
OvwDB Usage (OVwDB API)	The application can access the OpenView Windows database that manages all object and field data displayed on the NNM map
OV SNMP APIs	These APIs provide direct access to the SNMP protocol
OV Install Process	The application complies with HP OpenView's installation process
OV Process Management API	Allows an application to communicate with the various Unix processes included in NNM. For example, if the operator shuts down HP OpenView, the integrated application is shut down gracefully
Tracing/logging	When integrated at this level, an application will provide status and diagnostic information when it encounters unexpected conditions
File placement	The application follows guidelines in the HP OpenView Programmers Guide that helps avert problems with conflicting file naming and usage

Table 3.4. Third-Party Applications for Network Node Manager—by Function, Listing Integration Levels Supported

	Device-specific applications	
Vendor	Product	Integration levels
3Com	LinkBuilder, NetBuilder, LanPlex Manager	OSF/Motif, menu bar, loadable MIB, OV SNMP API, event integration, file placement
Acsys	Paragon	OSF/Motif, menu bar, loadable MIB, OV SNMP API, event integration, OVwDB Usage
AT&T Paradyne	Acculink	OSF/Motif, menu bar, loadable MIB, OV SNMP API, event integration, file placement, OV Help, OV Install Process, OV Process management, Tracing/Logging, OVwDB Usage
Bay/SynOptics (Premier Partner, OEM Partner)	Optivity	OSF/Motif, menu bar, loadable MIB, OV SNMP API, event integration, file placement, OV Help, OVwDB Usage
Cabletron	Spectrum for OpenView	OSF/Motif, menu bar, loadable MIB, OV SNMP API, event integration, OVwDB Usage
Chipcom/3Com (Premier Partner)	ONdemand NCS	OSF/Motif, menu bar, loadable MIB, OV Help, file placement
Cisco Systems	Crescendo Manager	OSF/Motif, menu bar, loadable MIB, OV SNMP API, event integration
Cisco Systems	CiscoWorks	OSF/ Motif, menu bar, loadable MIB, OV SNMP API, event integration
ConWare	NEMA	OSF/Motif, menu bar, loadable MIB, OV SNMP API, event integration, file placement, OV Help, OV Install, Application Status Information
DCS Dialog	LANconnect Security Manager, Accounting Manager	OSF/Motif, menu bar, loadable MIB, OV SNMP API, event integration, file placement, OV Help, OVwDB Usage, OV Install Process, OV Process Management, Tracing/Logging, Application Desktop, Application Status Information, Problem Resolution Text, Predefined Actions
ForeSystems	Foreview	OSF/Motif, menu bar, loadable MIB, OV SNMP API, event integration, file placement, OVwDB Usage, OV Install Process, OV Process Management
Gandalf (OEM Partner)	Passport	OSF/Motif, menu bar, loadable MIB, OV SNMP API, event integration, file placement, OV Help, OVwDB Usage, OV Install Process, OV Process Management, Tracing/Logging, Tracing/Logging, Ingres, Usage

Table 3.4. *(continued)*

	Device-specific applications	
Vendor	Product	Integration levels
General DataCom (OEM Partner)	ENmacs	OSF/Motif, menu bar, loadable MIB, OV SNMP API, event integration, file placement, OV Help, OVwDB Usage, OV Install Process, OV Process Management, Tracing/Logging
Hirschmann	StarCoupler Manager	OSF/ Motif, menu bar, loadable MIB, OV SNMP API, event integration, file placement, OV Help, OVwDB Usage, OV Install Process, OV Process Management, Tracing/Logging, Application Desktop, Application Status Information, Problem Resolution Text, Predefined Actions
LANNET (Premier Partner, OEM Partner)	MultiMan OV	OSF/Motif, menu bar, loadable MIB, OV SNMP API, event integration, file placement, OV Help, OVwDB Usage, OV Install Process, OV Process Management
Motorola Codex (OEM Partner)	9000-UX	OSF/Motif, menu bar, loadable MIB, OV SNMP API, event integration, file placement, OV Help, OVwDB Usage, OV Install Process, OV Process Management, Tracing/Logging
N.E.T.	FrameXpress Manager	OSF/Motif, menu bar, loadable MIB, OV SNMP API, event integration, OVwDB Usage
Optical Data Systems (ODS) (Premier Partner, OEM Partner)	LANvision	OSF/Motif, menu bar, loadable MIB
Racal (OEM Partner)	CMS 6000	OSF/Motif, menu bar, loadable MIB, event integration, file placement, OVwDB Usage, OV Install Process, OV Process Management, Tracing/Logging
RAD Network Devices	MultiVu	OSF/Motif, menu bar, loadable MIB, OV SNMP API, event integration, file placement, OVwDB Usage, OV Install Process, OV Process Management
Telco Systems	MVX	OSF/Motif, menu bar, loadable MIB, event integration, SNMP APIs, OVwDB Usage, OV Help, OV Process Management
UB Networks (OEM partner)	NetDirector, AccessEmpower	OSF/Motif, menu bar, loadable MIB, OV SNMP APIs, event integration, file placement, OVwDB Usage, OV Install Process, Application Desktop
Wellfleet/SynOptics	Site Manager	OSF/Motif, menu bar, loadable MIB, event integration
Xyplex	ControlPoint	Menu bar, OV Help, loadable MIB, event integration, OV Install Process, file placement

Traffic monitoring and analysis applications		
Vendor	Product	Integration levels
Axon Networks	LANServant manager	OSF/ Motif, menu bar, event integration, file placement, Application Desktop, Application Status Information
Concord Communications	Trakker	Menu bar
Frontier Software	NetScout Manager	OSF/Motif, menu bar, loadable MIB, OV SNMP API, event integration, file placement, OVwDB Usage, OV Help, OV Install Process, OV Process Management, Tracing and Logging, Application Desktop, Predefined Actions
Network General	Distributed sniffer	OSF/Motif, menu bar, loadable MIB, event integration, file placement
Network Application Technology	EtherMeter	OSF/Motif, menu bar, loadable MIB, Application Desktop
Wandel & Goltermann	IDMS Manager	OSF/ Motif, menu bar, OVwDB Usage, loadable MIB, OV SNMP API, event integration, file placement

Help desk and Trouble-Ticketing Applications		
Vendor	Product	Integration levels
CA/Legent (premier Partner)	Paradigm	OSF/Motif, menu bar, Ingres Usage, OV SNMP APIs, event integration, tracing/logging
Metrix	OpenUpTime	No integration supported
Peregrine Systems (Premier Partner)	PNMS/IPAS	menu bar, OV Help, OV SNMP APIs, event integration, OV Process Management, file placement, Application Desktop
Prolin Automation	Pro/HelpDesk	OSF/Motif, menu bar, OV SNMP APIs, event integration, OV Install Process, OV Process Management, Tracing/Logging, Application Desktop, Application Status Information, Problem Resolution Text, Predefined Actions
Remedy (Premier Partner)	AR System	OSF/Motif, menu bar, OVwDB Usage, event integration, file placement, Application Desktop, Application Status Information, Problem Resolution Text, Predefined Actions

Physical asset and cable management applications		
Vendor	Product	Integration levels
Accugraph (Premier Partner)	MT923	OSF/Motif, menu bar, OVwDB Usage, Ingres Usage

Auto-trol	Konfig	menu bar, OV Help, OVwDB Usage

Table 3.4. *(continued)*

Physical asset and cable manaagement applications		
Vendor	Product	Integration levels
ComConsult	CCM	OSF/Motif, menu bar, OVwDB Usage, OV SNMP APIs, event integration, OV Process Management
Dornier	Cable and Configuration Manager	menu bar integration, event integration, predefined actions
Isicad (Premier Partner)	Command	OSF/Motif, menu bar, OV Help, OVwDB Usage, Ingres Usage, OV SNMP APIs, event integration, Tracing/Logging

Unix server, database and applications monitoring applications		
Vendor	Product	Integration levels
Legent	AgentWorks	OSF/Motif, menu bar, OV Help, OVwDB Usage, Ingres Usage, loadable MIB, event integration, file placement
Network Partners	Trapper	OSF/Motif, menu bar, loadable MIB, OV SNMP APIs, event integration, OV Install Process, OV Process Management, Tracing/Logging, file placement, Application Desktop, Application Status, Information, Predefined Actions
Open Network Enterprises	M.O.O.N.	OSF/Motif, menu bar, event integration, OV SNMP APIs
Platinum	DB-Vision	OSF/Motif, menu bar, OV Help, loadable MIB, OV SNMP APIs, event, integration, OV Install Process, Tracing/Logging, file placement, Application Desktop, Application Status Information, Problem Resolution Text, Predefined Actions

Legacy management, other		
Vendor	Product	Integration levels
Boole & Babbage (Premier Partner)	Command/Post	OSF/ Motif, OVwDB Usage, OV SNMP APIs, event integration
Bridgeway	EventIX	
GenSym	G2	OSF/Motif, menu bar, Ingres Usage, OV SNMP APIs, event integration, Tracing/Logging
Independence Technologies	SNMP Agent	OSF/Motif, Ingres Usage, loadable MIB, event integration, OV Process Management, Tracing/Logging, Application Status Information, Problem Resolution Text

	Legacy management, other	
Vendor	Product	Integration levels
Ki Networks (Premier Partner)	DNM	OSF/Motif, menu bar, OV Help, OVwDB Usage, Ingres Usage, event integration, file placement, Application Desktop, Application Status Information, Problem Resolution Text, Predefined Actions
Landmark	TMON for Unix	OSF/Motif, menu bar, loadable MIB, OV SNMP APIs, event integration, OV Install Process, file placement, Application Desktop, Application Status Application Information, Problem Resolution Text, Predefined Actions
Network Computing, Inc.	LANAlert	OSF/Motif, menu bar, OV Help, OVwDB Usage, OV Process Management, Tracing/Logging, file placement
Onion Peel Software	Productivity Series	OSF/Motif, menu bar, OV Help, OVwDB Usage, OV SNMP APIs, OV Install Process, OV Process Management, file placement
Peregrine Systems	OpenSNA	OSF/Motif, menu bar, OV Help, OVwDB Usage, loadable MIB, OV SNMP APIs, event integration, OV Install Process, OV Process Management, file placement, Application Management, file Information, Problem Resolution Text, Predefined Actions Predefined Actions
Peregrine Systems (Premier Partner)	StationView	OSF/Motif, menu bar, OVwDB Usage, OV SNMP APIs, event integration, OV Process Management, file placement, Application Desktop, Application Status Information, Problem Resolution Text, Predefined Actions
Peregrine Systems (Premier Partner)	ServerView	OSF/Motif, menu bar, OVwDB Usage, OV SNMP APIs, event integration, OV Process Management, file placement, Application Desktop, Application Status Information, Problem Resolution Text, Predefined Actions
Perform	SAGE	OSF/Motif, menu bar, OV Help, OVwDB usage, event integration, OV Install Process, OV Process Management, file placement
Platinum	X-fer	OSF/Motif, menu bar, OVwDB Usage, loadable MIB, OV SNMP APIs, event integration
Raxco	Backup.unet	OSF/Motif, menu bar
Raxco	Print.unet	menu bar
Raxco	Security Toolkit/Unix	menu bar
SAS	SAS CPE for Open Systems	OSF/Motif

Table 3.4. *(continued)*

	Legacy management, other	
Vendor	Product	Integration levels
Securix	BoKS	OSF/Motif, menu bar
SNMP Research	MLM Configuration Tool	OSF/Motif, loadable MIB
Telemon	TelAlert	menu bar, event integration
Unison Software	Maestro	OSF/Motif, menu bar, OV Help, OVwDB Usage, loadable MIB, OV SNMP APIs,event integration, OV Process Management, Application Process Management, Application Desktop, Application Status Information, Problem Resolution Text, Predefined Actions
WilTel	WilView/ OpenView Link	OSF/Motif, menu bar

For even tighter integration, the applications developer may choose to use the OpenView Windows API (OVwAPI) that is supplied with the HP OpenView SNMP Developer's Kit. Even applications using the OVwAPI, however, must create Application Registration Files.

HP OpenView Certification Testing

HP provides certification testing for the various integration levels. Third-party applications certified to provide at least one area of integration with HP OpenView may display the label *Certified Partner*. Vendors who have passed certification tests for integration at all levels earn the label *Premier Partner*.
Integration levels subject to certification are as follows:

- User interface (OSF/Motif-compliant, menu bar, OVwAPI usage, etc.).

- Data integration (use of RDBMS to store object attribute information, and support for enrollment dialog or other menu bar access facility for displaying object attribute information).

- Event integration (use of HP OpenView Event Subsystem, with online help describing event; event registration, generation, and usage).

- Protocol integration (protocol and device management, SNMP API usage; MIBs must be loadable with the HP OpenView MIB loader; MIBs must follow relevant RFCs, etc.).

- Product support integration (application's file placement must not conflict with HP OpenView, Premier Partner, or other Certified Partner applications; support for HP OpenView tracing and logging facility for debugging purposes; etc.).

The number of third-party vendors and applications supporting OpenView NNM is an advantage, as it gives the customer many options for building a more comprehensive management solution. In practice, however, a single copy of NNM can support no more than two to four third-party applications without adversely affecting performance—assuming NNM is running on a midrange workstation. Typically, customers will integrate a trouble-ticket application with NNM, and perhaps a traffic-monitoring application. One or two device-specific applications such as CiscoWorks or SynOptics Optivity may be launched from OpenView, although many customers instead use SunNet Manager for router and hub management.

Thus, it is not unusual for organizations to maintain both SunNet Manager and HP OpenView NNM, or IBM NetView for AIX. Unfortunately, neither Sun, HP, nor IBM support links to competing management systems. Applications for synchronizing maps and correlating events between disparate management systems are available from several independent software vendors, however. In particular, Micromuse offers an application called NetCool/OMNIbus for collecting, prioritizing, filtering, and correlating events from multiple copies of SunNet Manager, HP OpenView NNM, and IBM NetView for AIX, in any combination. Bridgeway Corp.'s MapSync utility can be used to synchronize network topology maps across multiple copies of these same management systems, again in any combination.

Integration between NNM, IT/Operations, MeasureWare/PerfView, and IT/Administration

The level of integration between Network Node Manager, IT/Operations, MeasureWare/PerfView, and IT/Administration is more or less limited to the user-interface level and SNMP event passing. Each product maintains its own separate databases. PerfView supports a Data Source Integration (DSI) interface, allowing users to integrate existing shell scripts as well as IT/Operations commands; this requires a bit of work on the part of the administrator, however.

Operational and architectural integration

There are architectural reasons for the lack of tight integration between these four HP products. NNM is designed to communicate with SNMP agents. IT/Operations deploys HP-proprietary RPC-based agents that are optimized to collect large quantities of information in bulk operations. IT/Administration also employs HP-proprietary RPC-based agents that are different than (e.g., not interoperable with) IT/Operations agents. PerfView communicates with its agents using Berkeley sockets. HP is expected to migrate these three products to standard Open Software Foundation Distributed Computing Environment (OSF DCE) RPC-based agent communication mechanisms. The procedural code will still be HP-developed.

Strategic integration

HP's strategy is to synthesize IT/Operations, MeasureWare/PerfView, and IT/Administration into a single, seamless offering that supports the concept of *Process Centers* for problem, performance, and configuration management. As Fig. 3.1 shows, NNM provides *Common Services* underneath the Process Centers. Within this architecture, IT/Operation's role is that of a universal *problem collector*, for events from routers, hubs, and other network devices, as well as from Unix computers. According to HP, this approach will provide one common process for handling a problem, whether it comes from the network, servers, databases, or applications.

This approach can be beneficial because it allows customers to streamline their operations support staff by merging aspects of network management, systems administration, and database administration under one common interface. This is a radical step for many customers who have established traditional organizational boundaries between network and systems management.

Figure 3.2 depicts the architectural outline of the Process Centers concept. Figure 3.3 illustrates the evolution of the HP OpenView product set toward the Process Center architecture. It is important to note that HP's strategic direction includes de-emphasizing Network Node Manager as a standalone

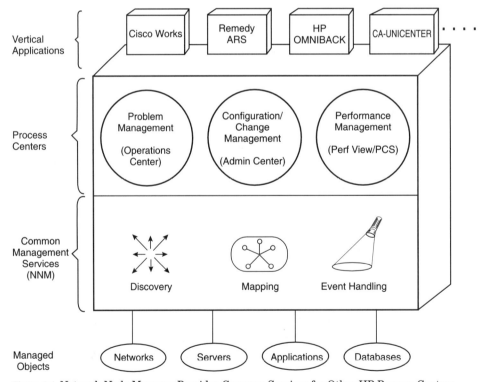

Figure 3.1 Network Node Manager Provides Common Services for Other HP Process Centers

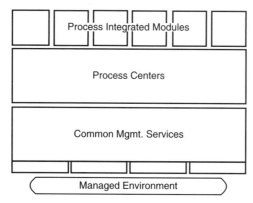

Figure 3.2 Architectural Outline of HP's Process Center Concept

product. Instead, NNM plays a supporting role, and it is likely that HP will bundle NNM in with IT/Operations and IT/Administration in future offerings.

In 1995, HP inaugurated a Solution Framework program for IT/Operations and IT/Administration that is similar to the Solution Partners program for NNM. Thanks to the Solution Framework program, HP has won several major vendor endorsements for IT/Operations, including those from Computer Associates, Legent, Oracle, SAP, and Unison Software. HP hopes to attract major database vendors into the program, and has promised to open up its application programming interfaces on IT/Administration in 1996.

Currently, the integration points for IT/Operations in the Solutions Framework include the following:

- Application Desktop
- Application Status Information
- Problem Resolution Text
- Predefined Actions

Application desktop. Application Desktop is an interface providing a consistent way of presenting and invoking applications, scripts, and commands. Operators can tailor the parameters and entry points as needed.

Application status information. Through the Application Status Information interface, IT/Operations collects status information from a given application. For applications that write to logfiles, the IT/Operations Logfile Encapsulation service extracts and classifies the application information. IT/Operations also can capture SNMP traps and treat them as collected messages.

Problem resolution text. Users or vendors may provide message-specific help text to operators to help them resolve problems faster.

Predefined actions. Users or vendors may preconfigure corrective actions to assist operators in solving problems. An action can be a shell script, program,

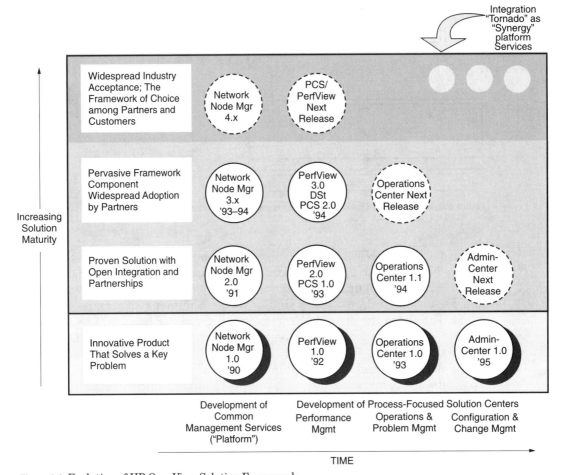

Figure 3.3 Evolution of HP OpenView Solution Framework

application trigger, or other response. These actions can be designated as auto-matic, operator-initiated, or operator-driven.

Chapters 11 and 12 discuss IT/Operations, IT/Administration, and MeasureWare/PerfView in greater detail.

Evolution toward Distributed Management

As previously mentioned, NNM was introduced primarily as a single-operator product capable of supporting typically fewer than 1000 and no more than 2000 nodes in an average configuration. Prior to NNM 4.0, the graphical user interface (GUI) client process was tied to the server facility; multiple operators were supported only through X displays. Prior to NNM 4.1, the inability of multiple copies of NNM to share information efficiently exacerbated this prob-lem, and made it difficult for organizations with large networks to deploy NNM as an enterprise-wide management solution.

HP recognized these limitations and enhanced NNM by splitting off the GUI client from the server in version 4.0, and by adding new capabilities for manager-to-manager exchange of topology and event information in version 4.1. Figures 3.4-3.6 show the evolution of NNM through these major architectural enhancements.

The architecture of NNM 3.3, as shown in Fig. 3.4, supports multiple operators through X displays only. Redirecting displays is highly resource-consumptive; also, multiple operators typically function in read-only mode, and one operator cannot see what the other operator is doing.

NNM 4.0, also called Tornado Release I, splits the GUI from the server, supporting a true client/server architecture, as shown in Fig. 3.5. In NNM 4.1 (Tornado Release II) the distributed capability was extended to support distributed polling and topology data collection.

According to HP, the enhancements made in NNM 4.1 can enable active management of up to about 25,000 IP devices. This assumes deployment of multiple Network Node Manager consoles in a hierarchical or cooperative arrangement. In addition, customers may purchase NNM Entry, a low-end version of NNM that is capable of monitoring no more than 100 devices. Because of the 100-device limitation, NNM is not widely used, although it does have applicability at remote branch offices, for example. A sample architecture for distributed management using NNM 4.1 is shown in Fig. 3.6.

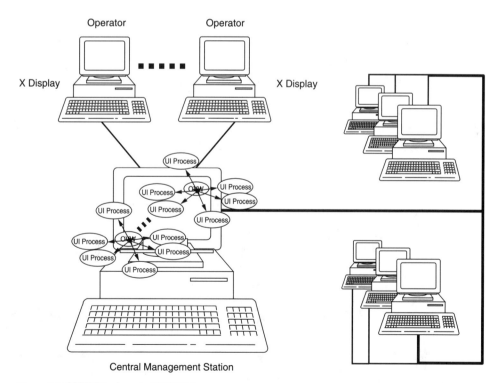

Figure 3.4 OVW Displays in NNM 3.3

NNM 4.1 supports distributed management through the following facilities:

- Distributed internetwork discovery and monitoring (DIDM)
- On-demand submaps and large-map viewer
- Filters for reducing the amount of extraneous data
- Event forwarding from remote stations
- Distributed threshold monitoring for localizing the collection of SNMP trend data

As Chap. 4 describes in detail, NNM 4.1 adds and extends certain key NNM processes to support sharing of topology and event data between multiple NNM consoles. The ability for multiple NNMs to share data is the key to achieving distributed management with OpenView. Data sharing among NNMs also allows the product to be deployed in several architectural models, including the following:

- Fully centralized
- Centralized/hierarchical

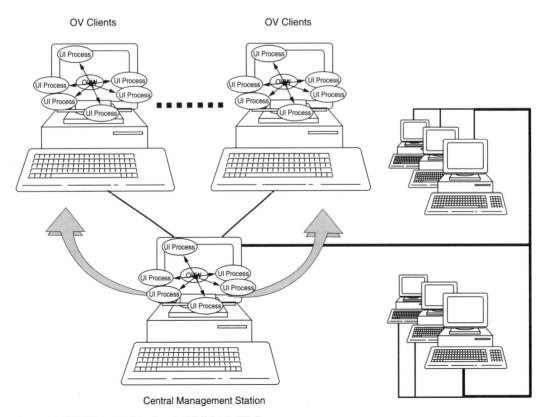

Figure 3.5 OVW Remote Displays in NNM 4.0 (TR I)

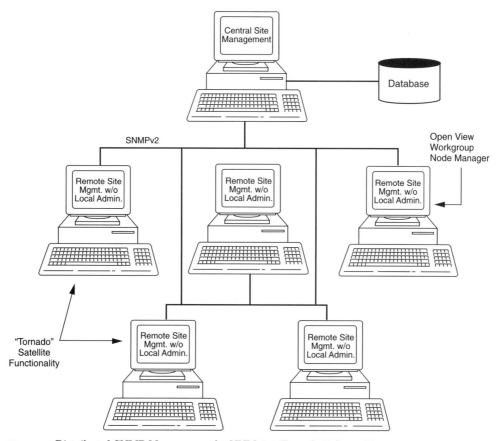

Figure 3.6 Distributed SNMP Management by NNM 4.1 (Tornado Release II)

- Hierarchical
- Cooperative/independent

NNM can be deployed to follow a fully centralized management model in which the entire network comprises a single management domain, and one management station performs all monitoring and data collection for that domain. In essence, all NNM deployments prior to release 4.1 were constrained to follow this model if no third-party applications were used to extend NNM's capabilities. Figure 3.7 depicts a fully centralized approach (Hewlett-Packard 1996).

A fully centralized approach has the advantage of being simpler to configure than the alternatives. However, if polling must occur over wide area links, the model can be inefficient. Typically, no more than 2000 nodes can be actively managed using a fully centralized approach.

Starting with release 4.1, NNM can support a centralized-hierarchical approach in which operators are located at a central management station, but

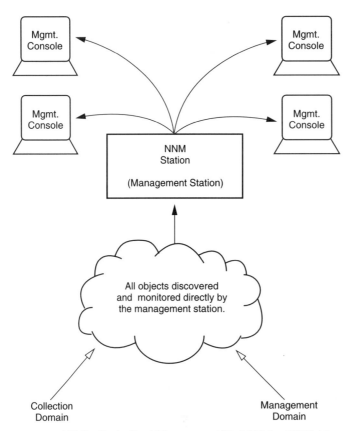

Figure 3.7 A Fully Centralized Management Model Using NNM 4.1

one or more local *collection stations* are deployed throughout the network to perform local discovery and polling. Collection stations are the same NNM software as management stations, except that they are listed as managed objects in the management stations domain. Figure 3.8 depicts a centralized-hierarchical management model.

All topology data and trap events are forwarded from the collection stations to the management station. The collection stations perform localized threshold monitoring (forwarding threshold events). The advantage to this model is that collection stations perform localized discovery and polling; traffic over the wide area is reduced. Scalability increases, tenfold or more, in the number of managed nodes. This model is more complex to properly configure and there is risk involved in relying totally on unstaffed collection stations for gathering data.

NNM 4.1 also supports a hierarchical management model, which allows collection stations to act as independent management stations, as shown in Fig. 3.9.

It is important to note that NNM 4.1 does not suport multiple-level hierarchies, as topology and status data can be forwarded only once. If data is forwarded from one collection station to another, that same data cannot be forwarded again from the second collection station to a management station.

The advantage of a hierarchical approach is that it takes full advantage of NNM's distributed features for optimal scalability, which is particularly valuable in multisite, geographically dispersed network configurations. However, this model can be difficult to configure; collection station topology filters must be carefully selected to forward only objects of interest to the management station; similarly, discovery and monitoring must be tuned for efficiency but without suppressing critical data that should be forwarded. Because management station and collection station domains may overlap, care must be taken to properly configure map filters. (Discovery, topology, map, and event filters are discussed in Chap. 4.)

Finally, NNM now supports a cooperative/independent management model, which may be appropriate in networks with independent sites wishing to share information at the boundaries of their management domains. Figure 3.10 depicts a cooperative/independent management architecture.

Again, care must be taken when configuring discovery, topology, event, and map filters. Configuration may be complex, depending upon specific network

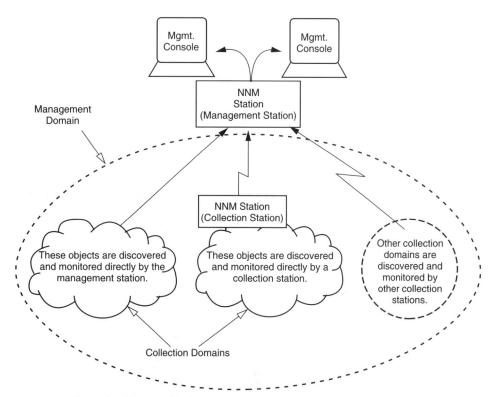

Figure 3.8 A Centralized-Hierarchical Management Model Using NNM 4.1

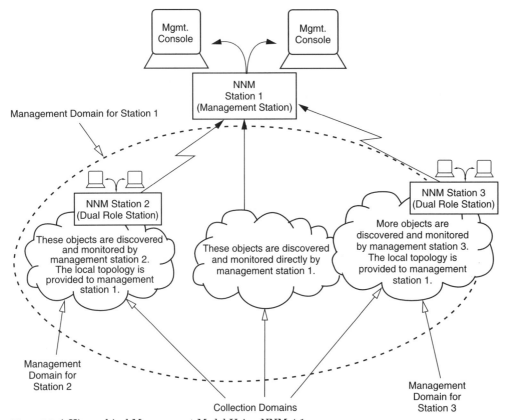

Figure 3.9 A Hierarchical Management Model Using NNM 4.1

requirements, as a management station might have a hierarchical as well as a cooperative relationship, depending upon topology and event data passed back and forth. Points of failure must be considered, particularly in the areas of management domains that are not overlapping. When deployed properly, the cooperative/independent architecture can be highly scalable and efficient.

Summary

HP OpenView NNM is the market leader for open systems network management. The product acts as a foundation upon which other management applications can be layered; these applications may be developed by HP, third parties, or customers. HP enjoys significant support from third-party software developers. HP has created a certification program for testing integration levels between OpenView products and third-party applications.

Until 1996, NNM lacked distributed management capabilities. However, with NNM 4.1, new processes and filters were added to support sharing of

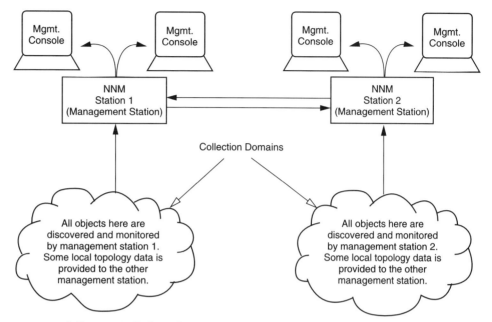

Figure 3.10 A Cooperative/Independent Management Model Using NNM 4.1

topology and event data between multiple copies of NNM. These enhancements allow NNM to be deployed according to several different management
models, including fully centralized, centralized/hierarchical, hierarchical, and
cooperative/independent.

Using HP OpenView Network Node Manager

This chapter describes how to use HP OpenView Network Node Manager (NNM) to perform five basic tasks: discover the network, map the network, load SNMP MIBs, browse SNMP MIBs, and handle SNMP traps. Support for the distributed discovery and event forwarding features of NNM 4.1 also are described. These basic functions are fundamental to supporting the critical tasks of collecting and analyzing SNMP data, as described in Chapters 5–6.

The first step for using NNM is to become familiar with the key Unix processes, or *daemons*, in the software responsible for accomplishing the basic NNM functions. These Unix processes, the names of which are printed in *italic type* in this book, sometimes are referred to as *applications*.

NNM Processes

NNM includes a number of task-specific processes that carry out different jobs. There are two basic types of NNM processes:

- Background processes are global processes that run continually during normal operations.

- Foreground processes are invoked when the OpenView Windows (*ovw*) user interface starts up.

Background processes

The process responsible for initiating and monitoring all other background global processes is *ovspmd*, NNM's process manager. The *ovspmd* oversees a number of processes including *netmon,* responsible for discovering the network; *ovtopmd* which maintains the topology database; *trapd*, which receives and logs SNMP traps; *ovactionid,* which identifies traps; and *snmpCollect,*

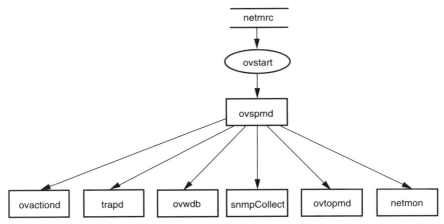

Figure 4.1 Background Processes at Manager Startup

which collects SNMP data. Starting with NNM 4.1, two new processes replace *trapd*: *ovtrapd*, and *pmd*. These processes, along with *netmon, ovtopmd, ovactionid*, and *snmpCollect* are child processes of *ovspmd*, as shown in Fig. 4-1 (Hewlett-Packard 1993).

In addition, *ovspmd* monitors the critical *ovwdb* process that controls NNM's OpenView Windows object database. By default, *ovwdb* uses a TCP socket bound to port 9999; for OpenView Windows to work, no other OpenView application can use port 9999.

It is important to note that *ovwdb* will shut down if the system runs out of virtual memory. The performance of the GUI also will suffer when NNM runs out of physical memory and begins swapping. To reduce memory requirements, an administrator can lengthen polling intervals or unmanage less critical nodes. Alternately, the administrator can stop collecting MIB data on selected MIB objects.

Several background processes depend upon other processes to operate properly. Background process dependencies are listed in Table 4.1 (Hewlett-Packard 1993).

Table 4.1. Background Process Dependencies

Background Process	Dependencies
netmon	ovwdb, trapd, ovtopmd, and snmpd
ovtopmd	ovwdb and trapd
ovwdb	no dependencies
snmpCollect	ovwdb, trapd, and ovtopmd
trapd	no dependencies
ovactionid	trapd

Foreground processes

Foreground processes are initiated when the OpenView Windows user interface is invoked. The parent process of the user interface is *ovw*; it initiates and monitors the map drawing process *(ipmap)*, the display of SNMP traps *(xnmevents)*, the MIB browsing process *(xnmbrowser)*, the SNMP MIB loading process *(xnmloadmib)*, the process for polling MIB objects *(xnmcollect)*, the process for graphing polling results *(xnmgraph)*, and the process for customizing SNMP polling procedures *(xnmsnmpconf)* (See Fig. 4-2). There are many other foreground processes, as described in (Hewlett-Packard 1993).

The *ovw* process provides NMM's graphical user interface, including the hierarchy of submaps depicting network layout and node status, and the set of pull-down menus for accessing applications and map operations. At startup, *ovw* reads registration files to define both the symbols used in the map, as well as the applications that are integrated at the menu-bar level. Modifying the registration files is one way in which users can customize NNM.

Network Discovery

NNM discovers the addresses of IP network nodes via the *netmon* process, storing network-level connectivity data in NNM's IP topology database. Because *netmon* discovers only IP addresses, third-party products must be used in conjunction with NNM to discover SNA, DECnet, IPX, and other non-IP protocol addresses.

The *netmon* process employs both SNMP-based polling and ICMP requests to discover network topology, status, and configuration changes. First, *netmon* uses SNMP to query a nearby router's routing and address resolution protocol (ARP) tables. The results of the query yield IP addresses of neighboring routers, to which *netmon* sends additional SNMP query for more addresses. This procedure is repeated over and over, yielding the addresses of more and more routers.

If a network is connected to the Internet, *netmon* easily might start discovering routers outside the boundaries of the organization's network (Waldbusser 1995). Administrators can limit discovery by using a seed file *(seedfile)* and carefully configuring the subnet masks on the routers identified in the seed file.

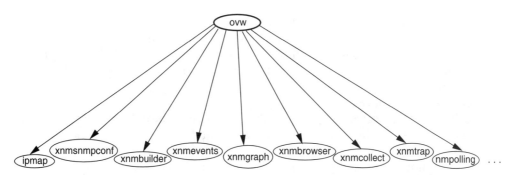

Figure 4.2 Foreground Processes Started from ovw

Netmon's ability to discover network nodes also is affected by the options chosen for *netmon* in the configuration (startup) file, *ovsuf*. (For more information on *ovsuf*, see Hewlett-Packard 1993.) *Netmon's* behavior is affected by the contents of the SNMP Configuration Database *ovsnmp.conf*. This database associates a status monitoring interval with the specified nodes, e.g., it controls how often *netmon* monitors the status of nodes.

The default SNMP configuration database is stored in the */usr/OV/conf/ovsnmp.conf_db* directory.

There is a corresponding shadow file—these two files are kept in sync by the *xnmsnmpconf* process. HP provides hard-coded defaults for the SNMP Configuration Database, including a polling interval of 5 minutes, a time-out value of 0.8 seconds, and a retry count of 3 attempts.

Tip: If NNM's performance is degrading (for example, it takes a long time for the map to reflect event notifications), you may try lengthening the polling interval—particularly for noncritical network nodes—or reducing the retry count or the time-out value. Doing this, however, probably will increase the number of events generated, including more of the nonmeaningful events.

There are several important observations to be made about NNM's discovery function:

- The *netmon* process is optimized for routed, rather than bridged, environments.

- The *netmon* process works best if all routers support SNMP agents.

- Administrators can use *ping* to supplement automated discovery when, for example, *netmon* fails to discover non-SNMP nodes. Alternately, customers can add the node manually to the IP topology database.

As it gathers IP network addresses, the *netmon* process populates NNM's IP topology database. IP topology data is stored as a series of ASCII (flat file) tables. The first series of tables describes network-level connectivity data, the next series describes segments, the third describes nodes, and the final series of tables describes node interfaces.

Distributed discovery, as supported in NNM 4.1, is described later in this chapter.

Updates to the IP topology database are made on a continuous basis from information collected by *netmon* from *managed* nodes. Administrators can designate important nodes as managed. Managed nodes are polled for status and configuration on a regular basis. Nodes left *unmanaged* are polled only on demand—that is, when an administrator initiates a specific request to poll that particular device.

NNM's IP topology database initially is created by the *ovtopmd* process before it is populated by *netmon*. *Netmon* usually can discover several hundred nodes during the first hour, depending upon the model of workstation used. However, it is not unusual for complete discovery to take up to 8 hours or more.

Network Mapping

NNM's map-drawing facilities can help administrators obtain meaningful views of network topology. Understanding a network's topology is fundamental to most other network management tasks, including effective fault isolation, performance analysis, and capacity planning. The network's logical topology is depicted through a series of maps generated by the *ipmap* process.

NNM's *ipmap* process is an OpenView Windows *(ovw)* application that constructs a graphical map using data obtained from the IP topology database. The map is hierarchically organized into submaps, reflecting the same hierarchy found in the IP topology database tables—e.g., internetworks, networks, segments, nodes, and interfaces.

When *ipmap* is first invoked, it talks with *ovtopmd* to bring the graphical map up to date with the IP topology database. This synchronization phase may last several minutes or more initially. Synchronization may recur periodically as *netmon* discovers new nodes. Synchronization of multiple "collection station" databases in NNM 4.1 are discussed later in this chapter.

The *ipmap* process is invoked automatically whenever the OpenView Windows user interface *(ovw)* starts up. There is an important relationship between *netmon* and *ipmap*, since *netmon* is continually retrieving status information and feeding it into the IP topology database. If the polling intervals are too frequent for the network's size, *netmon* may not be able to keep pace. As a result, updates to the map may lag several minutes or more behind actual network events. If this occurs, it may then take five minutes or so for an icon to turn red after a device goes down.

The solution to this problem is to lengthen the polling interval, reduce the retry interval, or designate less critical nodes as *unmanaged* so that *netmon* does not need to keep checking their status. Using multiple copies of NNM to divide the network into multiple domains is yet another option, and one that has been made more attractive by the introduction of distributed management features described later in this chapter.

Users can edit the network map by adding or deleting symbols. Table 4.2 shows the symbols describing objects in the internet, network, segment, and node submaps.

The internet submap represents the highest level view of the network, showing gateways, networks, and the connections between them.

The network submap represents the next level down, showing an IP network as a collection of segments and connections such as routers, bridges, and hubs.

The segment submap displays an individual segment's topology, be it a bus, star, or ring.

Finally, the node submap is the lowest level submap provided by *ipmap*. It displays the interfaces discovered by *netmon*. Users can add other symbols and information to describe individual nodes.

Users can specify whether or not *ipmap* should automatically create all submaps for all networks and segments. For very large networks, it may be

Table 4.2. Map Symbol Types

Submap Level	Symbols
Internet	Network: Internet
Network	Network: IP
Segment	Network: Bus
	Network: Star
	Network: Token
	Network: FDDI Ring
Node	Connector: Gateway
	Connector: Bridge
	Connector: Multiport
	Connector: Repeater
	Connector:Generic
	Interfaces
	Cards: Generic
	Cards: IP
	Cards: Serial
	Cards: Star LAN
	Cards: FDDI
	Cards: Token-Ring
	Cards: X.25

NOTE: If *netmon* discovers a node that has no particular IP topology behavior and no SNMP sysObjectID, ipmap will assign it a default symbol of type Computer:Generic.

wise to be selective about generating submaps, since the procedure can become very resource-consumptive.

Users should note that map editing cannot take place during the *ipmap* synchronization phase. It also is important to remember that deleting an individual map symbol does not automatically delete the corresponding object from the IP topology database. To delete an object in the IP topology database, all symbols representing that object must first be deleted from all submaps.

Loading MIBs

NNM supports the ability to load any standard or enterprise-specific SNMP MIB. The *xnmloadmib* process installs MIBs allowing administrations or NNM applications to browse, query, or manipulate the variables in those MIBs.

All loaded MIBs are written into a single ASCII file called */usr/OV/conf/snmpmib*. The *xnmloadmib* process compiles this list to produce the binary file */usr/OV/conf/snmpmib.bin* that is used by SNMP applications.

While the *xnmloadmib* process makes MIB loading a straightforward operation, it is not unusual for administrators to experience problems loading new MIBs. The syntax of the new MIB may be incorrect—this is hardly rare.

Additionally, the object label in the MIB module must be unique. For example, if the mnemonic name for an object ID component is used more than once in the module, the second object will show up in the MIB tree under the first object, sharing the common component name. As a result, SNMP queries will fail because the translation from the mnemonic object name to the numeric object ID (OID) will be incorrect. Workarounds for this problem are offered in (Hewlett-Packard 1993).

MIB Browsing and Graphing

NNM allows administrators to browse any MIB loaded with *xnmloadmib* as well as HP enterprise-specific MIBs and standard SNMP MIBs that come pre-loaded with NNM. The *xnmbrowse* process supports point-and-click traversal and viewing of SNMP MIB variables and values. The values may be graphed or displayed in text form. *Xnmbrowse* is user-friendly, allowing administrators to access the MIB browsing facility from the menu bar.

NNM provides two tools for displaying MIB data—the *xnmgraph* process and the *xnmappmon* process.

Xnmgraph is a Motif-based graphing utility that can graph real-time SNMP data or historical SNMP data obtained from binary files created by the *snmpCollect* process. *Xnmgraph* is a flexible tool supporting more than two dozen options for customizing the appearance and statistical content of the graphs produced.

Xnmappmon is more of a development tool that enables existing SNMP management applications to be integrated into the NNM menu bar. The *xnmappmon* process encapsulates output of terminal-based commands into a consistent, integrated presentation with the OpenView Windows look and feel. *Xnmappmon* also supports a large number of options for greater flexibility.

Handling SNMP Traps

NNM distinguishes between raw SNMP traps and events. Traps are sent by SNMP devices and received by the *trapd* process (*ovtrapd* process in versions 4.1 and higher) at either the TCP or UDP port 162, logged into a trap log file, and multiplexed to local applications. (In contrast, events are not raw traps from devices, but rather messages from NNM processes such as *netmon*. An SNMP trap becomes an event once *trapd* has received it and has reliably broadcast it to all OpenView processes that have registered for that trap. The relationship between *trapd* and other NNM processes is shown in Fig. 4.3. Traps and events stored in the logfile include the fields listed in Table 4.3. The *ovtrapd* process is described later in this chapter.

Administrators can specify that traps be forwarded to applications running on different management stations—the traps are forwarded to standard UDP port 162. Trap forwarding can become somewhat tricky when traps are to be forwarded to remote management stations on different subnets. Instead of ending up on UDP port 162, these ports are sent to TCP port 162.

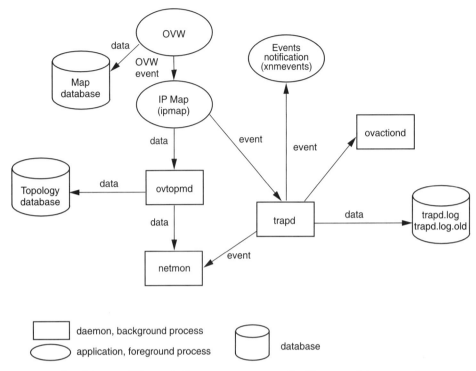

Figure 4.3 Trapd Logs and Forwards Traps to netmon, ovactionid, ovtopmd, ipmap, and xnmevents

Table 4.3. Trap Fields

Field	Meaning
Seconds	The time stamp (Time the trap was received in seconds since 00:00:00 GMT January 1, 1970).
Cat	Category number
Time	The formatted time stamp (readable equivalent to seconds)
EventSrc	Source (IP address) of the trap or event
SWSrc	Software source of the trap or event—includes dates on which OpenView component generated the event (as defined with the *trapd.conf* file)
Desc	A description of the trap or event (as defined with the *trapd.conf* file)
Sev	Numerical severity of the event
OID	The SNMP Object ID of the device generating the event
Gen	The SNMP generic trap number (for OpenView-generated events, this number will be 6).
Spec	The SNMP specific trap number
OvObjID	The OpenView OID (0 if not available)

NOTE: For OpenView-generated events, the Enterprise OID will always be .1.3.6.1.4.1.11.2.17.1

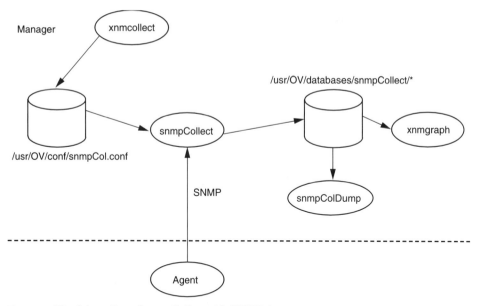

Figure 4.4 The Interaction of *snmpCollect* with SNMP Agents

SNMP Data Collection

NNM's *snmpCollect* process collects SNMP MIB values from managed nodes at user-defined polling intervals, optionally logging them to two types of files: binary data files (a new file is created for each individual MIB variable) and a separate OID file containing the OID, syntax, and units for each MIB variable. Figure 4.4 shows the interaction of *snmpCollect* with SNMP agents.

The *snmpCollect* process can be used to compare collected data values against user-defined thresholds, generating events when the thresholds are exceeded. The process of setting and adjusting thresholds is discussed in more detail in Chap. 7

NNM provides no prepackaged mechanism for automating complex responses to specific network events other than logging and displaying alerts. However, by dumping the *snmpCollect* files and sorting through them, it is possible to write scripts that trigger specific actions based on results of the data file search. It also is possible to sort through *snmpCollect* files to produce a more refined categorization of managed nodes. Administrators can take advantage of refined groupings to drive data collection processes in a more efficient manner—in essence, to customize NNM to implement policy-based management.

Administrators should be aware that *snmpCollect* will stop running if the disk is full. If there is a danger of running out of disk space, the administrator can lengthen the polling interval or stop storing logged data altogether and simply monitor for thresholds. The administrator also can use the Unix *cron* facility to schedule periodic removal of old *snmpCollect* files.

Tip: If Network Node Manager's performance begins to degrade noticeably, another option is to increase the queue limit on outstanding SNMP requests. This is done by increasing the *-n* option (NumberConcurrentSNMP) on *snmpCollect.* The higher the number, the better the throughput—however, this will increase SNMP traffic on the network.

Processes and filters for distributed management

NNM 4.1 contains new processes and filters supporting efficient exchange of topology and event data between two or more NNM consoles. Specifically, NNM 4.1 supports distributed discovery, event forwarding, and distributed thresholding.

Processes and filters for distributed discovery

Starting with NNM Release 4.1, several global background processes can be deployed in distributed fashion on remote collection stations. As Chap. 3 notes, a collection station is any NNM station acting the role of a remote data collector, gathering information about its managed domain. Collection stations appear as managed objects from the management station. By executing the following command from the management station:

$OV_BIN/xnmtopoconf -print

one can spot the collection stations as managed.

Figure 4.5 shows the key processes involved in a distributed deployment of NNM. The *netmon* and *ovtopmd* processes described previously in this chapter feed selected topology data from remote collection stations to *ovrepld,* a new process that replicates topology data at the central management station (Hewlett-Packard 1996).

The *ovrepld* process is responsible for replicating the remotely collected topology data in the management station's SQL topology database (controlled by *ovtopmd*). As such, *ovrepld* is the key process for supporting distributed discovery.

It is important to note that *ovrepld* does not discover any data on its own; it passively forwards only data derived from the *netmon* process local to the collection station onto a central management station. It also is important to note that *ovrepld* replicates only topology data; it does not forward event data, nor does it interact with or affect any other databases, such as those controlled by *ovwdb, snmpCollect,* or *ovw.*

The *ovrepld* process is responsible for synchronizing data between collection stations and management stations. Figure 4.6 depicts a typical relationship between collection and management stations. The *ovrepld* process sends topology data from a collection station to the management station as specified by the topology filter. As the upcoming section on filters describes, objects rejected by a topology filter remain in the collection station's local topology database. HP provides predefined filters, as described in the next section; a filter definition language is supported.

A full topology synchronization causes a complete check of every attribute of every object reported by the remote collection station (Hewlett-Packard 1996). This includes adding objects found by the remote collection station that are unknown to the management station, and deleting objects from the management station that are unknown to the remote collection station.

A full synchronization is performed by executing the following command:

nmdemandpoll -s collectionstation

The output of this command includes status of the synchronization process, information about the objects processed, and warnings about objects with conflicts or errors.

After synchronization, *ovrepld* interracts with the management station's topology database only to provide updates on changes in status and topology, as forwarded by remote collection stations. There is a 5-minute default for interval between status checks. If a check fails, the following progression occurs:

- First failure: *collection station warning* event
- Second failure (10 minutes): *collection station minor* event
- Third failure (15 minutes): *collection station major* event
- Fourth failure (20 minutes): *collection station critical* event

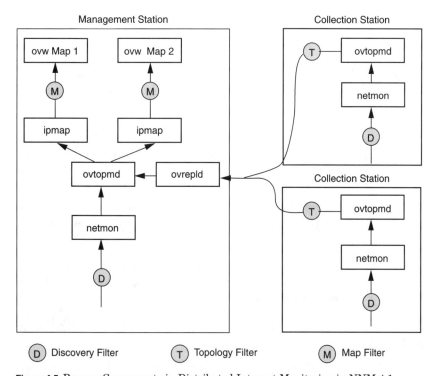

Figure 4.5 Process Components in Distributed Internet Monitoring in NNM 4.1

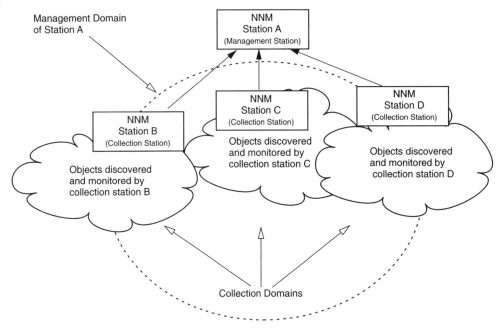

Figure 4.6 Management and Collections Domains

Topology Filters

The proper use of filters is essential for efficient and effective deployment of the distributed capabilities of NNM 4.1. Each filter's function is to control the exchange of information between collection stations and management stations by suppressing unnecessary information, thereby reducing excess traffic—particularly over WAN links.

NNM 4.1 supports two basic types of filters:

■ Data stream filters that permit some objects to proceed, and others to be blocked. Downstream from the data stream filter, the data stream includes only those objects accepted (passed) by the filter.

■ Set-defining filters that are applied to a pool of *candidate* objects evaluated. Only those objects meeting specified criteria can remain in the set of *valid* members.

Topology filters are technically data stream filters, although their net effect is to create a new set-defining filter at the management station. NNM 4.1 supports the following predefined filtering criteria:

■ No filter: forward all topology data from the collection station to the management station.

■ *sysObjectID*: forward nodes with/without a specific *sysObjectID*.

- IP address: forward all objects inside/outside a specified IP address range.
- Vendor: forward all objects from a specified supplier.
- Physical address: forward all objects with a particular physical address.
- All Token-Ring segments.

Configuring topology filters actually involves configuring the *ovtopmd* background process. Additional nonstandard filters may be defined by creating a special ASCII text file using the filter definition language specified in (Hewlett-Packard 1996). NNM supports simple filters as well as filter expressions, which are a combination of previously defined filters. Table 4.4 lists the many objects and attributes for which filters can be defined. This list represents a subset of objects and attributes in *ovwdb*.

The same conventions for defining nonstandard topology filters can be used for defining additional discovery, map, and persistence filters. Map filters and persistence filters are described briefly in the following paragraphs.

Map filters

Map filters are useful for tailoring map views for specific operators. This is important because a management station's management domain can't be made operator-specific. It may not be desirable for all operators accessing a management station to view the entire domain. Map filters can be applied on a per-operator basis to tailor the operator's view to present only relevant map objects.

The attributes used to create map filters include, but are not limited to, the following:

- No filter: all objects
- Connectors, networks, and segments only
- Nodes with specific *sysObjectID*
- Bridges, hubs, and their segments
- IP address ranges: objects inside/outside a particular address range
- SNMP-only: only those nodes supporting SNMP

Map filters are classified as set-defining filters. They may be configured from the NNM interface.

Persistence filters

Persistence filters are supported to provide backward compatibility with applications written for versions of NNM prior to release 4.1. With some of these applications, problems may arise if an object is filtered out and the application expects it to be kept in memory. By defining a persistence filter for that object, NNM ensures that any submap containing that object will be made a persistent submap.

Table 4.4. Objects and Attributes for which Filters can be Defined in NNM 4.1

Object Type	Filterable Fields in Object	Field Type
Node Object	isBridge	Boolean
Node Object	is Connector	Boolean
Node Object	isCollectionStationNode	Boolean
Node Object	isHub	Boolean
Node Object	isIP	Boolean
Node Object	isIPRouter	Boolean
Node Object	isMcClusterMember	Boolean
Node Object	isNode	Boolean
Node Object	isRouter	Boolean
Node Object	isSNMPSupported	Boolean
Node Object	vendor	Enumerated
Node Object	IP Hostname	String
Node Object	IP Status	Enumerated
Node Object	Selection Name	String
Node Object	SNMPAgent	Enumerated
Node Object	SNMP sysDescr	String
Node Object	SNMP sysContact	String
Node Object	SNMP sysLocation	String
Node Object	SNMP sysObjectID	String
Node Object	TopM Interface Count	Integer
Interface Object	isInterface	Boolean
Interface Object	isIP	Boolean
Interface Object	is Address	String
Interface Object	IP Status	Enumerated
Interface Object	IP Subnet Mask	String
Interface Object	Selection Name	String
Interface Object	SNMP ifDescr	String
Interface Object	SNMP ifName	String
Inter-face Object	SNMP ifPhysAddr	String
Interface Object	SNMP ifType	Enumerated

Object Type	Filterable Fields in Object	Field Type
Interface Object	TopM Network ID	Integer
Interface Object	TopM Segment ID	Integer
Interface Object	TopM Node ID	Integer
Segment Object	isBusSegment	Boolean
Segment Object	isFDDIRingSegment	Boolean
Segment Object	isSegment	Boolean
Segment Object	isSerialSegment	Boolean
Segment Object	isStarSegment	Boolean
Segment Object	isTokenRingSegment	Boolean
Segment Object	Selection Name	String
Segment Object	IP Segment Name	String
Segment Object	IP Status	Enumerated
Segment Object	TopM Interface Count	Integer
Segment Object	TopM Network ID	Integer
Network Object	isIP	Boolean
Network Object	isNetwork	Boolean
Network Object	IP Address	String
Network Object	IP Status	Enumerated
Network Object	IP Network Name	String
Network Object	IP Subnet Mask	String
Network Object	Selection Name	String
Network Object	TopM Default Seg ID	Integer
Network Object	TopM Interface Count	Integer
Network Object	TopM Segment Count	Integer

Persistence filters are set-defining filters. While persistence filters provide the advantage of preserving backward compatibility with older applications—at the expense of some effort—they also may reduce the performance gains offered by NNM's new On-Demand Submap feature, described in the following section.

On-demand submaps

NNM's *ipmap* process creates a hierarchy of several submap levels, including root, IP internet, segment, and node. Prior to NNM 4.1, all submaps were kept in memory; to improve performance, submaps may now be designated as transient—created and removed only as necessary. Transient submaps are created and maintained by *ipmap* process. A typical hierarchy of transient submaps is depicted in Fig. 4.7.

As noted previously, it may be necessary to designate certain submaps as persistent if older NNM applications expect objects in those submaps to remain in memory.

Event Forwarding and Distributed Threshold Monitoring

Event forwarding and distributed threshold monitoring are supported by two new processes, *ovtrapd* and *pmd*. These processes together replace NNM's *trapd* process.

The *ovtrapd* process is similar to the older *trapd* process in that it receives SNMP traps and inform-requests on port 162 via UDP. *Ovtrapd* can now buffer these traps, and then pass them to the Postmaster process, *pmd*. In addition, *ovtrapd* automatically provides an inform-reply to inbound SNMPv2C inform-requests, an important evolutionary step toward full support of forthcoming SNMPv2 standards.

The inclusion of *ovtrapd* and the Postmaster *pmd* process offers several advantages over the earlier NNM releases, including the following:

- Guaranteed arrival: The use of TCP instead of UDP to route events between various NNMs and third-party applications guarantees that forwarded events will reach their destination.

- Buffering: *ovtrapd*'s ability to can buffer traps means NNM can handle massive bursts of up to 2000 SNMP traps per second.

- SNMPv2 support: Provision of support for inform-requests is an important step toward realizing the security and effiency benefits of forthcoming comprehensive SNMPv2 support.

Figure 4.8 illustrates the relationship between these processes.

Two existing NNM interfaces, *xnmtrap* and *trapd.conf*, also have been modified to support event forwarding.

Event forwarding is primarily concerned with forwarding traps from collection stations to management stations. However, traps represent only

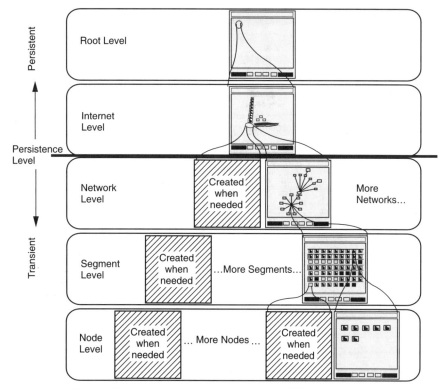

Figure 4.7 A Typical Hierarchy of Transient Submaps in NNM 4.1

asynchronous events; events triggered by local monitoring of thresholds also can be forwarded from collection stations to management stations.

Summary

NNM is fundamentally a collection of many processes. Users can control the effectiveness and efficiency of these processes by configuring their many options and filters. Starting with Release 4.1, new processes and filters have been added to support distributed discovery, event forwarding, and threshold monitoring.

Finding the optimal configuration of these processes and filters takes patience, effort, and skill. Each network is different, and although default configurations provide a good starting point, NNM can be optimized only through careful observation and testing. Understanding and anticipating this optimization process is important for managers as they adjust their expectations of what HP OpenView NNM can and cannot do for their organizations.

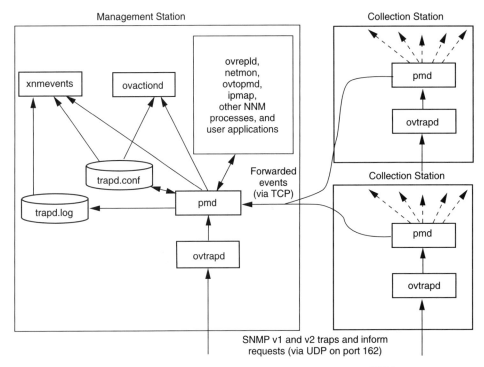

Figure 4.8 The Relationship between Processes in the Event Subsystem in NNM 4.1

5

Data Collection Using HP OpenView

Data collection is a broad term with many different connotations. There are as many different types of data collection as there are types of data. For our purposes, we define data collection as the logical and/or physical retrieval and storage of information on the network and/or network elements. Using this definition, we can examine the types of data that HP OpenView Network Node Manager (NNM) collects from the network. As we have seen in earlier chapters, NNM manages node status for TCP/IP networks. However, NNM also is the building block for management and data collection of other protocols and environments.

In this chapter, we will focus on how NNM polls the network using SNMP for node discovery and topology changes, as well as for gathering current status of devices throughout the network. We will see how NNM uses SNMP to collect data for both IP and non-IP nodes. We also will see how remote monitoring and segment-level data collections are supported. Finally, we will examine how data is collected from various interconnect devices, and how the element manager applications for these interconnect devices aid NNM with device management.

Network Node Manager and Data Collection

HP OpenView NNM is a platform for configuration, fault, and performance management of TCP/IP networks. However, NNM can only provide these management functions if the management system can communicate with network devices, and the devices include SNMP agents that are actively collecting data using the Management Information Bases (MIB, RFC 1212). The main functions of NNM are as follows:

- Automatically discover network devices throughout the network.
- Map these discovered devices in a logical layout.

■ Regularly poll the devices to maintain information about their current operating status.

Node Auto-discovery

Node auto-discovery is the process by which NNM collects information on the network devices, and automatically displays the devices in a logical map showing current operating status. Several factors are critical for auto-discovery to produce an accurate map. First, it is essential for the subnet mask to be correct for the management station and the default gateway (router). Second, the default gateway must be configured correctly and support SNMP. Finally, in order for the network nodes to be discovered, the nodes must be able to respond to a ping request.

Auto-discovery typically works best when there are many routers on the network and the routers are configured with SNMP agents. As we examine the details of the auto-discovery process, it is easy to understand why the routers are so important.

As Chaps. 3 and 4 discuss, when NNM starts it launches a process called *netmon,* which discovers nodes on the network. The *netmon* process is aided by a special file known as the seed file. The seed file is a manually created data file that consists of a list of network addresses, including the default router. After *netmon* discovers the default router, *netmon* uses information from the default routers' *arp* cache and route tables to discover additional nodes. Depending on the size of the network, auto-discovery can take up to 8 hours or more. After each node is discovered, it is placed on the map in its logical location.

Mapping

The NNM map is a collection of submaps arranged in a hierarchy from the root, or internetwork, to the networks, segments, nodes, and interfaces. For example, when an icon of an IP network is selected, it explodes into a submap showing the different segments on that network. This hierarchical view makes network navigation relatively easy and intuitive. The submaps are a collection of windows that contain common menu bars and a palette for displaying nodes (Fig. 5.1). The nodes are displayed as icons using shapes, symbols, and colors to display the network objects and their status.

NNM uses the application IP Map to produce the map of the discovered nodes. This application combines the *netmon* process with the topology manager, *ovtopmd,* to update and display the network maps. IP Map automatically loads when NNM starts and continually monitors the network, discovers new nodes, and automatically makes the necessary updates to the map.

Events, alarms, and traps

One of the most important features of NNM is the ability to alert the user when a problem occurs on the network by changing the colors of the node or nodes on the map. NNM accomplishes this by polling the SNMP agents of the

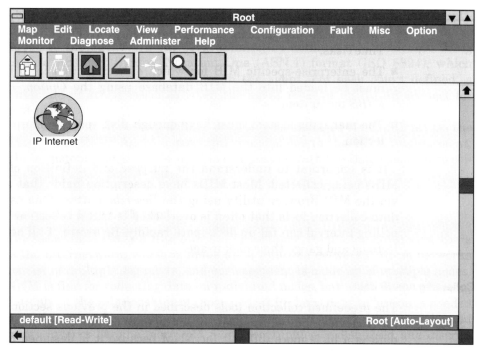

Figure 5.1 HP OpenView NNM Icons

devices to determine their operating status. If there is a problem, or a given condition exists, the agent on the managed device generates an alarm. An *alarm* is a specific condition that occurs when a preset value of a particular MIB variable is exceeded. The alarm triggers an event, which in turn determines the type and number of event notifications to send to the management station, as well as altering the color of the icon. A *trap* is an alarm sent from the SNMP agent to the manager, without an explicit request from the manager, when an error occurs or threshold exceeds.

Collecting SNMP MIB data

NNM contains predefined data-collection tools under the *Options: Data Collection & Thresholds: SNMP...* menu item. These data-collection tools allow you to collect MIB information from nodes at regular intervals and store the collected MIB data on the management station (RFC 1155). This type of data collection is useful in determining thresholds for a MIB variable that causes the generation of alarms, which in turn creates events that alert the user that a threshold has been exceeded. The prerequisites and requirements necessary for using the data-collection tools are as follows:

- The node for which data is being collected must support SNMP.
- The MIBs to be collected must be identified.

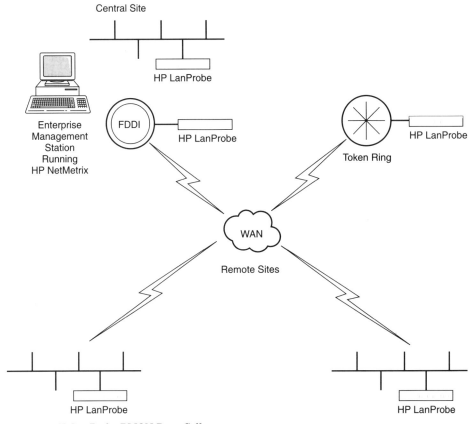

Figure 5.3 HP LanProbe RMON Data Collectors

- Matrix: Statistics on the traffic matrix tracking host-to-host conversations.
- Filters: Allow packets to be filtered according to preset values.
- Capture: Allows packets to be captured on a filtered equation.
- Events: Control generation and notification of events including SNMP trap messages and alarms.

NNM can be used to browse the RMON MIBs and query the MIBS, but NNM does not include a built-in application to easily manage the RMON devices. Fortunately, HP developed the NetMetrix applications to integrate with NNM and provide this functionality.

HP Data Collectors

There are three HP tools that can be applied to the task of data collection: HP NetMetrix, HP LanProbes, and HP Power Agent. They are descibed in succeeding paragraphs.

HP NetMetrix

HP Netmetrix is an integrated suite of applications providing comprehensive distributed monitoring and analysis using standards-based (RMON) data collectors. The applications are tightly integrated with the NNM platform and support Ethernet, Token-Ring, and FDDI. The NetMetrix suite consists of the following applications:

- Enterprise utilities, which consist of historical statistics/baseline, automated trending, reporting, alarms, node statistics, traffic matrix, RMON status, and Token-Ring RMON Extensions.

- Load monitor, which provides graphical view of network traffic load by multiple parameters including time, source nodes, destination nodes, protocol types, and packet sizes.

- Internetwork monitor, which provides relational information on data from multisegment networks. Provides end-to-end analysis of network traffic within segments as well as traffic between routers.

- Protocol analyzer, which provides packet filter and capture capability displaying detail, hexadecimal, and summary decodes. Supports real-time analysis as well as saved trace files to allow postprocessing.

- NFS monitor, which measures the Network File System (NFS) traffic on the segment. Also provides measurements such as response times, rejects, and errors for both the NFS server and clients.

- Traffic generator, which allows the generation of traffic in order to simulate a specific traffic pattern.

The NetMetrix applications can be launched standalone without NNM. In the Standalone mode, applications are launched from a window called the Agent Toolbox. Each RMON device in the database is represented by a triangle. Standalone mode is useful for smaller networks, but is not recommended for larger networks because the mapping and event configuration that NNM provides are not available. The NetMetrix applications are much more effective as a complement to NNM and together provide a powerful integrated network management and monitoring platform.

HP NetMetrix is compatible with any RMON-standard data collector. This is important as more and more interconnect vendors such as Bay Networks, Cabletron, 3Com/Chipcom, and Cisco, to name a few, are integrating RMON-based data collectors in their network devices. As we have seen, the RMON offers an effective way to collect data and monitor internetwork segments. However, RMON is only part of the solution and does not provide all of the necessary data. Fortunately, NetMetrix offers more complete distributed monitoring capabilities using the RMON extensions provided by the HP LanProbes and HP Power Agents.

HP LanProbes

HP LanProbes are stand-alone devices that are RMON-based data collectors that support Ethernet and Token-Ring. The LanProbes are noninvasive devices that are connected to the network segment and monitor all traffic on that network segment. LanProbes support all groups of RMON, but more importantly, provide the HP RMON extensions that enhance their monitoring capabilities. The LanProbes are available in a variety of memory configurations ranging from 1MB to 16MB of RAM, depending on the number and complexity of the data collection necessary for the segment. LanProbes are easily configurable using a terminal or terminal emulation on a PC, and the new LanProbe III probes support in-band, as well as out-of-band Serial Line Internet Protocol (SLIP) connections.

HP Power Agent

The HP NetMetrix Power Agent is an RMON-standard software agent that runs on either an HP or Sun workstation. The Power Agent supports all nine groups of Ethernet RMON, as well as Token-Ring and FDDI. The Power Agent extensions do the following:

- Provide support for 64-bit counters, allowing the agent to handle rollover values that increase rapidly.

- Implement three extended groups for monitoring upper-layer protocols (RMON is limited to the data-link layer of the OSI model).

- Provide unique method for MIB access via query group extensions allowing the correlation of time, host, and protocol statistics.

The Power Agent consists of two cooperating Unix daemons, *netmd* and *rmond* (Fig. 5.4). The *netmd* process monitors the segment, collects the data, and stores the data in shared memory. The *rmond* process receives the SNMP requests, accesses the collected data in shared memory, and responds to the SNMP request.

One final note on the relationship between the HP NetMetrix applications and the LanProbe/Power Agents: Not all applications are currently supported by both data collectors. For instance, applications such as NFS Monitor and Traffic Generator are supported by the Power Agents, but not LanProbes. On the other hand, some statistics, especially Token-Ring statistics are supported by LanProbes, but not Power Agents. It's important to know which Netmetrix applications are necessary for the specific network environment in order to know which data collectors are best suited.

HP Embedded Advanced Sampling Environment (EASE)

HP EASE is an architecture that uses statistical sampling to gather information about network traffic. Through the use of statistical algorithms, EASE captures network traffic information to recognize traffic patterns and to estimate actual traffic activity from the information contained in the sampled packets. Statistical sampling is a method commonly used in industrial quality control, financial auditing, and other areas where exhaustive analysis is not feasible or is too expensive to perform.

EASE provides a macroscopic view of traffic analysis on the entire network and can quickly identify the source of network problems. EASE is designed to monitor traffic characteristics that include bandwidth utilization, frame rates, broadcast or multicast storms, as well as error rates on the entire network. EASE does not collect and report data about every packet passing through the network. To look at every packet on high-speed networks would require a great deal of processing power for the monitoring and processing device. A huge amount of disk storage would be required to maintain data on every packet and to store it over a period of time. Fast computers with lots of memory can be very expensive. Detailed analysis is best applied when problems have been isolated and further information is required.

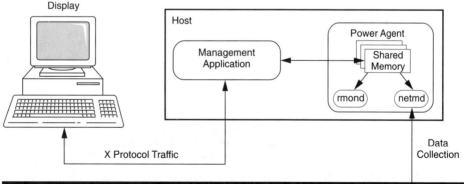

Figure 5.4 HP Power Agent Processes

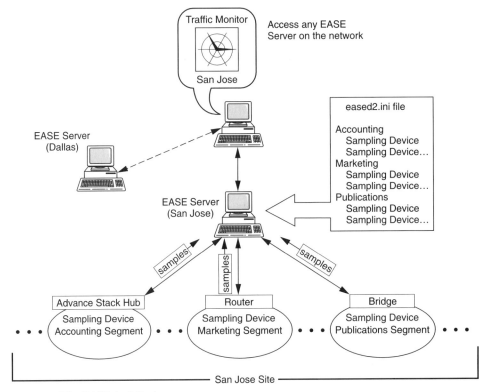

Figure 5.5 The EASE Architecture

As networking speeds increase to 100 Mbps and beyond, EASE is a technology that can be used to accomplish fast and economical traffic monitoring for the entire network.

Figure 5.5 shows the architecture of EASE. There are four main components in this architecture:

- Sampling segments
- Sampling devices
- HP EASE servers
- HP EASE applications

Sampling segments

In using EASE applications, an enterprise network is organized into sampling segments and is used to conveniently refer to certain areas of the network. The sampling segment is important because the user needs to know where traffic patterns are concentrated. Users want to view sources, destinations, and different types of communication traffic between nodes in the different areas of the network.

The term *segment* usually refers to a type of cable connection (e.g., coaxial, twisted-pair, or fiber) between devices. A sampling segment, however, does not refer to a backbone or to specific cable connections. A *sampling segment* is defined as the following: The area of the network between any two or more devices that filter traffic passing through them or that do not propagate network traffic through their interfaces. For example, LAN switches, bridges, and routers are most commonly used to filter traffic that passes through them. Therefore, the area of the network bounded by LAN switches, bridges, or routers are sampling segments. But extenders, repeaters, and hubs do not filter traffic passing through them; they remain within the sampling segment. Figure 5.6 shows a very simple example.

Sampling devices

A *sampling device* is one that contains the HP EASE agent software. The agent performs the sampling function. The EASE agent is embedded in network devices such as HP EtherTwist and HP AdvanceStack hubs, bridges, and routers. Since these network devices are present throughout the enterprise network, they provide the most effective way for sampling traffic on the network. Agents can be embedded into HP Traffic Probe and the HP LANProbe II/III. These probes can be used to sample parts of the local area network where there are no network devices that support the EASE agent.

The function of the EASE agent is to sample packets on the segment where it resides, and to forward the samples across the network immediately to a centralized location to be decoded and analyzed by the the EASE server.

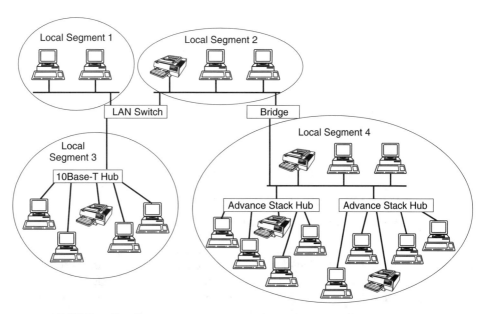

Figure 5.6 LAN Sampling Segments

Rather than burden the sampling device with this excess processing, packet analysis is performed at the server. Since SNMP is supported by HP network products, the sampling devices use SNMP to communicate with the EASE server.

The sampling device acts as a sampling instrument for the segment on which it resides. For example, the sampling device samples packets on a LAN segment using a (default) statistical mean value of 1/400 packets. In other words, on average, the sampling device will sample 1 in 400 packets. This does not mean that every 400th packet is sampled. Statistical sampling is used because there may be cyclic processes present on a network—such as a ping that occurs once every minute—that could synchronize with a sampling rate. When a packet is sampled, it is not decoded or analyzed by the sampling device. Instead, the packet's header information is encapsulated in an SNMP trap and sent to the HP EASE server. The EASE server analyzes the packet's header information and maintains a database of traffic activity.

HP EASE Servers

The EASE server collects and processes samples from sampling devices distributed throughout the network. This provides representative data about each sampling segment. Most of the processing related to the data collection and analysis occurs on the EASE server. Decoding each sampled packet, the EASE server is capable of analyzing protocols, such as 802.2, 802.3, Ethernet, SNAP, HPXSAP, ICMP, IP, UDP, TCP, IPX, XNS, DECnet Phase 4, and AppleTalk Phase 2. Based on its analysis, the EASE server compiles traffic information. For example, the EASE server keeps track of what device is doing the most talking on each segment. The results of the data processing, and not the packet header information, is stored in the EASE server database which is designed for optimal storage and retrieval of real-time information.

The location of the EASE servers are flexible; they can be installed in the segments or outside the segments.

EASE applications

There are two main applications:

- HP OpenView History Analyzer
- HP OpenView Traffic Expert

History Analyzer is a network traffic monitoring tool that allows a view of historical data over time. Sampled packets are analyzed and a database of historical traffic patterns are stored in the EASE server. History Analyzer can show a trend of where and what network activity occurs most frequently. Trend information helps the user make network changes without using the trial and error method for network planning. For instance, the user can optimize network performance by evenly distributing network activity or the user can plan ahead for additional resources to meet growing needs.

The following selection criteria help to identify information needs:

- Address mappings
- Network traffic levels by layer (e.g., MAC layer)
- Top talkers
- Top error sources
- Top broadcasters
- Profile of server by clients (bytes sent and received)
- Profile of clients by servers (bytes sent and received)
- Profile of services by servers
- Profile of services by clients
- Utilization on segment
- Protocol usage on segment
- Errors on segment
- Error breakdown for address
- Service traffic level

Depending on the selection, various presentation alternatives are available. Figure 5.7 shows the number of frames/second for MAC-addresses. The other alternative is to display segment errors related to the number of transmitted frames (Fig. 5.8). Also, the number of bytes exchanged between communication partners may be selected and displayed (Fig. 5.9).

Traffic Expert is a traffic management tool that displays the flow of network traffic graphically and recommends actions to maximize network availability. Traffic Expert provides an adaptive management system that continuously learns and adapts to the network's behavior. Traffic Expert uses the same database information on the EASE server as History Analyzer. This lets the user view both the dynamics of the network topology and the traffic characteristics: volume, type, usage, and flow directions.

Traffic Expert consists of two tools—the Report Generator and the Workgroup Analyzer. Report Generator provides the user with daily reports recommending various actions to optimize the traffic flow. Workgroup Analyzer provides a graphical display of traffic flows related to the actual network topology. The use of Traffic Expert together with History Analyzer (viewing traffic flows over time) provides a powerful set of tools for detecting emerging traffic problems, identifying possible solutions, and planning changes needed to ensure optimal performance.

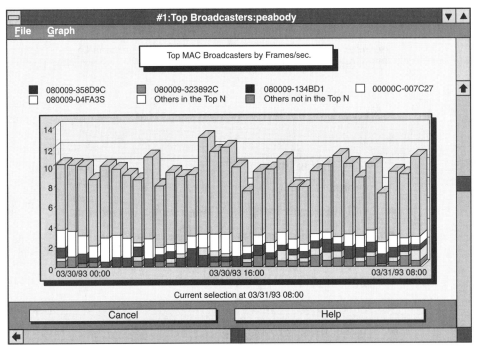

Figure 5.7 Frames Per Second by MAC Address

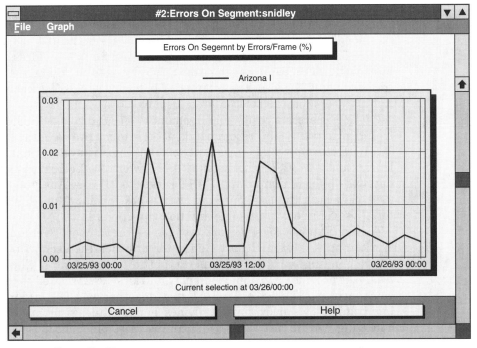

Figure 5.8 Errors Per Frame

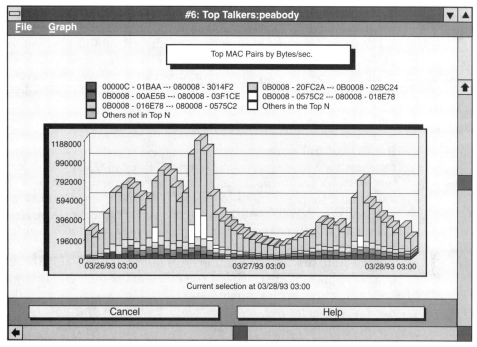

Figure 5.9 Bytes Per Second

Standalone EASE sampling probes also are supported. They can communicate with the servers as embedded probes do. The expected price of the EASE probes in both cases is very low in comparison with RMON probes. Due to the capability of reducing overhead, EASE offers an interesting alternative to RMON probes.

Collecting Data from Routers and Hubs

Almost all vendors of networking equipment deploy SNMP agents on their interconnection devices such as routers, bridges, switches, concentrators, and hubs. Many industry-leading equipment vendors not only are integrating SNMP agents, but also are integrating RMON in their equipment. These vendors are continually developing *element managers* that allow users to manage devices using a graphical user interface (element managers are discussed in more detail in Chap. 9). It is impossible to cover in this text every solution from all of the vendors. Therefore, we will attempt to cover the interconnect device genre as a whole.

The primary management objective of most interconnect vendors is to provide device management and enhancing network management capabilities. Device management refers to tasks such as configuration, warm boot, port status, and environmental status (operating temperature, power supply, etc.). Enhanced network management capabilities might include port statistics, backplane statistics, etc., with the ability to view a graphical representation of the device and its modules and/or ports. Since NNM is considered the industry standard for network management, all of the element managers are designed to tightly integrate with the platform. Each vendor offers a unique solution. Depending on the type of interconnect device, however, certain characteristics and limitations apply to the majority of these vendors.

Routers

Routers generally are regarded as the most critical network device on the most common type of network architecture, the collapsed backbone. Because all internetwork traffic must transverse the routers, it is assumed that this is the most likely source for data collection. The first thing we must do is differentiate between gathering statistics on the *performance of the router* versus using the router to gather statistics on the *performance of the network*. It seems like a subtle point, but there is a big difference.

Some statistics from the routers are important and must be monitored constantly to prevent unscheduled downtime of the network. Information such as port utilization, errors, broadcasts, route tables, etc., is critical for maintaining certain operating levels of performance on the network. Most leading router vendors, including Cisco and Bay Networks (formally Wellfleet Communications), do a fine job of providing users with this information via SNMP, using enterprise specific MIBS for the device. This MIB information can be gathered and managed using NNM. However, gathering statistics on the performance of the network is not always practical for the router.

The primary function of the router is to route traffic from one network segment to another as quickly and efficiently as possible. When network traffic becomes heavy, the router is expected to work even harder to ensure timely delivery of the packets. If routers are used for data collection and protocol analysis as a secondary function, for instance, under heavy traffic loads the router will divert more of its resources back to its primary focus of routing traffic. Therefore, at the time in which network statistics and traffic information are most critical, the router is least effective in gathering this information. This paradox is a problem faced by most router manufacturers. Under normal operating loads, resource sharing between routing traffic and data collection functions might not be a problem. Also, if the segment is not considered critical, the disadvantages are not that great. In any case, before using the router as a data collector for network performance, check the other options available.

Hubs and concentrators

Much like the router, the hub (concentrator) is a likely candidate for data collection because of the role it plays in interconnecting other network devices. Unlike the router, the concentrator does not have the task, and therefore overhead, of routing traffic between networks. Most concentrators on the market offer mixed topologies with multiple segments. This allows the network to consist of Ethernet, Token-Ring, and FDDI and still collapse into a single concentrator. The advantage of this type of architecture is the ability to collect data from these different topologies from a single device.

The device management of a hub allows configuration, warm boot, and shutdown via SNMP, much as routers do. The hubs also typically provide port status through alarming, enabling users to manage devices down to the individual port level. A key feature of hub-based network management is the ability to collect data from multiple segments simultaneously from the backplane. Many of the more advanced hubs and concentrators also support port switching, which allows network segments to be redefined and ports to be dynamically configured using SNMP. This is a powerful feature for administrative tasks such as moves, adds, and changes.

Unlike routers, hubs are much more suitable for RMON because they are not burdened with the processor-intensive overhead that routers incur. Some hub vendors have integrated RMON into the management module. Many vendors use a separate module that takes up a slot in the chassis, or a daughter board that piggybacks onto the network module. Some implementations include RMON, MIB II and enterprise-specific extensions. NNM provides the SNMP platform and mapping facility as well as the event configuration and data collection tools. HP Netmetrix adds value to these hub-based RMON products by supporting any RMON standard implementation. Protocol filtering, history, alarms, and multiple views allow Netmetrix to take advantage of these hub-based data collectors.

Advantages of some hub-based product versus the standalone products such as LanProbes are:

- Supports multiple segments
- Costs less per segment
- Does not require additional rack-mount space

Disadvantages of the hub-based probes are:

- Not all RMON groups supported
- Nondedicated test devices
- Limited packet capture and decodes
- No baseline facilities
- Performance considerations
- Reduced port count if dedicated chassis slot required

Some final thoughts on the comparisons of dedicated LanProbes versus hub-based probes have to do with product maturity and future directions. Under current specifications, HP LanProbes are superior integrated remote monitoring solutions providing all groups of RMON simultaneously. As hub-based probes become more sophisticated, they will offer the same degree of integration as LanProbes and Power Agents. This type of dedicated monitoring tool requires its own processor and memory and this requires space in the hub. It is clear, however, that as more and more interconnect vendors invest in RMON development and partner with data collection vendors, including HP, that hub-based probes will continue to improve.

Finally, as new networking technologies become part of mainstream networking (i.e., ATM, cell-switching), the clear boundaries between independent segments will become blurred, to the point that each port will be a different segment. At that point, segment-based statistics will have no relevance. In that case, the advantage may go to hub vendors offering backplane-based data collectors that allow analysis of network trends and traffic patterns.

Other devices

Routers and hubs are the primary interconnect devices capable of providing SNMP and RMON data for the NNM platform. Devices such as switches, bridges, gateways, multiplexers, and WAN equipment also can be managed via SNMP. Many of these devices support not only SNMP MIB II, but enterprise-specific MIBs as well. In particular, switches and high-speed bridges are becoming the collapsed backbone focal point in many networks, and consequently bear much of the same responsibility as routers in terms of interconnecting the collapsed backbone. Devices in this important role must support network management and data collection to monitor status as well as performance.

Summary

This chapter focuses on how NNM polls the network using SNMP for node discovery and topology changes, as well as for gathering current status of devices throughout the network. NNM contains predefined data-collection tools that allow administrators to collect MIB information from nodes at regular intervals and to store the collected MIB data on the management station. NNM can be used to browse the RMON MIBs and query the MIBS, but NNM does not include a built-in application to easily manage the RMON devices. Fortunately, HP has developed other applications such as HP NetMetrix to provide this functionality. HP NetMetrix, HP LanProbe, and HP EASE can be used in combination to round out HP OpenView's data-collection capabilities.

Chapter

6

Diagnosing Faults

Fault diagnosis is a classic real-time activity. Any delay in isolating and resolving a problem can seriously affect the productivity of users.

Critical success factors for the fault diagnostic process include a powerful platform to receive, process, and correlate messages, events, and alarms; diagnostic policies to be invoked on the basis of processed information; and intelligent agents that are capable of extracting essential information from managed objects.

This chapter provides a brief overview of the fault management process, pointing out HP OpenView's role in fault diagnosis. Third-party applications for fault diagnosis, including hub management applications and expert systems, are discussed in depth.

Introduction to the Fault Management Process

Fault management can be subdivided into the following phases (Fig. 6.1):

- *Data collection* includes detecting that something went wrong in network equipment or facilities. It also includes the gathering of basic data about symptoms. Data gathering is greatly facilitated by messages, events, and alarms that are generated by managed objects and network management systems. This phase also deals with isolating the fault to the failing component.

- *Diagnosis of faults* concentrates on the determination of the problem's cause and its solution. This phase includes assignment of responsibilities to staff members and the tools that assist fault diagnosis.

- *Bypass, work-around, and recovery* address the rapid deployment of procedures to circumvent the problem in order to restore service to the users.

- *Resolution* involves restoring service and undoing bypass and workaround actions after repair and replacement actions have been taken.

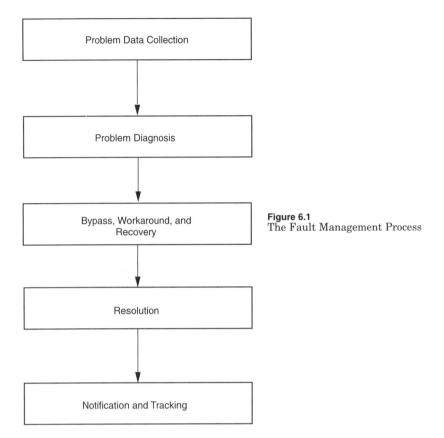

Figure 6.1
The Fault Management Process

- *Notification and tracking* is the final phase and involves notifying users, tracking open problems, closing trouble tickets, analyzing faults, comparing resolution actions with history data, and analyzing trends.

These phases are supported by multiple management applications and products that are integrated under the umbrella of major network management platforms such as HP OpenView NNM. A complete solution must include applications supporting the following capabilities:

- Knowledge base to maintain experiences with past faults and their resolutions.

- Query tools to search knowledge bases of trouble tickets for identical or similar problems.

- Change-management interface to query previous changes to determine whether they are related to the fault being diagnosed, and to generate change requests for solved problems.

- Asset-management database to get inventory and configuration data to complete trouble tickets.

- Accounting interface to provide accounting and charging for customer support services.

- Trouble-ticketing system to help route and dispatch trouble tickets to the right subject matter experts.

This chapter addresses in depth the second phase of fault management, fault diagnosis.

Messages, events, and alarms

Messages, events, and alarms are generated in networks in order to supervise status of managed objects. There are two broad alternatives for obtaining information about network status:

1. Manual processes: When managed objects are not performing as expected, users notify a central help desk or *client contact point* by means of open trouble tickets, e-mail, or the phone. Both fault and performance related notification is included.

2. Automatic processes: Agents can automatically extract status information from managed objects. Depending on the level of intelligence of agents, they can store the information and wait to be polled by the management station. Or they can interpret status information and generate messages, events, and alarms.

The problem data collection phases are shown in Fig. 6.2. Most organizations rely on a combination of manual and automatic processes for status monitoring.

Messages usually report on the *status* of network elements or managed objects. Status is the measurement of the behavior of an object at a specific instant in time. Status is represented by a set of status information items and their assigned values at a specified time.

An *event* is a change in the status of the managed object, a change that meets predefined conditions that determine whether notification is necessary. Typically, status is changing constantly. An event is characterized by changes that are significant to problem diagnosis. The occurrence of an event is reported via an *event report*, which contains information such as the type of event, the status that changed, the probable cause, and the effect of the event on the managed object.

Event detection involves monitoring the status reports of managed objects for event occurrences. There are three general types of status messages: continuous, unsolicited, and solicited. A management system or agent that supports event detection compares all status changes against the criteria for generating an event, and will generate an event report when these criteria are met.

Event detection can be done within a managed object or externally, from outside the object. One or both mechanisms may be used, although both forms of

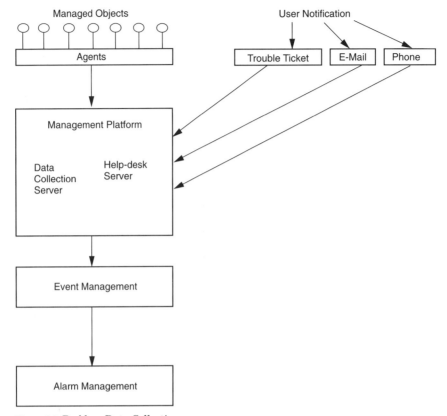

Figure 6.2 Problem Data Collection

event detection perform essentially the same function. Typically, internal event detection is a function of the object itself and is closely integrated with the other functions of the object. External event detection uses status reports made available by the managed object and performs event detection independently. This may be done in a process immediately adjacent to the managed object—an external monitor, for example. It also may be done within a management system in any of the functional areas.

Management applications capable of examining status reports over time can watch for status changes. When a change is detected, it is evaluated to see if it meets the event generation criteria. If these criteria are met, then an event is generated for the status change. Event generation criteria are used to determine the significance of a status change to the management of the managed object. If the change is determined to be significant, an event report is generated. Criteria must be set for each class or type of managed object, and may vary for object instances.

Events typically take the form of either CMIP event reports or SNMP traps, as described in Chap. 2.

Events may be filtered, logged, discarded, or used as input for triggering other events or corrective actions. By itself, HP OpenView NNM merely logs and displays events; filtering and command triggering is accomplished via user-written scripts. Later sections of this chapter describe third-party applications that can augment the fault diagnostic capabilities of HP OpenView.

Filtering

In order to reduce the volume of messages, events, and alarms, many network administrators deploy filters. HP OpenView NNM provides a limited set of filters. A more advanced paradigm is *multilayered filtering*. Figure 6.3 shows an example of multilayer filtering in which the first filter (a simple filter) eliminates certain message or event types, the second filter combines events into alarms, and the third filter sets priorities for each of the alarms.

Filtering can be built into message or event processors. The location of these processors differs, depending on the management architecture. SNMP-based

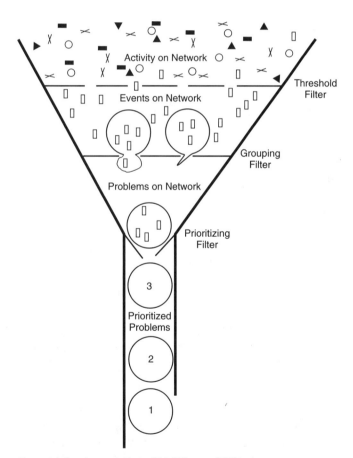

Figure 6.3 Implementation of Multilayered Filtering

systems implement these processors into the management station; CMIP-based systems implement more filtering into agents. Systems management products such as HP IT/OperationsCenter often use intelligent, agent-based filters that communicate data over remote procedure calls (*RPCs*).

SNMP agents have two alternatives for informing management stations about status of managed objects:

1. An agent can send a trap to the manager if something important occurs. In SNMP implementations, this is the exception rather than the rule.

2. The manager can send a request to the agent to obtain information. Normally, the SNMP manager polls agents for information, relegating agents to a passive role.

In diagnostics, both information alternatives are important. Traps can trigger the initialization of the diagnosis process; polling agents help to progress with diagnosis. The challenge in using SNMP is to minimize communication overhead and still obtain all of the information necessary to identify and resolve problems.

HP OpenView as Focal Point for Diagnosing Faults

HP OpenView can receive data from various sources. NNM can receive SNMP traps and data; with HP OpenView DM, messages, events, and alarms may be carried by SNMP, CMIP, or XMP. Once they arrive at OpenView, platform functions are applied to interpret, process, present, and report the results.

As mentioned previously, HP OpenView NNM supports only a limited set of filters. To guarantee an efficient processing of SNMP data, many HP customers use third-party applications such as the NerveCenter application from Seagate/Netlabs, or other expert systems.

Figure 6.4 shows the NerveCenter model.

NerveCenter can deal with all types of traps, not just with those that have been standardized with SNMP. Vendors have the option of defining traps for their specific needs. These traps send information about a specific device (a hub, for example) from that vendor. Decoding the transmitted information is the responsibility of NerveCenter.

Thresholding with NerveCenter is discussed in more detail in Chap. 7. The following sections describe how OpenView's diagnostic capabilities can be augmented by hub management applications and expert systems.

Hub diagnostics applications

Hubs play an increasingly important role in networks. Independently from the logical topology of networks, hubs maintain the physical structure. In many installations, hubs are the concentrators for Ethernet and Token-Ring segments, routers, bridges, brouters, FDDI and ATM nodes, and monitoring equipment. In collapsed backbones, the integration level around hubs is even higher. On the other hand, management applications in or for the hub could help to isolate faults at the port level, advising and dispatching engineers to the right place. Basically, data collection technologies are available, transporting management information is supported by various protocols, and management applications help to interpret data and launch the necessary platform function to alarm networks and systems operators.

The next section includes several examples that demonstrate the important relationship between OpenView and hub-management applications. While hub-management applications typically support multiple types of management platforms, this section concentrates only on the collaboration with HP OpenView. The focus is on those features that can assist diagnostics.

Level of interaction with OpenView

Most major hub vendors make an effort to support multiple management platforms. The integration level differs, depending on the features and services the platform vendor supports. In case of HP OpenView, there are many possible integration points; it is up to the hub vendor to select the right ones. Due to the need

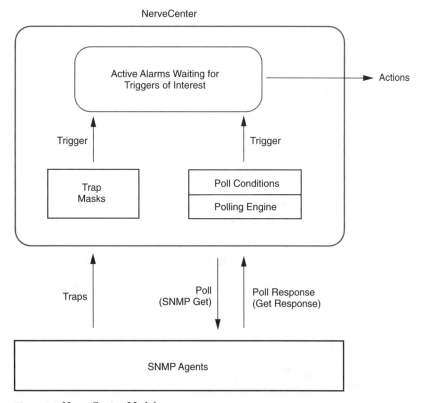

Figure 6.4 NerveCenter Model

to support multiple platforms, hub vendors typically do not offer deep integration, and this situation is not expected to change in the near term. One exception is Cabletron's support for hub management by Spectrum—the integration is deep because the same company is providing a platform (Spectrum) with built-in hub-management capabilities. In other cases, integration levels vary widely.

Management functionality

Management functionality usually includes the following items:

- Central management of a certain number of hubs.

- Management of Ethernet, Token-Ring, and FDDI from a single management station.

- Maintenance of a network map displaying the physical and logical topology, including its hubs, servers, clients, routers, bridges, and other equipment.

- Maintenance of a graphical view of the hubs and the current state of their components.

- Management and surveillance of each module and port in the networks, enabling, disabling, or toggling any port or module.

- Measurement of key fault and performance indicators in Ethernets, Token-Rings, and in FDDI. These indicators support real-time analysis on utilization levels, response time, and error statistics.

- Maintenance of filters to reduce the number of messages and events sent to the management station. At the same time, alarms are triggered when certain conditions occur.

- Setting of thresholds for key fault and performance indicators.

- Downloading firmware from the management station to change configuration, to activate redundant links, and activate or deactivate data collection.

- Logging for further analysis of all alarm messages generated in the network or in its components.

- Support of security features to better control the access to station addresses. If an unauthorized address appears, the management station is expected to turn off that port.

- Agent-to-agent communication within the hub supports information exchange via a communication backplane. This capability allows all hub information to be gathered, viewed, and configured by attaching a single SNMP manager to a single management card.

These functions usually are supported by most hub vendors. Special functions are provided by some of the vendors. For example, Optical Data Systems (ODS) has added optional hardware-based management and reliability features to its FDDI management capabilities. These features include:

- Per-port monitoring that provides the capability to learn each port's MAC address and detect when this address changes. In addition, it can detect MAC frame problems that are difficult to isolate even with the best FDDI protocol analyzers.

- Analysis of the traffic generated on each FDDI port.

- Detection of which station caused a lost token.

- Detection of no-token MAC frames, which can be caused by hardware or software faults. With current technology, this condition can be detected only on a ring through a binary search, in which a two-tap logic analyzer is used to bind the fault domain; then human intervention is required to move the taps during the search. ODS can detect which port is causing this condition without human intervention.

- Detection of when and which station on the port is stuck in beacon mode and can detect this beacon much more quickly than the 9 seconds taken by the RMT (Ring Management). This makes possible a faster recovery of the network.

- Statistics logic, which includes programmable counters as well as other management-support functions.

- Ring mapping, which determines which stations are connected into ports, is a valuable topological mapping capability and provides more accuracy than a software-based approach algorithm.

- Network utilization counters, which allow network management to determine the approximate amount of network bandwidth consumed by attached stations. This feature can be valuable for per-port billing applications.

- FDDI stations, which can waste bandwidth by holding the token and not transmitting. ODS modules measure both transmission time and holding time to determine true network utilization.

- Four configurable counters, which can count frames of various types including destination address, source address, frame length, frame control field, and selectable patterns occuring at selectable points within the first 256 bytes of the frame.

- Capture of the source address of beacon frames.

ODS has added sideband management access ports to the Ethernet, Token-Ring, and FDDI management cards. The new auxiliary ports provide network managers with a convenient and consistent way to diagnose problems even when the network goes down. They also can be used for standard network maintenance such as software downloads without taking up bandwidth on the primary links. The Ethernet ports can be used to manage all cards in the hub regardless of media type via a single homogeneous sideband network.

Database support

In most hub-management applications, the database is expected to be used locally in the hub. Typically, it is not a very extended database, nor does it support many attributes. Only the most important configuration and fault management-related data are maintained. Typical attributes include:

- Redundancy definitions for alternative configurations
- Inventory of hub components
- Communication data for each hub (name, IP address, MAC address)
- Hub status
- Filter parameter
- Bridge parameter
- Alarm definition
- Thresholds
- Textual comments on ports, cards, power supply

Usually, flat files with proprietary attributes are in use.

Network maps

Graphical representation usually is supported for a logical view, physical view, and for hub details. The OpenView platform supports all these views with OV map.

LANVision hub tool is ODS' comprehensive management solution. Its graphical user interface is based on OSF/Motif to provide system-level configuration and resource allocation, for simple point-and-click management of ODS intelligent hubs and other networking components. It allows the manager to assign users and devices dynamically to logical network segments via GUI interfaces, thus allowing the network manager to focus on configuration, planning, and proactive network management.

Cabletron's hub-management application offers a topology view of FDDI that provides connection information for FDDI networks. Device topology views allow managers to evaluate the actual port-to-port connections for actual packet paths using Cabletron hubs. In each view, a variety of hub labels (such as name, address, and special comments on location) may be included and displayed.

An application view helps to dynamically display applications supported by the hub (e.g., routing, bridging, monitoring). For example, the Unified Management View from ODS makes it possible from a single instance of a hub view to collect status or statistics from Ethernet, Token-Ring, and FDDI management cards present in the Infinity hub chassis. It is a new way to view information from multiple MIB lookup tables for different agents. From the same hub view network, administrators are able to set up specialized RMON tables to gather specific network traffic information. Third-party products, such as Cisco routers and Fore ATM switches may be supported the same way.

Ethernet indicators

Hub-level indicators provide information about data transmission results on a logical hub. These statistics consist of multiple physical level port statistics. Typical statistics required for diagnostics and performance analysis are:

- Peak traffic in the segment within a specified time window
- Average traffic in the segment for a specified period of time
- Current traffic at the time of the last sample
- Total packets received
- Total bytes received
- Missed packets
- Number of cyclic redundancy check (CRC) errors on the segment
- Frame alignment errors on the segment
- Collision rate in the segment for a specific period of time

Token-Ring indicators

Token-Ring indicators consist of hard and soft error, and of general performance statistics. Hub vendors usually support most of the following indicators for hard errors, soft errors, and general errors. Hard error indicators include:

- Ring purges by the active monitor
- Number of times input signal is lost
- Beacons in the ring for a specified period of time

Soft error indicators include:

- Number of line errors
- Number of burst errors
- Number of AC errors
- Number of abort sequences
- Number of lost frames
- Number of receive data congestion errors
- Number of frame-copied errors
- Number of token errors due to token loss or frame circulation
- Number of frequency errors

General indicators include:

- Cumulative number of bytes on the ring for a specified period of time
- Frame count
- Average and peak utilization level
- Average and peak frame rate
- Bytes per second on average or peak
- Average frame size for a specified period of time
- Current and peak number of stations on the ring
- Current operating speed of the ring

Configuring local area networks using the hub

Many hub vendors support software downline-loading to support configuration changes. To download firmware, all MAC addresses and all IP addresses in the various types of networks the hubs are supporting must be unique. The following example deals with SmartLink from ADC Fibermux to configure Token-Rings. The status window shown in Fig. 6.5 offers the following fields for configuration:

- Max stations in ring: A read-only field that indicates the number of stations on the ring.
- Split ring on beacon: Clicking on this field enables the SmartLink in the selected hub to split the ring when beaconing occurs. A check mark means the ring will be split.
- Auto-beacon isolation: Clicking on this field enables the Token-Ring SmartLink in the selected hub to automatically isolate a beacon condition. A check mark means automatic beacon isolation will occur, as long as the Split Ring on Beacon also is enabled.

Status information also is provided when:

- Rings are joined (the ring is whole) or isolated (a beaconing area of the ring is split off).
- Beacon Isolation is active (the auto-beacon isolation feature is actively isolating a beacon condition) or inactive (beacon isolation is not in use).

Network media modules can automatically identify and correct data paths if a failure occurs on media modules or links. Usually, any port to any location can be assigned in the hub. This method provides for more flexibility in setting up redundant data paths. ODS provides redundant devices using transceivers. Modules that are not inherently identified as having redundant pairs can be configured and controlled to provide redundancy. Two ports can be attached to the same uplink location. One port is enabled, the other disabled. Hardware

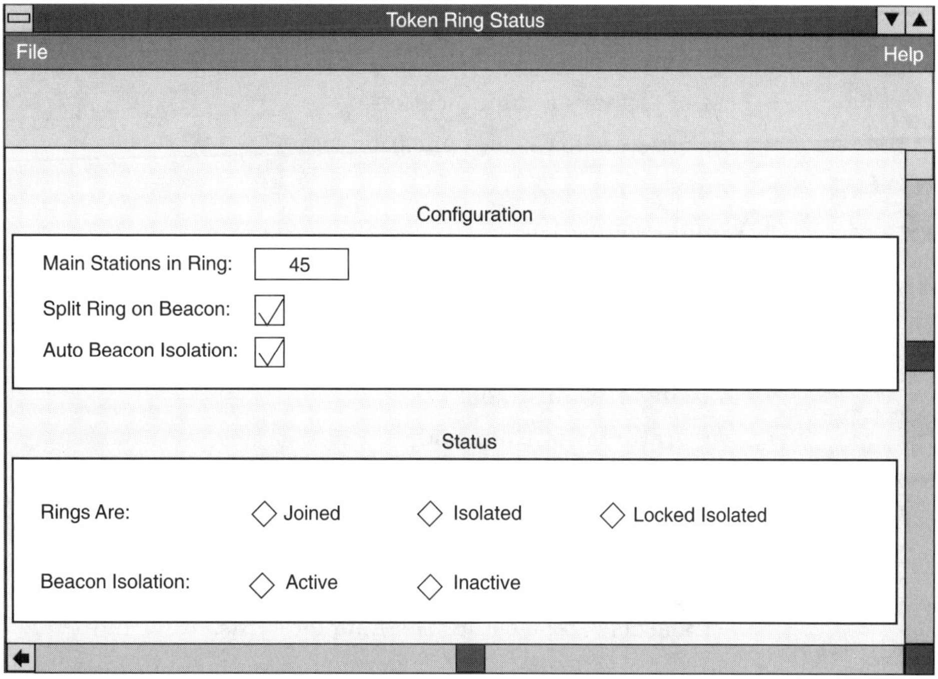

Figure 6.5 Token-Ring Certification Window—ADC Fibermux

sensors monitor the heartbeat signal of the link. The port enabled and providing the active LAN connection is deemed the primary port. The other is noted as the secondary redundant port. If the link fails on the primary port, the secondary port is automatically enabled to reinstate the LAN connection. If the original primary port regains its link integrity signal, the port remains disabled to avoid an oscillating effect between the two ports.

Redundant ports can be configured using SNMP. Network management stations can poll individual Ethernet ports for the MIB variable receive link. Intelligent decisions can then be made to enable ports or to reassign them to other backplane segments, without human intervention.

Many vendors go even further and use the hub to control and configure not only Ethernet, Token-Ring, and FDDI, but also bridges, routers, terminal servers, SNA gateways, and ATM switches. There is little doubt that hubs play a very important role of centrally managing complex structures.

Threshold alarms

The right setting of thresholds against all hub and port indicators helps to recognize proactively any performance bottlenecks and deteriorating hub conditions. Figure 6.6 for Cabletron hubs shows a typical alarm window for repeaters. Similar alarm-setting windows are available for other components. Most vendors differentiate between threshold alarms and trouble alarms.

Threshold alarms include all the indicators supported for ports and hubs. *Trouble alarms* may include the following:

- Loss of primary communication
- Loss of secondary communication lost
- Power failure
- Nonfunctioning port
- Nonfunctioning card
- Beaconing
- No token available
- Humidity over threshold
- Temperature over threshold
- Fan failure

With SNMP, alarms may be implemented in the form of traps. Writing and implementing traps is a real differentiator among vendors. Customization time and expenses must not be underestimated.

Most alarms can be set for the hub, for cards, or for individual ports.

SNMP and RMON Support

SNMP and RMON are considered by vendors as the basis for generating, collecting, processing, and transferring management data. The support of SNMPv1 is a must; RMON is built in by cooperating with RMON probe vendors; and SNMPv2 may be supported very soon. Basically, these standards are helpful, but are not without limitations.

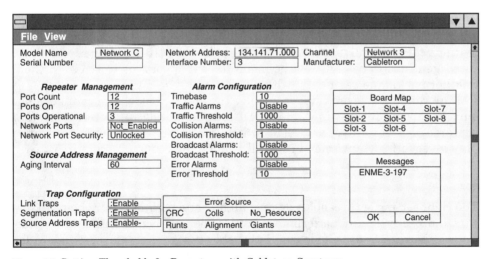

Figure 6.6 Setting Thresholds for Repeaters with Cabletron Spectrum

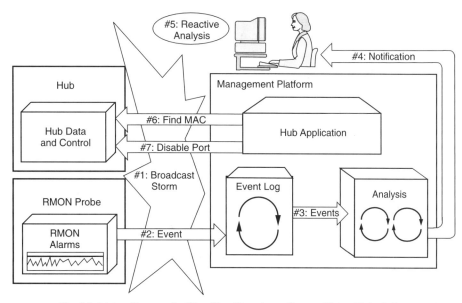

Figure 6.7 The Multistep Process for Handling Broadcast Storms Using Today's Reactive Network Management

A central pillar of a vendor's hub management strategies is the use of *smart agents* that provide distributed intelligence throughout the network, enabled by the use of RMON technology (Bailey 1996). Polling of these intelligent agents by the central management station can generate a considerable amount of network traffic, however, and vendors therefore are trying, where practical, to make these agents capable of correcting problems locally according to preset policies. This type of proactive approach frees up the platform for more higher-level functions, while enhancing scalability of the overall solution.

Figure 6.7 shows a broadcast storm. In such a case, the network administrator uses a RMON-application to identify the MAC address of the offending node. The administrator must then use a hub application to find the port to which the MAC address is connected, and manually disable the port. Because the two applications cannot interact, the network administrator must intervene to solve the problem. As the figure illustrates, seven steps are required to disable the offending port.

Ungermann-Bass's Access/EMPower moves beyond intelligent SNMP agent technology by empowering the hub not only to collect and reduce data, but to analyze, correlate, and respond to the data in real time based on preset policies without intervention from the management platform. This represents a far more distributed approach to management automation than can be achieved using traditional network management platforms. UB implements key platform-like features in the agent:

■ An event management system with which applications may integrate via APIs in order to act on events within the hub.

■ An application API that allows applications to both interact and access common data stored in the extensible SNMP agent.

■ A structured, system-like environment that supports the deployment of applications in a real-time environment. This includes standardized software installations, a version tracking system, and a mechanism for dynamically linking and loading applications during run time.

Distributing self-management responsibility to the hub frees the network management platform for a more crucial role as an application platform for historical analysis, planning, accounting, problem management, systems management, inventory control, and policy creation. Policy-based management is based on the concept that policies can be written to represent a predefined approach for dealing with a network event or condition such as a broadcast storm or bandwidth contention. These policies allow network managers to capture the knowledge that is used to solve a problem so that it can be applied automatically whenever the problem occurs again.

Figure 6.8 shows an example of how the NetStorm Terminator application running under Access/EMPower can change the reactive response to a proactive response. In this case, the network administrator can define a broadcast storm policy that makes use of both RMON events and hub data so that an informed decision can be written. It also uses the embedded port-to-MAC address mapping database maintained by Access/EMPower. An RMON rising

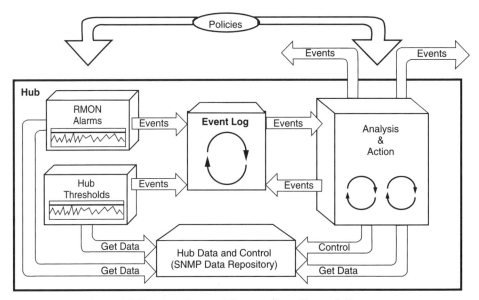

Figure 6.8 Using Access/EMPower to Respond Proactively to Network Events

threshold of approximately 1000 broadcasts/second results in an event logged by RMON in the internal event management system.

NetStorm receives the event from the event management system and proceeds to turn on RMON HostTopN study to gather additional critical data about the broadcast storm. NetStorm Terminator evaluates this data based on user-defined policies, such as what degree of broadcast traffic may be generated by a single host. If the offending host exceeds this limit, NetStorm logs to the event-management system an event that contains the MAC address of the offending host. This event will be forwarded as an SNMP trap to the network management station. NetStorm continues its work. By consulting the embedded MAC-address-to-port mapping database, it identifies the hub slot and the individual port to which the offending host is attached. After determining that the port does not exceed a *number of devices per port* policy, it disables the port and reports the corrective action to the event-management system. After the time period specified in the policy, NetStorm re-enables the port.

Using Expert Systems

The following principles are true in the area of fault management by expert system:

- Human expertise for fault diagnostics is rare.

- It is difficult to educate new experts.

- There is a definite demand for this expertise.

- The activities of problem determination, diagnostics, and resolution can be well-defined, and solutions do exist.

- Problems are complex, and there usually is no time to consult references and seek outside help.

- Mistakes and delays may impair the service level of all networks and systems, and, consequently, all business.

The general architecture is displayed in Fig. 6.9 (Terplan 1995).

Table 6.1 illustrates two examples of generic filtering rules. These rules are prepared without explicitly indicating the network component with which they deal. But the inference engine of the expert system can search the configuration database to identify the failed or degraded component.

Unsolved questions with expert systems

There are some unsolved problems related to the use of expert systems for fault dignostics assistance. They include:

- The time required for problem determination must not be longer than the time it would take the network operator to determine the problem.

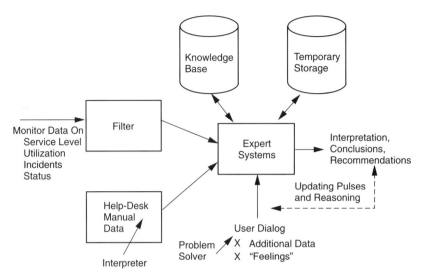

Figure 6.9 Structure of an Expert System

**Table 6. 1: Sample Operational Control Rules of the
Knowledge Base**

Example 1: Response time

WHENEVER RESPONSE TIME FOR ANY APPLICATION VARIES BY
       3 SECONDS
           IF INCREASE
                SEND MESSAGE "SERVICE LEVEL PROBLEMS" TO OPERATOR
                ACTIVATE RULES FOR CATEGORY: RESPONSE TIME
                                                  NETWORK TIME
                                                    HOST TIME
           IF DECREASE
                SEND MESSAGE "LOAD ON LINKS COULD BE INCREASED"
                TO OPERATOR

Example 2: Link failure

IF PROBLEM WITH ANY COMMUNICATIONS LINK
      THEN
              DEACTIVATE THE ROUTERS ON THE LINE
                    IF FREE BACK-UP-LINES IN THE POOL
                        THEN
                            SELECT THE FIRST
                            CHANGE THE ROUTER CONFIGURATION
                            ACTIVATE THE NEW CONFIGURATION
                    ELSE
                            SPEED UP DIAGNOSIS
            IF DIAL OUT OK, ROUTER OPERATIONAL
ELSE
           CONCENTRATE ON FEPS, MODEMS, AND SWITCHES OF THE LINE

- Volume of network elements may require thousands of rules, unless rules may be symbolically formulated.

- Dynamic network changes may require frequent updates in the knowledge base.

- The interpretation and synthesis of message groups are more complex than initially estimated, due to the difficulty of determining the start and end of events relevant to a certain symptom.

- A fairly large number of instruments may be required to identify the actual network status, and the expert system should interface with all of them.

Present and near-future expert systems' implementations may provide the answers soon. Product examples are given later in this chapter.

Expert systems can be used to augment the fault-diagnostic process. These applications are in most cases stand-alone applications, and usually are not linked to platforms. There are, however, several possible integration points:

- A configuration database that is maintained by the platform product.

- Status information about all relevant managed objects. Platforms are the receivers of such information; they easily can forward it to the expert system.

- A processor powerful enough to execute a large number of rules within a short period of time. Most powerful platform products are Unix-based and run on fast processors.

- High-quality presentation service to display conclusions and recommendations to the users. Platforms also can help provide this service.

The next section provides several examples of expert-systems applications and their applicability to fault diagnostics. The examples also show how those applications can be connected to platform functions.

G2 real-time expert system

G2 is an expert systems tool from Gensym Corp for developing large, real-time applications–process control, CIM, telecommunications, network monitoring, automatic testing, manufacturing, and the like, in which hundreds or thousands of variables are monitored concurrently. Application areas include production management involving online monitoring and control, planning and scheduling, quality monitoring and assurance, fault diagnosis, and operations management.

G2's architecture is based on a combination of object-oriented representation and a rule-based paradigm that provides hierarchical systems modeling, knowledge-based reasoning, temporal inferencing, real-time scheduling, dynamic real-time control, simulation modeling, and communications facilities to external data sources.

Key features of G2 include:

- Real-time inferencing, supporting both backward and forward chaining, daemons, and rule prioritization.
- Object-oriented graphics engine and editor.
- Structured natural language front end.
- Networking and integration support for Programmable Logic Controllers (PLCs), Distributed Control Systems (DCS), and databases.

G2 provides a highly graphical, object-oriented development environment based on the principle of application development via subclassing of generic objects and their associated classes. This object-oriented foundation also supports the creation of class libraries, and the organization of objects into collections or frames—referred to in G2 terminology as object *frames*. In G2, frames can represent both real-world objects and their relationships to other objects. Libraries can contain not only class definitions, but also rules, models, and any other knowledge associated with an application.

The object purist might object that G2, like most of the artificial intelligence (AI)-derived tools, does not support strict encapsulation in the sense that it is supported in languages like Smalltalk and C++. G2 does have classes and instances, inheritance, and polymorphism. It also supports attributes and methods. In addition, it supports daemons and generic rules that are outside the object hierarchy, and can access information in various classes and instances, as needed. Gensym, like other AI companies, has found that strict encapsulation causes large systems to execute too slowly. Thus, G2 provides a slightly different use of objects than one finds in the object languages.

The G2 development environment is dynamic and interpreted, allowing a developer to test an application iteratively at any stage of the development process, thereby foregoing the need to recompile the application every time a change is made. Although G2 is written in LISP, it is so wrapped in C that a developer is completely shielded from having to deal with LISP. No knowledge of LISP is required, because LISP provides no interfaces. Moreover, developed applications are delivered in C through the innovative use of translation technology that converts source code to runtime object code. These same translators allow applications to run using a minimum of system memory.

Creating applications in G2 is accomplished largely by icon-based development, wherein the user graphically depicts objects and their relationships, and by a structured natural language interface (for creating, editing, adding, and retrieving rules and knowledge) using English-like syntax.

G2's natural language interface is structured, in the sense that it prompts or guides the user to enter the proper syntax by providing a list of appropriate selections. The user can avoid searching the list by typing the first few letters of the command rule, or object. The interface "jumps ahead" to the desired item, whereupon the user merely double-clicks with the mouse to enter the command. Users also can retrieve knowledge on the basis of attribute, such as problem type, object type, and so on.

G2's object-oriented functional design and structured natural language interface, coupled with its simulation capabilities make it an exceptional tool for dynamically modeling complex plant operations, as well as for developing classes of "generic" knowledge that can be used to develop other applications.

G2 provides a dynamic simulation capability that provides for testing and evaluation during application development. *G2 simulator* is a special kind of data server that provides simulated values for variables and parameters. Simulated values mimic values occurring naturally in production, and can be sampled from actual values taken from room sensors and other control systems operating online. Using the simulator, G2 allows the user to simulate components of applications for a number of uses; for example, to test a knowledge base, run a simulation in parallel with a working process, use simulation models to selectively run and reset parts of a simulation, expand an application safely, and plan control strategies.

The user can simulate anything from normal system operation to obscure failure states at any time. For example, the user can test a knowledge base before deciding how to connect it to applications, or simulate the occurrence of rare states while speeding up the simulated time, thus gaining the ability to anticipate and plan for unusual situations (e.g., a decline in process efficiency caused by a solvent beginning to wear out).

The G2 simulator can provide simulated values while G2 is controlling real operations. Thus, the user can simulate any part of an application while running online under G2, given certain time constraints. In effect, this means that G2 can be used for simulations to perform a number of operations involved in developing and/or maintaining an application, including:

- Checking unreliable sensors for accuracy while they are operating, by regularly comparing observed values with expected values.

- Continuing to secure operations using simulated values if a real sensor fails.

- Estimating states that cannot easily be observed by sensors, and using these estimated values in control schemes.

- Keeping a simulated history of a variable to aid in diagnosing parts failures.

- Testing the effects of adding new hardware devices (e.g., controller, power equipment, etc.).

Integration of G2 applications is made possible by G2 Network, G2 Standard Interface (GST), and Telewindows.

G2 Network is a distributed communications architecture that allows G2 to communicate with external data sources that include: other G2 applications, control systems, PLCs, telemetry systems, power equipments, other simulation programs, databases, and so on.

G2 network also allows concurrent multiple access to G2 applications via Telewindows. Telewindows' multiuser client-server architecture allows G2 applications to run on server workstations, and to create multiple remote user seats on PCs. Telewindows also permits any number of authorized users to have a proprietary restricted access to G2 applications over network connections.

Regarding portability, G2 applications can be run on other platforms, without platform-specific alteration. Knowledge bases developed on one hardware platform can be run on other platforms and the GUIs remain identical. GSI is Gensym's standard general-purpose programming tool for developing interfaces from G2 to databases, control systems, and other external data sources. Using GSI, a developer first writes codc (in C or Fortran), which is then linked with GSI interfaces. GSI also provides libraries and example interfaces written in C and Fortran. These can be modified by the user for particular applications.

RTWorks from Talarian

RTworks addresses the problem of efficiently processing and displaying real-time data in a meaningful way for complex system applications. The RTworks suite of products is a set of powerful tools that help the developer build time-critical monitoring and control systems. Its design features separate processes for data acquisition, data recording and playback, data distribution, inferencing, and graphical user interface. RTWorks can be used for applications where a large number of data variables must be acquired, distributed, analyzed, and displayed in real time.

The RTworks architecture is inherently distributed and is based on a client-server model of computing. Interprocess communication is provided by a dedicated message server. The RTworks suite of products provides several integrated client process types (Fig. 6.10). An application is composed of multiple processes of various types working together. Process types can include both RTworks products and user-defined processes.

This distributed architecture provides for flexibility in deploying applications. By distributing the functions of an application over independent processes, an application can maximize throughput and response. Applications may also expand across multiple processors in a heterogeneous network if added performance or fault tolerance is necessary. The major RTworks process types are:

- The Interprocess Communication Server (*RTserver_*): Allows the RTworks processes to communicate with each other, as well as with user-defined processes.

- The Interference Engine process (*RTie_*): Uses rule-based inferencing, statistical functions, threading functions, objects, and classes to analyze history and current data in real time.

- The Human Computer Interface process (*RThciTM*): Provides an operator with a point-and-click graphical user interface.

- The Data Acquisition process (*RTdaqTM*): Acquires, filters, and groups the incoming data and sends it to the RTserver for distribution to other processes.

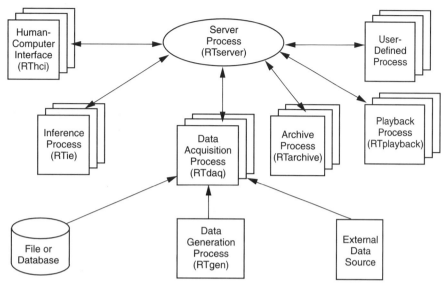

Figure 6.10 *RTWorks* Architecture

- The Data Archive process (*RTarchive_*): Records the rapidly changing messages and data onto a permanent storage medium (e.g., disk).

- The Data Playback process (*RTplayback_*): Retrieves data and messages from archive files and plays them back to other RTworks client processes or user-defined processes.

- The Data Generation process (*RTgenTM*): Allows a user to generate test data files which can be read by any of the RTworks processes. Tools are provided to insert ramps, spikes, and sine waves into the data.

The RTworks interprocess communication scheme allows these processes to be distributed among one or more nodes of a homogeneous or heterogeneous network. Messages are passed using *datagroups*, which are identifiers that specify the destination of the messages. Message traffic and processing can be optimized using this mechanism.

All RTworks processes are independent and can run in a stand-alone configuration. To facilitate independent testing, processes may receive data from a file, through shared memory, or from other processes via RTserver. Additionally, each process may log incoming and outgoing data to facilitate multiple-process debugging. RTworks processes also may be embedded within other existing bodies of software.

RTworks, written in industry standard ANSI-C, provides a completely open architecture where user-defined C, C++, and Ada functions can be linked directly with the various RTworks client processes. Also, external user-defined processes can join an application as a client and send and receive messages with other client processes in the application group. The RTworks Callable Function Library is available to user-defined processes, allowing them to take full advantage of RTworks' powerful message distribution and processing facilities.

All RTworks components support high-speed performance for time-critical applications and are designed to operate continuously in mission critical applications without requiring garbage collection.

RTWorks is in operation at SWIFT (Society for Worldwide Interbank Financial Telecommunications), headquartered in La Hulpe, Belgium. SWIFT operates a sophisticated computerized international telecommunications network that provides members with fast, responsive, and secure automated transmission of financial transactions. Currently, SWIFT has more than 3600 users, mostly banks, in 91 countries and processes approximately 2 million transactions a day. Because of the high number of users and transactions, the user support (or help desk) areas within SWIFT are critical to the success of the company. SWIFT has three support centers: one in Culpepper, Va., another in the Netherlands and a backup disaster center in Belgium.

In a support environment, especially in a financial telecommunications company, the support area receives numerous telephone calls each day. Customer problems range from communications trouble at the user's end, to difficulties at SWIFT's end, or problems at an intermediate carrier's point. Some calls are simply informational queries such as, "What is the currency code for Brazil?"

Since SWIFT is a telecommunications company, one can obtain information about the network through events, which provide information about the state of the network and any known network problems involving customers

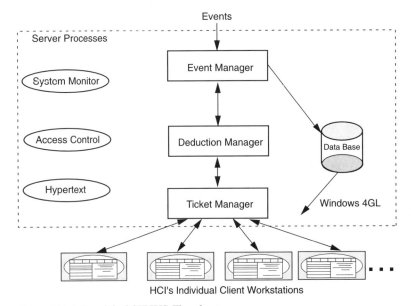

Figure 6.11 A Simplified SIRIUS Flowchart

or SWIFT components. For instance, an event is generated each time a user successfully logs on the network, is aborted from the network, or enters an incorrect password or command. These events can be captured and fed into an expert system with appropriate reasoning knowledge.

Talarian Corporation's RTworks was used by SWIFT as a key component of SIRIUS (SWIFT's Intelligent Resource for International User Support), an expert-system-based help desk (Fig. 6.11). SIRIUS is an intelligent, productivity enhancement project for SWIFT's user support centers. It is comprised of real-time deductions, events processing, an event manager, hypertext manuals, electronic messaging calendars, a scheduler, a front-end interface to SWIFT's internal e-mail and problem management system, a system monitor, a database for storage and retrieval, and a graphical user interface. SIRIUS was written on HP workstations using RTworks, C, Unix processes, Ingres, and Motif.

All of the SIRIUS processes, including those that do not use RTworks rules, communicate via an IPC mechanism written around the RTworks server. This has greatly simplified the entire design process, and makes it easy to communicate with external processes. The RTworks server has proven itself to be the robust central point of the entire SIRIUS project.

RTworks was used by SWIFT's developers for three primary tasks:

- The RTserver and RTworks Interprocess Communication (IPC) protocol is used to connect SIRIUS modules across the network.

- High-level reasoning is performed in the RTie inference engine.

- The Ticket Manager uses a combination of the RTie and rules, along with C code, to provide a cooperative groupware manager of trouble tickets.

In addition, SWIFT developed a custom human-computer interface for the system that connects to the RTserver and is based completely on Motif widgets and C code.

SIRIUS contains two inference engines and knowledge bases. One knowledge base deals with the parsed events and the other expert system deals with handling the tickets and the cooperative groupware nature of SIRIUS. As any process, or module, within SIRIUS is totally independent of every other module, modules communicate only via SIRIUS's custom IPC mechanism. SIRIUS uses a custom IPC protocol that was built on top of Talarian's RTworks server. This IPC allows standardized structures to be passed from one SIRIUS module to another SIRIUS module independently of where the modules are located. The high-level reasoning was prototyped using RTworks rules.

The Ticket Manager (TM) is the portion of SIRIUS that handles deducted tickets. The TM is responsible for maintaining the set of open tickets known to SIRIUS. When a ticket is generated, the TM stores the ticket in Ingres for backup purposes and then makes the ticket available to coordinators by sending it to all the SIRIUS HCI's for display. The Ticket Manager is written using a combination of the Talarian inference engine, rules, and C code.

Summary

HP OpenView provides standard and advanced services that may successfully be utilized for diagnosing faults and proactively monitoring network equipment and facilities. Large networks with many hubs may overload the platform with too many messages, events, and alarms. Special applications may help prevent network overhead and platform overload. This chapter has addressed add-ons for the platform such as NerveCenter and various expert systems intended to help speed up diagnostics. The other alternative is to give policy-based capabilities to hubs for more intelligent local diagnostics and decision making. A combination of both approaches will guarantee a strong fault diagnostics solution to networks and systems users.

7

Fine-Tuning the Fault Management Process

Chapter 6 provided several examples of how collected data can be used to diagnose network faults and to establish network baselines. This chapter describes how to fine-tune the fault-management process by applying polling and thresholding techniques more effectively with Network Node Manager, and by using the Seagate (formerly NetLabs) NerveCenter application to perform more sophisticated polling and data analysis. As this chapter will show, management by exception and policy-based management are two important techniques for maximizing fault management efficiencies.

Management by Exception

As described in previous chapters, HP OpenView Network Node Manager relies on (SNMP) GET commands to collect values of critical MIB variables. By logging values over the course of several weeks, an administrator can determine a range of values describing normal behavior for that MIB variable. It is now time to set threshold boundaries defining the normal range. The first step in setting thresholds is to change NNM's Collection Mode from *Store, No Threshold* to *Store, Check Thresholds*. NNM then will generate an event, in the form of a trap, whenever a specified threshold is crossed. Thresholding supports *management by exception* in that the NNM console alerts the operator only when an exception condition has occurred.

It is advisable to assign a unique trap number identifying each new alert; the available trap numbers range from 1001 to 1999. If no trap number is assigned, the NNM default trap number — 58720263 — will be used.

NNM supports several options involving thresholds:

- Absolute threshold or percentage threshold
- Threshold on MIB value, or MIB expression
- Threshold by itself, or with rearm values

Thresholds can be set only on MIB values described in numeric terms, such as counters, gauges, integers, addresses, and time ticks. HP suggests checking absolute values of MIB variables that count errors, such as interface errors (*ifInErrors, ifOutErrors*). Checking percentage values makes more sense for statistics describing aggregate traffic (*ifInOctets, ifOutOctets*). Generally speaking, any abnormal increase in error rates indicates a problem, while an increase in overall traffic may not indicate a problem unless the networking device is about to become overloaded or otherwise become a bottleneck.

In general, thresholds most often are set on MIB values. This may make no sense when monitoring counters, however, as the counter just increases continually until it rolls over. NNM allows administrators to monitor a counter's rate of change by supporting the ability to set thresholds on a MIB expression.

Finally, a threshold can be associated with a rearm value. Rearms are useful for preventing NNM from generating multiple alarms when a MIB variable keeps bouncing around the threshold value. For example, an administrator can set a threshold defining the highest acceptable value of a MIB variable, and then set a lower rearm threshold. NNM then will generate an event when the first threshold is exceeded, but if the value continues to bounce around this threshold, all succeeding events will be suppressed until the value crosses the lower point of rearm (Fig. 7.1). NNM generates a rearm event if this lower point of rearm is crossed, and another threshold event the next time the higher threshold is crossed.

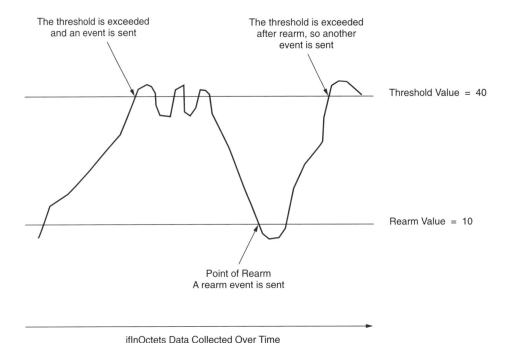

Figure 7.1 Effects of Rearm in NNM Event Generation

By using rearms, then, it is possible to reduce the number of events that NNM must handle. This capability, however, is rather rudimentary, and it does not suppress many other types of meaningless or secondary events that confuse and obscure what's really happening on the network.

Adjusting Thresholds

Once the network administrator has defined a set of thresholds, it is time to put them to the test. After about a week or so of network operation, the administrator probably will be able to identify thresholds that were set too conservatively. For example, if events are generated several times a week or more on a given threshold but there is no degradation in network performance, it may be wise to set the threshold higher and/or the rearm value lower.

After a period of time, when it seems that the adjusted thresholds are functioning as accurate indicators of network health, the administrator may then set the data collection mode to *Don't Store − Check Thresholds* to conserve disk space. However, different administrators have different philosophies about the value of logging historical data.

In a typical fault-monitoring cycle, minor monitoring and thresholding adjustments are made from time to time as new problems are identified and corrected, and as the administrator learns more about the network's specific behavior patterns. Figure 7.2 depicts the typical fault management cycle.

Policy-Based Management

Policy-based management can help simplify the time-consuming process of managing hundreds of network devices. Categorization is the essence of policy-based management. Once similar types of objects are grouped together, it is a straightforward procedure to create policies for managing the same things the same way.

However, NNM out of the box does not implement policy-based management. Instead of letting the user define a single policy for managing a selective group of objects, NNM allows administrators to sort nodes and configure data collection based on only three criteria:

- Whether the node supports SNMP
- Whether the node currently is managed or unmanaged (a user-specified condition)
- According to SNMP object identifier (OID)

As described in earlier chapters, administrators can sort through *snmpCollect* files and define like groups of devices based on values of specific MIB variables as well as on SNMP OID.

An alternative to sorting and script writing is to deploy an off-the-shelf application that supports a more sophisticated polling paradigm out of the box. Two such applications are Network Health from Concord Systems and

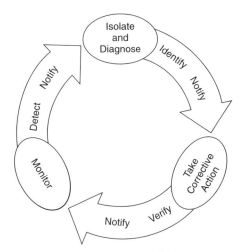

Figure 7.2 Fault Management Cycle

TrendSNMP+ from DeskTalk Systems. Both products support automated performance reporting, and can assist network administrators in baselining and trend analysis, as discussed in Chap. 8.

Another third-party application with more sophisticated polling features is Seagate/NetLabs' NerveCenter. NerveCenter primarily targets enhanced fault management rather than reporting. NerveCenter supports dynamic selection of monitored and polled elements to help administrators concentrate on just the managed objects of interest. Property groups allow administrators to create different classes of managed objects for defining the scope of polls and alarms.

Thresholding with NerveCenter

In 1994, HP announced an agreement with NetLabs, Inc., to integrate its NerveCenter alarm processing technology with Network Node Manager. (In 1995, NetLabs was acquired by Seagate Technology.) NerveCenter previously existed as an element of NetLabs's DiMONS management platform (Terplan 1995), which no longer is marketed. NerveCenter also is embedded in Sun's Solstice Enterprise manager, described in Chap. 1.

NerveCenter makes it easier to configure more complex polls, thereby reducing the number of events generated by NNM. When used properly, NerveCenter can make NNM a more scalable solution. NerveCenter provides three mechanisms for reducing network management traffic overhead: property groups, event-directed polling, and smart polling. Multiple NerveCenters also can be distributed, enhancing scalability, as shown in Fig. 7.3. Organizations can use remote, stand-alone NerveCenter applications to detect and handle local network problems, forwarding designated events to a central HP OpenView Network Node Manager for cross-domain coordination.

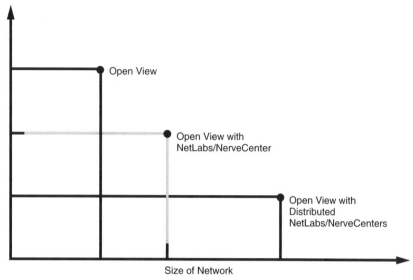

Figure 7.3 Increasing NNM's Scalability with NerveCenter

NerveCenter allows administrators to group similar objects and set threshold conditions, polling rates, and automated responses collectively on an entire group in one operation. This grouping capability reduces the need for scripts.

NerveCenter is a rules-based, distributed application for correlating and responding to network events. The last three releases of NerveCenter have provided successively more features for synchronizing collected information and managed devices with HP OpenView NNM.

NerveCenter supports the notion of conditional-state polling, a mechanism that is much more sophisticated than the simple use of thresholds and rearms. The conditional-state polling feature allows NerveCenter to detect and respond to a sequence of related events, rather than just to each individual event in isolation. To filter secondary or meaningless events, the administrator can use the criteria of event order or event persistence; combinations of these criteria also can be used.

Conditional states are depicted in the form of state diagrams, which define both the sequence of event detection as well as the automated actions taken upon receipt of specific events. While it requires a lot of thought to develop effective state diagrams, NerveCenter makes the process easier by providing a GUI with step-by-step instructions.

As shown in Fig. 7-4, each circle represents one stage in a detected sequence of events. Each arrow represents a transition between states. In this simple example, an event is generated after NerveCenter receives three successive traps in less than a minute. Without NerveCenter, NNM would generate an event at each circle — i.e., after each trap. It is easy to see that use of this state diagram can suppress unnecessary events; the number of events suppressed depends on the device as well as on the load on the network.

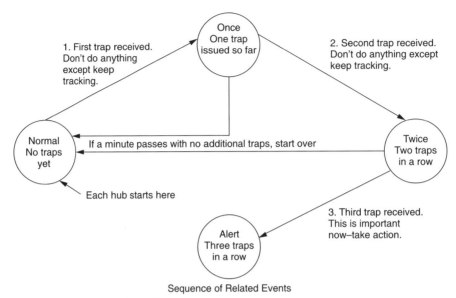

Figure 7.4 NerveCenter State Diagram

To support fault diagnosis and tuning, operators define what MIB information should be collected via polling. Any single poll collects information about only one object, except when smart agents are used. When a poll is set up for, say, hubs, the operator defines its polling rate, trigger names for invoking actions, and poll conditions. Poll conditions consist of one or more relational expressions.

Using NerveCenter, operators can create a relational expression selecting attributes from an attributes list of the object under consideration. Conditions may be modified during the diagnostic process. Additionally, conditions may be chained by multiple expressions — resulting in a fewer number of polls. In this way, poll conditions can be created that automatically evaluate the MIB data in practically any combination. Setting and modifying polling conditions may be driven by the results of previous polls. NerveCenter also can recognize results originating in RMON probes.

NerveCenter's Action Router feature allows administrators to define what actions should be taken based upon polling results. There are two components to the Action Router:

1. Rules, with the associated actions to take.

2. An engine that evaluates the status of specific alarms to see if the rules apply.

These features are extremely important when diagnostics are conducted in an automated or semiautomated manner. In this function, NerveCenter begins to approach the capabilities of an expert system. Actions that can be triggered by NerveCenter include:

- Sending e-mail
- Paging an operator
- Invoking a Unix command or script
- Logging data to a file
- Sending a trouble ticket
- Turning a poll on or off
- Generating an SNMP trap
- Issuing an SNMP SET command
- Generating an OpenView NNM event

For example, the ActionRouter may page different personnel, depending upon the device's location, type, or time of day. Figure 7.5 illustrates an automated action that has different definitions based on time of day.

Any of these actions can be defined at any point in the event sequence — i.e., at any circle in the state diagram. Multiple actions can be invoked as easily as a single action. Polls can be turned on or off at any point in a state diagram. This feature, called *smart polling*, allows administrators to control SNMP traffic overhead to a degree. Figure 7.6 shows an example of smart polling in which secondary and tertiary routers are polling for specific MIB variables only after NerveCenter detected sluggish performance on the primary router.

NerveCenter also can be configured to log data based on correlated network events. Although NNM can be configured to log threshold data, it cannot turn the logging activity on or off based on network behavior. The administrator,

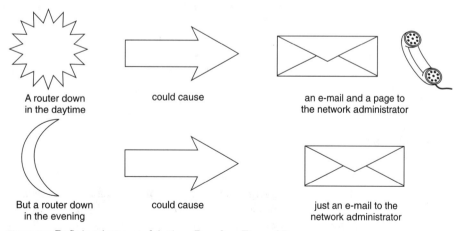

Figure 7.5 Defining Automated Actions Based on Time-of-Day

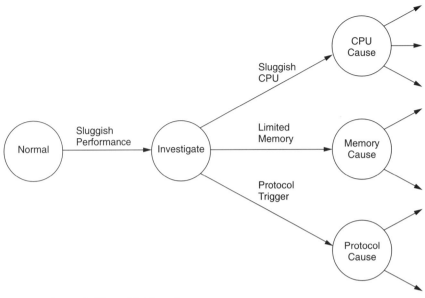

Figure 7.6 Smart Polling with NerveCenter

however, can designate "Log" as a state-diagram transition action; the resulting log will contain only entries that correspond to a detected sequence of events. Log data can be selectively deleted either manually or automatically.

In March 1996, Seagate released a version of the product called NerveCenter Pro, which supports cross-device correlation. Prior to this release, NerveCenter was not optimized for cross-correlating faults from multiple nodes and device interfaces into a single alarm message.

An enterprise NerveCenter Pro application costs approximately $15,000; a remote NerveCenter license for a single administrator and a single operator costs approximately $7500.

Although NerveCenter complements HP OpenView, it is not fully integrated with it; current implementations result in duplicate polling and other overlapping capabilities. Full integration of NerveCenter into OpenView would require modifications of OpenView event management, MIB entries, trap interpretation, and storage mechanisms.

State diagram examples

Development of NerveCenter state diagrams is largely a trial-and-error process that requires a thorough understanding of SNMP, familiarity with the network's behavior, patient observation, and educated guesswork. NerveCenter is an attractive alternative for administrators seeking to automate the process of grouping devices and configuring complex thresholds.

The following is an example from a leading international energy corporation. This company is using NerveCenter and HP OpenView Network Node Manager in combination to manage a network comprising more than 30,000 managed objects, including approximately 1000 routers, bridges, and hubs. The company has defined the following thresholds for router-specific alarms:

- Poll: *RtrOpStatUp*
- Poll: *RtrOpStatDown*
- Alarm: *RouterLinkStatus*
- Property group: CISCO

Figure 7.7 depicts the state diagram describing the following polling sequence. The *RtrOpStatUp.(SUBNETID)Poll* and *RtrOpStatDown.(SUB-NETID)Poll* poll the *ifAdminStatus* and *ifOperStatus* attributes — but only for those devices assigned to the CISCO property group.

The *RtrOpStatUp.(SUBNETID)Poll* checks whether the *ifAdminStatus* and the *ifOperStatus* for each interface equals *up*. If this condition is met, the transition is made to *Normal* state, and the severity is set to *Normal*.

The *RtrOpStatDown.(SUBNETID)Poll* checks whether the *ifAdminStatus* equals *up*, and whether the *ifOperStatus* equals *down*. When this condition is first detected, the transition is made to *LinkProblem* state, and a severity of *Major* is assigned.

If this condition happens a second time within the 3-minute polling period, the alarm is escalated to the *LinkDown* state with a severity of *Critical*. If the router becomes *unReachable*, the transition is made to the *unKnown* state with a severity of *Warning*. When the router becomes reachable again, the transition is made to *Normal* state with a severity of *Normal*. All transitions are reported as alarms to the OpenView Event system.

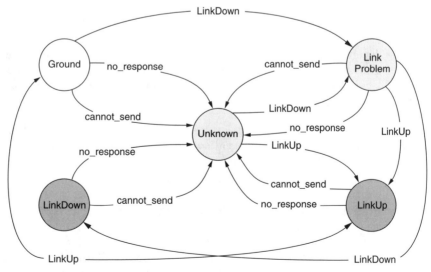

Figure 7.7 RouterLinkStatus State Diagram for NerveCenter

In addition to this router polling configuration, the company has established separate polling configurations for each subnet for the purpose of reducing network management traffic and eliminating the need to correlate all network events. NerveCenter pings the circuit-side of the remote router to see if it is reachable; if the ping responds, then the circuit-port of the router can be reached, and all polls directed to the subnet on the other side of the circuit are turned on. However, if the circuit-port cannot be reached via ping, then the circuit is set to *Critical* and all subnet-specific polls (polls directed to that subnet) are turned off until the ping responds. Subnet-specific polls are not forwarded to NNM. The company also has used NerveCenter to define state diagrams for directing polling of HP-UX system disk utilization and Bay Networks hub status. More information on the use of NerveCenter is provided in App. C.

Feeding Results into Trouble Ticket Systems

Although HP OpenView NNM supports fault detection and isolation, the product by itself provides no capabilities for tracking problems. As a result, customers must purchase and use add-on trouble-ticket systems such as Remedy Action Request (AR) System, Peregrine ServiceCenter, or Platinum Apriori.

There are many trouble-ticketing and help desk products available that can be integrated with HP OpenView at the event level. This chapter focuses on Remedy's AR System, one of the most popular choices for adding trouble-ticketing support to an OpenView-based environment.

AR System opens, tracks, and closes network events on a per-operator basis using an interactive process similar to e-mail (Desai 1996). AR System features a flexible, client/server architecture suitable for customization. From a technical standpoint, the AR System offers two options for integration with OpenView:

- Menu bar integration: The HP OpenView operator launches AR System from the *ovw* GUI.

- Event-stream integration: When AR System receives an OpenView event, the AR System's *arovd* daemon compares it to the user-supplied list of events and opens a trouble ticket if a match is found. Nonmatching events are discarded.

The *arovd* daemon works in conjunction with AR System's OpenView Registration Tool (*arovui*), allowing developers to specify SNMP traps that map into AR System entries (Desai 1996).

Customers can control the appearance and content of all AR System trouble ticket forms and reports. AR System also supports creation of macros to automate responses to events. AR System creates a historical audit trail of logged problems. End users as well as operators can make inquiries to the AR System database to support problem analysis. In 1995, Remedy introduced a new *Flashboards* feature for visually displaying, in graphical form, the number of open/acknowledge/closed trouble tickets in the AR System.

Flashboards assists large operations in particular by providing a real-time gauge of problem-tracking activities.

Summary

HP OpenView NNM is an excellent collector of data; in addition, it supports flexible polling and thresholding techniques for fine-tuning the fault management process. Third-party applications such as Seagate NerveCenter can be used to perform more sophisticated polling and data analysis. Management by exception and policy-based management, two important techniques for maximizing fault management efficiencies, are more easily supported when tools such as NerveCenter are used in combination with NNM. The fault management process can be further improved by automatically feeding event data into trouble ticket systems such as Remedy AR System.

Analyzing Data

Baselining is the process of taking snapshots of a network or system when it is healthy (Huntington-Lee 1994a). This involves capturing data over time to determine *normal* values of network or system statistics. Once a performance baseline is established, it can be compared to ongoing network behavior. This enables administrators to spot anomalies and to solve impending problems before they turn into network catastrophes. Baselining is a necessary prelude to capacity planning.

The Importance of Baselining and Capacity Planning

ISO defines four general types of performance management attributes that may be monitored for baselining purposes (Udupa 1996):

- Counters, which are numeric values, both settable (read/write) and nonsettable (read-only) that can only be incremented; counters wraparound when maximum values are reached.

- Gauges, which are dynamic variables that can be incremented or decremented.

- Thresholds, either maximum or minimum; events are generated when thresholds are crossed.

- Tidemarks, the indication of the highest or lowest value of a gauge.

These types of indicators can be used to monitor the performance of a multitude of network or system characteristics, including:

- Utilization: bandwidth, CPU, memory, etc.

- Errors: packet, disk, cache hits/misses

- Activity: user logons/logoffs, disk activity, printer activity, traffic volume, etc.

Organizations with large, multisegment internetworks stand to gain the most from the cost benefits provided by baselining. Any time routers are carrying traffic over the wide area, significant cost savings can be realized by optimizing network configurations. Unfortunately, most organizations today lack performance data they need if they are to optimize effectively (Huntington-Lee 1996b).

There are several alternatives to establishing baselines and creating useful performance reports:

- Rely on limited performance reporting capabilities of hardware-based monitors.

- Develop reporting capabilities in-house, using data collected by monitors or open management platforms such as HP OpenView.

- Out-task performance reporting to a specialized service provider.

It can be risky to rely on hardware-based monitor reports that provide little in terms of long-term trending information. Too much guesswork is involved, and, without access to trended data, the ability to predict impending trouble is greatly reduced.

Many network administrators have developed reporting capabilities in-house, using data collected by monitors or open-management platforms such as OpenView. This can be a time-consuming process, even when administrators are well-versed in the practice of baselining and script writing. In-house development can yield highly customized results, but maintaining the code and report templates may be problematic if there is staff turnover, or when network infrastructure changes.

Third-party automated performance monitoring tools can help provide that data in usable format while reducing the time it takes to create useful reports. As a rule of thumb, any organization with several or more backbone routers will benefit from deploying some sort of optimization, capacity planning, or automated performance reporting tool.

There are several automated performance reporting tools available that can complement an OpenView-based solution. As a rule, these tools duplicate to some degree OpenView's polling and/or database functions. Still, many customers find that the value of these tools more than compensates for the cost of redundant functions.

Automated Performance Reporting Tools

This section describes how four products, Concord Network Health and DeskTalk TRENDsnmp+, BBN StatsWise, and SAS CPE for Open Systems, can be deployed in an OpenView environment to support baselining and analysis.

Concord Communications' Network Health

Concord Communications introduced its Trakker traffic monitor in 1991. With the successful introduction of the Trakker Billing and TrakReport applications three years later, Concord helped to define the market for automated reporting facilities. Network Health represents a bold step for Concord, as it is completely software-based and does not require Trakker probes for data collection.

Network Health includes the Universal Poller and analysis and reporting features. The Poller application collects SNMP and RMON data, feeding it directly into an SQL database.

Network Health reports are produced daily on a scheduled basis by the product. The first page of the report depicts network performance for the previous day, compared to the baseline.

Concord offers a more off-the-shelf approach to baselining than its competitors. Network Health automatically collects data via its Universal Poller, and reduces data over time, creating a baseline of network performance. Once the baseline is developed, daily performance reports compare network activity to the baseline. Both LAN (Ethernet) and WAN (Cisco router) reports are offered, as are reports on Frame Relay performance.

Network Health provides easily understood reports on WAN as well as LAN activity. The daily canned reports are easily produced, and provide valuable information. The *Health Index* reports are unique in the manner in which they highlight service levels, and use linear regression analysis to predict when noticeable performance degradation is expected to occur.

Table 8.1 lists many of the prepackaged reports provided by Network Health.

DeskTalk TRENDsnmp+

DeskTalk's first commercial offering, TRENDsystem, was positioned as an application suite designed to augment SunSoft's SunNetManager. TRENDsystem

Table 8.1. Concord Network Health Performance Reports

Report Title	Function
Daily Network Volume	Daily traffic for preceding 30+ days
Hourly Network Volume	Traffic per hour for preceding 24 hours
Hourly Health Index	Utilization in a stacked bar chart, showing various types of errors, discards, etc.
Situations to Watch	Top 10 problem areas
Volume Leaders	Identifies network segments or WAN links with the highest volume of activity during the previous day
Ranked Volume/Bandwidth/Health Index Leaders	Compares leaders in volume/utilization, etc., to their past rankings
Health Index Leaders	Prioritizes top 10 problem areas
Volume/Health Index Change Leaders	Highlights portions of the network that changed the most
Daily Volume compared to Baselines	Each hourly volume datapoint is plotted against a *typical* volume for that hour
Utilization detail	The percentage of time that each segment or WAN link has spent at various utilization levels

added a relational database, installation aids, and development capabilities to the popular management platform.

In 1995, DeskTalk repackaged and significantly enhanced its base technology, and ported it to other non-Sun platforms, particularly IBM AIX running on the RS/6000 system. DeskTalk also now supports TRENDsnmp+ on HP OpenView.

As as result, DeskTalk has enjoyed a new measure of success selling into IBM shops accustomed to performance analysis and capacity planning tools on the mainframe. In some cases, TRENDsnmp+ is seen as a replacement for SAS tools on the mainframe; but increasingly, TRENDsnmp+ is being used in conjunction with SAS CPE for Open Systems. In fact, SAS and DeskTalk are exploring a potential marketing partnership to leverage this synergy.

Telephone companies represent another new area of success for DeskTalk. DeskTalk is selling TRENDsnmp+ as a customer premises equipment (CPE) reporting tool for telcos that sell network management services. TRENDsnmp+ collects data from the routers on the customer premises; this data is then fed into the telco management application that products detailed call accounting and billing reports.

DeskTalk offers several versions of its TRENDsnmp performance reporting software:

- TRENDsnmp (SNMP-only agents and management station interface)
- TRENDscout (GUI and analysis software for use with Frontier NetScout probes)
- TRENDrmon (RMON agents)
- TRENDsnmp+ (SNMP and RMON agents/management station)

Both TRENDsnmp and TRENDsnmp+ include an embedded Sybase RDBMS; tools are available for mapping to other RDBMSs.

The purpose of TRENDsnmp+ is to collect SNMP and RMON data in an efficient manner (using distributed agents or RMON probes), compress the data, and store it in an easily accessible SQL database. TRENDsnmp+ converts raw counters into userful delta values and rates, and creates logical tables of related statistics. Data is summarized and aged according to user-specified parameters.

TRENDsnmp+ employs several data reduction methods:

- Rolling up over time
- Aggregating data into rate tables
- Individual aging on a per-table basis

In 1996, DeskTalk released TRENDsnmp+ version 3.2. The following paragraphs summarize the enhancements in this release.

Grade of Service (GOS) reporting. GOS reporting is targeted at supporting service-level agreements. GOS converts historical performance statistics into meaningful graphical displays using a weighted stacked bar chart format. GOS allows the user to select any set of SNMP or RMON metrics and assign a grading scale (indicating relative importance) to each selected metric. An overall grading scale (such as excellent, good, fair, poor) is applied to the weighted metrics. This information allows network service providers to concentrate on areas where performance is substandard. Included are several preformatted reports, such as an Ethernet GOS report describing network utilization, errors, collisions, and broadcasts.

GOS can be set up with metrics from any SNMP MIB, allowing users to develop customized GOS reporting for routers, servers, LAN segments, and WAN links.

Database replication. TRENDcopy provides incremental, periodic, filtered database replication service to a backup server. Replication can be ad hoc using a command-line interface; or it can be scheduled. Database tables can be created or incrementally copied to another database. Copying can be triggered via user-specified criteria such as thresholds, time spans, or sets of nodes, so that the new database contains only the information required for the reporting applications.

Satellite database servers. TRENDsnmp+ pollers support satellite database servers, TRENDremote, for more fully distributing the data collection activity. TRENDremote allows the data to be collected and stored for a period of time at any physical location. Incremental, periodic data transfer can be triggered from a satellite location into a regional or central data repository. At least one copy of TRENDcopy must be purchased and installed at the central or regional server to support TRENDremote.

TRENDsnmp+ supports a number of canned reports. The following preformatted exception reports are included in the TRENDsheet option:

- Node availability
- Network bandwidth utilization
- Excessive errors

Customized reporting is based upon manipulation of query files created by the Trend report builder. The Grapher allows selection of color, pattern thickness, and name of the line. Table 8.2 lists performance reports provided by TRENDsnmp+.

DeskTalk provides extensive libraries for MIB-II reports, Ethernet RMON reports, and Token-Ring RMON reports. The Cisco 10.0 Report Library includes the following statistics:

Table 8.2. DeskTalk TrendSNMP+ Performance Reports

Report Title	Function
Hourly Packet Counts by Size (Ethernet)	Octets in, broken down by size (64, 65-127, 128-255, 256-511, 512-1023, 1024-1518)
Serial Line Quality (Hourly)	Ratio of input to input errors; Ratio of output to output errors
Hourly Input Utilization Frequency Distribution	Pie chart with percentage breakdowns (0-20%, 20-60%, 60-100%)
Hourly Interface (Total Bytes)	(Total bytes received/total bytes sent)
WAN Link Usage	Utilization broken down by input, input errors, output, output errors

- Hourly CPU and memory utilization
- Hourly CPU and memory utilization distribution
- Hourly router health (GOS)
- Hourly serial interface health (GOS)
- Daily worst interfaces
- Interface hourly percent utilization by protocol
- Interface hourly traffic by protocol
- Serial line hourly percent utilization by protocol
- Serial line hourly traffic by protocol

BBN StatsWise

StatsWise is positioned as an SNMP network capacity planning tool that can capture data efficiently and illustrate trends. BBN defines capacity planning as encompassing trend analysis, load balancing, and configuration planning.

StatsWise runs on Sun SPARCstations operating SunOS, or HP-UX 9000 systems operating HP-UX. The product can interoperate with SunSoft's Solstice Domain Manager (formerly SunNet Manager), HP OpenView Network Node Manager, and Cabletron Spectrum.

StatsWise was first introduced in August 1995. The product consists of three components:

- A poller that collects SNMP MIB II, Cisco private MIB, and user-defined MIB data; a MIB compiler is provided. Stored data is regularized for future access and manipulation.
- A DataServer engine designed to store sparse, time-series data in ASCII (Intermediate File Format) form. The data is accessible by client applications connecting via TCP/IP.

■ The Cornerstone client application, an analysis tool for generating graphs and reports.

Using the poller, administrators can group monitored devices into *collections*, with each collection assigned a different polling rate. StatsWise can be used to gather detailed information about how the network is behaving over time.

Administrators may choose to disable the StatsWise poller, and instead use data collected by popular management systems such as SunSoft's Site Manager, Hewlett-Packard's HP OpenView Network Node Manager, Cabletron Spectrum, and IBM NetView for AIX.

The data regularization process includes:

■ Conversion of counters to deltas

■ Compensation for counter wraparound and router resets

■ Dynamic linking of data

■ Construction of a flowchart by a workmap

StatsWise also includes a dataset editor for manipulating and storing data. Customers may purchase the poller and DataServer separately if they do not wish to use BBN's Cornerstone analysis module.

Table 8.3 lists the prepackaged reports included with StatsWise:

A variety of graphical report forms are supported, including X-Y line plots, scatter plots, bar graphs, histograms, and 3D surface plots. A WorkMap feature builds an icon-based flowchart of each analysis, allowing users to trace their steps in analyzing the network. StatsWise includes a scripting language for producing customized reports, and a developer's kit for customizing StatsWise screens.

SAS CPE for Open Systems

SAS CPE was first developed and used by SAS Institute to manage its own large internal network. Drawing from SAS Institute's existing statistical analysis applications, the vendor applied its technology for data organization, analysis, and trending to the task of reporting on systems and networks.

SAS benefits from its experience of serving a large installed base of customers using other SAS applications. SAS's biggest challenge is repackaging a very powerful and sophisticated technology in a form that is used easily by busy network administrators who might not be familiar with statistical analysis concepts. To help address this challenge, SAS has published a "Getting Started with SAS CPE and HP OpenView" document that outlines for users detailed procedures for configuring SAS CPE for Open Systems when deploying it with HP OpenView.

In 1996, SAS introduced a "dashboards"-like function for monitoring activity, as well as a PC-based interface — to help push product visibility to higher levels within the organization (e.g., non-SAS technicians). The PC interface will provide service-level type information and reports.

Table 8.3. BBN StatsWise Performance Reports

Report Title	Function
Line utilization	Line graphs of line utilization % vs time
Line utilization summary	Box plot graph of line utilization summary (median, upper and lower quartile, upper and lower adjacent values)
Line utilization mean day	Line utilization over an average (mean) day, including max, min, and mean curves
Total traffic Kb/sec	Two graphs for each interface selected: —line graph of total traffic vs time —histogram of total traffic vs count both graphs are in Kb/second
Router availability	Line router availability % vs time
Discard rate report	Four graphs for each interface selected: —line graph of packets discard rate in vs time —line graph of per packets discard rate out vs time —histogram of each/count vs discard rate percentage
Router IP load	Line graph of IP loading vs time Histogram of IP load distribution of packets/sec vs count for each router selected Similar graphs for total network (a summation of routers selected
CPU utilization	Graphs CPU utilization against time
Select and plot variables	Line graph vs time, and histogram of MIB variable values
Line utilization distribution	Distribution plot of interface utilization % vs count (histogram)
Min/max/mean	Mean value, min value, and max value for a selected MIB variable against a 24-hour time period (line graph)
Total traffic in packets/second	Two graphs for each interface selected: —line graph of total traffic vs time —histogram of total traffic vs count both graphs are in packets/second
Interface availability	Line graph of the percentage of time the interface was available
Errors rate report	Four graphs for each interface selected (two for line in, and two for line out) —Line graph packet error rate in vs time —line graph per packet error rate out vs time —histogram of each/count vs error %
Aggregate variables	Line graph vs time and distribution plot of selected MIB variable values
CPU Utilization distribution	Histogram of CPU utilization percentage vs count
Average packet size report	Four graphs: —average packet size (in octets) vs time —histogram of packet size vs count —min/max/mean line graph of average packet size over a 24-hour period —box plot of distribution of packet size

The core technology of SAS CPE for Open Systems resides in software that converts collected data into SAS datasets, called the *Performance Data Base*, a proprietary database. Data is reduced according to an aging scheme (days, weeks, months, years).

SAS CPE for Open Systems does not perform its own polling, instead using data collected by popular management systems such as HP OpenView, SunSoft Solstice Domain Manager (SunNet Manager), IBM NetView for AIX, and Cabletron Spectrum. SAS picks up data from HP OpenView in one of two ways:

- From output of the *SNMPcollect* process, SAS retrieves binary data.
- From user-specified files, SAS reads ASCII data.

For both HP OpenView and IBM NetView for AIX, SAS CPE performs "cleanup" with respect to data synchronization and timestamping. SAS also offers a "generic" facility for interfacing to Unix systems other than HP, IBM, and Sun.

SAS CPE allows administrators to set and maintain acceptable service levels for users of open systems and networks. SAS can reduce, process, and reformat data and present it in forms that allow experienced technicians to monitor baselines of system performance.

SAS CPE's strengths include sophisticated data-reduction mechanisms, and the ability to perform synchronization, transformation, and data cleanup. SAS is a powerful system and, in the hands of an experienced technician, it can be used to transform raw data into meaningful information. SAS bills this as *data warehousing*:

- Providing access to data and cleaning it up.
- Organizing data, not according to how it was logged, but how it will be used.
- Adding *business intelligence*, formatting data appropriately so it can be used in a meaningful way.

SAS CPE for Open Systems provides approximately 30 predefined report templates, many of which are geared for analysis of computer system server performance. Selected templates describing network performance are listed in Table 8.4.

Users can apply a variety of statistical analysis methods against this data, including smoothed plot (single variable), single-variable box plot, two-variable regression analysis, scatter plot of hourly means, high/low mean, stacked plot, two Y-X axis plot, and other graphical representations.

Product comparisons

Table 8.5 compares selected features of the four automated performance reporting tools discussed in this chapter.

**Table 8.4. SAS CPE for Open Systems
Performance Reports**

Network Reports

RPC client errors across machine/network

Input packets/second (MIB II)

Output packets/second (MIB II)

TCP retransmissions versus segments/second (MIB II)

TCP bad rcv packet types

Packet rcv error types

System Reports

CPU saturation by machine

CPU load averages by machine

CPU usage breakdown

Input packets to input errors by machine

Output packets to output errors by machine

Paging activity by machine

Network error percentage by machine

Output packet-to-collisions by machine

Network collisions across machine

Disk activity

UDP errors by type by machine

TCP errors by type by machine

Network I/O by machine

15 minute load average across machine

Weekly exception report by machine

Top 10 CPU busy (weekly)

CPU usage by day across machine

Top 3 disk drives (MB/sec)

Top 10 disk drives (MB/sec)

Disk usage across machine

Load average profile by whole day

Mean I/O rates across machine

Mean network error rate across machine

Collisions across machine

Resource utilization report across machine

NFS server activity by machine

NFS client activity by machine

Mean NFS/RPC error rates across machine

Capacity Planning

Baselining and capacity planning are closely related activities. The following section describes how customers may use a baselining/planning tool from NetSys to support capacity planning for networks based on Cisco routers. The NetSys product is not specifically integrated into HP OpenView, although it can complement Cisco's CiscoWorks application, which can be launched from OpenView.

NetSys offers several baselining and capacity planning tools for Cisco-based networks, including Connectivity Baseliner, Connectivity Solver, and Performance Tools. Performance Tools must be used in conjunction with the Connectivity Tools (Huntington-Lee 1995b).

The Connectivity Baseliner product constructs an enhanced network topology map based on information in Cisco configuration files and routing tables. User-specified Cisco router configuration files are copied into a specified directory under the Source Code Control System (SCCS), and then parsed to create the baseline model of the network.

The Connectivity Baseliner performs more than two dozen integrity checks across routers to identify potential configuration problems. These checks include verifying static routes, detecting inconsistent bandwidth configuration statements, and identifying invalid access list statements. The Integrity Checks include IP Integrity Checks, IPX Integrity Checks, Remote Source Route Bridging Integrity Checks, SNA STUN Integrity Checks, and AppleTalk Integrity Checks.

Connectivity Solver enables administrators to perform what-if scenarios using the baseline and simulation of failed links or nodes to determine the impact of network problems and changes. The Connectivity Solver can simulate:

- Protocol mismatches
- Access list mismatches
- Encapsulation problems
- Source-route bridging configuration problems

The administrator saves the changes made to the router configuration files in a NetSys working directory. The configuration files may be downloaded into the network at any time, at the administrator's discretion.

The Connectivity Solver supports the following functions:

- Load connectivity requirements and analyze them.
- Create new connectivity requirements and analyze them.
- Create new scenarios for what-if analysis.
- View routing tables.
- Perform routing table modeling and simulation.
- Modify all device parameter settings (routing algorithms, static routes, default networks).

Table 8.5. Comparative Features of Automated Performance Reporting Tools

Feature/ Function	BBN	Concord	DeskTalk	SAS
polling/data collection	Includes SNMP-based Poller; can also make use of data from SunSoft Site Manager, HP OpenView, and Cabletron Spectrum if the poller is disabled	via distributed Universal Poller agents, polling SNMP and RMON agents	via distributed DeskTalk polling agents or RMON probes (such as Frontier NetScout); polling policies can be defined by groups of MIB objects	Obtains data from SunSite Manager, Cabletron Spectrum, HP OpenView, IBM NetView for AIX, HP MeasureWare (does not include its own poller)
data collected	MIB II, private MIB (Cisco); a MIB compiler is included for reading other private MIBs	RMON, MIB-II, private MIBs (Cabletron MMAC hubs, all Cisco routers, Bay 3000 hubs, most 3Com hubs, some UB hubs, Alantec). A frame relay module is forthcoming	RMON, MIB-II, frame relay DTE, Host Resources MIB; some private MIBs; selected RMON groups (statistics, history, host and matrix)	Processes data collected by SunSite Manager and Cabletron Spectrum (MIB II, private MIBs including Cisco, Cabletron); also processes data from HP's PCS (MeasureWare)
devices monitored now	Cisco routers; MIB compiler provided for other private MIBs; out-of-the-box support for more devices planned for 1996	Cabletron MMAC hubs, all Cisco routers, Bay 3000 hubs, most 3Com hubs, some UB hubs, Alantec); support for RMON2 (via Axon) is forthcoming; support for Frontier forthcoming	Cisco, Bay, Cabletron, Frontier NetScout Domain View (supports NetScout extensions and subnet level monitoring)	Does not collect data directly from devices
Operating systems supported	Sun SPARC (SunOS) or HP-UX 9000	SunSPARC running SunOS Solaris; will run on HP-UX in 1Q96	SunSPARC or running SunOS or Solaris, or IBM RS/6000 running AIX	SunSPARC (Solaris), HP-UX 9000, or IBM RS/6000 AIX

■ Generates router IOS delta command files for changes made within the Solver.

NetSys's future strategy is to apply its Connectivity Tools and Performance Tools technology to other vendors' products — particularly switches. At this time, however, NetSys does not plan to support any routers other than Cisco's. NetSys is a privately held company; its investors include Cisco Systems and several venture capital firms.

Out-Tasking Alternatives

Automated performance reporting tools can help alleviate the maintenance burden, but tools still require installation, deployment, configuration, customization, and maintenance. Canned facilities give users a jump start, but making full use of a tool still requires time and talent. Again, network administrators with the skills and time to address performance reporting in complex, mixed environments are in the minority. The growth of network monitoring services is expected to mirror and even exceed the growth of automated performance analysis and reporting tools.

Performance monitoring services such as NETracker from International Network Services (INS) target this critical need for internetwork performance-reporting-without-pain. More full-service providers, such as Bell Atlantic Network Integration (BANI), Network Enterprise Services (NES), and BBN Systems and Technologies offer performance reporting in context with in-band monitoring and fault management. While performance reporting has long been offered by full-service outsourcers, it has only been within the past two years that a new class of vendors has emerged, providing much more narrowly targeted offerings, called *out-tasking*. There are a variety of out-tasking services available today, ranging from desktop inventory, asset management, and backup/recovery, to LAN/WAN performance analysis and reporting.

Because out-tasking providers specializing in performance reporting provide it as a service, customers don't have to deploy new systems or software themselves. The service provider installs data-collection software on, typically, a 486 PC running either Windows NT or SCO, at the customer site. The software, which supports a distributed polling capability, polls routers, typically once an hour, 24 hours a day. The software converts raw data into trended reports, in weekly or year-to-date format. In some cases, the reduced statistics are downloaded via modem during off hours to the vendor's central processing site, and hardcopy reports are shipped overnight to the customer once a week. In other cases, customers use the local system's GUI-based interface to pull the reports off the machine.

Table 8.6 compares the benefits and limitations of both tools and services for performance reporting.

Summary

Baselining is the process of taking snapshots of a network or system when it is healthy. Baselining is a necessary prelude to capacity planning. There are several alternatives for establishing baselines and creating useful performance reports, including relying on the limited performance reporting capabilities of hardware-based monitors, developing reporting capabilities in-house, using data collected by monitors or open management platforms such as HP OpenView, deploying automated performance reporting tools, and out-tasking performance reporting to a specialized service provider. The appropriate decision depends upon the network requirements and skill levels of the organization's staff.

Table 8.6. Automated Performance Reporting Tools Compared to OutTasking Services

	Tools	Services
Strengths	User can customize report content/format at will. User feels "in control" of reporting efforts.	Saves time—no need for installing, configuring, maintaining reporting tool. Saves money—can be less expensive than purchasing tool, acquiring training, devoting staff time to configuring/maintaining tool. Provides a "process" for baselining/reporting that most organizations lack. User leverages the expertise of other specialists.
Limitations	Cost of enterprise-wide deployment may be high, requiring diligent cost-justification. Network complexity can make tools difficult to optimize. Some training/maintenance involved (varies peer tool).	Cost of the solution is obvious, making it more difficult to justify in some organization. Users believe they can do it themselves more cheaply. Users do not want outsiders having access to network performance/configuration data.

Maintaining the Network

Maintaining the network is one of the network administrator's most important duties. In the OSI Specific Management Functional Areas (SMFAs), which include fault management, accounting management, configuration management, performance management, and security management (Fig. 9.1), the routine tasks of network maintenance are primarily in the configuration management area. All of these functional areas are important, however, if a network is to be properly maintained. The OSI SMFA standard defines *configuration management* as that which "identifies, exercises control, collects data from, and provides data to open systems for the purpose of preparing for, initializing, starting, providing for the continuous operation of, and terminating interconnection services." Using this standard definition, network maintenance really consists of moves, adds, and changes.

Network maintenance is the most time-consuming part of the network administrator's job. Because of the amount of time and effort spent on network maintenance, it is a vital function of network management. The key to effective network maintenance, like most things, depends on proper planning. Considering Maslow's hierarchy of needs and how it relates to network management (Fig. 9.2), the most basic need is to fix network problems. If a device is down, the administrators must concentrate on fixing that problem first, before undertaking any of their other duties. Therefore, if the base of Maslow's hierarchy of needs is to "fix" the network, the next level is maintenance of the network.

New client/server applications are forcing administrators increasingly to rely on the corporate network. Fortunately, HP OpenView and other management tools are continually evolving to aid in the support and maintenance of these ever-growing networks. As new high-speed technologies become more cost-effective, the network configurations become more dynamic. Router maintenance is extremely important to the corporate and WAN backbones. Reconfiguring one or two routers in a small network is not a problem. When administrators must maintain several hundred routers on a regular basis, however, the need for proper tools is magnified. The new hubs and concentrators

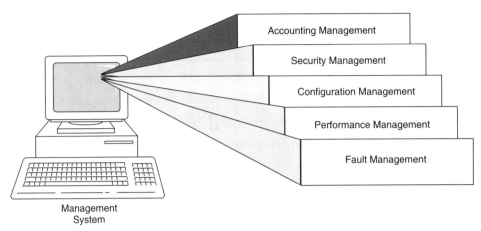

Management
System

Figure 9.1 OSI Specific Management Functional Areas (SMFAs)

offer switching technology, allowing administrators to reorganize workgroups "on the fly" via software. This significantly increases the complexity of hub maintenance.

Most networks consist of multiple protocols as well as older legacy systems. SNA environments are likely to share the network backbone with the TCP/IP environment. Most companies cannot simply eliminate the SNA environment. This represents a significant maintenance problem, because the network must support the time-sensitive data of SNA.

Another potential maintenance hazard is the cable plant. Physical layer documentation and mapping reduce the amount of necessary cable plant troubleshooting and maintenance. Moves, adds, and changes become much simpler when administrators and network technicians have accurate cable plant information. In this chapter we will focus on the task of network maintenance.

Planning the Network for Effective Maintenance

Proper network planning can make network maintenance a more palatable job. The old adage, "An ounce of prevention is worth a pound of cure," is certainly true concerning networks and network management. Research has shown that network administrators spend a good portion of their time re-engineering the networks because of lack of planning for the initial design. This is assuming, of course, that there was an initial design. A network management platform such as HP OpenView depends heavily on proper planning.

Planning the management system

The management platform, element managers, the number of concurrent managers, and management personnel skill sets are a few of the components that must be considered during the planning required to deploy HP OpenView Network Node Manager successfully. For example, the types and number of third-party element managers to be supported (e.g., hub managers, router managers, trouble-ticketing applications) are key factors in determining the proper management hardware platform. Each of these element managers has unique requirements for amounts of CPU, RAM, disk space, swap space, and overall performance of the management workstation or server. The number of concurrent managers (i.e., the number of administrators simultaneously using Network Node Manager's *ovw* user interface) has an impact on the amount of resources necessary for the management hardware. (For more information on this topic and associated estimated costs, see Chap. 19.)

To understand the virtual memory requirements of NNM, it's necessary to calculate the resources needed for each process. As Chap. 4 describes, NNM is comprised of both background (global) processes and foreground processes. Tables 19.3 and 19.4 in Chap. 19 depict the breakdown of both global processes and additional user processes for each occurrence of the *ovw* session. It is important to note that those resources are for NNM only; one also must consider resources necessary for the operating system, kernel, user processes such as *init*, X, VUE, etc., as well as those resources necessary for the aforementioned element managers. Using multiple element managers with multiple concurrent users can quickly add up to a significant investment in the management workstation or server.

Another important aspect of proper planning is considering the skill and training of the administrators who will be using the network management applications. Many administrators have vast networking experience, but do

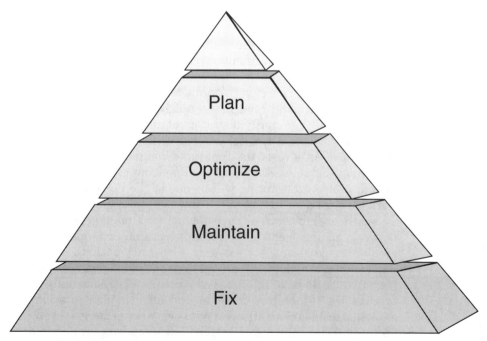

Figure 9.2 Maslow's Hierarchy of Needs for Network Managers

not possess the Unix skills necessary to maintain and administrate the management system properly. By the same token, many Unix administrators do not have experience in the administration of networking or internetworking devices. Even when network administrators have the requisite skills and experience, they must be trained in the OpenView environment. The lack of trained, experienced SNMP network managers remains one of the single most important roadblocks in many of the most visible implementations.

Planning the addressing and subnetting

One of the simplest ways to eliminate much of the burden of network maintenance is to develop a well-planned address scheme with proper subnetting. Many administrators are constantly reconfiguring their networks because insufficient planning went into allocating the proper addressing and subnetting scheme for growth. Many of these networks will function without proper subnet masks, but the routers must work much harder than necessary to make certain packets reach their intended destinations. HP OpenView NNM absolutely depends on proper subnetting during auto-discovery, and many mapping inconsistencies often are traced back to an inconsistent subnet mask on one of the routers.

Choosing Management Tools

In determining what tools are necessary for network management and network maintenance of the client/server environment, it is important to understand and differentiate between managing the network and managing network devices. While this may seem like a subtle difference, it actually is a big difference. HP OpenView NNM is merely the foundation on which to build the network management environment, and can provide a view inside the network. If proactive management with less, or even simplified, human intervention is the goal of network management, however, then OpenView NNM provides us with the road map—but it does not take us all the way. While NNM certainly can notify operators of an impending problem, it is limited in the kind of action it can take to solve the problem. Network administrators should have an idea of the types and complexity of problem notification and resolution the network management system must provide. The area of expert system problem resolution will be one of the biggest growth areas of the network management industry, one that will take us well into the next century.

Equally as important as choosing network management tools is choosing the network management or systems integrator to implement the system. Few companies possess the necessary personnel with the proper experience to implement a complete, integrated network management system properly. Even if companies do have the necessary personnel, it is usually more cost-effective to have the integrators come in and offer implementation and installation expertise to ensure an effective network management solution. HP has a list of about 45 factory-trained HP OpenView integrators throughout the country.

Maintaining the Client/Server Architecture

The network has become the corporate lifeline, extending from headquarters to remote offices, and even to employees' homes. This proliferation of the network has caused anxiety and concern for network and systems administrators. Client/server applications have increased not only the amount of traffic, but also the types of network traffic. For instance, access to a database server requires enough bandwidth to support the number of users necessary, but networks that support time-sensitive information, (e.g., voice, video, SNA traffic) require isochronous bandwidth, and network failures or outages can wreak havoc.

Fortunately, there are new network management applications that not only manage status of network devices, but also manage the other pieces of the client server puzzle including systems, databases, and applications. As applications have been downsized into distributed computing, the network has become part of the transaction. Therefore the fault tolerance of the application is only as secure as the weakest link of the network.

The dynamics of the new corporate structure also is affecting the amounts of traffic on the networks. As telecommuting, video conferencing, and rotating four-day work weeks become more prominent, the job of administrators to effectively maintain and ensure adequate network performance becomes even more challenging. These potential problems, coupled with shrinking network budgets (management wants more service for less money) have led many to seek refuge in automated, network management platforms such as OpenView NNM. The problem with this is that NNM by itself provides only a view into the network and network devices. While NNM can significantly enhance the administrator's ability to locate a problem on the network, its ability to configure devices, or actually fix the problem without human intervention, is not (as yet) sufficient.

In order to maintain the distributed computing environment properly, additional applications are necessary. These applications, integrated with OpenView NNM, offer a well-rounded suite of tools to maintain and monitor the network proactively. As new distributed computing applications develop, the need for more bandwidth, fault tolerance, and guaranteed delivery will increase the need for a more reliable, fast, and stable network.

Maintaining Network Elements

Network elements have become increasingly more sophisticated and intelligent. These network elements support a plethora of packet-switching, cell-switching, and other advanced technologies. Fortunately, most vendors of these intelligent internetworking elements also have implemented SNMP element managers to graphically manage these devices running on top of HP OpenView.

Element managers provide administrators with graphical, port-level views of the network elements to allow easy recognition and maintenance. The user can click on the device icon, which explodes the element manager application. Most element managers offer graphical views of the network devices and can quickly determine port status, reconfigure ports or segments, and quickly and easily monitor the health of the device via some sort of "dashboard" read-out feature. Of significance is the ease of use and ease of maintenance. This helps save time by reconfiguring *virtual ports* on the equipment, instead of physically locating a port and swapping the data cable. The helps to reduce configuration management drastically in terms of both labor and time. It is not uncommon for network device element managers to be among the first applications integrated into NNM.

There also have been recent advancements in smart applications such as HP IT/Administration that allow administrators to perform configuration management from a central interface to different platforms and other third-party hardware. As Chap. 12 discusses, HP plans in future releases of IT/Administration to provide configuration support for critical network devices as well as systems.

In addition, advances in agent technology supporting distributed intelligence allow administrators to manage databases, applications, and systems, as well as the network. As agent technology continues to develop, and database access becomes standardized into a common data repository, true distributed management of distributed computing will continue to become more flexible and much more powerful.

Maintaining the router

The router is the cornerstone of the corporate backbone, and with good reason. Router configurations, maintenance, and monitoring are critical to the performance of the internetwork. As routers employ new high-speed technology such as ATM, SMDS, Frame Relay, and high-speed LAN segments, they become even more critical. Because of the inherit overhead of the router, constant maintenance and monitoring are necessary to ensure the router does not create a bottleneck. As the network reaches to the most remote sites, router maintenance is critical if remote users are to access the corporate backbone with an acceptable level of performance.

NNM has several built-in menu items for managing Cisco routers (predefined macros using the Application Builder). Similar applications can be added using the Application Builder to manage other SNMP devices gathering any of the MIB data for that device. Most administrators, however, prefer some sort of graphical representations of the MIB information. NNM, for instance, also allows users to display the MIB information as a line graph. One of the most popular element managers for managing routers is CiscoWorks from Cisco Systems.

Cisco Systems: CiscoWorks

CiscoWorks is a modular suite of SNMP applications for managing Cisco routers. CiscoWorks consists of two main groups: Operation Series and Management Series (Table 9.1). The Operation Series applications are the applications used to maintain the network on a regular basis. The applications help with routine router administration and management tasks. The

Table 9.1. CiscoWorks Components

Management Series	Operation Series
CiscoWorks Reports	CiscoView
Sybase Data Workbench Report Writer	CiscoConnect
Integrated Relational Database	Workgroup Director
	Health Monitor
	Path Tool
	Software Manager Global Command Facility
	Configuration File Manager
	Global Command Facility
	AutoInstall Manager
	Security Manager

Management Series allows administrators to use the Cisco routers as data collectors (much like the probes in Chap. 5) and offers trend analysis for network traffic. In this segment we will focus on the Operation Series as it applies to maintaining the network.

The Operation Series consists of the following applications:

- CiscoView, which allows operators to quickly view a graphical representation of the Cisco router's physical configuration. Provides point-and-click controls for configuration.

- CiscoConnect, which offers customers with Internet access additional support from the Cisco support organization. Constructs a customer network profile and registers with Cisco.

- Workgroup Director, which allows operators to monitor and control the Cisco Catalyst and FDDI workgroup concentrators.

- Health Monitor, which provides graphical "dashboard" view of router activity, allowing operators to monitor the router status quickly and easily.

- Path Tool, which depicts graphically the logical path between source and destination address of packets as well as other statistics including network speed, error rates, and utilization.

- Software Manager, which allows administrators to centrally manage, distribute, and upgrade router software on routers throughout the internetwork.

- Configuration File Manager, which organizes and manages router configuration throughout the internetwork.

- Global Command Facility, which enables administrators to create scripts for groups of routers to be uniformly configured with common commands.

- AutoInstall Manager, which works with the auto-install feature built into the entire Cisco router family.

- Security Manager, which allows administrators to assign rights to groups and create administrative domains.

CiscoWorks integrates with HP OpenView NNM for the SunOS 4.1.3 platform, as well as HP-UX 9.05. CiscoWorks supports menu bar integration and event integration. CiscoWorks uses Sybase as the relational database management system (RDBMS) and can synchronize to the NNM database. One of the most significant enhancements to the CiscoWorks family is the CiscoView application. It drastically simplifies router maintenance and configuration, saving both time and valuable technical resources for other more advanced tasks. Table 9.2 lists the resources necessary for operating CiscoWorks.

Maintaining the network concentrator

Aside from the router, the most important internetworking devices are the *concentrators*, which distribute the networking topologies from the backbone to the desktop. While they may or may not represent a critical element, such as the routers, on the corporate backbone, they can require significant maintenance. The new concentrators that support port-switching can pose an especially difficult configuration problem. While they certainly enhance flexibility and allow administrators to distribute users to *virtual workgroups*, they also require network management and maintenance to ensure performance.

Fortunately, the vendors have designed sophisticated element managers that enable administrators to quickly and easily reconfigure the network segments on the fly. This offers a tremendous advantage over the old cable-swapping techniques from the wiring closets. Port-switching hubs and concentrators, along with hub management systems, have given the administrators the equivalent of *virtual wiring closets*. As networks become increasingly more geographically dispersed, these features prove to be invaluable timesavers for network administrators. Many routine tasks of moves, adds, and changes can be accomplished in seconds.

While there is not room in this text to cover all of the features of even one element manager, let alone several, we have chosen vendors that are among the more popular and have the most sophisticated features.

Table 9.2. System Requirements for CiscoWorks for HP OpenView

Hardware	Operating system	RAM	Disk space	Swap space
HP 9000 Series 700/800	HP-UX 9.x-9.05	64MB	1GB	128MB
Sun SPARCstation	SunOS 4.1.3	64MB	1GB	128MB

Bay Networks: Optivity 5.0

Optivity 5.0 is the Unix-based SNMP management system from Bay Networks (formerly Synoptics/Wellfleet) that integrates with HP OpenView NNM. Much like CiscoWorks, Optivity 5.0 is a suite of modules providing graphical information for managing Synoptics equipment. The latest version has been significantly enhanced from the 4.x version to include many of the features that were available only for the SunNet Manager platform. The primary features of Optivity provide graphical views for fault, performance, and configuration management. The new features for release 5.0 include Autotopology, SuperAgent, and Fault Correlator.

The Autotopology mapping feature discovers the Synoptics hubs, concentrators, routers, and switches, providing graphical views to the network configuration. The Fault Correlator automatically detects and analyzes events on MIB II, Synoptics, as well as Synoptic-partner devices, forwarding the intelligence to the Optivity console and thereby eliminating the waves of useless, redundant events.

Like many vendors, Bay Networks has placed a great deal of emphasis and development on software agents. The Optivity SuperAgent is the mechanism by which Bay Networks implements distributed management. One of the most significant features of Optivity is the LAN Architect. The LAN Architect offers flexible configuration management by using drag-and-drop capabilities for soft-configuring both the switched and shared-media workgroups. This is in effect, the Optivity version of the *virtual wiring closet*.

Optivity is available for HP OpenView NNM on HP-UX 9.0x, SunOS 4.1.x or Solaris 1.1.x. Optivity is one of the more tightly integrated element managers, including menu bar integration, database integration, and OV SNMP API integration. The applications help administrators understand the physical as well as the logical relationships of the network devices, allowing the devices to be managed as a system instead of as a collection of network devices. Table 9.3 lists the necessary resources for running Optivity 5.0.

ChipCom Corporation: ONdemand

ChipCom, now a division of 3Com Corp., offers a line of network management products for managing ChipCom hubs, concentrators, and switches. ChipCom has also partnered with several vendors, including HP, to integrate remote monitoring, RMON, and data collection. The ChipCom ONdemand Management solutions are built around two platforms: ONdemand Network Control Systems (NCS) for hub management and ONdemand SwitchCentral for switch management.

The ONdemand NCS offers a graphical user interface for managing Ethernet, Token-Ring, and FDDI networks. Administrators can determine hub, module, or port status quickly and easily as each network device is displayed in its current physical and logical configuration. The comprehensive and intuitive views of the ChipCom hubs and concentrators offer easy point-and-click buttons for routine tasks. The NCS ONdemand also enhances configuration

Table 9.3. System Requirements for Bay Optivity for HP OpenView

Hardware	Operating system	RAM	Disk space
HP 9000 Series 700/800	HP-UX 9.x-9.05	64MB	250MB
Sun SPARCstation	SunOS 4.1.3	64MB	1GB

and maintenance, allowing administrators to reconfigure the network down to the port level on the fly.

The ONdemand SwitchCentral Management Application complements the NCS, providing a GUI-based control system for the ChipCom StarBridge Turbo and the Galactica Network Switching Concentrator. Switch management is critical. The ability to maintain vital port statistics and virtual workgroup statistics, and the ability to switch on the fly, make SwitchCentral a powerful complement to the ONdemand NCS. One of the more powerful features of ONdemand SwitchCentral is the Forward/Blocking capability at the port level, which makes possible workgroup firewalls and isolation using software controls. The software also provides backplane statistics on the switch in order to analyze workgroup utilization trends and monitor utilization and error statistics.

ChipCom is one of the leading hub vendors in RMON integration. With agreements with HP and AXON, ChipCom has aligned itself with industry leaders in providing a road map for integrated RMON. While hub-based RMON may not be suitable for every situation, it is gaining in popularity. ChipCom also has had the foresight to develop its network management around the distributed paradigm. This will give them a strong advantage in the future with the emergence of distributed management and SNMPv2. Table 9.4 lists the resources necessary for running ONdemand NCS; Table 9.5 lists system requirements for ONdemand SwitchCentral.

As networking devices become more intelligent and sophisticated, it is important that element managers continually develop in order to help alleviate some of the time-consuming maintenance involved. It must be said that while element managers are powerful tools for effective network maintenance when correctly implemented, they can be misused or unused if not implemented correctly.

Maintaining SNA Environments

Maintaining IBM's System Network Architecture (SNA) environments traditionally have been left to mainframe concentric applications such as IBM's NetView for MVS. While this is an adequate solution for the SNA environment, NetView does not manage the TCP/IP networking environments. (For more information about IBM's management solutions, see Chap. 15.) Many administrators must be cross-trained in order to manage and support both types of architecture. This alone is a challenging proposition. Trying to manage the disparate systems with separate management tools makes this task even more difficult. There also are direct costs involved, such as for training, hardware for the systems, staff, upgrades, and service contracts. Fortunately, Peregrine Systems is meeting this challenge with the OpenSNA management system.

Peregrine OpenSNA

OpenSNA provides graphical management of IBM SNA networks integrated with HP OpenView NNM. The OpenView-based manager works with the host-based intelligent agent, providing distributed management architecture. Following are major features of OpenSNA:

- Auto-discovery of the SNA network, including VTAM applications and devices
- Automatic creation of the SNA network on the OpenView maps
- Real-time status
- VTAM command and control via menu bars or command prompts
- Optional integration with NetView

OpenSNA consists of the management application SNA Manager, which handles the user interface and the discovery of the SNA network, the SNA Agent that runs on the SNA Host, and the SNA Proxy that provides communication between the manager and agent (Fig. 9.3). The SNA Manager provides the mapping features of OpenSNA, which are identical to the IP maps, thereby greatly reducing the learning curve for administrators. The root map depicts the SNA Network as a separate network (which of course it is) alongside the IP internetwork (Fig. 9.4).

The SNA Agent runs on the SNA host (MVS only) and communicates with VTAM in order to get network status. The SNA Agent receives requests from the SNA Manager and issues the corresponding VTAM request in order to carry out the action. The SNA Agent can interface with a number of facilities, including NetView, that allow administrators to issue NetView commands.

Table 9.4. System Requirements for Chipcom ONdemand for HP OpenView

Hardware	OS	RAM	Disk space	Swap
HP 9000 Series 700/800	HP-UX 9.03	48**MB	30MB	128MB
Sun SPARCstation	SunOS 4.1.3	48**MB	15MB	128MB

**Required to manage 32 hubs, 1MB for each additional hub

Table 9.5. System Requirements for ChipCom ONdemand SwitchCentral for HP OpenView

Hardware	Operating system	RAM	Disk space	Swap
HP 9000 Series 700/800	HP-UX 9.03	24MB	24MB	48MB
Sun SPARCstation	SunOS 4.1.3_U1	24MB	24MB	48MB

The SNA Proxy is the background process that allows the SNA Manager to communicate with the SNA Agents. The SNA Proxy is the OpenView registered address for all of the SNA devices. It communicates directly to each of the SNA subareas and directs information to the appropriate SNA Agent.

The auto-discovery process is handled via the event messages from the SNA Agents. The SNA Manager uses the event information to build, or update, the OpenView map automatically. Status and topology changes are depicted automatically if *ovw* is running (if not, the maps are updated the next time *ovw* is launched). OpenSNA offers administrators a common management platform for managing the SNA and IP networks. The time-sensitive SNA traffic can be carefully monitored and easily managed with the graphical user interface. This common interface offers administrators a familiar platform from which to manage and maintain the desperate environments. Table 9.6 lists the resources necessary for running OpenSNA.

NeTech EView

EView/Open from NetTech is another third-party application that supports management of SNA elements from an OpenView workstation. By filtering alerts and alarms on the OpenView workstation instead of on an SNA mainframe, EView/Open reduces expensive mainframe cycles consumed by network management activity and network management's dependency on those resources. EView/Open Tools can:

- Perform equivalent downsized NetView functions.
- Automatically represent SNA devices and their status.
- Trigger platform automation actions.
- Manage SNA resources.
- Identify and depict current configuration of the SNA network.
- View all SNA resources.
- Filter alerts and messages at the workstation level.
- Identify location and cause of a failure on the SNA network.
- View multiple domain SNA networks in a single view.

- Use an interface to a downsized problem management system.
- Use an X Window interface to view SNA data.
- Use menu-driven SNA operator commands.

NetTech's logical-to-physical SNA correlation (LPC) process is an EView/Open option. The LPC option allows automatic physical to logical topology correlation for SNA physical units on LANs. This provides dynamic tracking of SNA devices' physical locations.

NetTech's problem manager interface, PMI, extends IBM's mainframe Info/Manager high-level application programming interface, API, to the open system workstation problem manager application environment. The PMI option allows the capability to selectively transfer and update trouble ticket reports to and from the mainframe and workstation problem managers.

Maintaining DECnet Environments

Much like the problem associated with the SNA networks, the Digital Network Architecture (DNA) and VAX/VMS DECnet systems require special tools to manage their legacy systems. Digital Equipment Corp. offers its own management solution based on IBM NetView for AIX, called PolyCenter on NetView. (For more information about PolyCenter on NetView, see Chap. 16.) Customers seeking to integrate DECnet management under HP OpenView NNM or NetView for AIX have another option: DEC Network Manager, DNM, from Ki Networks.

Ki Networks: DEC Network Manager

Ki Networks's DNM gives HP OpenView users a single management interface, transparently providing multiprotocol organizations with a simple management solution. DNM is designed for monitoring, configuring, and displaying

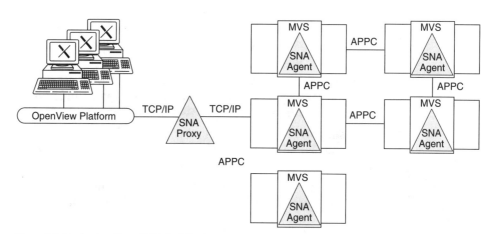

Figure 9.3 Peregrine OpenSNA Architecture

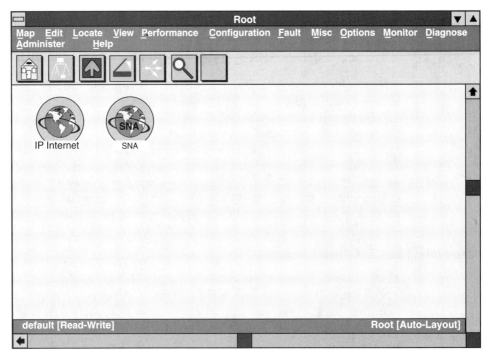

Figure 9.4 Peregrine OpenSNA Map

the DECnet and Local Area Transport (LAT) networks. As a result, DNM reduces the maintenance of these environments. The DNM product family consists of the DECnet Node Manager, LAT Node Manager, DECnet Automated Response and Profile Center (ARPC), and LAT ARPC.

The DECnet and LAT Node managers offer the complete set of DNM functions and features including the following:

- Fully integrated Map and Node Status: Allows users to select DECnet nodes, LAT servers, LAT services, and Maintenance Operations Protocol (MOP) devices monitoring the status changes.

- Single view submap management: Provides DECnet node, LAT terminal server, and MOP device availability and status via single-view management of individual DECnet, LAT, and MOP submaps.

- Polling support: Auto-discovery of configuration data and device status on any user-specified set of DECnet nodes, LAT terminal servers, and LAT ports; also provides passive auto-collection of MOP devices.

- Reliability and monitoring capabilities: Performs baseline determinations via NNM's graphical analysis of collected historical DECnet, LAT, and MOP counters.

The DECnet and LAT ARPC allow administrators to automate responses to DECnet or LAT events, and configure and monitor via command line interface. The DECnet and LAT ARPC also provide the baselevel functionality of the DECnet and LAT Node managers at only half the price. Table 9.7 lists the necessary resources for the DECnet and LAT Node Manager; Table 9.8 lists system requirements for the DECnet and LAT ARPC.

Physical Layer Planning and Maintenance

HP OpenView NNM focuses on the logical management of the network and network devices. One of the areas that NNM does not address is in the physical layer management (i.e., cable plant, building layouts, floor plans, cable trays, and physical equipment layout).

Physical management is important for network maintenance for a number of reasons. First, if there is a problem on the net, the administrator is likely to need the physical location of the device, especially if the device is not responding to software. However, the most important aspect of physical layer management falls under the configuration category. The moves, adds, and changes that we have been focusing on in this chapter often require physical relationships between the devices. It also is important to manage the database information providing graphical and text records of the cabling and communication infrastructure, as well as logs, trouble tickets, fixes, etc. Without these tools, administrators can become lost in the maze of cables, connectors, and misplaced equipment. There are element managers available that integrate with HP OpenView to provide this vital information, allowing administrators to relate the physical and the logical. Two of the leading cable plant applications are developed by Accugraph and Isicad.

Accugraph: MT923

The MT923 application from Accugraph provides a comprehensive set of tools to aid in tracking, managing, and controlling all of the physical elements of the network. MT923 helps administrators with the documentation of the moves,

Table 9.6. System Requirements for Peregrine Systems OpenSNA for HP OpenView

Hardware	Operating system	RAM	Disk space	Swap
HP 9000 Series 700/800	HP-UX 8.07 HP-UX 9.x required for APPC	8MB Additional for 2000 SNA nodes	10MB additional for 2000 SNA nodes	100MB

Table 9.7. System Requirements for Ki Networks DECnet and
LAT Node Manager for HP OpenView

Hardware	Operating system	RAM	Swap
HP 9000 Series 700/800	HP-UX 8.0, 9.0, 9.03, 9.04, 9.05	64MB- 128MB	192- 384MB
Sun SPARCstation	SunOS 4.1.3_U1, Solaris 1.1.1, 2.3	64MB- 128MB	192- 384MB

adds, and changes, as well as with the physical layer (cable plant) documentation using the electronic network modeling system. The MT923 consists of the following modules:

- Physical design: Using the built-in graphics capabilities, administrators can design and model the campus, including all network components. MT923 includes a database attached to the design, allowing detailed input about each network component. During routine maintenance, administrators can simply click on the device to determine the location and how it fits into the network.

- Cable management: Cable types, lengths, and wiring assignments can be included in the electronic model.

- Connectivity analysis: Point-and-click access to the physical and logical location of the devices on the network.

- Asset management: All of the networking and communications assets are tracked with this system. This aids administrators in determining information such as date installed, price, and warranty information. This application also can be used to include noncommunication assets such as copiers, furniture, tools, etc.

- Moves, adds, and changes management: Tools such as the Equipment Bay Modeler (MT972) offer the ability to create the graphics from the database information. It automatically updates the drawings as database changes are made. Maintenance techniques such as auto-population and data inheritance provide quick, effective data entry and maintenance.

The Accugraph MT923 integrates with HP OpenView NNM on the HP-UX 9.0x and Solaris 2.3.x platforms. MT923 also integrates with trouble-ticketing applications such as Legent's Paradigm and Remedy's Action Request system. Table 9.9 lists the resources necessary for operating the MT923.

ISICAD: COMMAND

ISICAD COMMAND is a physical network management application similar to the Accugraph application. COMMAND provides both the graphical front end and the industry-standard relational database system. The strengths of COMMAND are its ability to track and display the smallest details of the data and voice communications networks. COMMAND can display the entire schematic, showing not only the wall jack or physical location, but also cable paths, trays, cable pairs, connector pin-outs, MUXes, repeaters, and patch panels. This detailed schematic is invaluable in system and network maintenance because it gives engineers and technicians a detailed network blueprint. COMMAND can simultaneously manage the database of the network inventory, costs, warranty information, or other attributes.

COMMAND offers a WAN module that provides the ability to create and trace WAN circuits, virtual circuits, links, channels, and MUXes. The graphical display shows the relationship of the circuits to the network and to one another. COMMAND also provides bandwidth management by indicating which channels or circuits are free, and which are in use. These tools help make configuration management and WAN maintenance much easier. Table 9.10 lists the necessary resources for COMMAND.

Summary

Maintaining the network is a complicated, time-consuming, and costly function of network administrators. HP OpenView gives administrators the foundation with which to combat this problem. Designing the network and the network management system requires planning and analysis in order to get the proper tools and the proper platform. Applications are being developed that will need more and more bandwidth, placing greater demands on networks and their administrators.

Maintaining critical network elements such as routers and hubs can be complicated and difficult, but can be relatively routine when using the sophisticated network element managers integrated closely with the NNM platform. Legacy systems and the maintenance of those systems require resources and tools, and integration into open systems management platforms makes maintenance much more cost-effective. Finally, physical cable plant and asset management are a critical element in the maintenance of the network.

Table 9.8. System Requirements for Ki Networks DECnet and LAT ARPC for HP OpenView

Hardware	Operating system	RAM	Swap
HP 9000 Series 700/800	HP-UX 8.0, 9.0, 9.03, 9.04, 9.05	64MB	192MB
Sun SPARCstation	SunOS 4.1.3_U1, Solaris 1.1.1, 2.3	64MB-128MB	192MB

Table 9.9. System Requirements for Accugraph MT923 for HP OpenView

Hardware	Operating system	RAM	Swap
HP 9000 Series 700/800	HP-UX 9.05, 9.07, 10.1	64MB	1GB
Sun SPARCstation	Solaris 2.3, 2.4, 2.5	64MB	1GB

Many tools available integrate with HP OpenView NNM to help network administrators and engineers solve problems associated with network maintenance. Network maintenance will not be completely conquered in the foreseeable future. Network maintenance is part of a cycle that will continually require new, more sophisticated, "smart" applications to help administrators stay at least on an equal footing with the problems.

Table 9.10. System Requirements for Isicad COMMAND for HP OpenView

Hardware	Operating system	RAM	Swap
HP 9000 Series 700/800	HP-UX 9.x, 10.0, 10.1	64MB	1GB
Sun SPARCstation	Solaris 2.3, 2.4, 2.5	64MB	1GB

Chapter

10

Telecommunications Management

Carriers face continuously increasing requirements for providing the transport infrasructure for information highways. As a result, the network fabric must be redefined significantly. New services drive the demand for higher bandwidth, including services such as telemedicine, telecommuting, long-distance learning, online museum archives, home banking, desktop video teleconferencing to remote coworkers, file transfer, and real-time surveillance. These applications drive the demand for new and changed telecommunication technologies including advanced telephony, wireless for voice and data, broadband and mass-market broadband utilizing phone lines, and TV cables. All of these require dramatic changes in management functions and instruments.

New Requirements for the Management Framework

To acquire a new and viable perspective of the management environment, one must begin by recognizing that the network fabric is amorphous. Topology, configuration, and element components will be ever-changing. The management model must recognize that each task the network will perform places its participating elements in a state of multidimensional virtual identity.

On one dimension, bandwidth spectrum over the same connection will constantly change. On another dimension, the view of that bandwidth and related service will change on a user-by-user and provider-by-provider basis.

The management and support environment model must maintain a view of the total network fabric and its ever-changing state. It must, therefore, be all encompassing, multidimensional, and able to change its relationship with each network element on a virtual basis. Important attributes of the new management model are:

- Object orientation
- Expert analysis
- Standards and open systems
- Rapid development

Object orientation

Object-based technology is specifically geared to allow logic to be built in an *organic* fashion, and forms the basis of a new network management environment. By combining the behavior of a network element with its function, a series of attributes is established for its operation. These attributes, or objects, form the initial building blocks of a dynamic model.

Groups of objects with similar operating methods or processes can then be organized into classes. A series of switches, for instance, may have independent characteristics for which an object (attributes) would be defined. They all, however, switch traffic. The methods and variables of the switching procedures can be defined as a class. Classes and subclasses can be cut and pasted into other classes, allowing for a rapid, yet connected, definition of operation. When a new switch is added, its attributes would be declared in a new object, along with reference to its class, thus allowing it to be added to the management environment without disruption. Similarly, objects or elements can be removed from the definition of fabric content without having to update every other element defined to the fabric.

Interobject and interclass behavior are defined as relationships. Through the use of objects and relationships, a high degree of autonomy and independence is maintained, yet the entire network fabric can be modeled.

By defining relationships apart from the object attributes, a multidimensional structure is put in place that, when combined into a repository, forms a complete management information base. The organic nature of the object-oriented approach allows for the modeling of the network management and support environment as it actually is, rather than hard-coding it for what one thinks it might do. In this fashion, network elements are free to behave in whatever manner they might be called upon to behave. By using object-oriented technology as a network management and support environment fundamental, the unpredictable aspects of the network are not arbitrarily bounded, yet the action of the elements can be discretely monitored and tracked.

Expert analysis

With an object-oriented model definition in place, the boundaries inherent in traditional systems have been removed. The next fundamental that must be put in place is a method to handle the enormous amounts of information that must flow through the network management and support environment.

A data flow methodology must be implemented that not only will manage the data, but will make automated decisions about the data. Human managers, no matter the number, will not be able to keep pace with the torrent of information. Critical data will need to be prioritized. Noncritical data will need to be filtered. Alien data will require translation, and corollaries will be needed to transform status information into actionable events.

To provide the automated decision-making capacities that broadband network information traffic flow will demand requires the use of expert systems. With the aid of knowledge-based rules, automation can be applied to the interpretation of network events. These rules are dynamically modifiable, and contain the decision logic for event thresholding and correlation, alert generation, severity definition, and other message states.

The coupling of expert systems rules interpretation to an object-oriented, relationship-driven, managed information base creates a dynamic environment that is definable, actionable, and responsive in real time.

Standards and open systems

With a framework for a dynamic, real-time management and support system laid out, care must be taken to ensure that the framework is accessible to and flexible for a wide variety of networks, network elements, computing systems, and applications.

Adherence to standards and the use of open systems is fundamental to achieving flexibility and accessibility. Incorporating open operating environments, database environments, and systems interfaces will allow network and system management environments to interconnect to, and interoperate with, existing systems and network components.

Likewise, standards will allow providers to take advantage of market-available platforms, databases, and applications, as well as new developments in device technology and the ongoing *commoditization* of computing technology.

Standards compliance and incorporation also are vital to the network management framework. Because the depth to which the network provider's fabric must reach into that of a customer is unpredictable, the provider must be prepared to deliver network interfaces on a variety of levels.

The incorporation of such protocol standards as SNMP and CMIP will allow the provider's fabric to interface to the customer's fabric without concern for the physical topology. Standards, too, will play an important role in the interface to residential network service elements. Compliance with popular database and user interface standards will provide for direct support of content provider server technology. The SNMP importance is growing. In key areas, such as customer network management, it is providing customers a view and access into the telecom networks, LAN/WAN management, ATM management, etc. All will use SNMP in some form.

Beyond the support for device interface and interoperation, the use of standards and open systems provides a path to distribute the network management and support intelligence directly onto the elements themselves, thus allowing for both stand-alone and network fabric-based system management.

Rapid deployment

The final component to a successful management environment model for broadband is to place the power of the system directly into the hands of those network experts who will be responsible for operating and managing the environment.

Moving the system definition and customization directly to the business procedure, experts will be required to ensure rapid deployment of new service and device support. The dynamic and real-time nature of broadband networks will not be able to function if time windows must be carved out in order to relate functional requirements to programmers, who then must develop and test code.

The delivery of directions to the system, therefore, must be immediate and free of the intervening step of code development. The system interfaces must be graphical, intuitive, and highly manipulatable. Displays must be customizable to meet the viewing needs of the varying skill sets of the business process experts. This will require support of point-and-click, pop-up menus, and other standard commercial interfaces, plus the ability to use existing personal computers, workstations, and terminals.

Likewise, the dialogue with the system must be straightforward. Business experts and operators must be able to manipulate object definitions, relationships, and rules quickly and easily.

The display of network components, topology, and status must be zoomable from its highest level to its lowest, with the ability to balloon various components and segments on command. Operators must be able to view simultaneously the relationship between the graphical representation of the network and its elements, and the alert and conditional information associated with those representations. The human interface to the system, then, must be as sophisticated, yet as simple, as the underlying framework model.

This segment of the book represents the interests of service providers. In order to streamline these interests, many providers have united to define a common-platform computing model, the Service Providers Integrated Requirements for Information Technology (SPIRIT). SPIRIT is a model, and not a network management platform. It is important to remember that there are no off-the-shelf products available to meet the management requirements of the changing networking environments. Therefore, models must be carefully examined before customization of products can begin.

This chapter presents several models. The most important attributes of Telecommunication Management Networks (TMN) are introduced and the applicability of OpenView DM as core of the TMN platform is addressed. The in-depth practical example is based on the Alcatel Management Platform (ALMAO), using OpenView as the nucleus. A second example shows how Hicom PBXs from Siemens can be managed centrally by OpenView. A third example addresses the management of wireless networks using OpenView as the platform. There are a large number of solutions based on the OpenView platforms. Well-known examples involve trouble-ticketing (Action Request

System from Remedy), asset management (Command 5000 from ISICAD), application management (SAP from HP), modeling (Best/net from BGS Systems), and performance analysis and reporting (SAS from SAS Institute).

Current Status of Telecommunication Management Networks

The TMN effort is chartered by the International Telecommunications Union Telecommunications Standardization Sector (ITU-TS). Development began in 1988 and has been concentrated primarily on the overall architecture, using the Synchronous Digital Hierarchy (the international version of the North American Synchronous Optical Network, or SONET) technology as a target. The TMN techniques are applicable to a broad range of technologies and services.

The management requirements that helped shape the TMN specifications address planning, provisioning, installing, maintaining, operating, and administering communications networks and services.

The TMN specifications use standard CMIP application services wherever appropriate. One of the key concepts of the TMN specifications is the introduction of *technology-independent* management, which is based on an abstract view of managed network elements. Through this abstract view and a single communications interface, diverse equipment can be managed. Thus, TMN-managed networks can consist of both TMN-conforming and nonconforming devices.

The TMN specifications define an intended direction, with many details to be determined. The published TMN specifications address the overall architecture, the generic information model, the management services, the management functions, the management and transmission protocols, and an alarm surveillance function. Next, the TMN working groups will focus on the service layer, traffic (i.e., congestion), and network-level management.

Management systems that comply with the TMN principles reduce costs and improve services for the following reasons :

- Standard interfaces and objects make it possible to deploy new services rapidly and economically.

- Distributed management intelligence minimizes management reaction time to network events.

- Mediation makes it possible to handle similar devices in an identical manner, leading to more generic operations systems and vendor independence.

- Mediation makes it possible to manage and transparently upgrade the existing device inventory.

- Distributed management functions increase scalability.

- Distributed management functions isolate and contain network faults.

- Distributed management functions reduce network management traffic and the load on operations systems.

Many of the benefits that accrue from the TMN principles are directly due to its distributed architecture and to its mediation function.

The TMN architecture identifies specific functions and their interfaces. These functions are what allow a TMN to perform its management activities. The TMN architecture provides flexibility for building a management system by providing for certain functions to be combined within a physical entity. The following function blocks, along with their typical methods of physical realization, are defined within the TMN specifications:

- Operations Systems Functions (OSF)

- Workstation Function (WSF)

- Mediation Function (MF)

- Q Adapter Function (QAF)

Operations Systems Functions (OSF)

OSF monitors, coordinates, and controls the TMN entities. It is a TMN-compliant management system or set of management applications. The system has to make it possible to perform general activities, such as management of performance, faults, configuration, accounting, and security. In addition, specific capabilities for planning of operations, administration, maintenance, and provisioning of communications networks and systems should be available. These capabilities are realized in an operations system. The operations systems can be implemented in many ways. One possibility is a descending abstraction—for example, business, service, and network—wherein the overall business needs of the enterprise are met by coordinating the underlying services. In turn, the individual services are realized by coordinating the network resources.

Workstation Function (WSF)

The WSF provides the TMN information to the user. This typically consists of things such as access control, topological map display, and graphical interfaces. These functions are realized in a workstation.

Mediation Function (MF)

MF acts on information passing between an OSF and a Network Element Function (NEF) or Q Adapter Function (QAF) to ensure that the data the MF emits complies with the needs and capabilities of the receiver. MFs can store, adapt, filter, threshold, and condense information. The MFs provide the abstract view necessary to treat dissimilar elements in a similar manner. MFs also may provide local management to their associated NEFs. (In other words, the MF may include an element manager.) The MF function is realized in a mediation device. Mediation can be implemented as a hierarchy of cascaded devices, using standard interfaces. The cascading of mediation devices and the various interconnections to network elements provide a TMN with a great deal of flexibility. This also allows for future design of new equipment to support a greater level of processing within the network element, without the need to redesign an existing TMN.

Q Adapter Function (QAF)

This connects non-TMN-compliant NEFs to the TMN environment and is realized in a Q adapter. A Q adapter allows legacy devices (i.e., those that do not support the TMN management protocols, including SNMP devices) to be accommodated within a TMN. A Q adapter typically performs interface conversion functions, that is, it acts as a proxy. Network Element Function (NEF) is realized in the network elements. They can present a TMN-compliant or noncompliant interface. This would include such things as physical elements (switches), logical elements (virtual circuit connections), and services (operations systems software applications). Figure 10.1 illustrates the functions within a TMN environment. The portions that are outside the TMN environment are not subject to standardization. For example, the human-interface portion of the workstation function is not specified in the TMN standard.

Within the TMN specification are well-defined reference points to identify the characteristics of the interfaces between the function blocks. The reference points identify the information that passes between the function blocks. The function blocks exchange information using the Data Communications Function (DCF). The DCF may perform routing, relaying and internetworking acting at Open Systems Interconnect (OSI) layers 1 to 3 (i.e., physical, data link, and network layers) or their equivalents.

These functions are performed in the data communications network. Figure 10.2 shows the reference points (F, G, M, Qx, Q3, X) that have been defined by the TMN specification. These reference points are characterized by the information that is shared between their endpoints. The reference points are further explained as follows (Reeder 1995):

- F is the interface between a workstation and an operations system and a mediation device.

- G is the interface between a workstation and a human user. The specification of this interface is outside the scope of TMN.

- M is the interface between a Q adapter and a non-TMN-compliant network element. This interface, which is not specified by the TMN effort, is one of the most important, as today's networks primarily consist of devices that do not comply with the TMN standard.

- Qx is the interface between a Q adapter and a mediation device, a TMN-compliant element and a mediation device, and between two mediation devices.

TMN Function Blocks

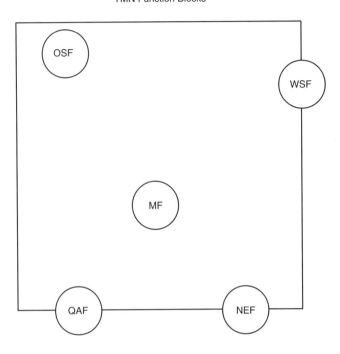

Notes:
MF   Medium Function
NEF   Network Element Function
OSF   Operations Systems Function
QAF   Q Adapter Function
WSF   Work Station Function

Figure 10.1 TMN Function Blocks

- Q3 is the interface between a TMN-compliant element and an operations system, a Q adapter and a mediation device, a mediation device and an operations system, and between two operations systems.

- X is the interface between operations systems in different TMNs. The operations system outside the X interface may be part of a TMN or a non-TMN environment. This interface may require increased security over the level required by the Q interfaces. In addition, access limitations may also be imposed.

Currently, only the Q3 interface has been specified to any degree of detail. The definition includes its management protocol (CMIP), alarm surveillance capabilities, and operations on the generic model used to describe the network. Alarm surveillance is a set of functions that enables the monitoring and interrogation of the network concerning alarm-related events or conditions.

The information model presents an abstraction of the management aspects of network resources and the related support management activities. This model consists of the management protocol object classes required to manage a TMN. Information about these objects is exchanged across the TMN-standard interfaces.

The TMN specifications provide a generic information model that is technology-independent. This independence allows management of diverse equipment in a common manner, through an abstract view of the network elements. This concept is vital for TMN to achieve its goals. The generic information model also serves as a basis for defining technology-specific object classes. The resulting specific object classes still support a technology-independent view, while enabling more precise management. For example, there could be a TMN definition of a switch that could be used to perform common management

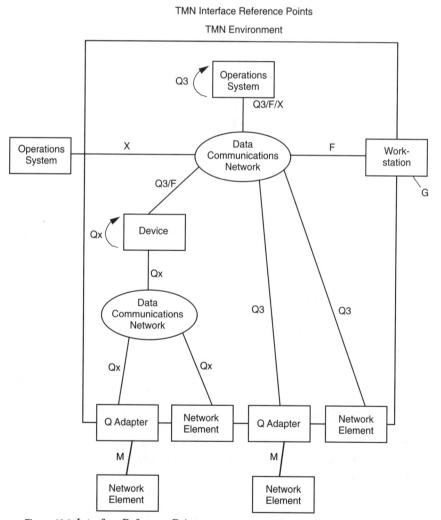

Figure 10.2 Interface Reference Points

activities, such as provisioning or performance gathering. In addition, this generic switch definition could be extended to cover the peculiarities of a particular vendor's switch. The extended definition could be used for such specialized activities as controlling the execution of diagnostic routines. TMN generic modeling techniques can be used by a resource provider or management system provider to define its own objects.

The TMN specification contains an information model common to managed communications networks. This model can be used to generically define the resources, actions, and events that exist in a network.

Capabilities of HP OpenView Distributed Management Products

HP OpenView Distributed Management (DM) products supply the leading, standards-based environment for building Telecommunications Management Network (TMN) or Operational Support Systems solutions. HP has combined strengths in network management protocols, distributed computing, telecom industry experience, and partnerships that, built with the help of the industry's leading companies, provide a rich set of features and solutions.

The platform is widely used as a software foundation for deploying TMN/OSS network element management and network management solutions. The platform provides a Motif-based graphical user interface and multiple management protocol services and stacks. The developer's kits are used to create custom applications, which are deployed on the DM platform.

The products based on this platform are focused on meeting the reliability, performance, distribution, and standards needs of telecom equipment and service providers. HP provides multiple protocols (CMIP and SNMP) for building OSI and mixed-protocol solutions. HP also supplies a TL1 proxy development kit and customization services for integration of TL1 devices. OpenView DM-based solutions are actively deployed in telecom operational support systems around the world. A large number of system integrators and solution partners also make significant contributions to the delivery of complete OpenView telecom solutions.

Driven by key telecom standards, the DM products support protocol, object, and service specifications defined by the International Telecommunications Union (ITU), International Standards Organization (ISO), X/Open, Internet Engineering Task Force (IETF) for SNMP, and the Network Management Forum (NMF). Extensive conformance testing is an essential part of each release. Full support for CMIP, CMIP over RFC 1006 (TCP/IP), and SNMP management protocols all are provided. This standards-based software delivers an interoperable and conformant platform.

OpenView is built on open systems enabling solutions to run on a variety of hardware platforms. DM products are built on an extensible architecture and are available on both HP and Sun computer systems. Additionally, the software has been licensed by leading computer vendors.

Figure 10.3 shows the architecture of the DM platform.

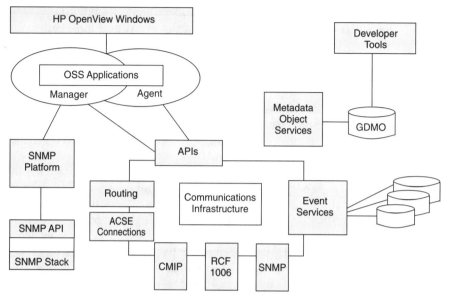

Figure 10.3 OpenView Distributed Management (DM) Platform

The Communication Infrastructure (CI) serves as the integration point for management protocol stacks such as CMIP and SNMP, management APIs, and related facilities stacks (routing, events, and association control). The Communications Infrastructure provides distributed message routing and access to applications and services through standard management protocols. It creates and manages associations, maps objects to network addresses and protocol stacks, and then routes requests, responses, and events. As the DM platform has been succcessfully deployed in many large telecom operational systems, application users can be assured of reliable delivery of critical management information.

Event management services collect, forward, and log network events and traps in a distributed environment. Event routing, filtering, logging, and administration are based on the ITU/ISO system management standards and are extended to include SNMP. These services provide full conformance to the AOM 221 and 231 profiles defined by the ITU. Other key features include filtering of both CMIP events and SNMP traps, scheduling, run-time reconfiguration for filtering of new user-defined events and traps, high performance routing, and support for multiple logs. These features result in interoperable and comprehensive event management across distributed networks.

The Event Management Services system consists of two basic elements: the event agent and the log agent. It also encompasses three basic management object classes: event forwarding discriminator, log, and log record. The event agents run on each OpenView DM node, and are responsible for routing and delivering events. The log agent runs only on management stations, where the event log maintains a history of events that can be used to diagnose, analyze, and tune the network. The metadata agent provides metadata information about user-defined notifications for the event and log agents to use, optionally, when filtering events. Figure 10.4 illustrates this service in more detail.

Telecom operators and network administrators today must be able to manage large numbers of events, or event storms, and identify the cause of problems rapidly and accurately. This is of particular importance in managing ATM switches and Sonet/SDH technology. The new extension of Event Management Services, called *event correlation*, is specifically designed to correlate event storms at a very high speed. It is supported on the OpenView DM platform. Event correlation involves processing multiple time-related events—as opposed to simple event filtering that treats each event independently. The benefit is a more extensive and sophisticated data reduction that includes the consideration of network topology and other factors. This technology facilitates and simplifies the development of management applications such as fault, performance, configuration, security, and service management. Using the concept of management by exception, this technology can cover essentially all management functional areas and enable operators to focus on exception events. It addresses two main real-world concerns:

- Handling of large volumes of events (event storms) from a single fault.
- Determining the fault that underlies the observed event (cause).

The technology is based on the notion of processing event streams in real time using simple processing elements that can be combined to produce sophisticated correlations. The event correlator supports events arriving out of order, a common phenomenon in a telecommunications environment due to delays incurred by network transmission equipment.

It is capable of accepting multiple streams of different types of events, correlating the events, then creating one or more streams of events. The resulting stream of events may be a subset of the original stream, or new event types with composite information taken from source events or external sources. This reduces the number of events and increases the value of information provided to the operator.

Object Services provide a Guidelines for the Definition of Managed Objects (GDMO) tool chain that compiles, stores, and provides dynamic access of object definitions. Metadata retrieval allows applications to dynamically interact with new objects. To help simplify development for CMIP protocol access, productivity tools are included with the developer kits. These tools convert GDMO definitions into object packages and automatically generate code, providing functions that are easier to use. More sophisticated developer productivity tools for GDMO object modeling, automatic manager, and agent C++ code generation are offered as companion products. The GDMO services help to ensure standards conformance for object definitions, increase developer productivity, and facilitate the building of dynamic applications.

The HP OpenView GDMO Modeling Toolset is an integrated suite of software tools for analyzing and designing OSI object models, focused on customers

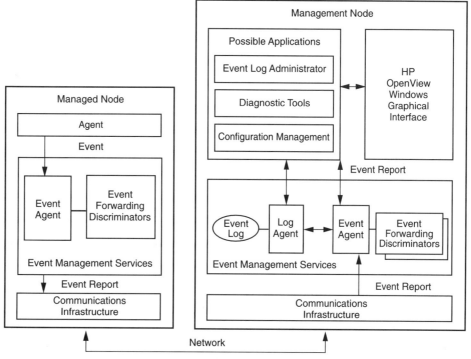

Figure 10.4 OpenView Event Management Services

building network management solutions. The tool suite increases the productivity of network management object modelers with powerful tools to graphically design and edit OSI network management object specifications. The GDMO Modeling Toolset allows multiple Managed Object designers to collaborate on object specifications and communicate object models to implementers.

Figure 10.5 shows the components of the GDMO Modeling Toolset.

To address the needs of application developers, the HP OpenView Managed Object Toolkit (MOT) automates a significant portion of the application development effort, resulting in immediate productivity gains. The MOT is composed of a class library and a C++ class generator. The class library incorporates both the software components that form the agent framework and the software components that provide access to managed objects for manager applications. Manager and agent are shown in Fig. 10.6.

The MOT class library provides the agent application infrastructure that automatically receives, validates, and routes CMIS requests to the appropriate object instance-handling routines. The MOT maintains managed object instance information and can provide an automatic reply, or the developer can customize the response operation and, for example, retrieve data from an external device, assisted by MOT-provided C++ classes. The MOT-based agent also provides an interface for transmitting notifications that the user has constructed.

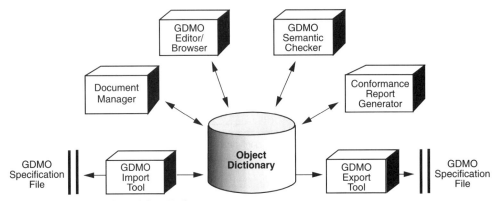

Figure 10.5 The GDMO Modeling Toolset

For manager developers, the MOT provides C++ classes that enable the developer to construct CMIS requests, and process received requests or notifications. The immediate benefits are:

■ Acceleration of agent application development by generating an OSI-conformant working agent directly from GDMO specification.

■ Generation of C++ classes and code from GDMO and ASN.1 which developers can easily customize to implement their agent-specific requirements and behaviors.

■ Customization of the generated agent one operation at a time.

■ Handling of the details of the receipt and transmission of CMIS requests and responses, including error responses, freeing the agent developer from the time-consuming task of implementing the CMIS handling routines.

The MOT infrastructure automatically handles scoped and filtered requests. The graphical user interface (GUI) provides network operators and administrators with a consistent view of the managed environment and seamless integration of management functions regardless of vendor or managed object type. OpenView Windows provides a common interface that simplifies both the development and use of management applications. Based on X11 and OSF/Motif technologies, OpenView Windows enables multiple application developers to combine diverse environments into a consistent, common environment for the user. This GUI serves as the key integration point for applications including the DM products, Network Node Manager, OperationsCenter, AdminCenter, Fault Management Platform, and a broad suite of partner HP OpenView applications.

The DM products extend the product structure and standards support, initiate a new open and high-performance architecture, and introduce a set of developer tools.

Two variations of the DM Platform are offered: DM Agent Platform and DM Platform. The DM Agent provides an unbundled version of the Communications

Infrastructure (CI) and its related components for building a variety of distributed management devices. The DM Agent can be used to create custom proxy devices, mediation devices, agents, Q-adaptors, and other intermediate platforms in distributed management environments.

The DM Agent Platform contains the CI and management protocol stacks. Services contained in the DM Agent Platform include the Event Management Services (EMS) which models the ISO definitions for alarms and logs, GDMO-based metadata services for compiling and online access of object definitions, and the Object Registration Services (ORS) which provide distributed knowledge of managed objects, instances, and physical addresses.

The full HP OpenView DM Platform contains all of the components of the DM Agent bundled with the HP OpenView SNMP Platform. The DM Platform is used for building manager-focused applications. HP OpenView applications, such as Network Node Manager and OperationsCenter, can run on top of the DM Platform. Any application that runs on the DM Agent Platform also runs on the complete DM Platform.

DM developer's kits provide APIs for interacting with HP OpenView Windows and managemnt protocols via the X/Open Management Protocol (XMP) and X/Open Object Management (XOM) APIs. Process control, tracing, and logging APIs are included so that applications can consistently integrate with HP OpenView process control and troubleshooting procedures. Extensive convenience routines and sample applications are included for developers. A lightweight API is supplied for creating SNMP-only management applications. The XMP and XOM APIs can be used for building portable, standards-based manager, agent, and combined manager/agent applications.

While there are a number of approaches for building applications, API-based mechanisms provide the most complete and highest performance solutions. Extensive documentation, a developer hypertext help system, tools, training, and consulting are available to help developers quickly move applications from development to delivery.

As with the platforms, two variations of the DM developer's kit are offered. The HP OpenView DM Agent developer's kit provides all of the libraries, header

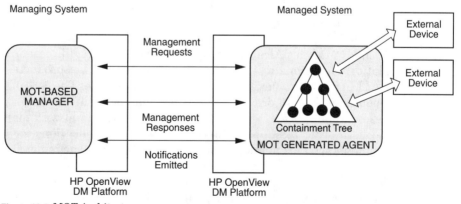

Figure 10.6 MOT Architecture

files, documentation, and tools needed to write applications that run on the DM Agent Platform. The developer's kit includes a copy of the runtime platform; therefore, developers do not need a separate copy of the DM Agent Platform to test applications.

The DM Agent developer's kit contains the XMP and related XOM APIs. The XMP API provides programmatic access to both SNMP and CMIS services, the Event Management Services, and metadata. XMP also includes a GDMO-based object definition package generator to simplify application development.

Programmatic control over association (connection) control, commonly referred to as *ACSE* control, is included. An XOM function generator and a hypertext online reference system also are included in the DM developer's kits to further increase developer productivity. A contributed file set provided with the developer's kit includes a public domain ASN.1 compiler, utility routines, and sample applications.

The DM developer's kit is used for building manager-side applications that will operate on the DM platform. The complete DM developer's kit contains all of the components of the DM Agent developer's kit and the SNMP developer's kit (OVw and Direct SNMP APIs). The DM developer's kit also includes a run-time copy of the complete DM Platform.

Public Switching System from Alcatel

The Alcatel Management Platform ALMAP 3 offers a homogeneous runtime system and a development environment. Its mission is to enable the fast and flexible development of standards-conformant management applications for distributed operations systems in a Telecommunications Management Network. These operations systems provide for the uniform management of all network resources and services in terms of the user interface, regardless of the architecture of the management solution.

ALMAP has achieved a coherent integration of proven market products, technologies and tools, such as the HP OpenView product family, the HP DCE product family, standard protocol stacks under HP (OTS/9000) and under Sun's SunlinkOSI, Marben/Retix protocol stacks, DataViews, UIM/X, and ClearCase.

ALMAP aligns to all major TMN and system management standards issued by ITU-T, ETSI, and ISO, as well as NMF/OmniPoint, SPIRIT, and to some extent OSF. Future plans will include OMG. In addition to market products, ALMAP provides Alcatel modules and tools, which fill essential gaps in the platform functionality as it is provided by the market products.

ALMAP is open, flexible, scalable, and extendible. The core of ALMAP is HP OpenView DM. It provides a flexible management framework for multiple hardware platforms, transportation protocols, and network management protocols in order to support the development of applications for network management, systems management, and application management.

HP's OpenView Communication Infrastructure has been selected by the Open System Foundation (OSF) for essential components of the Distributed Management Environment. This makes it a de facto industry standard. Figure 10.7 illustrates the central role of OpenView DM in the ALMAP platform.

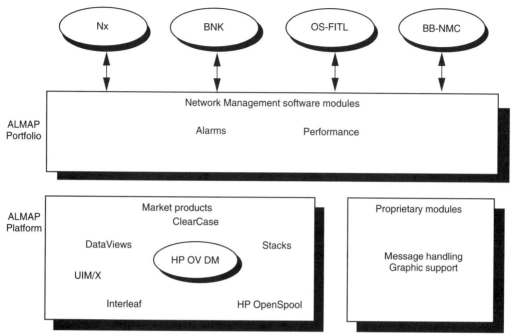

Figure 10.7 The Core of the ALMAP Platform: HP Openview DM

ALMAP is part of the Alcatel 1300 product family, which additionally contains the Alcatel Management Applications (ALMA). Together ALMAP and ALMA form a generic management system that can be used for the management of public and private networks: switching and transmissions systems, mobile networks, metropolitan area networks (MAN), broadband ISDN, virtual private networks (VPN), intelligent networks (IN), office communication systems, management systems, and networks.

Alcatel customers include public and private network operators, service providers, public authorities, energy providing companies, banks, and insurance companies.

ALMAP3 comes as a fine-granular open portfolio of packages. They have well-defined functionalities and a minimum of interdependencies, so that customers have the highest degree of freedom to select and combine a particular set of packages for their specific needs. Among those packages are:

- Members of the HP OpenView product family
- Protocol stacks
- CASE Tools

The software platform model of Service Providers Integrated Requirements for Information Technology (SPIRIT) defines a number of platform services. ALMAP is a platform in the sense of that model of NMF/SPIRIT, and it offers today nearly all of those services. Figure 10.8 depicts ALMAP's realization of the SPIRIT software platform model. It contains:

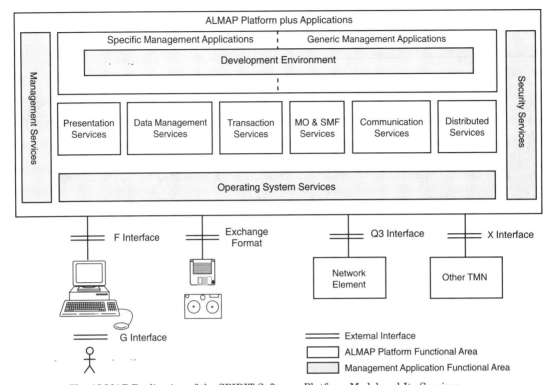

Figure 10.8 The ALMAP Realization of the SPIRIT Software Platform Model and Its Services

- Actual platform services
- Development environment
- Generic and specific applications

ALMAP 3 is SPIRIT-compliant in that the packages of ALMAP do realize precisely these kinds of services. There are slight differences, however, between ALMAP and SPIRIT. For instance, there are three SPIRIT services that will become available with ALMAP only in the future.

Table 10.1 shows the general purposes of services in a software platform, as seen by ALMAP. The same table also lists comparable services recommended by SPIRIT.

Further details on ALMAP can be reviewed in Case Study 4.

Managing PBXs with HP OpenView DM

Administration of voice systems, in particular of PBXs, is rarely integrated with platforms or with data network management products. All manufacturers working on solutions concentrate on two targets: administration of PBXs, and integration of PBX management into the management platform.

Table 10.1. The Services of ALMAP 3 Compared with SPIRIT

ALMAP service	Purpose	Differences compared with SPIRIT
Managed Objects and SMF Services	Handle managed objects and implement systems management functions as specified in the ITU-T X.700 series, such as Logging, Event Forwarding, Scheduling	These services are not explicitly mentioned in the Software Platform model of SPIRIT
Communications Services	Provide protocol stacks which realize the Q3 and X interface	None
Presentation Services	Handle the interaction between the human user interface devices (display, keyboard, mouse, etc.) and the system. They also implement the F and G interfaces as specified in the ITU-T M.3000 Series	None
Distributed Services	OSF/DCE services	None
Management Services	Support the management of the management platform, the management applications, and parts of or the whole TMN. These services go beyond the elementary Management Services that are, for instance, within OSF DCE	None
Operating System Services	Manage the fundamental physical and processing resources of a given machine	None
Generic Management of Applications	Management applications with a high degree of reusability, like generic services used by many management application, mediation services for protocol conversion, etc.	SPIRIT makes no distinction between generic and specific management applications
Development environment	Provides tools and techniques for the effective and efficient development of management applications	Is not as such part of SPIRIT, but may be seen as corresponding to the Programming Languages
Specific management applications	Management applications with a lower degree of reusability, and in general have to be developed anew for each management system	These management applications are defined in the ALMA (Alcatel Management Applications) Portfolio, and are not part of the ALMAP platform
Data management services	Manage persistent storage	ALMAP currently does not provide packages for these services, but will do so in the future
Transaction services	Coordinate resources in order to maintain transactional integrity over those resources	ALMAP currently does not provide packages for these services, but will do so in the future

Table 10-1. The Services of ALMAP 3 Compared with SPIRIT *(continued)*

ALMAP service	Purpose	Differences compared with SPIRIT
Security services	Enforce security policies on data and processing objects on the platform, data objects exchanged between platforms, and realize the security concepts of the customers and users of the platform	ALMAP currently does not provide packages for these services, but will do so in the future

The PBX Manager from the Dr. Materna Company offers a management Dr. application for Hicom-PBX systems from Siemens-Rolm. The PBX Manager is an add-on application that runs on multiple management platforms, including HP OpenView. Taking the standard services of the platforms, PBX Manager can concentrate on the special management needs of the PBXs. Features included in the first release are:

- Graphical visualization of the network of the PBXs, including equipment and facilities.
- Display of equipment and facilities through the use of standard icons.
- Status surveillance of networking components using standard SNMP agents.
- Visualization of status changes using multiple colors.
- Use of preprogrammed actions for status changes, such as opening a trouble ticket for certain faults.
- Correlation of faults from data and voice objects.

PBX Manager uses a hierarchy of protocols. Between managed objects — the actual PBXs — and the SNMP agents, native protocols are in use. Between the agents and the management platform, standard SNMP is in use. The proxy protocol conversion, native to SNMP, has been implemented in the SNMP agents.

Figure 10.9 shows the incorporation of PBXs and handsets into the visualization of computer networks.

The purpose of the PBX management solution is to integrate telecommunication equipment into existing network management systems. Corporate networks in particular can benefit from this type of integration. Corporate networks offer shared resources for voice and data transmission. Using this solution, the advanced event processing and event correlation service from HP OpenView can be fully utilized.

Managing Wireless Networks with HP OpenView Element Management Framework (OEMF)

The OpenView Element Management Framework (OEMF) is a powerful and comprehensive element management solution closely tailored to the needs of management centers in Groupe Speciale Mobile (GSM) and in other mobile telephony networks. By providing improved monitoring, control, configuration, and management functions, OEMF reduces operational costs and assists in the delivery of enhanced services to the customer. Simultaneously, through its open, standards-based architecture, OEMF provides a framework which supports and integrates other standards-driven applications, such as Inventory Management and Network Advisor, from HP Partners or from third parties.

The management of GSM is a complex task. Demand is high for real-time alarm processing, performance evaluation, and accounting data processing. Figure 10.10 shows the basic structure of GSM components. This structure consists of three principal parts:

- The Base Station Subsystem (BSS)

- The Network Subsystem (NSS)

- The Network Management Subsystem (NMS).

Other components are shown in Fig. 10.10

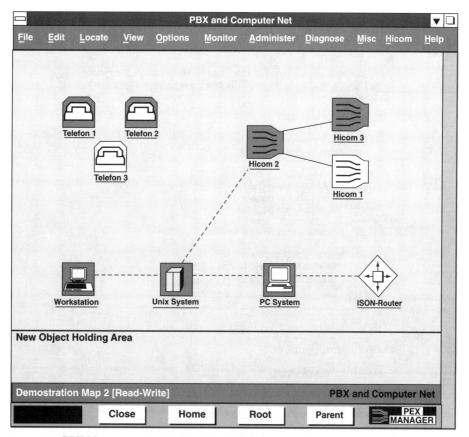

Figure 10.9 PBX Management with OpenView DM

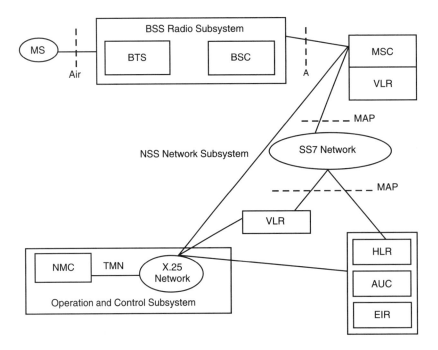

The GSM structure consists of three parts: the Base Station Subsystem (BSS), the Network Subsystem (NSS), and the Network Management Subsystem

BSS Radio Subsystem:
 BSC: Base Station Controller
 BTS: Base Transceiver Station
 MS: Mobile Station

NSS Network Subsystem:
 MSC: Mobile Switching Center
 HLR: Home Location Register
 VLR: Visitor Location Register
 AUC: Authentication Center
 EIR: Equipment Identification Register

Operation and Control Subsystem:
 NMC: Network Mangement Center

Figure 10.10 GSM Architecture and Components

OEMF addresses five key management requirements:

- Fault management
- Trouble-ticketing
- Performance management
- Graphical topology management
- Generic command facility

These applications are integrated within HP's OpenView graphical user interface, providing a consistent look and feel across all supported tasks. A wide range of additional management applications and services from third parties can be integrated into the same environment using integration points; OEMF supports CMIP, ASCII and proprietary protocols, including TL1.

Fault management

This component offers the following functionality:

- Integrated fault-gathering from equipment, regardless of type and vendor.
- Filtering, analysis, and correlation of network events.
- Integrated operator access in a highly graphical environment, with definable views based on operator profiles.
- Automatic paging and fault notification.
- Retrieval and viewing of history of alarms.
- Multiple security levels.

The application handles different event formats from different vendors and equipment. It also integrates seamlessly with other components of OEMF. The new event correlation services can be successfully implemented here.

Trouble-ticketing

This application uses client/server technology and an intuitive graphical user interface to provide an efficient way of responding to network faults. Work orders are created and distributed to local management centers or to field operations personnel, ensuring that all parties are kept informed of the fault and of the remedial actions being taken.

Because the application can directly access the fault information reported by a network element, trouble tickets can be created and dispatched automatically; if preferred, however, operators can enter further information onto the ticket before it is transmitted to operations.

The HP OpenView platform and its components offer APIs for third-party applications. In this case, AR Systems from Remedy can be used for trouble-ticketing and trouble-tracking. The server segment of the product is running on OpenView; the client segment runs on Unix under OST/Motif or on a PC under Microsoft Windows. This structure offers opportunities to distribute the ticket generation and tracking process. Both segments can be installed on the same hardware and software, if required.

Performance management

This application enables the operator to monitor network elements and display performance variables graphically or in reports. Other performance-related functions include historical reporting and network capacity planning.

The integration between OEMF's components enables the operator, for example, to define a performance threshold and have violations of that threshold automatically passed on to Fault Management for immediate actions. Another benefit of the integration is that operators have real-time access to information on how a fault, captured by the fault management application, is actually affecting network performance.

In managing wireless networks, performance and fault management are tightly connected to each other. Leading Technology, Inc., provides a powerful analysis and reporting solution. The product consists of a central performance database containing both raw counters collected at various sampling frequences, (e.g., every 15 minutes), and key summary values generated on a daily, weekly, and monthly basis by a data aggregation process. These summary values comprise totals, averages, busy hours, and busy hour totals of key parameters for different network elements. Parameter examples are: traffic carried, congestion levels, call failure levels, answer/seize ratios and so on.

Data is acquired from the network, from potentially multiple sources. These can be performance reports generated by Element Management Systems, or the network elements themselves, or consolidated performance data produced by Integrated Network Management platforms. Data is loaded into the performance database by the Performance Data Interface (PDI) at configurable intervals, such as daily, hourly, or on arrival. The reporting applications then access the performance database, performing analysis and presenting results in a variety of graphical and tabular forms. Reports are both routine and ad hoc.

Routine reports give standard graphical and tabular output. When initiated interactively, they are controlled by Motif-compliant applications, using standard Motif dialogues to control key report variables. There are three principal groups:

- Daily reports: element performance and network-wide reports

- Long-term trending reports: element performance and network-wide reports over longer periods

- Forecasting reports: element performance and network-wide reports with estimated saturation time

All reports can be sent to the operator screen, hardcopy, or file formats. Graphical reports can be plotted or saved in industry standard file formats, such as Encapsulated Postscript. Text reports are produced as ASCII text documents and Comma Separated Variable format for use by other desktop applications, such as spreadsheets. Both formats are managed and distributed by a report server.

Ad hoc reports and analyses are achieved through Kingfisher, a free-format, Motif-compliant graphical enquiry tool. Users can apply conditions to restrict data retrieved and expressions to translate the data retrieved. This can then be presented in different graphical ways, the user controlling the graph type, line styles and colors, graph annotation, and labeling. This process is fully interactive, allowing unrestrained analysis and visualization of data. At any time, a graph or tabular report can be saved as a Kingfisher procedure for rerunning at a later date, or for incorporation into the Metrica/NPR reporting application as a new menu option, or into a separate application which accesses the Metrica/NPR performance database.

The performance database is managed by the high-bandwidth Metrica database server. All other processes and reporting applications accessing the performance database do so as client processes to the Metrica database server, and can be distributed around a TCP/IP network of Unix workstations.

Metrica/NPR consists of:

- Operator specific developments: In the initial deployment of the system, the operator may make changes to the underlying data model and to the high level reporting applications. The system also may be integrated into a network management system or interfaced with OSS applications.

- Technology specific layer: This layer provides a base data model for the representation of performance data from technologies such as cellular GSM, TACS/AMPS and general wireline. A set of reporting modules generates a range of reports from this data and provides basic visibility of all performance counters.

- Metrica/NPR core: This layer provides the basic infrastructure for the management of the performance data that is provided by the network elements or element management systems. It is the configuration of subsystems in this layer that form the major part of initial deployment and it is the maintenance of these subsystems that form the bulk of system administration tasks.

- Metrica data management system: Metrica is a powerful data management system specifically designed for the storage, analysis, and presentation of technical data. The product is generally available and deployed in a wide range of applications for the management of wireless networks.

Figure 10.11 shows all components of Metrica/NPR.
For integration with HP OpenView DM, three options are available:

- Session-level integration
- Application-level integration
- Database-level integration

These are described in the following paragraphs.

Session-level integration. Metrica/NPR is based on standard Motif and X Window toolkits, and all components are accessible via simple Unix commands. This means that the user is able to run Metrica/NPR from the same workstation or X terminal as other applications using X Window and Motif.

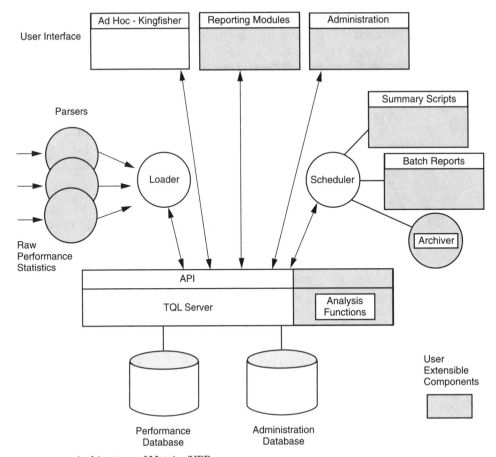

Figure 10.11 Architecture of Metrica/NPR

Application-level integration. There are two alternatives, depending on the place of the initiation: the network management platform user interface or the Metrica/NPR user interface.

From the network management platform user interface, Metrica/NPR reporting modules are implemented using the Metrica Technical Scripting Language (TSL). Users can produce new TSL scripts to provide new reports which analyze performance data. These TSL scripts can provide their own Motif-based user interface, or can be executed from a C program or Unix shell script. Thus, any C/Unix based network management system can initiate analysis of performance data and the production of performance reports. Figure 10.12 shows an example for this type of integration.

From the Metrica/NPR user interface, Metrica/NPR could potentially generate alarms and events related to performance data. This could involve thresholding on relatively complex conditions. Retrieval from other applications is possible as shown in Fig. 10.13.

Database-level integration. Also in this case, there are two alternatives depending on the initiation of data export and import: the network management platform user interface, and the Metrica/NPR user interface.

From the network management platform user interface, all Metrica/NPR data retrieval and analysis is performed using TQL, which is similar to SQL. This involves submitting queries to the performance database, and retrieving data. The TQL API is a C programming library; thus performance data can be returned to a C program for further processing. Any network management application of HP OpenView DM has full and flexible access to performance data managed by Metrica/NPR via the TQL API.

From the Metrica/NPR user interface, all Metrica/NPR reporting applications are implemented in TSL scripts. These can make calls to C programs, which in turn can make SQL queries into relational databases to retrieve the current configuration of the mobile network.

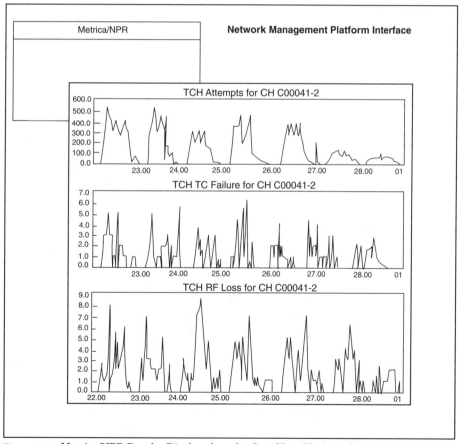

Figure 10.12 Metrica/NPR Results Displayed on the OpenView Platform Screens

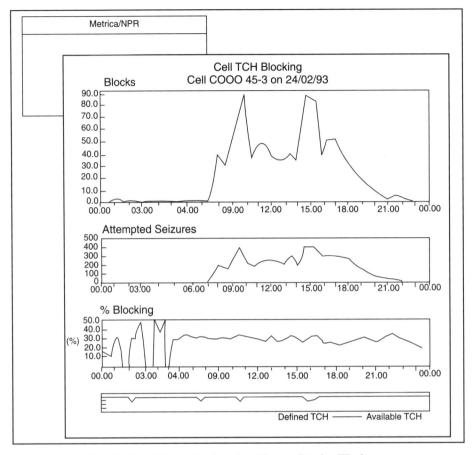

Figure 10.13 Platform-Collected Data Distplayed on Metrica Display Window

Graphical topology management

This application provides the operator with graphical displays of managed elements on the network, as well as their connection relationship. It also supports user defined "follow-the-sun" maps for daytime and nighttime operations; different filters and correlation rules can be applied and an SQL connection can be implemented to integrate with configuration databases.

The heart of this application is the concept of management by exception; operators are presented only with network elements reporting a fault. The topological view of the network is not used simply for reporting; it also can be used to configure the objects being displayed. Management domains can be defined, and the application integrates fully with the fault management and configuration management functions.

Generic command facility

This application enables the operator to act on network elements via a single, consistent graphical user interface. From the operator's viewpoint, it unifies and standardizes the network. Details such as the vendor, type, or protocol are hidden from view.

Summary

The examples in this chapter have shown the wide range of telecommunications management applications that can be built upon the HP OpenView foundation. In particular, the applications concentrate on the following:

- Services management for broadband networks including Sonet, SDH, ATM, and residential services such as video-on-demand.
- Provisioning and monitoring applications for broadband networks.
- Network monitoring for outsourced customer networks managed by telecommunications service providers.
- Customer gateways into public networks for real-time monitoring and management data.
- Integration with other management platforms for TMN compatibility and a single view from a multivendor environment.
- Element management systems for new equipment and new data communications services.

Using these applications, the service provider can improve competitiveness through:

- Faster service deployment, whether broadband, multimedia, or wireless, local, or international.
- Fewer isolated and incompatible management applications and systems.
- Better information for strategic development, network planning, service management, and customer care.
- More efficient network operation and problem resolution as well as greater security, reliability, and interoperability.

Two Hewlett-Packard products extend the value of the HP OpenView DM Platform for telecommunication companies, the HP Fault Management Platform (FMP) and the HP Distibuted Processing Environment (HP DPE).

The Fault Management Platform provides a set of services that management applications use to control event and alarm messages from diverse network elements and systems. It includes a Mediation Service that collects, stores, filters, and extracts messages, and an Alarm Management Service that displays and correlates alarm messages and external applications based on alarm data. The HP FMP enables telecommunications services providers to increase productivity, reduce costs, and improve the quality of real-time network monitoring and control.

The HP Distributed Processing Environment provides an Information Network Architecture-compliant platform for distributed telecommunications services and operations systems. Trader services and framework API simplify the development and deployment of distributed telecommunications applications.

Finally, HP provides a sophisticated event correlation system called HP OpenView Event Correlation Services (ECS). This is a highly distributed approach to event correlation, and is initially targeted at carriers and services providers. Chapter 18 provides more information on HP OpenView ECS.

Unix Systems Administration

Unix and NT Fault and Performance Management

Improving the availability of distributed client/server systems through automated fault management is a critical requirement today as customers seek to move applications off the mainframe and on to smaller machines offering better price/performance (Huntington-Lee 1995c). But the manageability and reliability of networked Unix and Windows NT servers are nowhere near mainframe quality, hence the need for systems administration products capable of monitoring and controlling client/server computers across the enterprise.

To address these challenges, HP has introduced the HP OpenView Solutions Framework, described below.

The HP OpenView Solution Framework

The HP OpenView Solution Framework for integrated systems management embraces these components:

- HP OpenView IT/Operations for operations and problem management
- HP PerfView and MeasureWare for resource and performance management
- HP OpenView IT/Administration for configuration and change management

Both IT/Operations and IT/Administration now include an embedded version of HP OpenView NNM (Fig. 11.1), giving customers new possibilities for integrating network and systems management within their IT organizations.

IT/Operations supports operations and problem management by collecting, grouping, filtering, and processing messages from a variety of sources (Fig. 11.2).

HP PerfView/MeasureWare supports resource and performance management (Fig. 11.3). MeasureWare agents can send information to IT/Operations; drill-down from IT/Operations to PerfView screens also is supported.

IT/Administration supports change and configuration management for files, users, and printers. The IT/Administration architecture supports a central

Enterprisewide Operations and Problem Management:

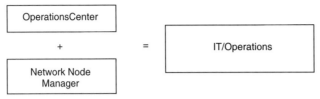

Enterprisewide Configuration and Change Management:

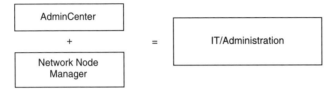

Figure 11.1 IT/Operations and IT/Administration Combined with OpenView NNM

object and model database combining information representing user-defined policies and processes with data describing the physical elements of the distributed computing environment. IT/Administration is discussed in more detail in Chap. 12.

In addition to these three core systems management offerings, IT/Operations, IT/Administration, and PerfView/MeasureWare, HP supports several function-specific areas of systems administration, including the following:

- Backup/restore management via HP OpenView OmniBack II

- Distributed print management via HP OpenSpool

- Software distribution via HP Software Distributor (also integrated in IT/Administration)

The remainder of this chapter will focus on the areas of Unix fault and performance management, including HP's solutions for these areas: HP IT/Operations and HP MeasureWare/PerfView.

An Introduction to Unix Fault and Performance Management

The Unix operating system provides embedded commands for monitoring operating system resources, processes, and peripherals. Many administrative tasks can be performed by editing configuration files and writing scripts (Nemeth 1995). Writing shell scripts is still the most widely used method for automating Unix administrative tasks. These tasks include, but are not limited to:

- Monitoring servers for status, performance, and impending problems (disk full, etc.).

- Troubleshooting — diagnosing problems when something goes wrong; tracking problems.

- Tracking resource usage and creating accounting/usage billing reports.
- Performing backups and managing storage resources.
- Adding/deleting new users or changing their access privileges.
- Installing new software.
- Auditing security.
- Managing printers and distributing reports.
- Scheduling jobs and balancing workload.

This chapter focuses on the first four bullet points, which fall under the general category of fault and performance management.

While Unix does support some inherent facilities for collecting fault and performance data (such as *iostat*, *lpstat*, etc.), these are low-level, arcane commands that must be triggered manually or on a scheduled basis, and may not be used effectively by the typical system operator. Even when understood, these commands yield statistics that look only at an individual system; no

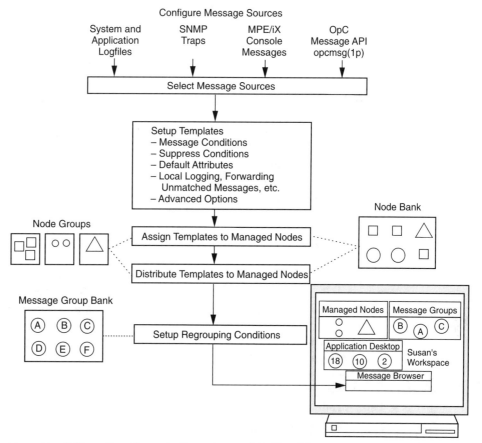

Figure 11.2 IT/Operations Supports Operations and Problem Management

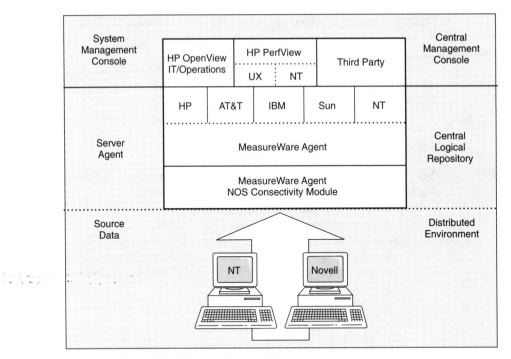

Figure 11.3 HP PerfView/MeasureWare Architecture

commands provide CPU utilization statistics across the entire distributed environment, for example.

There are a wealth of statistics hiding in Unix system logfiles. Unix does not include facilities for filtering logfile messages, comparing multiple statistics, or reporting on rates of change, for example. Without add-on tools, systems administrators must tend servers in person to guarantee server availability. The cost of maintaining onsite staff quickly becomes intolerable when servers are geographically dispersed throughout a corporation. At the same time, organizations cannot afford to let the availability of critical Unix systems suffer.

The complexity of Unix systems administration is compounded by interconnectivity to desktop and network operating systems, such as Microsoft Windows NT and NetWare. As a 32-bit, network-aware operating system, Windows NT is rapidly encroaching on traditional Unix territory. As a result, many organizations are seeking to streamline the management of both Unix and NT systems from the same console.

Several types of products can be used to automate Unix and NT systems administration, including:

- Intelligent agents (SNMP and RPC-based)
- Point-product applications or application suites
- Enterprise system administration consoles

Generally speaking, agents are low-priced software programs typically purchased in volume. Agents usually do not support their own graphical user interface (GUI). Instead, they collect data, perform functions locally, and report to a central management station. Agents may:

- Poll via SNMP

- Schedule execution of Unix commands.

- Monitor database activity and trigger alarms when thresholds are exceeded.

- Monitor systems or network activity and trigger alarms when thresholds are exceeded.

SNMP agents instrument the kernel with an SNMP Management Information Base (MIB). SNMP MIB implementations are designed for highly distributed architectures where it is assumed that topology information and critical alerts will be forwarded to a central SNMP-based management console.

However, SNMP MIB implementations are limited to the vendor's opinion of which Unix statistics are important enough to capture in a MIB. Although MIB builders usually are offered for extending the MIB, few systems administrators have the time or expertise to build a new MIB.

Product examples of SNMP-based agents include:

- IBM Systems Monitor for AIX

- The AgentWorks component of CA-Unicenter (formerly Legent)

- SNMP Research EMANATE

In contrast to SNMP agents, RPC/IPC-based agents are capable of supporting remote execution of Unix commands, providing more intelligence and local processing capabilities than available using traditional SNMP agents. But RPC-based agents are proprietary in nature and not generally interoperable with other vendors' management architectures. Product examples of RPC/IPC-based agents include:

- BMC Patrol

- CA Systems Alert component of Unicenter

- Digital System Watchdog

- HP PerfView/MeasureWare

- Tivoli/Sentry

- Open Enterprise Networks: *Managing Objects on Networks*

Point-products include function-specific applications for backup, software distribution, print spooling, and other tasks. Examples include HP OmniBack II and OmniSpool and HP Software Distributor.

Enterprise systems administration consoles are high-end products that, in some respects, support a *manager-of-managers* construct. The core function of an enterprise systems administration console is to capture messages from system logfiles, obviating the need for a human to watch a screen waiting for something important to happen. Messages may come from several sources:

- Syslog daemon (*syslogd*)
- SNMP traps
- Console messages from non-Unix systems (NT systems, proprietary mini-computers)
- Events created by other consoles
- Traps from network management systems
- Intelligent agents monitoring against user-specific thresholds

Some consoles are capable of capturing and processing any ASCII message. Once messages are captured, they typically are parsed and reformatted. When filtering occurs locally, unimportant or duplicate messages are discarded or logged, while important messages are forwarded to the central console. Filters typically are defined at the central console and downloaded to the local systems. Filtering criteria vary from product to product; all products have the capability to parse strings and look for keywords, such as "disk space full." When products support local filtering only, filtering often is limited to a simple accept or reject action. Centralized filtering allows for comparison of messages coming from multiple servers; rules-based capabilities support complex filters such as "accept only if three identical messages received within five minutes from same server."

Once reformatted and filtered, messages may be forwarded to operator console for display, or forwarded to a program or script for automated response. All products reviewed in this chapter support interfaces or development of scripts to reboot systems, trigger trouble tickets, and other remedial actions. Some products support more advanced rules languages in addition to scripting.

Messages that are suppressed may be logged locally. The facilities for viewing the log or creating reports vary widely from product to product. The capabilities of HP IT/Operations are discussed in the next section.

HP IT/Operations

HP IT/Operations, formerly known as OperationsCenter, is an enterprise systems administration console introduced by HP in 1993. Version 2.0 was introduced in August 1995. IT/Operations, an enhanced version of OperationsCenter that includes embedded NNM, shipped in 1996.

IT/Operations consists of a Management Server and distributed intelligent agents. The Management Server portion of OperationsCenter collects data, intercepts SNMP traps, regroups and forwards messages, controls the datastore for messages and actions, and installs the OperationsCenter agent software on managed nodes. IT/Operations supports manager-to-manager communications, providing a failover capability, as well as the ability to transfer control to a different management server on a scheduled basis. This functionality requires the purchase of an additional product, HP's MC/ServiceGuard.

IT/Operations agents intercept the following types of messages:

- SNMP traps.

- HP-MPE/iX console messages.

- Unix logfiles: IT/Ops agents encapsulate logfiles of applications and systems, extracting message information and checking status.

- Threshold-monitored objects: IT/Ops agents generate messages when thresholds are exceeded.

- IT/Ops messages: generated by an API or IT/Ops command.

IT/Operations agents are preconfigured to monitor HP OmniBack II, HP OpenSpool, and HP OpenStorage logfiles.

Filters and thresholds are applied at the agent level. IT/Operations agents filter messages on a simple accept-or-reject basis by comparing the content of ASCII text messages to user-defined strings. Messages matching suppress conditions are suppressed; all others are forwarded. Rules-based event handling *is not* supported. For example, the user cannot specify "if this message AND this message, then alert" or "alert only if you receive this message more than 3 times in one minute," and so on.

Message matching conditions include alert severity, node name, application name, message group, object, as well as message text (ASCII string).

Logfile templates are provided for defining default message attributes. The logfile encapsulator can be configured to collect, filter, reformat, and display logfile messages.

Threshold monitoring templates provided are of five basic threshold types:

- Maximum

- Minimum

- With reset

- Without reset

- Continuous

Programs and MIB objects may be monitored via thresholds; IT/Operations provides the following default monitors:

- Disk utilization 90 percent, interval 10 minutes, reset value 85 percent

- Process utilization 90 percent, interval 5 minutes, reset value 80 percent

- Swap utilization 75 percent, interval 5 minutes, reset value 70 percent

The matching criteria for SNMP trap include the following attributes:

- Node
- Enterprise ID
- Generic trap
- Specific trap
- Variable bindings

After filtering, data is converted into an HP proprietary format for presentation to the central IT/Operations management server. IT/Operations also can change the severity of the event in a message. The IT/Operations message format includes the following fields:

- Severity level
- Node
- Application
- Message group
- Object
- Message text

Automation

Automation is initiated at the management server unless the action is to be taken on the same managed node at which the message was intercepted. Automation at the management server provides for:

- Regrouping, which entails assigning a message to another message group.
- Starting nonlocal automatic actions.
- Forwarding the message to external notification interfaces, trouble-ticketing systems, etc.
- Initiating virtual console sessions on managed nodes.

Automation at the local managed node includes initiating local actions (rebooting, paging, e-mail, scripts, and other programmatic response). Alternatively, Operator-Initiated Actions may be predefined and started by the operator in response to a message, such as opening consoles on remote systems, broadcasting commands to multiple systems, starting management applications. IT/Operations establishes the network connection and system login to facilitate Operator-Initiated Actions.

Administrators must define in advance the corrective actions to be triggered for specific events. Administrators also can define *problem resolution* text (*Message Details*) for events not handled automatically.

IT/Operations can trigger *monitoring applications* as a corrective action. Monitoring applications include scripts, programs, and/or SNMP GETS for checking MIB variables. IT/Operations starts the monitoring application; values are returned to the IT/Operations API.

History and logging

The management server's history log can track and collect messages suppressed and/or forwarded. It also is possible to track the user-written Message Detail annotations associated with each event message. However, users must write scripts or use third-party tools such as Microsoft Access to pick up keywords and group messages into meaningful categories. The report writer is limited to the following six report types:

- All active messages, short report
- All active messages, detailed report (including operator instructions and message annotations)
- Selected active messages
- All history messages, short report
- Selected history messages
- IT/Operations error report: IT/Operations Management Server error messages

Customization and APIs

HP provides a GUI-based pulldown agent configuration tool that allows users to fill in the blanks to specify which log files to monitor and which strings to accept or reject. Incorporation of new or existing scripts is supported through the logfile encapsulation feature. IT/Operations provides the following APIs:

- Command API and a Library API for submitting OpsC messages and for delivering the current value of monitored objects (for threshold monitoring).
- Mainframe/legacy system API for triggering predefined actions for IBM systems (MVS, OS/2, and AS/400.) This API, for example, allows customers to configure Legent Prevail/XP and OperationsCenter to trigger automated actions when a mainframe problem occurs.
- Event correlation API for interfacing to Seagate NerveCenter and similar applications.

HP IT/Operations runs on HP 9000 series 700 or 800 computers running HP-UX. Its resource requirements include: 96MB RAM (128MB recommended), 200MB swap space, and 100MB storage for messages. Agents supported include HP-UX 9.X and 10.X, AIX and AIX 4, SunOS, Solaris 2.3 and 2.4, MPE/iX, AT&T GIS SVR4, Bull DPX, SGI IRIX, SCO UNIX, Sequent Symmetry, and Digital Unix (OSF/1). Agents for Windows NT shipped in mid-1996.

Like OpenView NNM, IT/Operations supports CA-Ingres and Oracle SQL databases. Pricing for HP IT/OperationsCenter is approximately $30,000 for the management server (console). List price for agents run approximately $2000 for a quantity of 1, with substantial discounts for bulk purchases.

HP IT/Operations supports filtering and recovery actions on the local agent only, making sophisticated rules-based processing nearly impossible. Some competing products, such as Ensign from Boole & Babbage, support a flexible approach whereby alarms can be defined either centrally or locally.

One of IT/Operations' biggest advantages in the marketplace is the strength of the HP OpenView and HP-UX installed base. Customers with HP products often cite the desire for "one-stop shopping" as an advantage of IT/Operations. IT/Operations also supports a manager-to-manager communications feature, enhancing scalability and fault tolerance of the solution. However, the product does not include embedded functions for backup, storage management, software distribution, workload balancing, user administration, or trouble-ticketing, as do some competing products such as CA-Unicenter. These functions are supported in extra-cost options provided by HP and third parties. Also, the IT/Operations console runs only on HP-UX, whereas competing products such as CA-Unicenter, Tivoli/Enterprise Console, and Boole Ensign run on multiple versions of Unix.

Table 11.1 compares features of IT/Operations to three competing products: Boole & Babbage Ensign, CA-Unicenter, and Tivoli/Enterprise Console (Huntington-Lee 1995c).

In February 1996, HP formally introduced major enhancements to the former OperationsCenter and AdminCenter products, both of which now incorporate

Table 11.1 Comparative Features of HP IT/Operations and Its Competitors

Function	Boole Ensign	A Comparison of product features CA Unicenter	HP	Tivoli TME
Alarms (logfiles)	Yes	Yes	Yes	Yes
Automation	Metalanguage	Scripts	Scripts	Prolog-type 4GL
Security	Yes	Yes	Yes	Yes
Job scheduling	Yes	Yes	Yes	Yes
Workload balancing	Third party (4th Dim.)	Yes	Third party (Unison)	Yes
Unix Resource accounting	No	Yes	Separate product— PerfView	Extra-cost option—Tivoli Sentry
Chargeback	No	Yes	No	No
Trouble-ticketing	Third-party interface	Yes, plus Third-party interface	Third-party interface	Third-party interface
Reporting	No	Yes	Minimal	Yes
Database monitoring	No	Extra-cost option—DB Alert	No	No
Applications discovery	No	Yes	No	No

a tightly integrated version of HP OpenView Network Node Manager (NNM) out of the box (Huntington-Lee 1996c).

These enhancements represent a further melding of systems administration and network management technology, a key point of HP's integrated management strategy. HP has renamed the two enhanced products to reflect this merger.

OperationsCenter is now known as IT/Operations; the new product provides topological views of the network infrastructure as constructed by NNM. According to HP, this will give MIS staff access to network information that may be helpful in determining causes of problems, such as server failures.

However, the primary end-user interface to IT/Operations interface is not be the NNM menu hierarchy, but rather the Application Desktop GUI that supports assignment of management tools and views to specific operator profiles. IT/Operations shipped with three predefined and preconfigured operator user roles: System Operator, Network Operator, and Integrated System and Network Management (ISNM) operator. Customers may tailor their own operator roles as well. The ability to delegate network and systems management-specific tasks among different operators according to skill levels and scope of responsibilities should help improve operator productivity while reducing duplication of effort, according to HP.

In addition to rolling NNM and OperationsCenter into one product, other enhancements to IT/Operations included a new toolkit encompassing NNM's MIB Application Builder and Data Collector, as well as enhanced communications to external applications such as trouble-ticketing systems via an API that recognizes and supports the use of local agent-based correlation.

Along with IT/Operations, HP also announced IT/Administration, the new version of AdminCenter that includes NNM at a price that is $5000 less than what customers must pay if they purchase the products separately. In addition, the bundled packages streamline the installation process and documentation set.

HP shipped IT/Operations in May 1996, at a starting list price of $40,000. Pricing for IT/Administration, which shipped in June 1996, starts at $17,000.

An Overview of MeasureWare/PerfView

PerfView is a centralized performance measurement tool originally designed to monitor HP operating systems. Over the years, HP has extended PerfView capabilities beyond Unix and MPE to embrace other vendors' operating systems. In mid-1995, HP introduced MeasureWare, a multifaceted product offering that brings PerfView-collected information on to the same console as data that measures the performance of networks, applications, and databases. MeasureWare includes an end-user interface component that can display information collected by selected HP and non-HP agents. One of these agents, MeasureWare agent, is the original PerfView agent with some important enhancements. The following section describes MeasureWare. Following that is a discussion of other related HP performance tools: PerfView, PerfView RX, and GlancePlus.

HP MeasureWare

HP MeasureWare's console component can graph, in real time, the statistics collected simultaneously by the MeasureWare agent, BMC's Patrol Agent, HP's NetMetrix agent, and the MeasureWare Transaction Tracker feature.

- MeasureWare displays system performance statistics.

- BMC Patrol displays database performance statistics.

- HP NetMetrix Internetwork Response Manager displays WAN/LAN link latency and node-status information across the network (network response time).

- Transaction Tracker measures the beginning and ending of a transaction to provide application response time, from the end-user's perspective.

MeasureWare collects the statistics from these several different agents, overlaying the graphs onto one display. The primary benefit of this is that it allows the administrator to visually detect patterns in the combined graphs that provide clues about sources of trouble. For example, if the MeasureWare graphs indicate that application response time increases when there is a spike in network traffic utilization, the administrator will know enough to first call up the NetMetrix application and investigate network links. Without this type of capability, the administrator must guess as to what area (network, server, database) to investigate first. In large, interconnected workgroups, this guessing game can consume precious hours or days.

MeasureWare represents an initial step toward viewing performance of the interconnected workgroup as a whole. Today, the correlation of system and network behavior must occur in the mind of the technician viewing the MeasureWare screen. As HP continues to refine and test artificial intelligence technology, this type of correlation will be supported automatically to greater degrees.

HP MeasureWare alarm conditions are automatically reported to IT/Operations. IT/Operations and MeasureWare are integrated at the agent level.

Products that compete with HP MeasureWare include Tivoli Sentry, IBM Systems Monitor for AIX, CA/Legent AgentWorks and, to a lesser extent, the CompuWare EcoTools/EcoNet suite for applications and database monitoring. Table 11.2 lists comparative strengths and weaknesses of MeasureWare and products from Tivoli, IBM, and CA.

PerfView

PerfView consists of two components:

- Motif-based performance analysis software, supporting alarm monitoring, filtering, and analysis capabilities running on HP systems.

- Agents: PerfView (now MeasureWare) intelligent agents that collect and monitor metrics on HP, Sun, and IBM systems.

Table 11.2. HP MeasureWare and Its Competitors

Vendor	HP	IBM	CA-Legent	Tivoli
Product	MeasureWare	Systems Monitor	AgentWorks	Sentry
Strengths	In-depth performance monitor; HP OpenView support	Affordable, comprehensive, supports distributed architecture for NetView AIX	Distributed architecture, multiplatform server, flexible standards based (SNMP)	Object-oriented, flexible, feeds into Console rules/based filtering
Limitations	Moderate to high price; focus on HP systems	Focus on IBM AIX; no message consolidation console	Pricing/ packaging issues since CA takeover	Lack of performance trending; complex to deploy TME environment

MeasureWare agents capture and log statistics, and determine if exception conditions exist. Whereas IT/Operations agents trigger alarms based on specific messages, MeasureWare agents are more sophisticated and can apply algorithms to compare current service levels, including response times, transaction rates, resource utilizations, and bottleneck indicators against predefined alarm thresholds. MeasureWare agents are capable of tracking approximately 30 system metrics. Typically, seven days' worth of data can be stored in the default configuration. Metrics collected include, but are not limited to:

- Total CPU utilization
- Active processes
- Peak disk utilization
- Physical disk I/O per second
- Memory utilization
- Memory management disk I/O per second
- Swap space utilization
- Packets I/O per second
- Cache hit rate
- User CPU utilization
- Active processes

The PerfView management console application includes three components; an Analyzer, a Monitor, and a Planner. The MeasureWare agents send raw performance data via Remote Procedure Calls (RPCs) from the alarm source (managed node) to the Analyzer for further analysis. PerfView console application then filters out irrelevant performance data, timestamping and logging the relevant data in system memory. The Monitor supports management-by-exception through centralized event monitoring and customized alarms. Alarm conditions can consist of thresholds and time duration elements for single measurements or combinations of multiple measurements. The Monitor displays alarm conditions, while the Planner provides linear forecasting models based upon historical data provided by the agents.

Both MeasureWare and PerfView console applications can manipulate data from non-MeasureWare agents through an extensibility feature called Data Source Integration (DSI). The DSI interface allows operators to monitor any resource, including MVS systems or the output of existing Unix scripts, through a proxy agent.

MeasureWare agents can automatically initiate local actions when thresholds are crossed. These actions include pages, e-mail, scripts, or other programmatic response.

PerfView RX

PerfView RX is an add-on application that can be used for long-term trending and capacity planning. PerfView RX can track more than 200 system statistics. The product identifies applications and processes using Unix system resources. A number of metrics can be displayed, including the login ID of each application or process.

PerfView RX allows concurrent graphing of multiple metrics such as total CPU utilization, peak disk utilization, disk I/O, etc. The display helps users spot the cause of system bottlenecks via flexible graphing options. Users can turn on or off the lines representing various metrics. The granularity of the graph can be adjusted for viewing of any trends or anomalies in system activity. Users can adjust the Y axis of the graph to more closely view lower-level activities.

Metrics displayed by PerfView RX include, but are not limited to, the following:

- CPU use during the interval (percentage of total and seconds)
- Number and rate of physical disk I/Os
- Maximum percent full of all disk filesets
- User CPU use during interval
- CPU use at real-time priorities
- CPU use for interrupt handling
- CPU idle time during interval
- CPU use for managing main memory contents
- Rate of system procedure calls during interval
- Number of disk drives configured on the system
- Average utilization of busiest disk during interval

- Number and rate of logical/physical disk reads, I/Os, writes, etc., during the interval
- Percent of logical reads satisfied by memory cache
- Number of configured LAN interfaces
- Number and rate of network file system requests during interval
- Main memory use (percentage of total)
- Swap space use on disk (percentage of total)
- Number and rate of memory page faults during interval
- Number of process swaps during interval
- Percent of virtual memory currently in active use
- Number of processing in run queue during interval
- Number of user sessions during interval

GlancePlus

GlancePlus is online diagnostic software that supports examination of performance data at the Unix system application and per-process levels. Problems with system CPU, memory, disk, and network utilization can be detected using the product. Information can be displayed in graphical or tabular form. GlancePlus supports user-specified performance rules for diagnosing problems; alarms can be triggered if problems are detected. In addition to supporting metrics on individual processes, GlancePlus allows several measurements to be combined and evaluated as one metric. GlancePlus graphs typically are used to show short-term performance history of cumulative and running average totals over the course of between 10 minutes and several hours.

GlancePlus includes a rules-based advisor facility. The product is capable of reporting on more than 600 system metrics.

Summary

HP is evolving its OpenView architecture toward a more distributed model. The release of HP OpenView NNM 4.1 in mid-1996 was the first significant milestone in this regard. Customers have been requesting this architectural improvement, as evident in Datapro's 1996 HP OpenView User's Survey described in Chap. 20.

HP also is evolving its OpenView Solution Framework to encompass a management philosophy of integrating the previously separate disciplines of network and systems management. HP believes that key management processes, including problem, change, configuration, and resource/performance management, can be applied consistently to networks and systems through an integrated approach. As a result, HP began bundling its NNM network management solution in the IT/Operations and IT/Administrations systems administration products in 1996. Few customers have undergone such radical change (see Fig. 11-4); merging network and systems management requires restructuring of internal IT organizations as well as the deployment of new products and processes. However, pressures to streamline IT organizations while managing new, complex network and computing technologies ultimately may force reluctant customers to embrace HP's viewpoint.

"Do you plan to merge, or have you already merged
your Network and Systems Management operations?"

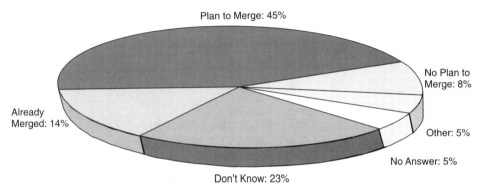

Figure 11.4 Customer Plans to Merge Network and Systems Management Operations. Source: 1995 OpenView Forum Users' Conference Survey

HP IT/Administration

In November 1994, HP announced a configuration and change control application it called AdminCenter. Now known as IT/Administration, the product joined OperationsCenter, now IT/Operations, and PerfView, now MeasureWare, as the third in a trio of major systems management offerings designed to complement HP's flagship network management offering, HP OpenView NNM. Together, these products form the foundation of HP's OpenView Solution Framework, as explained in Chap. 11.

While HP IT/Operations is primarily a fault management system and MeasureWare/PerfView addresses performance management, IT/Administration targets configuration and change control of software, peripherals, file systems, and even user-related data. HP designed IT/Administration to be highly object-oriented, in the hope that object orientation would help the product tackle the knotty problem of simplifying user administration in mixed environments. In an all-HP-UX environment with only a few servers, for example, an organization may get by with one or two HP-UX gurus to handle the process of assigning user IDs, passwords, privileges, and network IDs, and ensuring users have the right software loaded onto their workstations.

But in large geographically dispersed networks supporting several flavors of Unix as well as Windows NT and NetWare, it may be cost-prohibitive to retain enough technically adept systems administrators at each site to handle the mix of platforms. According to HP, IT/Administration potentially can enable one systems administrator to manage from 150 to 200 computer systems.

The distributed, heterogeneous network is precisely the type of environment in which IT/Administration should be cost-effective. The product supports a *process-oriented approach* to centralizing and automating the configuration of Unix systems and servers, users/passwords, file systems, and software. IT/Administration is process-oriented because it gives the customer a single, unified interface to the process of configuration across a potentially diverse set of entities, including devices, software, systems and subsystems, and users. As a result, HP customers will not need to deploy a different procedure for configuring each individual type of managed object in the environment of net-worked systems.

In addition, the ability to provide a consistent look-and-feel across a diverse set of management products has been a major selling point of the entire HP OpenView product suite. HP hopes that IT/Administration will reinforce that competitive advantage.

IT/Administration maintains an inventory of configured managed objects. The product also supports policy-based management, allowing an organization to assign different responsibilities to different systems administrations as appropriate by creating customized management domains.

Like IT/Operations, IT/Administration has two primary components: a management server and intelligent agents. The management server runs on HP 9000 series 700 and 800 computers operating HP-UX. HP offers agents for HP-UX, IBM-AIX, Sun Solaris, Novell NetWare, and Windows NT. Also like IT/Operations, IT/Administration primarily uses remote procedure calls (RPCs) instead of SNMP to exchange management data between agents and the management server. SNMP traps can be received and generated through the NNM facility now embedded in IT/Administration.

IT/Administration Concepts

IT/Administration allows customers to impose a new, organized method of administration on what may have been a very informally, if not chaotically, managed distributed computing environment. To deploy IT/Administration effectively, one first must understand the concepts it uses to enforce this organized approach to distributed systems management. Several of these key concepts include:

- Objects
- Roles
- Domains
- Policies
- Modes
- Queries

The following sections will briefly describe these concepts.

Objects

As an object-oriented system, IT/Administration uses abstraction to hide implementation-level details from operators and administrators. While this makes the product easier to use, the initial configuration and deployment of the system requires some study.

In the parlance of IT/Administration, objects are either *Abstract* or *Managed*. In either case, customers must understand fully the concept of inheritance to manipulate objects effectively. Abstract Objects are used to model the tasks of systems administration. Abstract Objects include the following:

- Templates
- Defaults
- Policies
- Domains

In addition, IT/Administration provides predefined Abstract Objects for management servers, administrators, and Object Classes.

A *default* is a predefined value for an attribute. A *template* is a special set of defaults that facilitate the creation of an object *instance,* or something real that is to be managed. A *policy* is a range of valid attribute values. A *domain* defines the management space. Policies and domains are described in more detail in later sections of this chapter.

In contrast to Abstract Objects, Managed Objects represent real devices and systems. Managed Objects are grouped into Object Classes supporting inheritance. An *Object Class* is defined as a group of objects with common attributes. Each Managed Object is represented by colored icons on the IT/Administration screen; status is indicated by color. IT/Administration provides the following 10 default object classes:

- Unix system
- User
- Group
- Kernel
- Swap space
- File system
- Software
- LP spooler
- Peripherals
- Interfaces

HP also provides default attributes for each of these 10 Object Classes, as listed in Table 12.1. In addition, users may define up to 10 additional attributes to an Object Class, including five integer attributes and five string attributes. These attributes are also inherited by subclasses.

The ability to group Managed Objects into Classes is a powerful feature. For example, it enables adminstrators to perform mass updates on all, or a subset of all, objects in the same class. This subset is called a *collection.* An administrator may want to create a collection of all PostScript printers in marketing departments across the company, and then perform a mass update such as a configuration change, on all printers in the collection. The collection can be generated by using the Query Result Table; in some cases, objects can be dragged and dropped on screen to create the collection.

The division of objects into Managed and Abstract is a reflection of IT/Administration's underlying design. In IT/Administration's architecture, the area responsible for Policies and Processes Representation is separate

Table 12.1 IT/Administration Object Classes and Their Attributes

Managed object	Attributes
Unix system	Hostname, release, license, model, vendor, system-ID, IP-address, link-level address, serial-number, system usage, admin-info
User	Login name, password, login-enable, user-ID, home-directory, shell, group, name, office-location, office phone, home phone
Group	Name, password, group-ID, members of the group
Kernel	Drivers, subsystems, kernel-parameters, device-parameters (each parameter is defined by name, state, and description)
Swap space	Available capacity, space-used, space-free, percentage of usage, swap priority, kernel entry; also device-file and type (including disk type and disk partition) or file system used
File system	For HFS/CDFS systems: device-file, mount-point, permissions, capacity, space-used, space-free, minimum free space, long or short filenames, file system check priority, disk partition
	For NFS systems: remote mount-point, local mount-point, permissions, capacity, space-used, space-free, exporting system info, export permissions (exported directory data, client-systems, and attribute information)
Software	Launches into HP Software Distributor (.SD)
LP Spooler	Printer, print destination, device-file
Peripherals	Vendor, product-ID, size, bytes-per-sector, interface, partitioning (name, size, device-file, in-raw-use, file-system)
Interfaces	Type (serial interfaces, centronics interfaces, SCSI interfaces, HP-FL interfaces), hardware path, and connected devices

from the area governing Systems and Network Representation (Fig. 12.1). Conceptually, the Policies and Processes area is an ¡image of all the "knowledge" in a systems administrator's mind. The Systems and Network area reflects the physical elements in the computing environment, such as systems, kernels, peripherals, files, users, and so on. These two areas, Policies/Processes and

Systems/Network, are brought together in the object and model database. The Model Processing area of IT/Administration operates on this data, forming a bridge between the images of the environment and the real world, as shown in Fig. 12.1 (Hewlett-Packard 1994b).

The Model Processing function of IT/Administration is central to the product's operation. The Model Processing function interprets object model definitions, applying user-specified policies to those definitions. Synchronization (described below) is handled by Model Processing. The Model Processing function also receives the administrator's request to change those policies to provide information about them. A Request/Action system selects the communication protocols and system commands needed to carry out the administrator's requests. As shown in Fig. 12.2, the communications protocols currently supported by IT/Administration are Distributed Computing Environment Remote Procedure Calls (DCE-RPCs) and the Simple Network Management Protocol (SNMP).

Roles

The abstract concept of *Roles* is important for understanding and deploying IT/Administration. IT/Administration provides two default Roles out of the box:

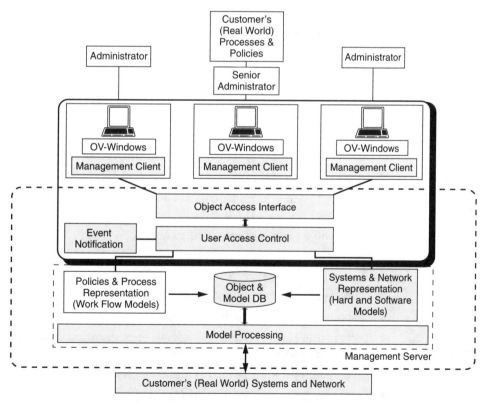

Figure 12.1 IT/Administration Architecture

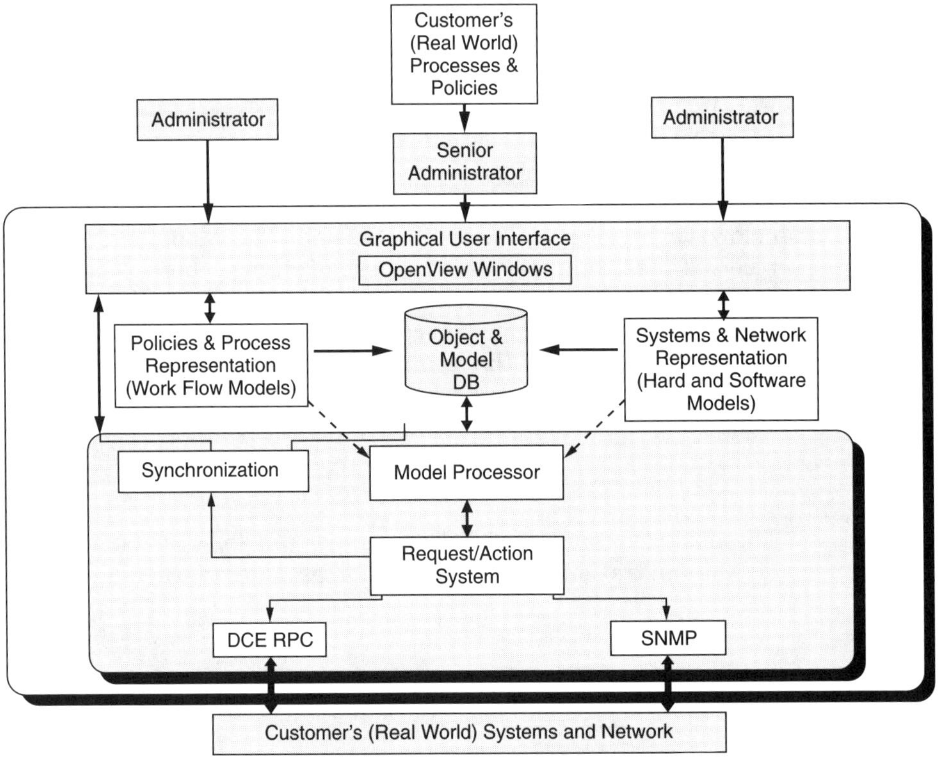

Figure 12.2 The Request/Action System of IT/Administration Supports DCE RPC and SNMP Communications.

Senior administrator:

- Responsible for defining, grouping, adding/removing managed nodes.
- Responsible for defining the roles of other administrators.
- Responsible for defining policies for object classes, their defaults, and templates.
- Responsible for modifying object classes.

Normal Administrator:

- Responsible for implementing systems administration tasks.
- Responsible for configuring the HP-UX operating system.
- Responsible for changing the kernel configuration if drivers/subsystems must be added.
- Responsible for adding/modifying user/group accounts.
- Responsible for setting up/altering file systems.
- Responsible for managing the LP spooler.

IT/Administration sets a limit of no more than three senior administrators per copy of IT/Administration. By default, a senior administrator also has normal administrator capabilities.

Domains

IT/Administration enforces the practice of dividing the distributed computing environment into domains, which are hierarchically organized in a tree structure. The highest domain is the Root Domain; the lowest domain consists only of managed nodes. The idea of containment is supported within domains; that is, a node such as a workstation, can be viewed as a "container" for all objects belonging to that node, such as interface cards, device drivers, and files in that workstation.

Domains and nodes are assigned to administrators, who are then reponsible for managing them. The concept of domains can be further refined by use of *management areas*. Management areas define administrator access rights to different groups of object classes; administrators can be assigned to specific management areas. For example, 10 Unix servers may comprise a management domain; one administrator is assigned the management area of Users, Groups, and Installed Software, while another administrator is assigned the management areas of Kernel and Disks. Management areas may overlap, just as domains may overlap. Table 12.2 shows the default management areas provided by IT/Administration.

One advantage of management areas is that they simplfy the process of defining access permissions for normal administrators.

Policies

Policies are one type of Abstract Object. Although generally speaking, *policy* is thought of as a set of authorized procedures, IT/Administration defines the word to mean a specific range of valid values for a selected object attribute. In other words, an IT/Administration policy ensures consistency throughout the managed environment by restricting the values of a parameter—be it the access rights of users in a particular group, or the minimal amount of free swap space on all the Unix systems in the managed domain, etc.

Only senior administrators can define policies, as sloppy policy management can lead to conflicts in valid values, giving rise to deadlocks. If a deadlock occurs, the senior administrator can disable the policy checking mechanism.

Modes

IT/Administration supports three modes of operation:

- Scheduled
- Immediate
- Simulated

Table 12.2 IT/Administration Default Management Areas

Management area	Object classes
Node	Unix or NT system
Users and groups	User, group
Unix kernel	HP-UX kernel, drivers, kernel parameters, kernel device
Disk	File systems, HP-UX disk configuration, exported directories, hardware interface, interface card, partition, swap
Installed software	Software management services, software remove option, installation option, software root, installed product, installed subproduct, installed fileset
Software depots	Software management services, software remove option, depot copy option, depot, depot product, depot subproduct, depot fileset
Spooling	LP Spooler spool, remote print protocol, printer link software, rlp daemon, LP printer model, remote cancel model, remote status model
Interface	Network cards, interface cards

Scheduled Mode is the default mode. The administrator must specify a date and time for the change to occur. To create a Scheduled configuration change, such as changing a user's access rights or scheduling a software distribution, the administrator must create a sequence of changes, called a *Change Group*, then enter a comment describing the change, and specify a date and time for the change to be downloaded. When changes are downloaded they are also tracked by the product's Change Audit Manager. The administrator responsible for the change is noted.

In contrast, changes made while the system is in Immediate Mode will take effect right away. Obviously, Immediate Mode must be used with caution. Any changes made in Immediate Mode are automatically logged in the Change Audit Manager.

Simulated Mode allows administrators to view how the system configuration will look once schedule changes are made. Upon entering Simulated Mode, the administrator selects a *simulation base*, which is one or more change groups. The system then displays the effects of the configuration changes in salmon on the screen.

IT/Administration provides a Mode Manager window for switching from one mode to another. The Mode Manager window is opened each time the product is launched or restarted.

Synchronization

IT/Administration provides an open, flexible mechanism for controlling, administering, and tracking changes made to the distributed computing environment. It is possible, even likely, that unauthorized changes sometimes will be made even when IT/Administration is installed in a real network. IT/Administration provides a synchronization facility for detecting unauthorized changes, such as a user-add or software download. A Synchronization Manager displays the differences between the network's real configuration and configuration as specified in the IT/Administration database.

Administrators can manually trigger the synchronization process, or it can be scheduled to occur periodically. Synchronization also can occur automatically, continuously. Synchronization messages can be displayed as alerts on the HP OpenView NNM Event Browser window.

Queries

Queries are used to gather information about the actual configuration of the managed computing environment. IT/Administration supports two types of queries: predefined and user-defined. IT/Administration provides a number of predefined queries. Logical operators (AND, OR, NOT) can be used in many combinations to create more powerful queries.

Integration with HP OpenView NNM and Other Systems

HP Software Distributor

IT/Administration includes the functionality of HP OpenView Software Distributor. This capability, found in the IT/Administration package under the *.SD* directory, includes a set of tools for packaging, distributing, installing, and removing software in networked environments. The bundled functionality of Software Distributor with IT/Administrations allows administrators to define consistent policies for software management across the enterprise. This includes distributing updated versions of software as well as taking inventory of existing applications in use.

HP Software Distributor (SD) comprises several architectural elements:

- SD Depot (process *swagentd*)
- SD Controller
- Target Systems, each supporting the SD agent (process *swagent*)

A central SD depot for storing software must be established. It can be set up on any supported Unix system, and need not be dedicated. The system should be accessible by all target machines. Since Unix is a multitasking operating system, the logical roles of an SD depot, SD control, and Unix target system could be combined in one or two machines. Software distribution to PCs, however, requires a separate PC file server and controller to govern the software for desktop systems.

SD has two modes of operation:

- Push, in which the central administrator on the HP-UX SD controller installs the software on the target systems. The SD command set need not be enabled on the target systems.

- Pull, in which end users are responsible for installing the software themselves; thus, the SD command set must be installed and enabled on the target systems.

Communication among the SD Controllers, the SD Depot, and the targets is based on DCE RPCs. The SD Controller must run on HP-UX, but agents can run on HP-UX, Solaris, SunOS, DOS, or Window/Windows NT systems. TCP/IP network connections are required.

Every system managed by SD is protected by a range of Access Control Lists (ACLs). Five different levels of permission can be granted by each ACL. SD authorization uses ACLs to determine the RPC caller's right to access a particular SD object in a particular way—read, write, etc. An object's ACL is searched for an entry that matches the caller. Once a matching entry is found, the access rights are compared with those required by the operation. If the necessary permissions have been granted, access is authorized, and SD proceeds with the request.

SD supports the POSIX 1387.2 standard specifying software packaging structure. This common packaging format enables software to be processed on any conformant system. To date, HP and Platinum Technologies are the only two major software distribution vendors to adhere to POSIX 1387.2 standards.

HP OpenView NNM

As mentioned previously, HP in 1996 bundled HP OpenView Network Node Manager (NNM) with IT/Administration when the product was renamed from AdminCenter. NNM's OVWindows process is installed on the management server with IT/Administration. However, the GUI can be displayed on a separate client station. IT/Administration can be launched from NNM, and is integrated with the NNM Event service. Similarly, IT/Adminstration is integrated with HP's Software Distributor to perform software installations under the change control policies specified using IT/Administration.

Third-Party Applications

The intial releases of AdminCenter and IT/Administration did not support published APIs; hence, there are no third-party applications yet marketed as integrated with IT/Administration. HP plans to open up these interfaces in

1997, if not sooner. IT/Administration's model-based reasoning facility, according to HP, also should enable integration with third-party and customer-written applications.

IT/Administration for Workgroups

In May 1996, HP introduced IT/Administration for Workgroups, an adaptation of IT/Administration designed for managing interconnected workgroups of Windows and Windows-NT based PCs. For more information on IT/Administration for Workgroups, see Chap. 13.

Competing Alternatives

Several competing products support the same or similar functions provided by IT/Administration. These products include Boole & Babbage Ensign, Computer Associate's CA-Unicenter, and Tivoli Systems' Tivoli/Admin.

Table 12.3 compares features and functions of IT/Administration with these competing products.

IT/Administration is similar in nature to Tivoli's Admin in that both packages are object-oriented and support policy-based management. Tivoli/Admin shipped well over a year ahead of IT/Administration, and now that IBM has acquired Tivoli, the product is expected to be more heavily marketed and more frequently updated. Ensign from Boole & Babbage competes with IT/Administration to some degree, but Ensign's ease of deployment allows it to be targeted at medium-size networks as well as at larger environments. CA/Unicenter is also a competitor to IT/Administration; however, CA's monolithic packaging tends to make that product more attractive for centralized environments and less attractive for highly distributed environments.

Summary

IT/Administration targets configuration and change control of software, peripherals, file systems, and even user-related data. HP designed IT/Administration to be highly object-oriented. As such, it is extremely flexible, but configuration requires some effort.

IT/Administration maintains an inventory of configured Managed Objects. The product also supports policy-based management, allowing an organization to assign different responsibilities to different systems administrations as appropriate by creating customized management domains.

IT/Administration is similar in nature to Tivoli's Admin, a policy-based user administration and security tool that takes advantage of Tivoli's object-oriented framework. Tivoli/Admin shipped well over a year ahead of IT/Administration. Ensign from Boole & Babbage also competes with IT/Administration to some degree, but Ensign's ease of deployment allows it to be targeted at medium-sized networks as well as at larger environments.

Table 12.3 Comparative Features of HP IT/Administration and Its Competitors

A Comparison of product features Function	Boole Ensign	CA Unicenter	HP	Tivoli TME
Automation	Metalanguage	Scripts	Scripts	Prolog-type 4GL
Backup	Yes	Yes	Extra-cost option—HP OmniBack	Extra-cost option
Recovery	Yes	Yes	Extra-cost option—HP OmniBack	Extra-cost option
Storage management	No	Yes	Extra-cost option— OmniStorage	Extra-cost option—third-party
File admin	Yes	Yes	Yes	Extra-cost option— Tivoli/FSM
Printer admin	Yes	Yes	Extra-cost option—HP OpenSpool	Extra-cost option— Tivoli/Print
User admin	Yes	Yes	Yes	Extra-cost option— Tivoli/Admin
Workload balancing	Third party (4th Dim.)	Yes	Third party (Unison)	Yes
File distribution	Yes	Extra-cost option— Software Delivery	Yes, via —Hp Software Distributor	Extra-cost option—Courier
Software distribution	Third party (Tangram)	Extra-cost option— Software Delivery	Yes, via—HP Software Distributor	Extra-cost option—Courier

IV

Interconnected Workgroup Management

OpenView Workgroup Node Manager and Other HP Workgroup Products

This chapter describes several HP products that address workgroup and inter-connected workgroup management. They are:

- HP OpenView Workgroup Node Manager (WNM), also called OpenView for Windows
- IT/Administration for Workgroups
- AssetView

In addition, the chapter discusses HP's migration strategy for bringing the functionalilty of Unix-based products, such as IT/Operations and NNM, to Windows NT environments.

An Introduction to HP OpenView Workgroup Node Manager

HP first introduced its Windows-based OpenView product in the early 1990s. The initial releases were aimed primarily at the OEM community. The product was successful in this form; major device vendor Cabletron, for example, added its own device-specific management to HP's Windows-based SNMP system, reselling the product by the thousands as Remote LANView, an entry-level hub management application.

In May 1993, HP announced an end-user version of HP OpenView for Windows, renaming it HP OpenView Workgroup Node Manager (WNM). To support the end-user customer base, HP bundled in several new applications, including a remote control PC software (a version of Intel's LANdesk DTRemote), a paging utility (a version of Notify!), and Visual Basic facilities for extending or building custom applications.

WNM still does not include any embedded features for many functions that customers generally associate with desktop or workgroup management, including PC hardware/software inventory, user administration, virus protection, software distribution, software licensing and metering, or trouble ticketing. WNM cannot actively manage PCs lacking SNMP MIBs—and that includes most pre-Windows95 PCs. While WNM supports browsing of Desktop Management Interface (DMI) components, few PCs installed today support DMI (for more information on DMI, see Chap. 2). Over the course of time, however, more PCs will ship with SNMP- and DMI-compliant subsystems.

Consequently, HP positions WNM as a desktop management *platform* upon which third parties can create client/server management applications. As with NNM, HP is counting on third parties to come forward and fill in the gaps by creating value-added applications that will complement the core OpenView WNM facilities described below.

Close to 50 third-party vendors have expressed some level of commitment to delivering HP-certified integrated applications for WNM. As of late 1996, only a handful of these vendors had completed the certification process, which requires icon-level communications in addition to menu-level integration. To meet customer demands for a more prepackaged solution, HP in 1996 introduced the Workgroup Node Manager Professional Suite.

This suite, which is sold through HP's reseller channels for under $2000, includes the following bundled applications:

- Symantec Norton Administrator for Networks (NAN)
- Network Integration's Windows NT and Novell NetWare server management
- A DMI Management Information File (MIF) browser and Remote DMI client

Symantec's NAN supports PC hardware and software inventory as well as software distribution and software metering. The product's hardware inventory facility supports more than 300 fields of information (Francett, 1995) and software inventory recognizes more than 1500 off-the-shelf applications. The software metering facilities support automatic rollup of license logs from multiple sites to a central site, and suite metering capabilities for predefined or user-defined suites. In addition to supporting Windows systems, NAN supports DOS, OS/2, and Macs running on NetWare, Vines, NT, LAN Manager, LAN Server, and PathWorks LANs. The version included in the Workgroup Professional Suite supports a five-client license for software distribution.

The DMI MIF browser is architecturally significant, but until more DMI-enabled components find their way into corporate networks, the capability will be underutilized.

In summary, WNM is a platform offering a few basic functions for desktop management; it can be easily enhanced by the addition of third-party and customer-developed applications to form a more comprehensive solution. In this respect, WNM is similar to HP OpenView Network Node Manager (NNM). It is important for customers to understand that WNM and NNM are very different products. WNM is *not* HP OpenView Network Node Manager running under

Windows. WNM has a different code base and different set of APIs—and a much different set of capabilities and limitations.

Using WNM

Differences between Unix and MS-DOS/Windows demand a different architecture for HP OpenView for Windows. These differences are evident in the user interface and application programming interfaces (APIs) in particular.

The user interface is Windows 3.1. HP enhances the environment with a Network Device Map and Alarm and Event Handling services. Applications interface to the map through the HP OpenView for Windows APIs. The map system provides background (bitmap), symbol, and submap support.

The Event Manager works exactly like its Unix counterpart. One important difference is the capability to link different sound files to various status files, allowing critical errors to sound like ringing alarms or to play back prerecorded human speech files. The Event Manager logs events in a Paradox database file.

The SNMP Manager is a higher-level MIB browser. It provides SNMP agent access and displays MIB information as graphics or text. The OpenView for Windows MIB compiler can exchange MIBs with its Unix counterpart. The SNMP Manager also features a block read and set utility, easing reading and configuring multiple MIB variables within the same device.

WNM provides facilities for discovering and polling IP and IPX network nodes, including bridges, hubs, routers, and IPX servers. To support these facilities, WNM includes embedded IPX stack and a TCP/IP stack from FTP Software. Banyan Vines/IP also is provided, as shown in Fig. 13.1 (Francett 1996).

Discovery

WNM supports two types of discovery: Basic (IP) and Extended (IPX). Both types are supported by background processes. While Basic Discovery behaves somewhat like HP OpenView Network Node Manager (NNM), Extended Discovery is not at all similar to the discovery processes supported by NNM.

Basic Discovery queries neighboring router ARP caches to discover and identify all IP devices. As with NNM, however, proper IP subnet masks should be supplied, as well as the IP networks you want to discover. Otherwise, the product may venture beyond your company's boundaries and begin discovering the entire Internet.

Extended Discovery uses NetWare diagnostic services to locate all IPX devices. SNMP *Get* commands are then used to identify the devices. Administrators can specify a maximum number of IPX nodes to be discovered.

Both Basic (IP) and Extended (IPX) discovery can be scheduled to run automatically, such as at night or over the weekend. Once discovery is complete, administrators can create a network map manually by selecting from the prepared list of discovered devices. Alternately, the Basic Layout command creates submaps according to a hierarchical structure, as shown in Fig. 13.2. Administrators may then manually annotate the submaps by adding notation or bitmaps, for example. Once submaps are customized in this manner, they should be renamed, otherwise they may be overwritten by WNM when the discovery process is run again.

Maps that are automatically generated may be confusing and list many more devices than necessary from a network administrator's point of view. Rather than pruning and annotating automatically generated maps, it might be easier to create submaps manually. The steps involved in creating submaps follow:

- List all devices to be represented on the map (note the network address of each device and its relation to the other devices).

- Organize the devices hierarchically into levels based on their network position, device type, or function.

- Create a *home* submap.

- Create second-level submaps.

- Add additional submaps as desired to create alternate views of the network (e.g., a view of all hubs, a view of all routers, etc.).

As one might surmise, even with NNM's discovery and map-generating features, the process of creating usable network maps and submaps is far from automatic. No matter what route chosen, the administrator will end up customizing the view, adding lines to show connectivity relationships, and inserting bitmap background maps and other graphical elements.

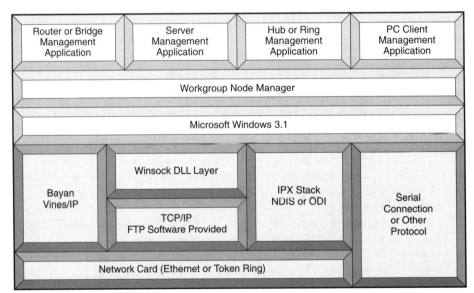

FTP   =   File Transfer protocol
NDIS =   Network Device Interface Specification
ODI   =   Open Data-link Interface

Source: HP OpenView Advisor, November 1995 ®McGraw-Hill.

Figure 13.1 HP OpenView Workgroup Node Manager (WNM) Architecture

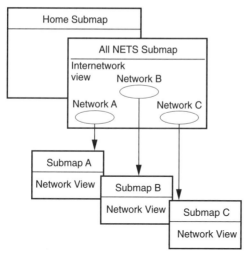

Figure 13.2 HP OpenView WNM Basic Layout Mapping Function

SNMP polling and trap facilities

WNM allows administrators to poll network devices at predefined intervals to obtain status and behavior information. WNM also monitors asynchronously generated SNMP trap messages that alert administrators of status change or failure.

To poll devices, the network administrator must create a list of devices based on IP or IPX address. Polling parameters must be selected, including:

1. Polling interval

2. Severity of alarm

3. Form of notification (update map, sound bell, or log)

The values of these variables may be displayed in various graphical outputs on the WNM screen, as listed in Table 13.1.

Administrators can use WNM to set thresholds on SNMP MIB variables so that alarms are generated when thresholds are exceeded. Alarms also may be generated by traps. WNM automatically logs all SNMP traps received, and administrators can specify that particular traps should update the WNM map or produce an audible alarm. Traps must be specifed by device class, as indicated by the system object ID, and trap ID.

Alarms

Alarms are generated by traps or when thresholds are crossed. Alarms may be logged, displayed on the screen, or they may trigger a sound on the console. Alarms also may be forwarded to other consoles.

The categories of alarm severity include:

- Critical
- Major
- Minor
- Warning
- Marginal
- Informational
- Disabled
- Unmanaged
- Normal
- Unknown

It is not difficult to imagine that an administrator would not want to be distracted by informational alarms. As a result, most alarms are merely logged. Administrators can display selected groups of alarms from the alarm log, although the filters are rather general. Alarm log filters include:

- Alarm type
- Object type
- Object name
- Object status

WNM provides only rudimentary facilities for filtering alarms. The product does, however, allow administrators to trigger an MS-DOS or Windows program when an alarm is generated. Information about the alarm can be passed

Table 13.1 SNMP Polling Graph Options for WNM

Command	Description
Polling	Polling sets the number of seconds between updates when a query (SNMP GET) is performed; the range is from 1 to 6000 seconds. For example, if polling is set to 5, polls will occur every 5 seconds. If zero (0) is selected, polling will occur only once, at startup.
Samples	Indicates sample size for displaying the query as a graph. If the sample size is set to 10 (the default), the graph will display the last 10 sample points—one point for each poll.
Community	SNMP devices can restrict access to MIB variables by using Community names; it is a very loose form of a password.
Graph type	3D bar, line
Graph style	Presentation style—vertical bars
Grid	A grid may be added to a graph; the default is no grid.
Legend	A legend may be added to a graph. The default is that legends are included.
Print color	Print the graph in color (gray is the default).

**Table 13.4. Differences between IT/Administration (Enterprise)
and IT/Administration for Workgroups**

IT/Administration for Workgroups	IT/Administration
Does not include NNM	Includes NNM
Does not support user-definable queries and policies	Supports user-definable queries and policies
Manages up to 250 nodes	Manages up to thousands of nodes
Provides 25 predefined PC queries	Does not include predefined PC queries
Does not support Administrator roles	Supports Administrator roles
Does not support Simulation mode	Supports Simulation mode
Requires HP-UX; can redirect display to PC or X terminal	Requires HP-UX

long-term costs of maintaining and upgrading their networks at reasonable levels. AssetView lets managers control range of assets, including PCs, workstations, laptops, cellular phones, and test and measurement equipment. The software can link with enterprise management platforms such as HP OpenView, facilities management software from Accugraph, and Norton Administration Metering from Symantec.

Controlling costs and achieving an optimum return from technology have become far more complicated in the distributed environment of this decade. Assets have become widely dispersed and less visible. Today, 80 to 85 percent of the technology budget is spent, not on hardware and software, but on soft costs, including purchasing, installing, and managing technology, and training and supporting those who are using it. This presents an opportunity, as well as a challange. AssetView helps customers to manage assets and increase productivity by providing the right information at the right time to make the right decision. AssetView provides software and services that:

- Optimize asset utilization
- Manage and control software licensing
- Identify and establish standards
- Reduce support costs
- Expedite migrations
- Maximize buying power
- Manage contracts
- Charge back costs
- Forecast for the future

The overall AssetView System architecture is shown in Fig. 13.5.

AssetView is part of a complex process including needs analysis and inventory steps. *Needs analysis* is an initial study that assesses existing asset man-

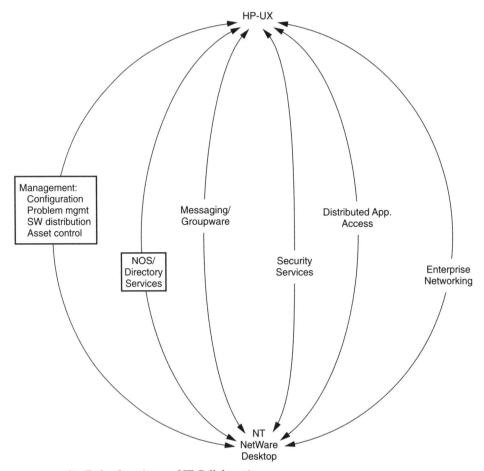

Figure 13.4 Six Technology Areas of IT Collaboration

agement processes and information needs. The analysis identifies areas in which savings will be achieved through better access to asset information. *Inventory* is a comprehensive inventory of assets produced by Hewlett-Packard or the customer. Trained specialists collect the data using automated tools and processes. Inventory can include any assets, whether networked or mobile, even noncomputer assets. Assets are bar-coded for efficient tracking in the future.

AssetView applications

Inventory data is loaded into AssetView, a comprehensive system providing up to 400 kinds of data for unlimited assets, whether networked or off-network, or even noncomputing, such as copiers and PBXs. Data includes user profiles, lease and maintenance contract details, acquisition costs, as well as component-level technical information.

Updating inventory data. The database is kept current through HP AssetLink, an integrated set of communication links. Moves, adds, changes, or deletes can be communicated via network linkages, e-mail, fax forms, and 800 numbers in the United States.

Management reports. Asset information is provided via any category the customer chooses: user, location, functional area, product type, manufacturer/vendor, lessor, etc. The user defines which reports are required and when reports are needed. Standard and customized reports are available on a regular or ad hoc basis.

Online access. Real-time access to data can be provided to network administrators, help-desk attendants, and other users, enabling drill-down for configuration, financial, user, and contract data. Online access can improve response time by providing user profiles, network connectivity, and service history.

Integration. AssetView can be linked to other applications for enhanced operations. For example, linkages can be made to network management such as

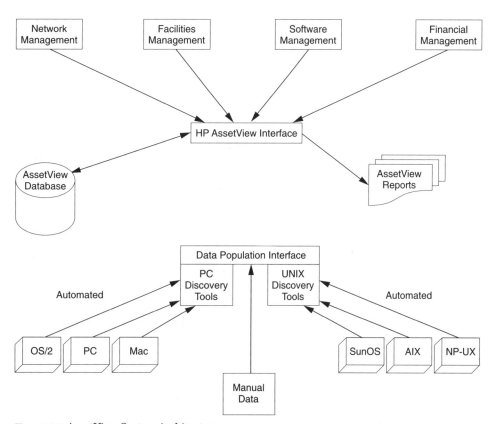

Figure 13.5 AssetView System Architecture

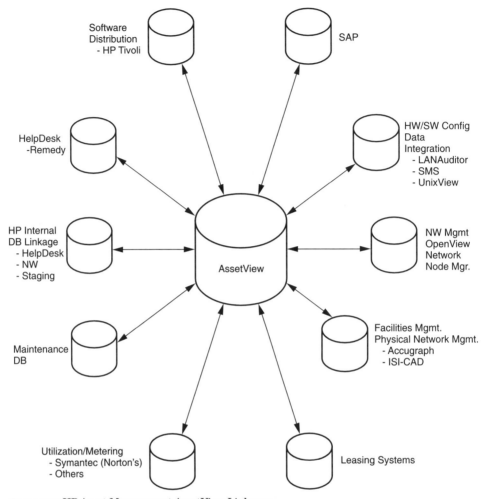

Figure 13.6 HP Asset Management AssetView Linkages

HP OpenView, help desk, change management, and facilities management applications. Linkages are shown in Fig. 13.6.

The principal features of the product include support for an unlimited number of assets, and multiplatform design, including Windows, DOS, Macintosh, or Unix platforms. More than 400 types of data can be included in the data repository. Assets can be located by geography, site, building, or office cubicle: identified by organization unit, such as subsidiary, sector, division, or department. Figure 13.7 illustrates the central repository indicating asset type, data categories, and data elements.

Asset types are not limited to networks. HP uses automated polling technology to maintain accurate data. HP also tracks off-network assets (laptops, stand-alone PCs, faxes), nonnetwork data such as employee identification, purchase orders, and data for regarding contracts, warranties, serial numbers, depreciation, and disposition, and even noncomputing assets such as copiers, PBXs, and others.

Worldwide capabilities include multicountry implementations to meet global customer needs.

AssetView is available as a product offering only, or as a combination of product and professional services. Table 13.5 shows the basic functions supported by AssetView product only, AssetView product combined with services, or services only.

Changeable plans are supported by the data repository. On the basis of this database, the user can change the selection of standard and customized reports, and order ad hoc queries as the need arises.

Linkages to other applications, including network management products, graphical representation of asset data, and links to other applications, are supported. Other links can be established to help-desk operations, procurement processes, and accounting/general ledger management.

The product supports a reasonable level of automation for asset discovery for multiple platforms to facilitate the population of AssetView. The need for manual population is minimal. Related services are provided for training, data validation, bar code inventory, and other services to ensure a successful implementation and life cycle of the product.

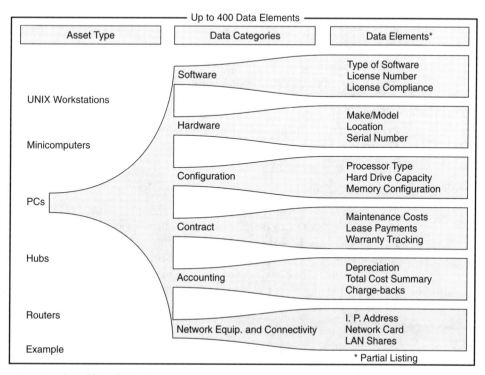

Figure 13.7 AssetView Central Repository

Table 13.5. Various Combinations of AssetView Product and Services

HP AssetView product only	HP AssetView product and services	HP services only
Customer builds and manages own program on HP AssetView	Customer builds own program on HP AssetView using HP services to "jump-start" the implementation	Customers outsource the process to HP and simply receive information where/when they want it
Option: HP performs needs analysis to guide implementation	HP AssetView; Option: HP performs needs analysis to guide implementation	Option: HP performs needs analysis to guide implementation
Option: HP performs inventory	HP performs inventory	HP performs inventory
Option: HP loads data	HP loads and validates data	HP loads and validates data
Option: HP integrates with other applications	Option: HP integrates with other applications	HP maintains database

Agent Support for Workgroup Environments

In March 1996, HP announced a series of enhancements to existing HP OpenView products involving extensions for supporting Windows NT and NetWare workgroup environments. These enhancements included NT and NetWare agents for IT/Operations, NT agents for MeasureWare, and NT agents for OmniBack II. At the same time, HP announced plans to port several products to NT, including NNM, NetMetrix, IT/Operations, and IT/Administration.

Table 13.6 lists the products, functions, and product release dates for workgroup agents. Table 13.7 summarizes the NT porting plans for key HP OpenView products.

Summary

HP OpenView is often seen as primarily targeting Unix-based open systems and networks. There are, however, a number of OpenView products for managing PC-based workgroups, including HP OpenView Workgroup Node Management, IT/Administration for Workgroups, and AssetView for tracking desktop and other connected assets across the enterprise. HP is migrating both the management server and agent portions of many OpenView products to full support for Windows, NetWare, and Windows NT systems.

Table 13.6. Workgroup Agents and Modules from HP

Workgroup agents and modules from HP	Product release date	Function
IT/Operations agent for Windows NT	1H96	Operations and problem management
IT/Operations agent for Novell NetWare	2H96	Operations and problem management
MeasureWare NOS Connectivity Module for NT NetWare	1Q96	Resource and performance management
MeasureWare agent for Windows NT	2H96	Resource and performance management
MeasureWare Database module for Windows NT	2H96	Resource and performance management
MeasureWare Client for Windows 3.x, 95, and NT	2H96	Resource and performance management
IT/Administration agent for Windows NT	2H96	Configuration and change management
IT/Administration agent for Novell NetWare	1Q96	Configuration and change management
Software Distributor agent for Windows NT and NetWare	2H95	Software distribution
OpenSpool Windows GUI for Windows NT	1H96	Print management
OmniBack II media agent for Windows NT	1H96	Backup management
OmniBack II disk agent for Win95	1H96	Backup management
OmniBack II disk agent for Windows NT	2H95	Backup management
OmniBack II disk agent for Novell NetWare	2H95	Backup management

Table 13.7. HP OpenView Products Supporting Windows NT

HP OpenView products supporting windows NT	Product release date	Function
Network Node Manager for Windows NT	2H96	Network management
PerView for Windows NT	2H96	Resource and performance management
NetMetrix for Windows NT	2H96	Resource and performance management
OmniBack II for Windows NT	2H96	Backup management
IT/Operations for Windows NT	Statement of direction	Operations and problem management
IT/Administration for Windows NT	Statement of direction	Configuration and change management

HP OpenView and Internet and Intranet Management

In mid-1996, Internet/intranet management became a major industry buzz-word, used cavalierly by many vendors seeking to add "freshness" to the positioning of their existing management tools. There is some substance to this trend, however, as more and more corporations explore use of the Internet—particularly the World Wide Web (WWW)—to gather information from global resources in a speedy manner, and to disseminate information both corporately and publicly. While *Internet* implies electronic commerce with outside suppliers and customers, the term *intranet* is used when Internet and WWW technologies are used strictly within the confines of an organization, with no or limited access to the outside Internet.

With the explosive popularity of Web use, the issues of Internet and intranet management have become relevant topics. At the same time, the Web is being considered as a replacement for X terminals for sharing management data among remote network administrators when no formal manager-to-manager communications have been pre-established.

A valid intranet/Web management strategy must examine several issues:

- Effective leveraging of Internet/Web technology by the corporation, including management of the Internet/intranet infrastructure.
- Management and testing of Web applications.
- Management of the actual Web servers.
- Management of Web page status.
- Monitoring of Web usage by employees.
- Establishment and enforcement of corporatewide Web usage policies.
- Use of Web as a vehicle for exchanging management data: Is it secure? Is it reliable? Is it efficient?

Any vendor's so-called Internet/intranet management strategy should be examined to see how these various points are addressed. At present, most vendors, including HP, address some subset but not all of the above requirements. This chapter considers these points when comparing HP's Internet management strategy to that of its chief competitor, Tivoli. A description of Platinum's Web application testing and capacity planning tools also are included. Before Internet/intranet management product comparisons can be made, it is important to understand more about the foundations of Web technology.

Web Technology

The World Wide Web is an Internet technology that is layered on top of basic TCP/IP services. The Web is now the most popular Internet application next to electronic mail (Schulzrinne 1996). Like most successful Internet technologies, the underlying central functionality of the Web is rather simple:

- A file naming mechanism: the Universal Resource Locator, or *URL*

- A typed, stateless retrieval protocol: Hypertext Transfer Protocol (HTTP)

- A minimal formatting language with hypertext links: Hypertext Markup Language (HTML)

URL

The Universal Resource Locator (URL) is part of a larger family of file naming mechanisms called Universal Resource Names (URNs), which are used to designate objects within the WWW. URLs name the physical location of an object; URNs name the identity without regard to location. Uniform Resource Citations (URCs) describe properties of an object. At this time, only URLs are in widespread use (Schulzrinne 1996). The URL is the *home page* address, such as:

http://www.int.snmp.com

Like TCP/IP, SNMP, and other popular protocols, URLs originally were considered to be temporary solutions until more powerful mechanisms could be developed. The simplicity and intuitive nature of URLs no doubt contributed to their rapid acceptance.

HTTP

HTTP is the protocol used for access and retrieval of Web pages. As such, it is widely viewed as the *core* Web protocol. It is an application-level protocol used almost exclusively with TCP. The client, typically a Web browser, asks the Web server for some information via a GET request. The information exchanged by HTTP can be any data type, and is not limited to HTML.

HTTP usage has surpassed that of older Internet access and retrieval mechanisms such as File Transfer Protocol (FTP), Telnet, and Gopher. These older services often coexist with and are supported by HTTP-based Web browsers.

HTTP is a simple protocol; its clients and servers are said to be *stateless* because they do not have to remember anything beyond the transfer of a single document. But HTTP's simplicity results in inefficiency; for a typical HTML page, the client first retrieves the HTML page, then discovers the potentially dozens of images contained within the page, and issues a separate HTTP request for each (Schulzrinne 1996). Each HTTP request requires a separate TCP connection. To overcome this multistep process, typical Web browsers may open several TCP connections at once, a practice that may overload slower-speed links.

HTTP is a textual protocol—all headers are transferred as mostly ASCII text—which simplifies the creation of simple browsers.

HTML

Web browsers have become widely popular because they all share understanding of a simple media type, HTML formatting language. HTML is easy to understand, and can be written by hand or generated from other text formats by translators (Schulzrinne 1996). HTML is actually a simple document type of the Standardized Generalized Markup Language (SGML).

HTML is simpler than *nroff* and other document languages in that it is not programmable. As a result, the descriptive capabilities of HTML are limited to low-level constructs, such as emphasis or indented lists. But because HTML parsers are rather forgiving of HTML coding violations, many Web pages contain coding "mistakes" used purposely to achieve particular layout effects on popular browsers (Schulzrinne 1996).

HTML is optimized for display rather than printing or storage. HTML has no notion of pages, making formatted printing difficult. Request for Comment (RFC) 1866 describes HTML 2.0 in detail.

Web browsers

Web browers function as clients, asking Web servers for information by using the HTTP protocol. Each request is handled by its own TCP connection and is independent of each previous request. As noted earlier, just the retrieval of one HTML page may require establishing several TCP connections. Consequently, network managers need to be aware of the resource limitations of their intranet infrastructure when rolling out Web applications, since Web usage is significantly resource-consumptive.

Examples of popular Web browsers include:

- Mosaic
- Netscape
- HotJava
- Webspace

These and other Web browers are being used more and more to support internally developed corporate Web applications, ranging from company job postings and notices about benefit policy updates, to supporting Lotus Notes-based groupware activities. In addition, Web technology is used to support commerce with the outside world. In many cases, Web servers capable of supporting this type of external activity can be purchased off the shelf. Examples of these types of Web servers include the following (Muller 1996):

- Connect Oneserver
- Navisoft/AOL Naviserver
- Netscape Commerce Server
- Open Market Webserver
- Secureware Secure Web Servers
- Spry Internet Office Web Server
- Spyglass Server

Hewlett-Packard currently supports or is planning to support the Navisoft/AOL, Netscape, and Open Market servers on HP-UX.

The next section includes a case study extracted from (Muller 1996) describing how HP IT/Operations can be used to manage a Netscape Commerce Server.

HP's Internet/Intranet Management Strategy

HP is targeting OpenView NNM at Internet/intranet infrastructure management rather than at Web servers and services. HP promotes a three-tier OpenView strategy for managing and leveraging the Internet:

- Manage the corporate Intranet infrastructure, including the network infrastructure, servers and Internet applications, and security.
- Manage the infrastructure of Internet service providers.
- Leverage Internet technologies in OpenView solutions.

The enhancements in NNM 4.1 significantly increased the product's scalability, making OpenView-based management of corporate Internet/intranet infrastructures possible. Management of Web servers and applications is largely provided by the generic server and application management capabilities of IT/Operations, described later in this section.

HP is targeting management of Internet service providers' infrastructures through its HP OpenView DM offering, described in Chap. 10, and HP OpenView Event Correlation Services, described in Chap. 18. Internet service providers may include carriers, cable companies, value added networks (VANs), and others.

Finally, HP is exploring and prototyping Web technology extensions to OpenView products, including the following:

- Web access to OpenView event repositories for problem management support
- Web access to the OpenView map
- Internet as a software transport vehicle

Using IT/Operations for Internet Management

As Chap. 11 describes, IT/Operations is capable of managing processes and applications running on any computer for which HP provides an IT/Operations agent. Supported systems include HP-UX, Solaris, AIX, SCO, and in 1997, Windows NT, among others. IT/Operations agents are capable of intercepting SNMP traps, Unix logfile messages, and events generated when IT/Operations agents detect threshold crossings.

The following case study, excerpted from (Muller 1996), describes how IT/Operations can be used to manage Netscape Commerce Servers.

Case study

The Netscape Commerce Server runs under HP-UX and supports secure electronic commerce and communications on the Internet and TCP/IP intranets. The server permits corporations to publish HTML-formatted documents (Web pages) and deliver them using HTTP. To ensure data security, the Netscape Commerce Server provides server authentication, data encryption, and user authorization. Communications support includes the Common Gateway Interface (CGI) and the Secure Sockets Layer (SSL) protocol.

To support manageability, the Netscape Commerce Server records several kinds of errors, all of which can be collected by an IT/Operations agent reading the server's logfile. These errors include the following:

- *Unauthorized*, which occurs when users attempt to access protected server documents without proper permission.
- *Forbidden*, which occurs when the server lacks file system permissions needed to execute a read or to follow symbolic links.
- *Not Found*, which occurs when the server can't find a document or has been instructed to deny a document's existence.
- *Server Error*, which occurs when the server has been misconfigured or affected by core dump, out of memory, or other catastrophic error.

HP provides an IT/Operations template for handling these errors. Users can devise proper responses, including forwarding events to the appropriate IT/Operations or database operators, or triggering a script for deleting hypertext links to documents that no longer exist, for example. Each error type described above can be associated with error codes. The most common HTTP error codes are as follows:

- **200** OK: Successful transmission, usually not recorded in error log.
- **302** Redirection to a new URL.

- **304** Use local copy. The client asked for a document, and the server told it to fetch the document from its cache.
- **401** Unauthorized. A proper username or password was not supplied.
- **403** Forbidden, access denied.
- **404** Not found, access denied. The user is told that the document doesn't exist (sometimes used to deter interlopers).
- **500** Server error, logged.
- **8181** Certificate has expired (a message for secured servers only).

IT/Operations agents are capable of collecting these error messages and forwarding user-specified events to the IT/Operations console for operator attention and problem resolution. For example, in the case of error 500 (server error), possible causes of the problem may include the following:

- CGI is not enabled on the Web server (preventing electronic commerce application from running).
- Permissions have not been specified properly.
- CGI script is not specifying a shell or other program to be run.
- Syntax error in the script.

Syntax errors typically are resolved by tweaking application scripts, which may be written in CGI, Practical Extraction and Report Language (PERL), or Tool Command Language (TCL). Many Web server applications for electronic commerce are written in C language and implemented with CGI, PERL, or TCL scripts.

Monitoring Web page availability with IT/Operations

IT/Operations can be deployed to monitor Web page status as well as Web server status. Specific functions supported include:

- Monitoring Web access logfiles and error logfiles
- Monitoring the HTTP daemon
- Viewing server access statistics
- Integrating the native Netscape administration and configuration tools into IT/Operations
- Starting up and shutting down the Web server and administrative interface
- Modifying access configuration

HP has developed a script that can be used by the IT/Operations agent monitor to check the availability of the Web server system, the HTTP port, and the Web page. The script uses the Korn shell, one of four major Unix command and script interpreters in use today. This script, designed primarily for Netscape Commerce Server, theoretically can be modified and extended to monitor other Web servers as well.

Tivoli's Internet/Intranet Management Strategy

On March 25, 1996, the Tivoli Systems division of IBM announced its *net.TME* Internet management strategy. The net.TME initiative is targeted primarily at corporate customers using Internet services for internal or intranet communications.

The net.TME is a four-pronged strategy, including new Tivoli products, new interfaces supporting third-party Internet management applications, new Internet management standards spearheaded by Tivoli, and Web-enabling enhancements to Tivoli's existing product line (Huntington-Lee 1996d).

Products

The first new product announced is Tivoli/net.Commander, a specialized, bundled version of Tivoli/Sentry, Tivoli/Courier, and the Tivoli Management Environment (TME) framework, all optimized for managing aspects of the Internet environment.

The first release of Tivoli/net.Commander focused on deployment and configuration as well as availability and performance management for NetScape on Solaris and Microsoft Information Server on NT (Fig. 14.1). Subsequent releases add support for user access control, including mail alias management and enterprise user console integration. That release will support additional Web servers, including Open Market, Spyglass on Unix, Lotus InterNotes, and IBM ICS on Unix and Windows NT.

Tivoli/net.Commander auto-discovers all Internet servers and services, creating icons for each on the management console. The product then establishes dialogues for configuration and deployment, enabling administrators to more easily set up parameters for new servers. The Tivoli/Sentry component provides a scrolling list of monitors including one that moniors the size of Web server log files to ensure that they do not grow so large that they affect performance.

Tivoli/net.Commander also makes it easier to configure load balancing via DNS round robin management. DNS Round-robin is a widely used process for managing multiple Web servers; it uses a table-lookup algorithm that automatically connects those attempting to access a Web site to the next available Web server.

The initial version of net.Commander also supports out-of-the-box browser deployment for NetScape on Solaris and Microsoft Info Server for NT. This capability, supported by Tivoli/Courier, allows central IT administrators to push client browsers down to remote desktops. The benefit to this approach is a greater degree of centralized control over browser deployment, as well as embedded *helper applications* provided by net.Commander, and a standard set of *bookmarks* available to all users across the enterprise.

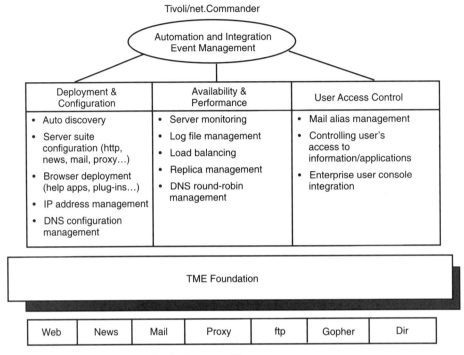

Tivoli/net.Commander

Figure 14.1 Tivoli/net.Commander for Internet Management

Typically, most end-user organizations today harbor a mish-mash of different browser versions and configurations across the enterprise, since individuals and departments simply FTP browsers down off the Internet at will. According to Tivoli, however, central IT staff is still held responsible for the performance and availability of these browsers, even if they were not deployed under the guidance of central IT organization.

Indeed, Tivoli believes that, as client/server systems evolve toward even greater degrees of network-centric computing, the degree of complexity involved in managing these systems will grow exponentially. Tivoli is positioning its distributed object technology, embodied in TME, as the only viable approach for managing the network-centric environment through a single, integrated interface (Huntington-Lee 1996d).

Tivoli's net.TME attempts to manage not only Web servers but also the new "cloud" of Internet services that include mail, proxy, news, gopher, directories, and FTP. When organizations deploy these Internet services, they enable a whole new class of Unix- or NT-based applications. Unlike traditional client/server applications supported by rigid, proprietary remote procedure call (RPC) connections to one or two servers, Internet-based applications can exhibit a truly global reach that is enterprise-or interenterprise-wide in scope. This environment poses a new set of management challenges.

Third-Party Application Support

One new challenge in particular is monitoring Web server activit: tracking who is *hitting* the Web server, and where. To this end, Tivoli also offers a Tivoli/Plus integration module linking Tivoli/Enterprise Console to a third-party application called Net.Analysis product from NetGenesis Corp. NetGenesis, a new company, is partially owned by McAfee and Tivoli.

Net.Analysis is designed to track and display real-time Web content usage. The product parses Web server logfiles and stores them in a relational database, allowing administrators to run reports showing who is hitting the Web site and which pages they are hitting. Currently, Net.Analysis is sold through McAfee's distribution channels; Tivoli sells Tivoli/Plus for Net.Analysis through its own direct sales and reseller channels.

Internet Management Standards

According to Tivoli, standards will be key to successful management of the Internet environment, simply because there are so many different Internet vendors and services with differing APIs and file formats. Because the ISV community won't be successful in this market unless standards are developed, Tivoli is spearheading a standards effort it calls Internet Management Standards, or IMS. IMS is expected to define standard APIs, allowing a management application to configure, monitor, and control access to Internet services such as mail, gopher, proxy, etc. IMS also will define a set of Java APIs in the future.

IBM, Sun, Spyglass, Netscape, and several other vendors have already publicly committed to the IMS effort as of this writing. Others are expected to endorse the fledgling IMS effort as time goes by.

Web-enabling TME products

The final plank of the net.TME platform is the introduction of Web-enabling technology to existing Tivoli products, including Web browser interfaces. This allows administrators as well as end users to access selected TME functions using a Web browser interface.

For example, laptop users will go through the Web browser to access Tivoli/Courier for the purpose of pulling down software distributions. The Web interface also provides an easier way for senior managers to obtain accurate real-time data on TME-managed resources, such as summarized reports tracking the number of software distributions completed or the problems detected and corrected automatically via TME.

Tivoli is correct in claiming that the scale of the computing environment has grown due to the proliferation of Web technology. Not only must network and systems administrators manage applications spanning multiple sites, but now face the possibility of inter-enterprise applications.

According to Tivoli, successful management of Internet environments requires an open, standards-based approach embracing a mastery of distributed object technology, as well as an integrating management of the existing client/server environment. Rather than managing individual servers, or using the Web with existing tools, Tivoli is seeking to promote use of an Internet Management Standard and to offer Web technology (integrated in TME).

Platinum Web Application Testing Tools

Platinum Technology is a leading supplier of database and systems management tools. In 1996, Platinum's Application Lifecycle Solutions division announced Final Exam Internet Test, a standalone environment for testing the reliability and performance of Internet-based commercial client/server applications. These tools test Web applications before they are deployed, and predict response time on clients and thresholds on servers. The Platinum tools can help administrators anticipate hardware requirements for handling resulting network (HTTP) traffic.

Final Exam Internet Test is not a real-time management solution, but an important capacity planning test suite. It supports HTML objects, providing an automatic capture/replay process to ensure thorough testing of applications that use Netscape and similar Web browsers. Final Exam analyzes the performance of clients and servers in Internet applications as they respond to various Web-user load levels. The product generates and monitors load stress tests under user-defined variable system loads.

Users can schedule, run, and control various load scenarios including unlimited numbers of virtual users on the load server, as well as real users on multiple client workstations. All clients, load servers, and web servers participating in the test session can reside anywhere on the Internet. All resulting data automatically is collected and collated. Status and load reports can be requested while the stress test is in progress, or at the conclusion. The reports provide statistical analysis and graphs illustrating performance results superimposed over the load status. Comparison of previous results to current results is also supported.

Final Exam runs on Windows 3.1, Windows NT, and Windows 95 as well as SunOS and Solaris. Additional Unix versions are forthcoming.

Summary

Internet/intranet management is a hot topic, due to rapid proliferation of Web-based technology through corporations and other organizations. There are many facets of Internet/intranet management. Like many vendors, HP is just beginning to articulate its Internet and intranet management strategy. The first emphasis of HP's strategy is management of the Internet/intranet infrastructure using HP OpenView NNM; IT/Operations can be deployed to manage Web servers and to monitor the status of Web pages.

Competitors such as Tivoli and Platinum also are articulating Internet/Web management strategies. Tivoli's strategy is broad, encompassing management of Web servers, Web services, and monitoring of Web usage. HP does not supply applications for Web usage monitoring. Neither HP nor Tivoli have put forth capacity planning tools optimized for Web applications, while Platinum has developed tools for testing Web applications and predicting resource requirements.

No single vendor's strategy as yet covers all important aspects of Internet/intranet management. By deploying open tools such as HP OpenView, however, customers can mix and match vendor solutions to a certain extent to achieve comprehensive management.

HP OpenView Derivatives

IBM NetView for AIX (SystemView AIX)

HP OpenView is perceived by many in the industry as a de facto standard for SNMP-based network and systems management. This perception is due to two factors:

- The large and growing installed base of HP OpenView Network Node Manager.
- The use of NNM as a basis for several competing SNMP management offerings from IBM, Digital, and AT&T/NCR.

Chapters 15 to 17 describe products from IBM, Digital, and AT&T/NCR respectively, pointing out similarities and differences between HP OpenView NNM and its derivatives.

Introduction to NetView for AIX

For more than 10 years, IBM has invested heavily in management-related products. Before 1991, there was a major void in IBM's product line with respect to SNMP-based solutions. To fill this gap, IBM chose to license OpenView NNM from Hewlett-Packard for its Unix-based solution, and NMC Vision from Network Managers for its DOS/Windows-based solution.

The licensing agreement between HP and IBM extended up to and including NNM Version 3.3. IBM did not license succeeding versions of NNM, the so-called *Tornado* releases described in Chap. 3, because IBM and HP have taken different directions in terms of product development. Unfortunately, this creates more work for third-party applications developers who must address the problems of porting code from one platform to the other to satisfy customer needs. This problem affects not only IBM and HP customers, but users of Digital's and AT&T/NCR's management solutions as well. As

Chapters 16–17 explain, Digital's solution is based on IBM NetView for AIX, while AT&T's products follow HP's development path.

NetView for AIX is one of several IBM management platforms offered in the SystemView Series family. IBM offers different solutions for managing mainframes, PCs, Unix workstations and servers, as well as databases and storage resources, LAN interconnections, network devices, and midrange computers — both IBM and non-IBM systems as well. IBM is constantly enhancing the functionality of its managed products. In addition to AIX, IBM offers solutions for managing the following environments:

- MVS
- OS/2
- AS/400
- Windows

Each of these platforms supports many additional point-product applications. In all, IBM offers more than 160 different management-related products.

For years, it has been the user's task to figure out how these products work together. Then, in May 1995, IBM announced an ambitious initiative called SystemView Series (code-named Karat), designed to integrate these products into a common object-oriented framework. Over time, IBM will transition management applications from all of its major environments to a framework based on IBM's System Object Model (SOM), Distributed SOM, and the Object Management Group's Common Object Request Broker Architecture (OMG CORBA), as shown in Fig. 15.1. This will allow third-party developers to build their objects on top of the IBM framework, as shown in Fig. 15.2. For users, this offers the potential for more tightly integrated management applications.

The initial release of SystemView Series, which shipped in mid-1995, focused exclusively on the AIX environment. This release was compromised primarily of existing NetView for AIX products, with the addition of two new items, Performance Reporter and System Administrator for AIX. *Performance Reporter* is an administrative application that supports service level agreement monitoring and capacity planning. Performance Reporter includes more than 50 IBM-provided generic reports, as well as a facility for producing customized reports. *System Administrator* will allow administrators to create groups of users, and apply policy for access privileges and concepts against groups of users. System Administrator builds upon current functionality in IBM's Systems Management Installation Tool (SMIT). Table 15.1 lists all of the product functions included in the initial release of SystemView AIX; the components added in SystemView for AIX Version 1 Release 2 (late 1995) are indicated by asterisks.

The late 1995 release of SystemView Series includes support for OS/2. The package provides applications for desktop management, problem management, console management, change management, and configuration management, as listed in Table 15.2. In 1996, IBM released SystemView for MVS, as well as

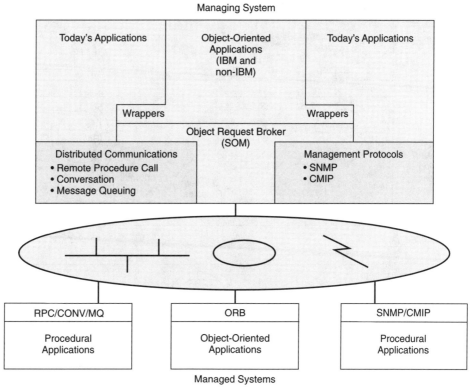

Figure 15.1 Evolution toward Object-Oriented Technology

enhancements for SystemView for AIX and OS/2. Functionality in SystemView for MVS is listed in Table 15.3. The AIX enhancements for 1996 included DataHub for AIX, Network Security Program (NSP), and Distributed Security Manager for AIX, as well as new products for print management, performance management, problem management, and change/configuration management. A SystemView Series offering for the OS/400 environment was introduced in 1996, as shown in Table 15.4. PC SystemView, supporting both Windows and Windows NT, was announced in 1996, as were agents for DOS, Novell, and MacOS environments.

SystemView Series is actually an evolution of existing IBM products into an integrated, object-oriented framework. For the user, the most tangible benefits of the new SystemView Series include the following:

■ Single user interface across AIX, OS/2, MVS, and OS/400 management products.

■ Single delivery mechanism; all products on a single CD, using CD showcase technology that allows users to select the product/function they want to buy at any time.

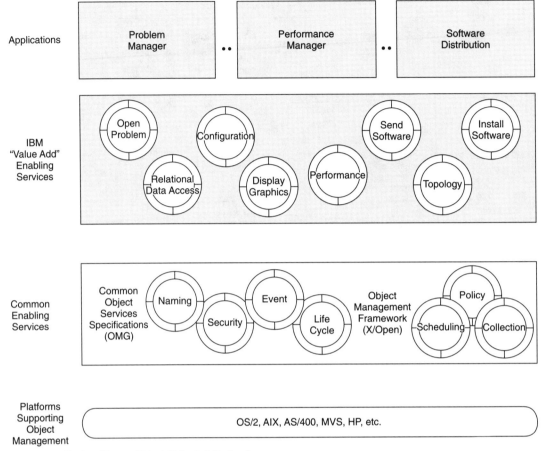

Figure 15.2 SystemView—Object-Oriented Technology

- Single view of shared management data (evolving over time).

- Evolution to object services (SOM/DSOM/CORBA).

Among the products included in the initial release were NetView for AIX, Systems Monitor for AIX, Trouble Ticket for AIX, LAN Management Utilities for AIX, NetView Distribution Manager, and management applications for IBM's bridges, routers, hubs, and ATM switches. Performance management for applications and SNA were added in Release 2.

The initial release of SystemView Series for AIX included 22 products on a single CD. This CD has one program identification number (PID) for licensing purposes (that number is *5765-527*), rather than 22 different PIDs, as traditionally has been the case. Users select the function/product they wish to use, call the IBM representative, and obtain the cryptographic key for unlocking that function. The customer is billed for that product. At any time

Table 15.1. SystemView For AIX—Initial Release

SystemView component	Function
NetView for AIX	Network management
Systems Monitor for AIX, Solaris, HP-UX	Network/systems management
LAN Management Utilities	LAN network management
Intelligent Hub Manager	Network device management
AIX Router and Bridge Manager	Network device management
ATM Camus Manager for AIX	Network device management
ADSTAR Distributed Storage Manager	Storage management
ADSTAR DSM Chent/Agent for AIX, Sun, HP-UX, DOS, OS/2, Windows	Storage management
Loadleveler for RS/6000 and SP	Workload management
Job Scheduler	Workload management
Print Services Facility/6000	Print management
AIX PPFA/6000	Print management
Performance Toolbox and Performance Aide	Performance management
RMONitor for AIX	Performance management
Performance Reporter	Performance management
**Performance Monitor for SNA	Performance management
**Performance Monitor for Applications	Performance management
Trouble Ticket for AIX	Problem management
AIX NetView Distribution Manager	Software distribution
AIX NetView DM Agent for AIX, HP-UX, OS/2, Windows	Software distribution
Distributed SMIT	Configuration management
Distributed SMIT Agents for AIX, Sun, HP-UX	Configuration management
Systems Administrator for AIX	Configuration management
AIX/6000 Security	Security control
DSMIT for Administration	Business management

NOTE: The components added in SystemView for AIX Version 1 Release 2 (late 1995) are indicated by asterisks**.

in the future, the customer may choose to unlock any additional products on the CD simply by calling IBM; no other licensing agreements need be negotiated. In addition, IBM has consolidated more than 100 price points into a list of 15 basic prices. This new sales and delivery mechanism is expected to drastically streamline IBM's sales and licensing products, making it easier for customers to order IBM management solutions.

Table 15.2. SystemView for OS/2 Workgroup

SystemView component	Function
Netfinity	Desktop management, operations management, problem management, configuration management
Distributed Console Access Facility (DCAF)	Console management
NetView Distribution Manager/2	Software distribution
Net Door	Change management
iFOR/LS	License management

Table 15.3. SystemView for MVS—Initial Release

SystemView component	Function
NetView for MVS	Network and systems management, console management
NetView Auto Bridge/MVS	Network and systems management
NetView Distribution Manager	Software distribution
NetView MultiSystems Manager MVS/ESA	Network and systems management
Automated Network Operations/MVS (ANO)	Network and systems management, console management
Sysplex Operations Manager (with Towers)	Network and systems management
Target System Control Facility	Network and systems management console management
NetView Remote Ops Manager	Console management
CICS Automation Option/MVS	Console management
IMS Automation Option/MVS	Console management
OPC/ESA Automation Option/MVS	Console management
OPC/ESA 1.4 Operations Planning and Control/ESA	Workload management
Display and Search Facility	Workload management
CICSPlex System Manager	Workload management
Resource Management Facility	Workload management
Job Entry Scheduler	Workload management
Report Management and Distribution System	Print management
Print Services Facility	Print management
Job Entry Scheduler	Print management
Resource Management Facility	Performance management
NetView Performance Monitor (NPM)	Performance management
Enterprise Performance Data Manager/MVS	Performance management

Table 15.3. SystemView for MVS—Initial Release (continued)

SystemView component	Function
Information/Management Family (Info/Man)	Problem management, change management, configuration management
Problem Management Bridge/MVS	Problem management
Systems Modification Program Extended	Change management
Software Manager/MVS	Change management
NetView Network Planner/2	Configuration management
Hardware Configuration Definition	Configuration management
ESCON Manager	Configuration management
Resource Access Control Facility (RACF)	Security management
Distributed Security Manager for MVS	Security management
SAA dpAccounting Manager/MVS	Business management
DataHub/2 (Control Point)	Database management
DataHub Support/MVS	Database management
ADSTAR Distributed Storage Manager	Storage management
Data Facility Storage Management System	Storage management

Table 15.4. SystemView for OS/400—Initial Release

SystemView component	Function
OS/400 Base Services	Network and systems management, problem management, configuration management, security management
OS/400 Graphical Operations	Network and systems management
Client Access/400	Network and systems management, configuration management
NetView for OS/2	Network and systems management
System Manager/400	Problem management, change management
ADSTAR DSM/400	Storage management
Backup Recovery and Media Services/400	Storage management
Performance Tools/400	Performance management
Performance Investigator/400	Performance management
Managed System Services/400	Change management
DataHub/2 (Control Point)	Database management
DataHub Support/400	Database management
DataPropagator/400	Database management

Object class libraries and other tools will help users build objects and applications for SystemView Series. In the future, SystemView applications will be capable of receiving management data from AIX, OS/2, DOS, and Windows clients supporting the Desktop Management Task Force (DMTF) Desktop Management Interface (DMI). Other vendors' DMI-compliant systems will be able to exchange management data with SystemView Series products. For more information on DMTF/DMI, see Chap. 2.

Product Overview: NetView for AIX

NetView for AIX is the core network management product in IBM's SystemView for AIX suite. NetView for AIX is targeted at managing multi-vendor devices on TCP/IP networks, providing configuration, fault, and performance management functions. It has many features for making the product easier to install and use. IBM's AIX Service Point program can be used to facilitate communication with NetView for MVS. Figure 15.3 shows principal components of IBM NetView for AIX.

Like HP OpenView NNM, NetView for AIX is an SNMP-based management system; however, NetView for AIX also can act as a service point for enterprise-wide NetView/MVS management system. IBM has expended considerable effort enhancing the core OpenView NNM code. Key IBM-developed value-added features of NetView for AIX include:

- End-user interface improvements, such as navigation tree, tool palette, and control desk.

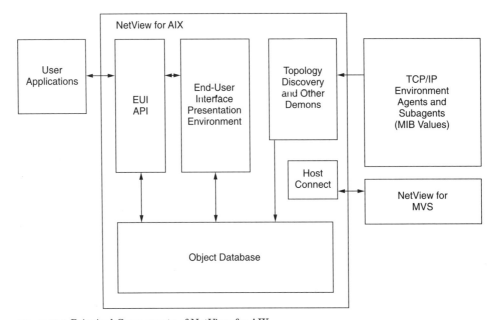

Figure 15.3 Principal Components of NetView for AIX

- Manager takeover function, which allows transfer of network management to a second NetView for AIX if the primary system goes down.

- Multiple database types, which support Ingres, DB2, Informix, Oracle, and Sybase.

- Distributed discovery, which cooperatively allows discovery and polling to be distributed via use of Systems Monitor for AIX/Mid Level Manager, facilitated by the *trapgend* subagent.

- Open topology API, which allows developers to create topology maps for networks of any protocol type, via the *gtmd* process.

- Filtering enhancements, which allow users and applications to control the type and volume of data received.

- NetView/MVS affinity, which allows trap conversion/filtering before being forwarded to NetView/MVS.

- Ease of installation, which provides for easier installation of NetView for AIX remote applications via SMIT/DSMIT.

- Third-party applications. NetView Association now offers more than 150 third-party applications.

Strengths

The primary strengths of NetView for AIX include ease of use, support for non-TCP/IP networks, and enhanced handling capabilities. In Version 3.2, released in June 1995, IBM added alarm filtering and event correlation features that are lacking in the OpenView NNM core. These enhanced alarm handling facilities are absolutely necessary for scalability.

Today, IBM positions NetView for MVS as the platform of choice for managing networks comprising tens or hundreds of thousands of nodes — chiefly because it can be scaled upward. By improving the scalability of NetView for AIX, IBM may in the future allow this product to overtake NetView for MVS in distributed processing environments. In response to customer demand, IBM also is developing SNA management applications for NetView for AIX. Additionally, IBM is emphasizing its support program, both for end users and for third-party vendors who join the NetView Association business partner program.

Another important advantage of NetView for AIX is the distributed management capability that is supported using Systems Monitor for AIX. While OpenView NNM is typically used to manage a few thousand nodes or fewer, IBM customers can increase the scope of management under NetView for AIX by distributing polling and discovery tasks among multiple RS/6000 workstations running the Systems Monitor for AIX agent or Mid Level Management (MLM). Figure 15.4 depicts how management processing can be offloaded from NetView for AIX onto multiple AIX workstations using Systems Monitor for AIX.

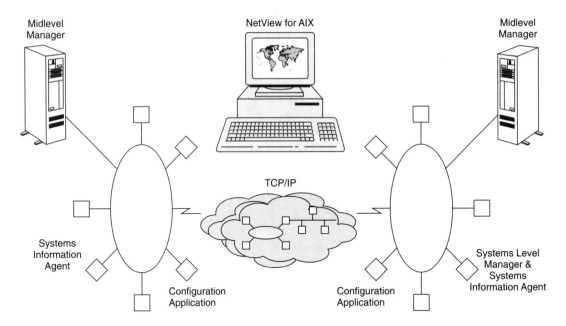

Highlights
• Local Systems Management and Automation
• Configuration Application

Figure 15.4 NetView feature for AIX System-Level Manager and Agent Configuration

Limitations

In order to make NetView for AIX a more successful product, IBM should further increase its focus on the AIX-based products and reduce emphasis on older, proprietary solutions in general, and on NetView for MVS in particular. This transition likely will occur slowly over the next five years.

To IBM's credit, the 1996 acquisition of Tivoli Systems should accelerate IBM's progress toward distributed, object-oriented implementations. Tivoli is considered an industry-leading supplier of object-oriented technology to the systems and network management industry.

Basic Platform Services of NetView for AIX

The basic platform services provided by NetView for AIX include device discovery and network mapping, distributed implementation, and manager-to-manager communications. The following sections describe these services.

Device Discovery and network mapping. Dynamic Network Discovery automatically discovers IP-addressable nodes and tracks IP network device adds and changes, keeping the network topology map current. In a typical configuration, 1000 nodes can be discovered in about 20 minutes. Automatic map drawing/redrawing (autotopology) is supported to a limited extent. The system continually verifies network device connection. Operators can save current network maps to compare with later maps; no sophisticated change management software is provided.

Alarm capability. NetView monitors IP network node status, and generates events if user-defined thresholds are exceeded; alarms can trigger NetView alerts. Users can configure polls for groups of objects and examine the states of multiple components simultaneously. Traps and events can trigger user-defined shell scripts and NetView alerts, and can receive RUNCMD commands from NetView for MVS. TCP/IP diagnostic routines include IP ping, TCP connection test, and SNMP agent test.

Distributed polling is supported using System Monitor for AIX agents. Users can install System Monitors on RS/6000 workstations throughout the network to offload automation of individual LAN segments and feed that information to a handful of NetView for AIXs.

Event filtering. Filtering rules can span multiple objects (groups) simulataneously, which allows users to monitor different states of objects in different groups, and allows users to complete boolean expressions to define thresholds. Filter Editor and Filter Control Interface allow managers to see graphical representations of selected SNMP events.

Alarm correlation. Alarm correlation is supported to some degree by the Event Correlation feature. Also, a problem diagnostic facility enables users to trace a specific data pattern to determine whether a network problem is related to that pattern. The network map can display packet routes for tracing; users can browse MIB to examine values. The SNA Manager/6000 application option of NetView for AIX can automatically trigger shell scripts or NetView for MVS RUNCMDs based on alerts to display probable cause or recommended solution text messages.

SQL Database. Flat file (ASCII) log of events and polled data is created. Topology data is stored in SQL databases, including Oracle, Ingres, Sybase, DB2, and Informix.

Support of protocols. SNMP (MIB I, MIB II) and remote monitoring are supported. Private extentions for IBM 6611 routers are offered to users. IBM NMVT's can be converted via Service Point applications. CMIP support is planned, but has not yet been implemented. Experimental implementations of SNMPv2 are available.

Users can browse performance-related MIB variables to examine, chart, or modify values. NetView for AIX maintains historical data based on built-in and user-defined threshold polling; this data can be graphed for analysis in pie/bar charts or line graphs, or it can be saved in ASCII files. Users can customize SNMP thresholds and traps, and can dynamically edit maps and set polling intervals determining how often the map is updated. Users can add new devices and device types via SNMP MIB Editor.

Application programming interfaces. APIs are provided for linking to Service Point applications. SNMP API and HP OpenView Windows API are included from Version 2. Support for OSF/DME Consolidated Management API (CM-API) also is included. The SystemView business partners' program offers additional APIs. NetView for AIX supports the AIX System Management Interface Tool (SMIT), providing command line interface for remotely logged users.

- Access control, based on AIX security and audit features. Graphical User Interface is based on OSF/Motif standards; users can edit the map with supplied map-editing tools. Menu bar function allows point-and-click access to View, Locate, Test, Edit, and Help functions.

- Distributed implementation and distributed database supports multiple users via a client/server implementation. As a Service Point product, NetView for AIX can be scattered at sites throughout the SNA network to feed information to central site NetView. The security features provide a pseudo-domain capability.

- Manager-to-manager communications can be supported using the AIX System Monitor for AIX/Mid-Level Manager. Customization of this product is time-consuming. NetView for AIX acts as a Service Point, accepting SNMP events and issuing an NMVT event to the main NetView console. NetView for AIX accepts mainframe NetView RUNCMDs via the AIX Service Point interface; receipt of RUNCMDs are acknowledged. Information flow between NetView for AIX and MVS is bidirectional. Figure 15.5 illustrates this cooperation between the products.

The SNA Manager/6000 application can serve as an enterprise management workstation, displaying SNA topology data and alerts. Furthermore, network topology and status can be exchanged with the NetView Multisystem Manager for NetView for MVS, allowing graphical display from mainframe Graphic Monitor Facility (GMF) and automation via the Resource Object Data Manager (RODM).

NetView for AIX runs on IBM RS/6000 POWERstations and POWERservers running AIX.

NetView for AIX Entry

The IBM NetView for AIX Entry program is a licensed program that provides comprehensive distributed management of heterogeneous, multivendor Transmission Control Protocol/Internet Protocol (TCP/IP) networks that have 32 nodes or fewer. Features include:

- Graphical object-oriented user interface that provides a view of heterogeneous networks at a glance.

- Dynamic Network Discovery, which allows TCP/IP network resources to be discovered, mapped, and monitored automatically.

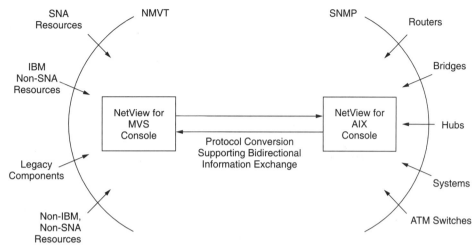

Figure 15.5 Cooperation between NetView for AIX and NetView for MVS

- System Management Interface Tool (SMIT) which facilitates installation with easy-to-use menus and help screens.

- Tools for accessing standard and enterprise-specific MIBs, building MlB applications, collecting MIB information and configuring events.

- User-configurable polling intervals to regulate the amount of traffic generated by the management station.

- Tools for diagnosing network problems by testing network connectivity, finding routes, and requesting network information from remote SNMP nodes.

Two-way communication between NetView for AIX Entry and NetView for MVS allows NetView for MVS to filter SNMP traps from TCP/IP networks according to user definitions and convert them into NMVT alerts. These, in turn, can be edited using the alert editor, filtered, logged, and sent on to NetView for MVS. Responses from NetView for MVS are sent to NetView for AIX via RUNCMDs through the AIX NetView Service Point.

NetView for AIX supports a manager takeover facility that lets one NetView for AIX console take over for another in the event of a failure. It also lets the platform discover additional devices, such as bridges and routers.

Databases can be distributed among multiple workstations to enhance performance and availability. The product features improved security capabilities, device discovery features, and event synchronization attributes. Version 3.2 improved the scalability of the platform, enabling it to better manage bigger environments, and pushing it into the role of the enterprise manager.

Today, most IBM NetView for AIX users use a single workstation to perform all management functions. By offloading the database to other machines, the management system will run faster and can be scaled up to manage larger networks and systems. As a result, users could have multiple database servers on different platforms supported by different operating systems.

Adding support for SNMPv2 will improve NetView's scalability, enabling distributed NetView for AIX managers to share data. For example, SNMPv2 will let one NetView platform act as backup to another, so if the primary manager fails, another automatically take over. The backup program in use today is not standards-based. Also, support for SNMPv2 enables one NetView platform to freely send or share management data with another NetView platform. None of these capabilities were possible with Version 1.

Other improvements in the new version include a more rapid discovery feature, as well as event and alarm correlation capabilities. The enhanced software lets users present events or alarms on one integrated window. In earlier versions, the NetView screen can integrate alerts from different resources, but they appear in different windows on the screen. The upgrade simplifies the task of monitoring, collapsing, and correlating multiple events.

Value-Added Applications from IBM

In order to meet user need, IBM has been developing and implementing management applications for the AIX platform. These applications target particular IBM devices, connections between various IBM management tools, and some process-specific applications. This segment gives a complete overview on IBM-based management applications.

Intelligent Hub Manager for AIX

The IBM Intelligent Hub Manager for AIX is a licensed program that facilitates and expands the management of LANs with IBM 8250 or 8260 Intelligent Switching Hubs. The product aids LAN management by collecting and reporting statistics per hub port and per LAN. This program offers LAN-level security by preventing unauthorized users from accessing the network. The product:

- Enhances network management for IBM hubs, improving network support productivity by providing a graphical interface for the fault, configuration, operation, and change management functions.
- Offers an expanded view of IBM 8250 and 8260 hubs with realistic graphics of various components, including color-coded status for operations and status notification.
- Allows administrators flexibility in assigning individual ports or modules to a LAN, and to isolate any module from the backplane for troubleshooting purposes.
- Discovers automatically the models of IBM 8250 and 8260 hubs and their installed modules.
- Provides network security by preventing unauthorized users from accessing the network.
- Provides an easy-to-use, context-sensitive online help facility.

Router and Bridge Manager for AIX

The IBM Router and Bridge Manager for AIX supports management of the IBM 6611 Network Processor (router), the IBM 2210 Nways Multiprotocol Router, the router blade in IBM 8250 and 8260 hubs, the IBM 8229 LAN Bridge and RouteXpander/2. The product can manage most other vendors' routers and bridges via SNMP. The ability to monitor each 6611's aggregate health of the protocols, network interfaces, and system function in a single view is an example of the value of this application. Router and Bridge Manager runs as an application on the NetView for AIX platform; additionally, the product provides unique features for managing APPN and Data Link Switching (DLSw) topologies.

Systems Monitor for AIX

The IBM Systems Monitor program serves two important functions for managing distributed heterogeneous environments:

- It can act as an intermediate SNMP manager, allowing for distribution of the systems and network management tasks into the network, thus freeing up the network management platform to manage larger, more complicated networks.

- It provides detailed system-level information on the systems on which it runs, so that the user can keep a close watch on the critical workstations to ensure that they are operating smoothly.

As a distributed SNMP manager, Systems Monitor can be used to monitor a customer-defined set of SNMP devices on a network, thus offloading this responsibility from the network management platform as shown in Fig. 15.6. By moving this function into the supported workstations on the network, the management platform is freed to manage larger, more complex networks. Systems Monitor has several key user-configurable functions that simplify management tasks. Sophisticated filtering, thresholding, and analysis are used to reduce the amount of data forwarded to the network management host, so that only the most crucial information is sent to the SNMP manager.

An automation capability allows Unix, SNMP commands, and shell scripts to be executed directly by Systems Monitor in response to the MIB data it monitors. With this capability, network and system problems can be solved with minimal intervention from the network operator. This Systems Monitor function reduces the amount of work that must be accomplished by the SNMP Manager and operator and also reduces network traffic.

IBM Systems Monitor consists of a Simple Network Management Protocol (SNMP) subagent which, when installed on supported workstations in the network, extends the enterprise-specific MlBs on the workstations on which it is running. The package includes System-Level Manager (SLM), Mid-Level Manager (MLM), and System Information Agent (SIA) functions. SLM can be installed remotely to collect periodical data for NetView for AIX.

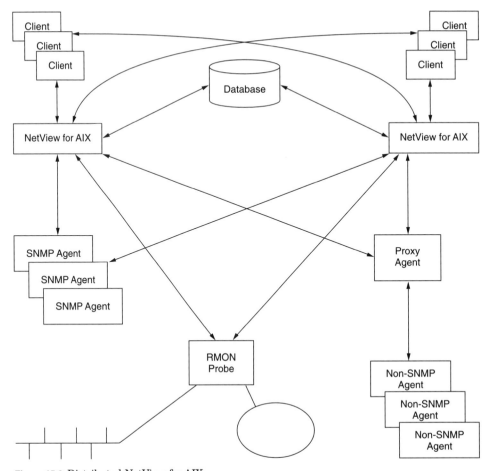

Figure 15.6 Distributed NetView for AIX

Systems Monitor agents are available for AIX, SunOS, Solaris, HP-UX, DEC Ultrix, and NCR/UNIX systems.

Performance Reporter for AIX

This application supports performance history reporting for distributed computer systems and includes more than 50 predefined reports. Performance data can be collected from AIX, HP-UX, Solaris, and SunOS systems. Performance Reporter can use data collected by Systems Monitor agents as well. Data is summarized before it is stored, according to user-defined storage policies.

NetView Distribution Manager (DM) for AIX

NetView DM for AIX is a software distribution tool that can distribute software over TCP/IP networks to AIX, OS/2, HP-UX, DOS, Windows, SunOS, and

Solaris clients. NetView DM for AIX, part of the SystemView for AIX product family, is not fully integrated with NetView for AIX.

Trouble Ticket for AIX

The IBM Trouble Ticket for AIX program is a licensed program supporting trouble ticketing, system inventory, and notifications. The application tracks the problem history of each device connected to the network, each software program installed on the network, and each service used by the network. Users have immediate access to problem histories. The system inventory provides detailed information on network devices, software applications, and external services that support network operations. Trouble Ticket for AIX supports the following:

- Creation and qualifying of initial problem and change records
- Linkage of problem and change records for joint tracking
- Automatic escalation procedures
- Automatic notifications
- Logging and annotation of all changes in the status of change and problem records

AIX Systems Network Architecture Manager/6000

The IBM AIX Systems Network Architecture Manager/6000 program is a licensed program that provides visibility and management of SNA subarea resources on NetView for AIX, using NetView on an MVS or VM platform. This product combines the strength of two platforms by allowing the customer to choose NetView for AIX as an operator workstation and manager of the TCP/IP network and NetView to integrate data for SNA. AIX SNA Manager/6000 provides:

- A graphical display of SNA subarea network topology and status to the LU level, including terminals and applications.
- A command line window which provides for sending NetView, VTAM, and MVS commands to NetView for AIX.
- The ability to view SNA alerts dynamically (or later) by selecting a resource from a submap.
- A means of easy navigation through the submap hierarchy to find failing resources.
- One set of commands to manage both SNA and TCP/IP resources.
- Customizable easy-to-use graphical interface, with the ability to customize aggregation thresholds and priorities using aggregation capabilities similar to those of NetView Graphic Monitor Facility.
- Quick access to SNA Manager/6000 information via InfoExplorer, the RISC System/6000 hypertext browser.

AIX LAN Management Utilities for AIX LMU for OS/2

LAN Management Utilities (LMU) supports monitoring of IP, IPX, and NetBIOS devies from a single workstation. Operators can retrieve configuration, performance, and fault information from Novell and IBM LAN Server nodes; and view system-level information about OS/2, DOS, Windows, and Novell clients as well as IBM PC LAN servers. IBM AIX LMU for AIX supports the following features:

- Extends the management capability the user has from NetView for AIX by providing support for clients and server on IBM NetBlOS and NetWare IPX networks.

- Saves resources by allowing consolidation of network management resources and skills at a single location.

- Improves problem management by integrating LMU and NetView for AIX management functions with common applications such as event handling and trouble ticketing.

- Shows system status at a glance through an easy-to-understand graphical view of the network, quick access to configuration, fault and performance data.

- Gives the flexibility to manage heterogeneous networks from a central location, or by distributing management task throughout the network.

LAN Network Manager for AIX

LAN Network Manager for AIX (LNM for AIX) provides SNMP management for Token-Ring, FDDI, and Ethernet LANs integrated into the NetView for AIX platform. Fault, performance, and configuration management are provided for FDDI hubs, including the IBM 8240 and IBM 8230 model 3; SNMP bridges, including the IBM 8229, IBM 8250, and IBM 8260; and the IBM 6611 router.

RMONitor for AIX

RMONitor is a performance management tool that collects, monitors, and indexes statistics from Token-Ring and Ethernet LAN segments. These statistics are collected from various RMON-compliant agents and include packet octet and error counters. RMONitor serves as a central point for managing the agents in a distributed management structure. It provides valuable information for those responsible for maintaining LAN performance, while enhancing the services that the LAN provides. RMONitor runs with NetView for AIX.

NetView for AIX Service Point

The IBM AIX NetView Service Point program is a licensed program that allows the AIX Unix environments to exchange network management information with the NetView for MVS program, enabling centralized NetView for

MVS network management for multivendor devices. As a gateway to the NetView for MVS program, the AIX Service Point operates in a screenless environment on a RISC or Sun workstation. AIX NetView Service Point supports the following characteristics:

- Utilizes System Network Architecture (SNA) Logical Unit (LU) 6.2 protocol for communicating network management informaton to NetView for MVS. This gives users a more efficient, flexible, and reliable way to send alert information to NetView for MVS and to execute distributed commands from NetView for MVS.

- Supports shared libraries so that Service Point applications can dynamically link with the service point. Application writers will no longer need to coordinate Service Point modifications with application modifications. Customers will be able to apply Service Point maintenance without impacting service point applications.

- Provides more detailed information on the program's APIs, problem determination techniques, installation, and customization, which enables more proficient and productive Service Point usage.

- Includes support for new NetView (S/390) subvectors to provide application writers with more flexibility in sending and receiving information from NetView (S/390).

- Provides TCP/IP enhancements to the Distributed Application Support Workstation feature to allow remote applications to specify which service point to access. This reduces costly network broadcast traffic.

TMN Workbench/6000

The Telecommunications Management Network Workbench/6000 is a set of AIX-based tools that simplifies the development of element, network, and service management applications that use the OSI agent/manager model and includes the following advanced functional capabilities:

- A compiler for the specification languages GDMO and ASN.1. This compiler helps to remove much of the routine work, such as the generation of code for the data structures. When used with the browser, the compiler creates a formatted view of the specification, making it more understandable for the programmer.

- A class browser and editor that allow the programmer to view graphically the formatted output of the compiler and to modify the specification or create new specifications.

- An X/Open Management Protocol (XMP) API tracer that helps developers test their applications.

- Database services including Metadata and Abstract Data APIs, which allow for persistence of class definitions and allow programs to manipulate OSI management objects interactively.

- A tool that enhances the developer's ability to specify and write agent applications. This tool generates code and provides an environment to quickly prototype and test the results.

IBM cannot meet all user needs for management applications. But Business Partners may help. This segment shows a representative mix of applications written by third parties. They include both device-dependent and device-independent solutions. There are many more; IBM's Management Applications Catalogue for NetView for AIX gives an up-to-date summary of all available products (IBM 1995).

Management Applications from Tivoli

In 1996, IBM acquired Tivoli Systems, a leading supplier of object-oriented technology for systems management applications. Tivoli offers a number of systems management tools including:

- Tivoli/Courier: software distribution
- Tivoli/Sentry: intelligent agent for monitoring systems performance
- Tivoli/Admin: for user and file administration
- Tivoli/Enterprise: for consolidating and processing messages from Unix system log files, NT systems, SNMP systems, and other diverse sources

The first three products overlap with existing IBM products, specifically IBM NetView Distribution Manager (DM), IBM Systems Monitor, and DSMIT. It is expected that, over time, IBM may somehow merge features of the Tivoli products into its existing product line.

IBM currently does not have a true equivalent to Tivoli/Enterprise Console. This product may become a strategic enterprise management offering for IBM.

The Tivoli/Enterprise Console provides enterprise-wide event and problem management that integrates the management of systems, network, databases, and applications. The Tivoli/Enterprise Console is a rules-based application that provides a centralized point to collect, process, correlate, and respond to events and alarms from network management systems, database management systems, and applications. Tivoli provides an event adapter for IBM's NetView for AIX network management systems. This adapter can forward any NetView for AIX event or alarm to the Tivoli/Enterprise Console for correlation with other types of events.

Multiple, distributed consoles are provided by the Tivoli/Enterprise Console. Each console view can be customized to provide each member of the IT staff with information relative to their responsiblities. Automatic responses are provided by the Enterprise Console. A graphical rules editor is provided as well as a toolkit for building event adapters.

Enterprise Management

HP must rely on Solution Partners to offer enterprise management solutions. Typical solutions incorporate legacy management, WAN, LAN, systems, and also desktop management. Applications do exist for each area; HP or third parties are responsible for the seamless integration.

In contrast, IBM has a much wider array of in-house solutions for the various areas of enterprise management. IBM supports more than 150 different management-related products. In addition to the AIX offerings described previously, other important platforms and some of their typical applications include:

- NetView for MVS platform
    - ~ Automated Network Operator
    - ~ LAN Automated Option
    - ~ Multisystem Manager
    - ~ Resource Object Data Repository
    - ~ NTuneMOn
    - ~ NTuneNCP
    - ~ Enterprise Performance Data Manager
    - ~ LAN Resource Extension and Services
    - ~ NetImpact
- NetView for AS/400 platform
    - ~ Systems Management Automation Offering
    - ~ Automation Operations Control/Automated Network Operations
    - ~ NetView Remote Operations Manager
    - ~ NetView Remote Operations Agent

HP does not offer such a rich choice of company internal applications; customers must turn to third-party applications for a complete OpenView solution addressing these same areas.

Summary

IBM's vast installed base represents many customers who may require one or more products referenced in this chapter. Therefore IBM is gaining in popularity as a platform for development of third-party applications. Third parties have been writing platform and product extensions for NetView for MVS for many years. Now, third parties are writing applications for NetView for AIX, for OS/2 and for Windows.

IBM's relationship with Digital Equipment Corporation will have an impact on SNA management directions. Digital's housing of NetView for AIX technology will provide interesting hardware and software alternatives for customers attracted to NetView. Polycenter NetView is a SNMP management system that supports extensions for DECnet management. NetView for AIX is running on Digital's OSF/1 operating system and Alpha AXP hardware. Polycenter Manager on NetView for AIX also manages Digital terminal servers and bridges. Database support is constantly extended and includes Oracle, Informix, Sybase and Digital Rdb OSF/1 databases.

Regarding IBM's entire network management product family, communication links exist between the products, and users may customize their IBM-dominated management environment by putting the emphasis on products best suited to their environment. Future SystemView releases will significantly simplify the integration of management applications across multiple platforms.

Many organizations are hoping to reduce operating costs and increase quality of service by integrating management of SNA networks under a Unix-based SNMP framework. Certain applications will support management solutions without using NetView for MVS. Most customers initially will seek to offload portions of mainframe NetView functions onto the SNMP platform to free CPU cycles and increase operator efficiency. Still, NetView for MVS will not be displaced totally in the near term.

Users may choose to deploy SNMP-manageable SNA servers as they migrate toward integrated TCP/IP-SNA management. IBM and third-party products act as bridges between mainframe NetView and SNMP platforms. Positioning NetView for AIX as an umbrella manager may, however, overstress the capabilities of this product. The use of SystemView Series may help to better balance application load between various platforms.

Digital Polycenter Manager on NetView

Polycenter is Digital's trademarked name for the set of products and services targeting the management of networks, systems, storage devices, and other resources. Included in the Polycenter suite are many point product solutions for open systems as well as for additional DECnet environments.

In August 1993, Digital and IBM announced a joint development agreement whereby Digital would license IBM's NetView for AIX, porting it to Digital's Alpha-based hardware running the DEC OSF/1 operating system. This product is now known as Polycenter Manager on NetView, and it forms the cornerstone of Digital's network and systems management architecture. Like NetView for AIX, Polycenter Manager on NetView shares a core code base with HP OpenView NNM. In September 1995, Digital released Polycenter Manager on NetView for Windows NT, a port of the Alpha-based Polycenter NetView product to Microsoft's Windows NT operating system. This port represented the first commercially available port of HP OpenView NNM code to the Windows NT operating system. HP's port is expected to ship in 1997.

Like IBM's NetView for AIX, Polycenter NetView includes core HP OpenView NNM code. Most core NNM processes described in Chap. 4 are included in both IBM NetView for AIX and Polycenter NetView; a few, such as *netmon*, have been modified. However, IBM has added an important process supporting non-IP discovery and mapping functions, called *gtmd*, that also is present in Polycenter NetView. Like IBM NetView for AIX, Polycenter NetView differs from HP OpenView NNM in the following respects:

- End-user interface improvements that include a navigation tree, tool palette, and control desk.

- Multiple database types that support Ingres, Informix, Oracle, Sybase, and Rdb.

- Open topology API that allows developers to create topology maps for networks of any protocol type using data collected via the process.

- Filtering enhancements that allow users and applications to control the type and volume of data received through Compound Status polling.

- Third-party applications; SystemView/NetView Association supports third-party developers porting to both the AIX and OSF/1 operating systems.

There are two facilities supported by NetView for AIX that are *not* supported by Polycenter NetView:

- IBM's Host Connection/Service Point functionality for communications with an IBM NetView for MVS

- Support for IBM's Systems Monitor for AIX via the system monitoring subagent *(trapgend)*

Polycenter NetView offers several advantages over IBM's NetView for AIX, including:

- Superior price/performance gains provided by Digital's Alpha processors.

- Additional GUI enhancements for ease of use.

- Event integration enhancements, making it trivial for any application to trigger an event card.

- DECnet and IP management capability from one platform.

- Integration with Digital value-added applications including PathDoctor for router trace facilities, and System Watchdog and Console Manager for systems administration support.

- Availability on the Microsoft Windows NT platform.

- Cooperation with Digital's ManageWorks solution for distributing polling and event management across PathWorks, LAN Server, and Novell LANs.

Going forward, Digital plans to offer integration between Polycenter NetView and Microsoft's and Novell's management systems. This integration is expected to include exchange of topology data with Microsoft's SMS. Also, Polycenter NetView soon will gain access to IPX topology, performance, and status data collected by Novell's ManageWise system, as shown in Fig. 16.1.

Strengths. The primary strengths of Polycenter NetView include NT support, price/performance, ease of use, support for DECnet management, integration with a unique set of DEC and third-party applications, and also some added alarm handling capabilities. Polycenter NetView NT offers even greater potential for price/performance benefits as well as outstanding ease-of-use features and integration with Microsoft Systems Management (MSM) Server and Digital's own Polycenter AssetWorks software distribution application.

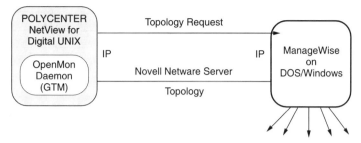

Figure 16.1 Polycenter NetView and Novell's ManageWise

Limitations. Polycenter NetView's arrival on the market was relatively late—several years after SunNet Manager and HP OpenView NNM, and about two years after IBM's NetView for AIX. This late entry has made it more difficult for Digital to persuade third-party applications developers to port to the OSF/1 platform. As a cosponsor of IBM's NetView Association, however, Digital can extend to its developers a strong third-party support program. Through the efforts of the NetView Association, the number of third-party applications for Polycenter NetView on OSF/1 had grown from only a handful in mid-1994 to more than 25 by mid-1995. Third-party applications for Polycenter NetView on OSF/1 are listed in Table 16.1. Digital is expected to increase its third-party support as it goes forward with its NT-based offering.

The acquisition of Digital's systems and network management technology by Computer Associates in April 1996 cast doubt on the status of Digital's Polycenter program. However, the NetView-based products were not acquired, to avoid breaching Digital's licensing agreement with IBM. Digital is expected to continue marketing and supporting Polycenter Manager on NetView until well into 1997 at least.

Digital Value-Added Applications

Digital provides a number of useful network and systems management applications that can be used in conjunction with Polycenter NetView. Each application, along with its area of focus, is listed in Table 16.2. Collectively, these applications manage a diverse set of environments, as shown in Table 16.3.

The following paragraphs highlight some of Digital's more significant value-added offerings, including PathDoctor, System Watchdog, Console Manager, FullSail, HubWatch, and DECnet Manager.

PathDoctor

PathDoctor allows users to diagnose network paths between any two IP network addresses. PathDoctor supports the private enterprise MIBs for Cisco, Wellfleet (Bay Networks), IBM, Proteon, and 3Com routers as well as Digital routers. PathDoctor also supports MIB rule expressions including the Frame Relay DTE Interface MIB.

Table 16.1. Third-Party Applications for Digital Polycenter NetView on OSF/1

Vendor	Application	Function
American Power Conversion	PowerNet Manager	UPS monitoring
Armon	OnSite	Traffic monitoring
Axon Networks	LANServant Manager	Traffic monitoring
BMC Software	Patrol	Database monitoring
BrainTree Technology	SQL Secure	Security management
Chipcom	OnDemand NCS, On-Demand SwitchCentral	Hub/switch management
Frontier Software	NetScout	Traffic monitoring
Gensym Corp.	G2	Expert system
Heroics	RoboMon	System monitoring
Independence Technology	iView Log Manager	Applications monitoring
Innovative Software	PowerCenter	Operations automation
Lannet	MultiMan/OSF 1	Hub management
Network-1	NET1-NetPanel	Rule-based inference engine
Notification Technologies	Attention!	Alert notification by paging devices
Ordinox Network	WINMANAGER	Systems management
Phoenix Network Technologies	Six2Dmcc	Command and alert interface from OpenVMS VAX to Polycenter NetView
Prolin Automation	Pro/Helpdesk	Trouble-ticketing
SoftLink, Ltd	FASTCopy Network Engine	Data and file transfer, software distribution
Systemetrics	PageMate	Alert notification to pagers
Technically Elite Concepts	Network Professor	Traffic monitoring
Victron BV	Wiz Kit	Protection software for Novell servers acting as clients of Unix servers
W. Quinn	Q*File UNIX, Q*Menu UNIX, DQR UNIX	Disk, file management; menu creation, storage management

Table 16.2. Digital Value-Added Applications

Application	Function	Integration with Polycenter NetView (PNV)	Environments supported
Manage-Works	LAN NOS and SNMP network management	SNMP trap forwarding to PNV	MS-Windows
Polycenter AssetWorks (PAW)	Software distribution, hardware/software inventory	SNMP trap forwarding to PNV; launching from ManageWorks and PNV NT; ability to share inventory data via "property sheets"	Windows NT-based; can distribute software to OpenVMS and many types of Unix
PathDoctor	Trace/diagnose a path between any two IP addresses	Standalone or launched from PNV	Alpha-OSF/1 V1.3 and higher
System Watchdog	Performance monitoring for systems, processes, and networks	Standalone, or trap forwarding to PNV	Alpha-OSF/1 Alpha-OpenVMS, VAX OpenVMS
Console Manager	Consolidates console messages; supports reboot, diagnostics of remote systems	Standalone, or trap forwarding to PNV	Alpha-OSF/1, RISC Ultrix, Alpha-OpenVMS, VAX OpenVMS
FullSail	File administration, user administration and performance monitoring	Standalone, or trap forwarding to PNV	Alpha-OSF/1 V3.0, Ultrix RISC
HUBWatch	Monitor and control all DEChub products and modules including DEChub900 Multiswitch, DEChub 900 GIGASwitch/FDDI	Standalone or launched from PNV	Alpha OSF/1 V.2 or higher, VAX-OpenVMS
DECnet Manager	Monitor and control DECnet IV nodes, DECnet OSI nodes, Digital LAN bridges, and terminal servers	Layered on top PNV	Alpha-OSF/1 V1.3 or V2.0
TeMIP	Toolkits for developing OSI Q3/CMIP applications for telecommunications management	Developer's kit only	Alpha-OSF/1, Ultrix
Networker Save and Restore (NSR)	Automates backup and recovery on networked computing environments	Standalone or complementary to PNV	Alpha OSF/1 V2.0x and V3.0x, VAX Ultrix
Advanced File System and Utilities	Increases file system integrity, availability with fast reboot and automatic online reconfiguration	Standalone or complementary to PNV	Alpha-OSF/1 V2.0 or later
Hierarchical Storage Manager (HSM)	Hierarchical storage management with optical disk support, archiving	Standalone or complementary to PNV	Alpha-OSF/1 V1.3 or later
Capacity Planner	Graphic modeling, "what if" analysis on changes to system configuration; workload planning	Standalone or complementary to PNV	Alpha-OSF/1, VAX OpenVMS, Alpha OpenVMS
Scheduler	Automated job scheduling	Standalone or complementary to PNV	Alpha-OSF/1, Alpha OpenVMS, VAX OpenVMS
Security Compliance Manager	Security policy configuration; detects and reports nonconformance	Standalone or complementary to PNV	Alpha-OSF/1, Alpha OpenVMS, VAX OpenVMS

Table 16.3. Environments Supported by Polycenter Products

Application	OSF/1	Open-VMS, Ultrix	AIX	SunOS Solaris	HP-UX	OS/2	Windows Windows /NT
Manage-Works							Windows server. agent; IP, IPX, NetBEUI agents
Polycenter AssetWorks (PAW)			Agent			Agent	NT server, agent; Windows, MAC, agents
Polycenter NetView	Server						NT server
PathDoctor	Server	Ultrix server					
System Watchdog	Server, agent	Ultrix server, agent; Open-VMS server, agent	Agent	SunOS agent	Agent		
Console Manager	Server, RS232	Ultrix server; Open-VMS server; RS232	RS232	RS232	RS232	RS232	
FullSail	Server, agent	Ultrix server, agent	Agent	SunOS agent; Solaris agent	Agent		
HUBWatch	Server	Open-VMS server					Windows server
DECnet Manager	Server						NT server
TeMIP	Server	Ultrix server					
Networker Save and Restore (NSR)	Server, agent	Ultrix server, agent	Agent	SunOS agent; Solaris agent	Agent	Agent	Windows agent; NT agent
Advanced File System and Utilities	Server, agent						

Application	OSF/1	Open-VMS, Ultrix	AIX	SunOS Solaris	HP-UX	OS/2	Windows Windows /NT
Hierarchical Storage Manager (HSM)	Server, agent	Open-VMS server, agent	Agent	SunOS agent	Agent		
Capacity Planner	Server, agent	Open-VMS server, agent; Ultrix agent					
Scheduler	Server, agent	Open-VMS server, agent; Ultrix agent		SunOS agent	Agent		NT agent
Security Compliance Manager	Server, agent	Open-VMS server, agent; Ultrix server, agent	Server, agent	SunOS server, agent; Solaris server, agent	Server, agent		NT server, agent

By providing real-time graphical displays of both forward and reverse paths, PathDoctor helps administrators to more easily diagnose IP routing and performance problems. Administrators can easily check routers and router interfaces for "bad" or "suspect" operations symptoms. These symptoms can be user-defined, and based on rule expressions from MIB-II or private enterprise MIB variables.

PathDoctor automatically graphs routing paths, showing vendor, type, and traffic information for specified routers and router interfaces. Congested or resource-constrained routers and interfaces can easily be identified via color-coded status displays. Administrators can customize alarm thresholds and rules to fit individual network behavior patterns.

PathDoctor can be operated as a nonintrusive application, as SNMP polling traffic is throttled to prevent diagnostic traffic from impacting measured operations. PathDoctor reads, but never sets, MIB variable values.

By providing path diagnostics and other valuable data, PathDoctor provides advantages over the *traceroute* function embedded with TCP/IP, which is restricted to providing only end-point usage, with no path diagnostics.

PathDoctor is more effective than using plain SNMP *route path* supported by OpenView NNM, as PathDoctor can provide more varied statistics describing performance between two specified end points.

System Watchdog

Polycenter System Watchdog consolidates server and workstation performance and event data collected from agents residing on distributed systems.

System Watchdog agents are designed to run on remote systems, detecting abnormal events and alerting operators or initiating automatic, user-specified corrective actions. The System Watchdog consolidator component can log all messages for later analysis, and sends e-mail or places phone calls to specified operators when particular messages are received.

System Watchdog agents monitor system, subsystem, network, and process events. System events include CPU errors, memory errors, Ethernet errors, and stopped processors. Subsystem events include disk errors, disk state errors, component interface problems, disk near-full conditions, printer problems, and shadow set problems. Network level events include node unreachable, node out of resources, node unknown, or other connection problems. Process level events including process looping, missing processes, missing batch jobs, device and batch queue problems, and queue manager problems.

System Watchdog supports policy-based management through flexible system monitoring schedules and user-defined monitoring sequences. By defining application-specific messages to the agent component, business application programs can be monitored by System Watchdog. Security schemes are supported for OSF/1 and OpenVMS environments.

Console Manager

Console Manager supports remote management of computer systems and attached printers by intercepting console messages appearing as output over RS-232C lines and/or printer ports. Messages are scanned for predefined text strings according to a pattern-matching algorithm. When specified strings are detected, Console Manager prioritizes them according to severity levels.

From Console Manager, operators can control these same monitored systems to reboot, run diagnostics, backup disks, and even install software. Each Console Manager application can control up to 200 systems or devices. Protocols supported include Local Area Transport (LAT), Telnet, and selected terminal emulation protocols.

Console Manager supports an OSF/Motif GUI with a map of monitored systems represented as icons.

FullSail

Polycenter FullSail consists of three components—Account Manager, File System Manager, and Performance Monitor—with a Motif-based front end. FullSail is somewhat analogous to HP AdminCenter, with added performance monitoring features.

The Motif GUI, called Navigator, allows an administrator to group managed systems into a *Management Set*. Among other things, this allows launching of either the Account Manager, File System Manager, or Performance Monitor application with a preselected management set. Management sets can be grouped by location (building, floor, etc.), department (finance, marketing, engineering), processor type, or other criteria.

The Account Manager application makes it easier to add, modify, delete, or review user accounts. The Account Manager supports NFS-mounted home directories; the application can be customized.

The File System Manager simplifies configuration and monitoring of file system mount points and other tasks, such as NFS mounts to hundreds of systems simultaneously.

Using the Performance Monitor, the administrator can monitor file systems on the network for availability and capacity. Administrators can set thresholds on key parameters such as load average, swapping rate, free memory, memory in use, disk throughput, buffer cache usage, and NFS statistics.

HUBwatch

The HUBwatch application supports SNMP-based monitoring and control of the entire range of Digital's DEChub product line, including modules within stackable hub offerings as well as high-end DEChub 900 MultiSwitch and GIGAswitch/FDDI equipment. In addition to collecting SNMP MIB variable information, HUBwatch can be used to balance network traffic and allocate bandwidth by using point-and-click facilities to easily switch modules, port groups, or individual ports to different LAN channels. HUBwatch also supports a serial line interface protocol (SLIP) interface, ensuring a consistent user interface for both in-band and out-of-band access.

DECnet Manager

DECnet Manager allows Polycenter NetView operators to monitor and control DECnet IV nodes and DECnet/OSI nodes. For DECnet IV nodes, Digital LAN bridges, and Digital terminal servers, this includes automatic discovery, autotopology, polling for status, and support for basic commands. Event support also is provided for DECnet IV nodes. Autotopology is not supported for DECnet/OSI nodes, but status polling and support for basic commands are provided. DECnet Manager also supports a Trace Route feature between any two DECnet IV or DECnet/OSI nodes.

DECnet Manager utilizes Digital's Network Information and Command Exchange/Network Control Protocol (NICE/NCP) to discover and communicate with DECnet IV nodes. DECnet Manager includes a facility for graphing key performance and utilization parameters for DECnet nodes, lines, and circuits.

DECnet OSI nodes are managed via Digital's implementation of the Common Management Information Protocol (CMIP). Digital LAN bridges are managed via the Remote Bridge Management System (RBMS) and terminal servers via Digital's Maintenance Operations Protocol (MOP).

The DECnet Manager application effectively replaces the older DECmcc/Polycenter Network Manager 200/400, and the DEC MSU/Polycenter SNMP Manager 300. DECnet Manager can be linked with the older existing products via event passing mechanisms. Users of DECmcc can continue to use customized DECmcc code with DECnet Manager.

Digital Products for Windows and Windows NT Environments

In addition to Polycenter NetView on OSF/1, Digital offers a Windows-based management system called ManageWorks, as well as two important Windows NT-based products: Polycenter Asset Works and Polycenter NetView on NT. Figure 16.2 shows Polycenter NetView NT's support of the Object Linking and Embedding (OLE) facility to Polycenter Asset Works. Both of these products offer technological advantages over the competition, and are well worth considering.

ManageWorks

ManageWorks is a versatile, affordable product for managing single-site LANs. The product is somewhat comparable to Hewlett-Packard's HP OpenView Workgroup Node Manager (WNM), described in Chap. 13. However, OpenView WNM is largely restricted to SNMP-based monitoring of LAN-attached devices. In contrast, ManageWorks supports not only SNMP device management, but also user administration and server management for Novell NetWare (IPX), IBM LAN Manager (NetBEUI), and Digital PathWorks LANs

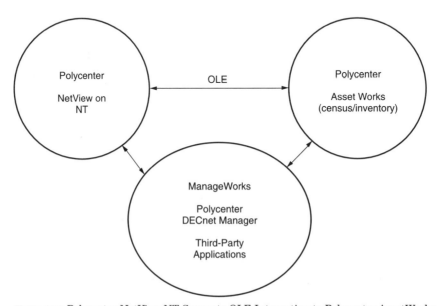

Figure 16.2 Polycenter NetView NT Supports OLE Integration to Polycenter AssetWorks

as well. ManageWorks focuses on end-user services much more strongly than does HP OpenView WNM.

For example, ManageWorks allows administrators to combine multiple NetWare administrative console functions under one GUI, meaning multiple NetWare servers can be managed simultaneously through a single window.

ManageWorks interfaces with NetWare consoles through standard NetWare APIs. The product also supports the OLE 2.0 object model standard, allowing users to embed OLE objects, icons, or files and link them directly into the ManageWorks interface. The ManageWorks Software Developer's Kit (SDK) provides access to the WinSock application programming interface (API), and the Microsoft Foundation Class (MFC) API set for viewers and management applications.

ManageWorks can pass SNMP traps to Polycenter NetView on OSF/1; the two systems will support soon the ability to share configuration data, as shown in Fig. 16.3. Distributed polling will be possible in forthcoming versions, creating a highly scalable solution.

Digital sponsors a business partners program for ManageWorks. Third-party applications supporting the ManageWorks platform include HelpStar from Help Desk Technology, AuditWare from Preferred Systems for NetWare server auditing, NetCon from Capacity for PC asset management and remote control.

ManageWorks is available in 16- or 32-bit versions, and supports Windows 95, Windows 3.x, Windows for Workgroups, and Windows NT.

Polycenter AssetWorks (PAW)

Polycenter AssetWorks (PAW) is a hardware/software inventory and software distribution tool that is layered on top of Microsoft's Systems Management (MSM) Server. Whereas Microsoft's product provides software distribution, remote PC control, and administration for Windows and Windows-NT systems, PAW extends the inventorying and software distribution capability to cover a variety of Unix platforms as well as OpenVMS over TCP/IP, DECnet,

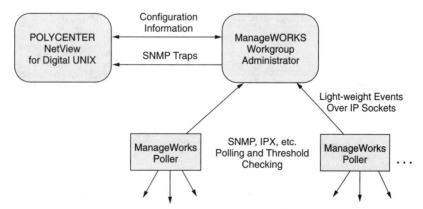

Figure 16.3 Polycenter NetView and ManageWorks Directions

and PathWorks networks. PAW also provides a reporting capability, a fundamental feature that MSM Server lacks. Because MSM Server does not provide automated reporting, customers must define and generate SQL queries to obtain reports. PAW does provide canned reports that can be customized extensively for frequency (daily, weekly, etc.), and by category (PCs only, Unix nodes only, etc.), output format, location, and scheduling.

PAW collects hardware and software inventory data automatically, once PAW agents have been installed in Unix and OpenVMS systems. PAW supports drag-and-drop software distribution to OSF/1, Windows, SunOS, Solaris, AIX, HP-UX, and Macintosh systems.

PAW can work in conjunction with Polycenter NetView on OSF/1 or NT by exchanging SNMP trap and topology data, as shown in Fig. 16.4. Polycenter NetView on NT affords a seamless interface with PAW. For example, Users can view *property sheets* of status and configuration information on failed distributions, thereby gaining critical event history for diagnostic purposes.

Summary

Digital's Polycenter suite includes many point-product solutions for open systems as well as for additional DECnet environments. The Polycenter Manager on NetView (both the OSF/1 and Windows NT versions) are derivatives of IBM NetView for AIX, which in turn is a derivative of HP OpenView Network Node Manager. All of these products share many of the core processes described in Chap. 4.

Digital has added several important enhancements to the NetView for AIX code base, including performance improvements, router management features, and enhancements for ease of use. In particular, Digital was the first vendor to successfully port the HP OpenView NNM code base to the Windows NT platform.

With the acquisition of Digital's systems and network management technology by Computer Associates in April 1996, the status of Digital's Polycenter program seems unclear. However, the NetView-based products were not acquired, to fulfill Digital's licensing agreement with IBM. Digital will continue to market and support Polycenter Manager on NetView until well into 1997 at least.

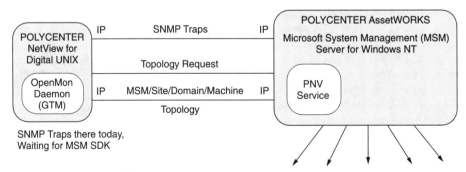

Figure 16.4 Polycenter NetView and Polycenter AssetWorks

17

NCR OneVision and OperationsAdvantage; AT&T OneVision

OneVision is an enterprise management strategy first announced by AT&T in 1994. At that time, the concept of OneVision was to provide end-to-end network and system management solutions for both commercial and telecom sectors. In the commercial sector, OneVision took the form of HP OpenView-based product sets and integrated applications. The OneVision direction in the telecommunications area was a bit more complex, including both HP OpenView Distributed Management (DM) technology and object-oriented middleware known as the BaseWorX Applications Platform.

In August 1995, AT&T announced its intention to spin off NCR, formerly AT&T Global Information Solutions (GIS), into an independent, publicly traded company come 1997. In late 1995 and early 1996, there was a certain amount of confusion and uncertainty over the future of OneVision. In 1996, NCR reaffirmed its decision to continue the HP OpenView-based OneVision strategy for its commercial customers. The following sections discuss the March 1996 release of OneVision products. The status of AT&T's version of OneVision is discussed separately following the NCR section of this chapter.

NCR OneVision Components

The core of the 1994 OneVision announcement was a technology agreement with Hewlett-Packard to license HP OpenView products, including the following:

- Network Management: HP OpenView Network Node Manager (NNM) would become the basis of OneVision Node Manager.

- Systems Management: HP IT/Operations (formerly OperationsCenter) would function as the core of OneVision OperationsAdvantage.

Part of this agreement called for AT&T GIS to port HP OpenView Network Node Manager (NNM) to NCR 3000 series hardware running NCR's MP-RAS Unix operating system. This product, known as OneVision Node Manager, has been supported through versions 4.0 and 4.1 (Tornado Releases I and II) of HP's NNM software.

As Chapters 15–16 explain, IBM and Digital modified HP's NNM code somewhat in fashioning their own network management offerings. In contrast, OneVision Node Manager is a direct code drop of NNM. Yet the OneVision product family and strategy as a whole can be differentiated from HP OpenView in several important respects, including the following:

- Support for managing SNA and asynch devices, in addition to TCP/IP

- OperationsAdvantage integrated application suites for systems management

Support for SNA connections is provided by the NCR Protocol Switch for OneVision System (PSW). This product provides an LU6.2 SNA transport interface for the OneVision NNM, as well as remote TCP/IP nodes. PSW enables remote TCP/IP LANs connected to an SNA backbone to communicate with and be managed by OneVision NNM. This is particularly useful in the banking sector, where SNA backbone networks frequently are connected with TCP/IP LANs at remote branches. Figure 17.1 illustrates the PSW connecting two TCP/IP LANs via an SNA wide area network (WAN).

Support for asynchronous device management is provided by NCR Computer Manager, discussed later in this chapter.

OperationsAdvantage and Bundled Solutions

OperationsAdvantage is a "best in class" integrated set of systems management applications targeted at NCR customers. NCR first announced OperationsAdvantage in 1995; in March, 1996, the vendor shipped Release 2.0 of the product suite. These applications include several developed by NCR as well as a number of HP products and value-added applications from third parties.

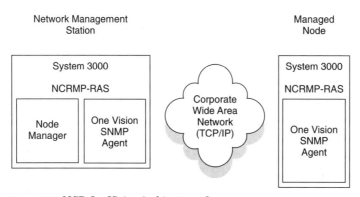

Figure 17.1 NCR OneVision Architecture Overture

Figure 17.2 depicts the NCR OperationsAdvantage architecture. HP IT/Operations serves as the systems management consolidation point; Oracle is the management data repository. OperationsAdvantage 2.0 can be launched from the IT/Operations screen. NCR-developed and other value-added applications of OperationsAdvantage 2.0 are integrated into IT/Operations so that events can be passed to the console in three ways:

1. Through the IT/Operations message API, which can be added to any application
2. Via SNMP traps
3. Via the reading of an application message in a logfile for event consolidation

While it draws heavily upon IT/Operations and other HP-supplied products, NCR OperationsAdvantage is differentiated from HP offerings in several ways:

- Default scripts: OperationsAdvantage includes unique default monitoring scripts for IT/Operations, and integration templates for NCR's TopEnd transaction monitor and NCR's Lifekeeper cluster management system.
- Management Bundles.
- Complementary Products.

The Management Bundles and Complementary Products can be considered the two primary components of OperationsAdvantage 2.0.

Management Bundles

With Release 2.0 of OperationsAdvantage, NCR is offering two distinct Management Bundles:

- Distributed Management Environment OA
- Data Center Environment OA

Each offering is based on IT/Operations. Customers may mix and match Complementary Products to round out either Management Bundle. NCR offers a single *OAinstall* installation facility supported by both Management Bundles. This utility provides a graphical front end that guides the user through the initial installation and setup processes.

One major benefit of the OA Management Bundles is that the feature eases the customer's burden of properly configuring hardware and software to support launch and, in some cases, of event integration between a number of complex and powerful packages. The result can be significant cost savings in terms of customer staff salary paid for the integration time and effort. Ongoing maintenance of the bundle also is reduced, provided the customer wants to stay on the same release levels supported in the bundle.

Distributed Management Environment OA is targeted at vertical markets, particularly banking and retail. It supports a large number of geographically

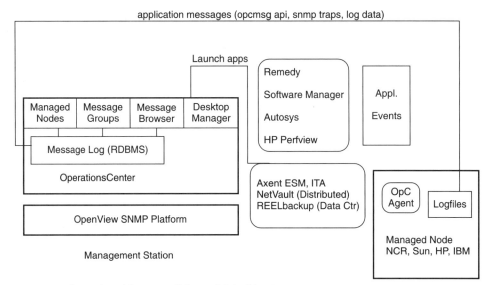

Figure 17.2 OperationsAdvantage Release 2.0 Architecture

dispersed business locations, such as retail outlets or local bank branch offices. Because these remote branch offices do not have technical staff on site, central monitoring of the computing environment is essential. NCR targets Distributed Management Environment OA at these organizations, particularly those supporting 50 or more remote sites. In addition, the Distributed Management Environment OA 2.0 assumes the presence of at least one midrange NCR server per branch or store, and traffic pattens supporting the forwarding of transactional data to a central site for corporate processing— typically over SNA, TCP/IP, or asynchronous connections.

Table 17.1 lists the products and functional areas included in the Distributed Management Environment OA 2.0. All of the applications in the bundle are, at minimum, preintegrated for the customer at the launch level. Remedy AR System, HP PerfView, NCR Software Manager, and Platinum AutoSys are additionally integrated at the event level. For example, the Remedy interface allows trouble tickets to be created automatically when events are received; closing a ticket can trigger acknowledgment of the OperationsAdvantage event.

Table 17.2 lists the productions and functional areas included in the Data Center Environment OA 2.0. The same integration levels apply for Distributed Management Environment. The Data Center Environment OA 2.0 is targeted at Unix-based data centers with a small number of large Unix processors, a local TCP/IP LAN/internetwork, and dedicated staff on site. A mainframe-like orientation also is assumed, although IBM equipment or protocols are not necessarily a prerequisite. Batch processing, massive amounts of stored data in DASD, disk arrays, optical jukebox, tape libraries, etc., are assumed to be present, as well as the use of decision support systems running off corporate databases.

Complementary Products for OA 2.0

The Complementary Products of OperationsAdvantage 2.0 include applications from NCR, HP, and third-party vendors (Table 17.3). The functional areas covered by the Complementary Products are broad, and include:

- NCR hardware cluster status monitoring
- Computer and asynchronous device monitoring
- Print/output management
- Job/resource accounting and charge-back
- Software license metering
- Disk and storage management
- Database monitoring
- Server performance monitoring and capacity planning

While the NCR Management Bundles provide a certain level of integration with IT/Operations out of the box, most of the Complementary Products have minimal integration with IT/Operations. Two exceptions are NCR LifeKeeper FRS and NCR Computer Manager. LifeKeeper FRS is integrated at the event level with IT/Operations, forwarding alerts to the IT/Operations console; NCR Computer Manager can forward its alarms to IT/Operations agents.

Table 17.1. Distributed Management Bundle for NCR OperationsAdvantage 2.0

Product	Function	Integration level
HP IT/Operations	Consolidation (fault management—systems)	Launch
NCR OneVision NNM	Consolidation (fault management—network devices)	Launch
Platinum Autosys	Job scheduling; administration	Launch, event
NCR Software Manager	Software distribution; asset management	Launch, event
AT&T NetVault	Backup; data management	Launch
HP PerfView	Server performance management	Launch, event
Remedy Action Request (AR) System	Problem management; trouble-ticketing	Launch, event
Axent OmniGuard Intruder Alert and Axent Enterprise Security Manager	Security Management	Launch

Table 17.2. Data Center Management Bundle for NCR OperationsAdvantage 2.0

Product	Function	Integration level
HP IT/Operations	Infrastructure (fault management—systems)	Launch
NCR OneVision NNM	Infrastructure (fault management—network devices)	Launch
Platinum Autosys	Job scheduling; administration	Launch, event
StorageTeck REELibrarian StorageTeck REELbackup	Backup, storage management; data management	Launch
HP PerfView	Server performance management	Launch, event
Remedy Action Request (AR) System	Problem management; trouble-ticketing	Launch, event
Axent OmniGuard Intruder Alert and Axent Enterprise Security Manager	Security Management	Launch

NCR management applications

The following paragraphs describe the NCR applications in the Management Bundles and Complementary Products portions of OperationsAdvantage 2.0. These applications span critical Unix and desktop systems administration functions such as software distribution, automated remote server management, and user administration. Included are:

- NCR Software Manager
- NCR Computer Manager
- NCR LifeKeeper
- NCR TopEnd

NCR Software Manager. Software Manager is a mature, reliable electronic software distribution application that has a strong customer base in both the retail and banking environments. HP's Software Distributor is a direct competitor to NCR Software Manager.

NCR Software Manager has a client/server architecture and supports distribution, installation, and deinstallation of packaged applications, in-house applications, and data files. The product supports attribute-based distribution (providing the ability to group targets rather than maintaining long lists), fan-out distribution, software copy count, and multiplatform/multiprotocol support.

NCR Software Manager consists of the following:

- Unix-based Central Manager
- Gateway servers supporting Unix SVR4 SCO UNIX, SunOS, Solaris, and HP-UX
- Agents supporting DOS, OS/2 Unix SVr4, SCO Unix, self-service terminals (SST), NetWare, SunOS, Solaris, HP-UX, AIX, Windows, and Windows NT.

A wide variety of targets and LAN and WAN protocols are supported including NetWare 3.X, StarGROUP LAN Manager 2.1, FTP PC/TCP for DOS 2.05 and PC/TCP for OS/2 1.2. Communication protocols supported include TCP/IP, LU6.2 over SDLC or X.25, OSI over X.25, SDLC, Ethernet, and TCP/IP on Token-Ring.

Table 17.3. Complementary Products for NCR OperationsAdvantage 2.0

Product	Function
NCR Computer Manager	Fault management (computer systems), asynch device management
NCR Hardware Manager	Fault management (NCR systems)
NCR Customer Support Facility	Fault/problem management (NCR systems)
NCR Job Accounting	Resource/asset management
NCR Disk Array Plus NCR Volume Manager and Administrator NCR Teradata Manager NCR Archive Storage Facility	Storage management Data management
NCR Lifekeeper Series	Data/transaction management
AT&T Commvault HSM (R)	Storage management
Axent Enterprise Access Control (R)	Administration
BGS Best/1	System performance management
BMC Patrol (R)	Database monitoring
CompuWare Ecotools (R)	Database monitoring
CompuWare EcoChargeback	Resource accounting/chargeback
Dazel Output Management System (R)	Printer management/administration
Gradient Licensing (R)	Software metering/asset management

(R) indicates reference sell product

NCR Computer Manager. NCR Computer Manager is designed specifically for Unix fault management. The product's strengths include multiplatform support, flexible configuration of agents, and support for secure manager/agent communications and a variety of WAN transports. The product also offers a Message Collector utility option for gathering asynchronously generated alarm messages across the network. The Message Collector utility allows a limited degree of network-wide filtering.

All NCR Computer Manager agents perform scheduled data collection—hourly, daily, or less frequently. The agent executes the appropriate Unix system commands to collect the statistics, and sends the results back to the Computer Manager. The product supports asynchronous alarm forwarding. Computer Manager agents can forward console error messages detected by the computer's operating system. These messages take the form of *Notice*, *Warning*, or *Panic* messages, depending upon the severity of the condition.

With NCR Computer Manager agents, customers can configure polling schedules, thresholds, and types of data. Computer Manager agents out of the box support proactive systems monitoring of more than 20 managed parameters, including those covering system configuration (kernel), file system configuration, user/group data, device inventory, maintenance logs, disk performance, overdue jobs, system utilization by user, system response time, and *sar* data.

NCR Computer Manager agents also support security management by monitoring for failed logins, *su* attempts, UUCP connections, and Set UID files. The product supports multilevel manager access and encrypted commands for enhanced security.

NCR Computer Manager is tightly integrated with IT/Operations. Computer Manager creates icons for all managed systems, forwarding all alarms to IT/Operations through the *opcmsg* API. IT/Operations can then associate Computer Manager alarms with the appropriate Computer Manager agent machines, including non-TCP/IP systems. This allows management of both IP and non-IP nodes at the OperationsAdvantage-IT/Operations console.

NCR LifeKeeper. LifeKeeper supports high availability and cluster management for NCR hardware systems. Integration templates provided with OperationsAdvantage allow customers to administer LifeKeeper components through the IT/Operations interface. Functions include administering and configuring cluster components; NCR's Distributed Lock Manager (DLM) application also is supported through this interface. In addition, the IT/Operations console provides a special message group called Application Availability for displaying LifeKeeper and DLM message. Clicking on this icon triggers a display of IT/Operations event messages initiated by LifeKeeper and DLM log messages.

NCR TopEnd. TopEnd is NCR's strategic middleware for application and transaction management. OperationsAdvantage supports management of TopEnd via the IT/Operations console as follows:

- Monitoring of TopEnd alerts
- Launching TopEnd's global administration facility from the IT/Operations console
- Administering TopEnd runtime managed nodes through the TopEnd global administration user interface

Customers must install an IT/Operations agent on each TopEnd runtime node to be managed. The IT/Operations logfile encapsulator can then monitor errors and other informational messages as logged by the TopEnd node. TopEnd messages are assigned to the application message group icon.

Third-party applications

Third-party applications in NCR OperationsAdvantage Management Bundles include:

- Remedy AR System
- Platinum AutoSys
- AT&T NetVault
- StorageTek REELibrarian and REELbackup
- Axent Omniguard Enterprise Security Manager and Intruder Alert

Remedy AR System. Remedy's AR System is a trouble ticketing and work flow management application supporting internal client/server help desk operations. Remedy ARS enables automated creation, transmission, escalation, and closure of action request trouble tickets. Remedy ARS comprises three tools:

1. Submit tool, for entering trouble tickets
2. Notify tool, for broadcasting messages to designated personnel
3. Admin tool, for setting up help desk policies and procedures

AR System is integrated with IT/Operations at the launch and event levels.

Platinum AutoSys. AutoSys supports job scheduling and job control across distributed Unix systems. Scheduling can be based upon predefined job dependencies, calendar events, or file arrival. AutoSys supports batch queue functionality, dynamic load balancing, and job execution across heterogeneous platforms. In addition, AutoSys supports interdependent processing and complex branching logic. Related tasks may be grouped into job streams and managed as one unit of work.

AutoSys also supports error recovery; jobs may be restarted or rerouted depending upon events. Error recovery procedures can also be automatically triggered. AutoSys generates events that can be stored in an Oracle RDBMS. AutoSys is integrated with IT/Operations at the launch and event levels.

StorageTek REELbackup and REELibrarian. REELbackup is a Unix-based backup system for backing up data to tape over a network. The StorageTek products support backup and recovery for the Data Center Management Bundle of OperationsAdvantage. (Note: Backup and recovery for the Distributed Management Bundle is supported by AT&T NetVault, described below.) The product is capable of multiplexing multiple backups onto a single volume; checkpoint restart and disk/file recovery is supported, as are data compression and encryption. Via automatic backup scheduling, unattended operations are supported. A real-time status monitoring facility is included. REELbackup complements the REELibrarian network-based tape management and cataloging application. REELibrarian has a client/server architecture supporting ad hoc tape usage through a centralized processing procedure which presents mount requests to tape operators.

Axent Technologies Omniguard Enterprise Security Manager (ESM) and Intruder Alert. Omniguard ESM and ITA provide security monitoring for OperationsAdvantage. ESM supports a GUI-based facility for configuring security policies over diverse computing and organizational structures. ESM tracks both current security status and trends over time. A variety of reporting formats are supported, including graphs, bar charts, and spreadsheets in both print and screen delivery modes. ESM is capable of monitoring whether security policies are being followed as prescribed. ITA supports real-time monitoring of system messages, commands, and statuses. ITA can forward these alerts via e-mail or broadcast, and can trigger automatic actions such as stopping Unix processes, disabling a user's account, remotely executing commands, or terminating a program.

AT&T NetVault. NetVault is a distributed tape backup application providing backup and restore capabilities for the Distributed Management bundle. NetVault has a client/server architecture, and supports unattended full, selective, or incremental backups with automatic scheduling. Simultaneous, multiple clients can be backed up to parallel drives. Data compression is done on-the-fly, and overflow management is supported for handling large files. Media supported include QIC, DAT, DLT, 3mm, Exabyte, and StorageTek.

AT&T OneVision

For more than 15 years, AT&T has marketed products supporting network and systems management in both the data and telecommunications areas. Many of AT&T's products are mature element management systems addressing special components of AT&T's carrier service offerings; others are targeted at managing customer premise equipment.

Over the last several years, AT&T has made several attempts to position these offerings as a comprehensive suite. In 1989, AT&T introduced the Accumaster Integrator for hierarchical integration of both voice and data element management systems. Three years later, AT&T began reselling NetLab's SNMP/CMIP integrated management platform under the AT&T StarSentry logo. At the same time, AT&T began working with Teknekron and other partners to develop a highly scalable object-oriented platform for telecommunications operation support systems (OSS) called BaseWorX. However, AT&T faced an enormous challenging when it came to integrating its broad range of products and services around three platforms: Accumaster, StarSentry, and BaseWorX.

Architectural Platform for Telecommunications Management Development

AT&T will develop future telecommunications management products and services around the integration of HP's OpenView Distributed Management (DM) platform and AT&T's existing BaseWorX technology. HP OpenView DM is described in more detail in Chap. 10.

By establishing a common core of platform technology and a unified structure for both BaseWorX and OpenView, AT&T hopes to more quickly bring to market management applications that span the customer premise (CPM), customer network (CNM), and telecommunications network (TNM) management domains and permit true end-to-end management solutions.

The AT&T BaseWorX Applications Platform offers comprehensive "middleware" capabilities facilitating the development of OSI network management and operations support systems (OSS) applications targeted primarily to the management of highly complex public telecommunications networks. BaseWorX supports the following attributes:

- Peer-to-peer support
- OSI X.700 CMIP support
- Operations, administration, and maintenance (OA&M) support
- Telecom Management Networks (TMN) support
- Operations Support Systems (OSS) support
- Development environment
- Runtime environment
- Common Management Information Service (CMIS) services
- ASN.1 compiler

The integrated platform architecture is structured around complementary "best in class" technologies from both platforms, which will be combined to form a core set of functionality for both. The core platform is intended to preserve compatibility with existing BaseWorX and OpenView DM applications and to permit application software portability while enabling interoperability at the management platform. The first phase integration provides:

- Common Applications Process Management: Integration of the BaseWorX platform Reusable Operations, Administration, and Maintenance (ROAM) components with Open View Process Management functions.

- Common Communications Structure for Management Applications and Services: Integration of the BaseWorX Common Communications Platform (CCP) APIs with the OpenView Communications Infrastructure and OpenView family of GDMO development tools.

- Common Application Programmer Interfaces: Use of XMP on the OpenView CI/OPI as the industry-standard API, with CCP APIs also supported for compatibility with existing BaseWorX applications and for offering a higher-level programmer interface for developer ease of use and productivity.

During this first phase, AT&T and HP will collaborate on the assessment of options for implementing CORBA-compliant object technology in the core platform, with the objective of developing a common architecture and implementation approach that could be implemented in a second phase.

During the second phase, AT&T and HP will focus on the implementation of common object technology, a common data repository, user interface integration, and any additional functionality identified through marketplace needs assessment.

Platform core extensions will be developed by both parties to meet the unique needs of particular application domains. Each such extension will utilize the functionality residing in the common core and be dependent on the common core. Through the concept of architecture profiling, the logical linking of appropriate core extensions to the common core platform, specific management domain profiles can be created. Examples of these may be CPM Application Architecture profiles, TNM Application Architecture profiles, and CNM Application Architecture Profiles, and combinations of these.

Figure 17.3 shows the three targeted management domain areas of OneVision. The figure also indicates which areas are supported by what platforms. As can

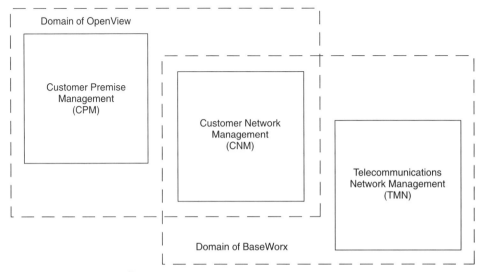

Figure 17.3 Management Domains

be seen, the primary goal of platforms integration is Customer Networks management (CNM).

The resulting CNM products will support an X.11 Windows/Motif user interface. The platform also supports the Tuxedo/T Transaction Monitor for distributed transaction processing. The Common Communication Platform (CCP) APIs from the BaseWorX platform, along with the XMP API from HP OpenView DM, will provide transport independence for OneVision applications. The OpenView Protocol Interface (OPI) derived from the OpenView DM platform, will allow customized stacks to be integrated with OpenView's postmaster daemon. OpenView DM also will contribute SNMP support, including an SNMP stack implementation, an SNMP MIB Browser, IP discovery and layout, and MIB application builder, as described earlier.

AT&T OneVision Overview

AT&T OneVision is designed to give AT&T customers a single, consistent view and control point for their public and private networks, comprising AT&T and third-party products and services.

The OneVision architecture represents a flexible approach for the management of heterogeneous resources and services supporting a business enterprise. AT&T is specifying an Application Integration Architecture to extend the interoperability of systems to interoperability of applications and services within systems. The architecture's specifications are based on de facto and international de jure standards (IETF/SNMP, ITUT/ISO) and specifications used by industry consortia (NM Forum, OMG, OSF, X/Open, and DMTF). The following section is a high-level description of the architecture and represents a vision that will be realized as more and more OneVision applications become available.

Levels of integration

The intention of the architecture is to allow for the integration of management applications and the information they deliver. It does allow for applications to integrate at various levels as described below, ranging from a very tight integration to a menu-level integration. The levels are presented in increasing levels of integration, with each level including the properties of the preceding levels.

Menu. In this level of integration, applications can be launched from the same menu bar in the graphical user interface (GUI). This level of integration allows a single point from which a variety of applications (including ISVs and third parties) can be launched, while sharing the hardware and operating systems and the software engine for the GUI.

Map. The next level of integration is at the iconic map level. Here, the integrated applications share the same map and the methods used in traversing the map for performing the management functions. This allows a common interaction paradigm for the management of equipment and services. This level of integration also defines the ways by which managed entities are grouped or structured, based on such user-defined characteristics as topology, geography, connectivity, responsibility, security, etc.

Events. In this level, the applications share the methods and mechanisms by which events are received, displayed, and processed in the same manner. This allows the users to treat, in the same manner, events that range from simple informational ones to notification of alarm conditions triggered by a possibly complex sequence of events and actions, without distinguishing the details of their origin (SNMP trap, CMIP notification, proprietary alarm, etc.).

Interoperation. Applications integrated at this level exchange information via the architecture's application programming interfaces (APIs). This is useful when there is a need for one application to base its function on information from another (e.g., a trouble ticket generated automatically based on information from another application about the down state of a printer). The specification of APIs for information exchange is crucial for this level of integration and is particularly useful for the development of applications by ISVs, third parties, and the various AT&T business units.

Database. In this level, the applications share the same means of data storage, and may even possibly share some of the schema in the database. This allows for the use of a single technology for data storage, and also allows information stored by different applications to be retrieved jointly in order to establish some relationship between the management information.

Data Model. In this highest level of integration, the applications view the data using the same model (SNMP SMI, CMIP GDMO, CORBA IDS); thus, the means of exchanging information, as well as retrieval and modification of persistent information, becomes very standardized. This allows for great efficiency in the manipulation of management information and avoids unnecessary replication of data by different applications. The use of the same model to represent the data allows the applications to establish relationships between the various information in an easier, structured manner. It also provides indirectly for the interoperability of applications.

The architecture is structured into layers: Management Solutions, Management Applications, Management Infrastructure, and Management Instrumentation.

The Management Solutions component shown in Fig. 17.4 builds upon the suite of management applications described in the next section. These solutions will be customized, installed, supported, and maintained as needed by the customer for whom the solution is tailored. The solutions can be provided in the form of professional services or outsourcing. They also can be offered as vertical solutions to specific industry segments such as financial banking, retail, or transportation. They can be offered as horizontal solutions such as end-to-end management of bandwidth across the customer's enterprise.

The Management Applications component, shown in Fig. 17.5, provides the user with three categories of management functionality. The first category, Management Support Applications, provides a suite of applications independent

Figure 17.4 Management Solutions

of the managed resources, such as Trouble Desk, Reports, Inventory, Accounting, etc. The second category, Management of Resources, provides a suite of applications for the management of computer and communications resources in the customer's premises. This includes applications for management of such resources as routers, hubs, desktop computers, etc. The third category, Management of Services, provides a suite of applications that enable customers to manage network services as provided and allowed by AT&T (e.g. InterSpan Frame Relay, 800 Service and SDN) and other service providers.

The Management Infrastructure, also referred to as *platform,* provides services based on the abstraction of commonly required services and functions that are used by most applications. As Fig. 17.6 shows, it is structured into four components: User Interface, Common Management Services, Management Distribution Services, and Management Information Services. The architecture provides Application Programming Interfaces (APIs) for exchange of information between these components and the applications. These APIs enable new management applications and new managed elements to be added with minimal impact on existing applications or managed elements.

Selected architecture features

Some OneVision architectural features of note include application-to-application communications, manager-agent communications, and platform communications. Supported facilities for application-application communications include:

- Interface Definition Language (IDL): The architecture allows applications to communicate via standardized object interfaces such as the OMG IDL.

- Remote Procedure Call (RPC): Applications also could use RPC mechanisms to implement services in a client/server environment.

Supported facilities for Manager-Agent communications include the X/Open Management Protocol (XMP). This interface is an API standardized via X/Open to enable management applications to send requests to, and receive responses and event reports from, agent systems (or management systems

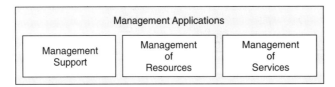

Figure 17.5 Management Applications

playing the agent role) using CMIP or SNMP. Applications using this interface in the architecture also use the X/Open ISO-Abstract-Data Manipulation (XOM) API for some of the associated services.

Supported facilities for Platform Communications include:

- Inter-Process Communication (IPC) within system: For the distribution of platform services between processes on the same system, the architecture uses APIs to hide the details of the underlying interprocess communication facilities such as pipes, sockets, message queues, semaphores, and shared memory.

- Inter-Process Communication (IPC) across systems: For the distribution of platform services between processes across multiple systems, the architecture uses APIs to hide the details of the underlying medium of transport (such as TCP/IP, OSI, StarLAN, Datakit, X.25) and the interfaces used (such as sockets and XTI/I1LI).

- Legacy Communications: The architecture provides APIs through which communications with legacy systems and elements can be maintained, and gradually migrated over time.

- Directory: The architecture provides APIs for accessing standardized directory services such as DCE Cell Directory Service (CDS), Internet Domain Name Service (DNS), and X.50a.

- Security: The architecture provides APIs for accessing security services dating to authentication and authorization. The security schemes are provided at different levels including login, object, map, network, and at the agent level.

Management information services. This component provides services for manipulation of stored management information, both persistent and volatile, and enables easy migration between database technologies by providing transparency of the actual means of data storage. Facilities supported include a data repository, persistent/transient data, class/instance data, and transaction services.

Management instrumentation. The instrumentation layer of the architecture provides an abstraction of the managed elements representing real-world entities (e.g., router or ATM switch) based on standardized (de jure and de facto), and in some cases proprietary, representations. Facilities supported include DMTF/DMI, SNMP, OSI/GDMO, and OMG/CORBA.

Management distribution techniques and model translation techniques. Management distribution techniques include support for proxy agents and smart agents. Model translation techniques include SNMP/CMIP MIB and proxy translation.

Reusable OA&M Services (ROAM). As applications become more complex, they need to be managed like the network they are designed to manage. One approach is to use the same mechanisms to manage the platform as are used to manage the environment. This creates a bootstrap problem, however, in that when the platform is misconfigured or failing, these functions will not be guaranteed to be operating properly. The Operations, Administration, and Maintenance (OA&M) components of the integrated platform deal with managing the applications via a separate, out of band, mechanism. This includes such areas as Configuration Management, Fault Management, Execution Management, Security Management, Performance Management, and system-wide OA&M services like Resource Management, Multiple Application Administration, and Software Fault Tolerance. In the interest of brevity, only Fault Management and Execution Management are discussed below.

Fault Management. The BaseWorX platform's Fault Management provides an application programming interface which is used by the platform and application processes to specify that internal processing errors have been detected. The resulting messages can then be routed to a number of different locations and/or collected and logged in a central location within the distributed complex. It provides capabilities for incorporating messages from other third party packages which log their error messages into package specific locations. It also has the ability to trigger specific actions based on the messages/alarms which are logged.

The fault management capabilities of the OpenView platform provide a mechanism for logging information in a consistent way on a per-machine basis. One important aspect of the logging facilities provided as part of the OpenView platform is that the implementation makes use of a high-speed shared memory queue, where messages are dumped to minimize the impact of message logging on the performance of the calling process. A logging daemon process, which is working asynchronously to the other processes in the system, picks up the messages which have been dumped into shared memory and logs them appropriately.

The initial integrated platform architecture includes both styles of log management as they exist today, and application developers can decide which option best suits their specific needs. The integrated platform also provides a

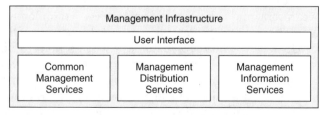

Figure 17.6 Management Infrastructure

capability to consolidate all fault messages into a single centralized log through the BaseWorX platform's log management facility by feeding OpenView messages into it. In a longer term we expect a greater consolidation of implementation, while maintaining existing interfaces for compatibility.

Execution Management. Execution Management services provide runtime management of the distributed applications in a heterogeneous environment. Both BaseWorX and OpenView support execution management. The integrated architecture combines these two functionalities by plugging the OpenView execution management under the existing BaseWorX execution management and then building appropriate linkages between the BaseWorX platform components and the OpenView platform components as part of the end application. This entails having the OpenView execution management server started up as a persistent daemon within the BaseWorX execution management environment, and interfacing the BaseWorX execution management daemon configuration descriptions to the appropriate OpenView OVstart and OVstop commands within that environment.

The advantage of this approach is that platform users have access to all of the functionality provided by both the BaseWorX platform and the OpenView platform. This includes the distributed execution management, the multiple application administration, and the flexible startup and respawn options associated with the BaseWorX platform, as well as the server dependency capabilities of the OpenView platform.

TMN Services

Both OpenView and BaseWorX have various level of services and functionality in the area of support for TMN and the related NM Forum OMNIPoint specifications. OpenView's focus to date has been to provide the industry standard interfaces and stacks for communicating across the TMN interfaces, whereas the BaseWorX platform has been focusing on producing technology which weaves those industry standard interfaces into a complete application construction environment, which has been specifically architected to support those interfaces in a seamless manner.

These two approaches are synergistic. The combination of the two represents a powerful mechanism that provides support for building TMN-based applications.

Object services and object communication

The integrated platform offers a choice for using the object services. BaseWorX platform users can continue to use the object services as implemented today in the BaseWorX platform and migrating with it to become OMG CORBA-compliant. The OpenView platform customers will be able to use the OMG CORBA technology, when it becomes available, from the OpenView platform.

The BaseWorX platform and the OpenView platform are consistent in their view and use of object communications in a distributed environment. Basically, the CORBA model is appropriate for use within an application or operations systems, whereas the TMN Q3 interfaces are more useful for interoperability between applications or operations systems. In response to the customer demand for a complete framework for developing OO TNM applications, the BaseWorX platform has implemented an object communications mechanism within a distributed application, while maintaining the TMN standard model of communications between the operations systems. The BaseWorX platform also has linked the two models of object communications via Interoperability Gateway Services to provide a local view of the external objects.

HP has based its OO strategy on OMG/CORBA technology. Although this component is not currently available in integrated platform, it will provide CORBA-based solutions for the management and communications of the objects in a distributed environment. These services will be used to provide a basis for integration between applications built on the platform structure, and to allow application functions to be spread across several machines to provide the overall solution to scale to manage very large environments.

Summary

OneVision is an enterprise management strategy first announced by AT&T in 1994. In August 1995, AT&T announced its intention to spin off NCR, formerly AT&T Global Information Solutions (GIS), into an independent publicly traded company come 1997. In late 1995 and early 1996, there was some confusion and uncertainty over the future of OneVision. In 1996, NCR reaffirmed its decision to continue the HP OpenView-based OneVision strategy for its commercial customers. The core of NCR OneVision is the use of HP OpenView NNM as NCR OneVision Node Manager, and the use of HP IT/Operations as NCR OperationsAdvantage. Release 2.0 of OperationsAdvantages includes support for suites of bundled applications for both Data Center and Distributed Management.

Meanwhile, AT&T has continued to pursue a OneVision strategy based upon integration of HP OpenView DM and BaseWorX. The integrated BaseWorX-OpenView platform provides a comprehensive set of functionalities and capabilities configurable to support the needs spanning customer premise management (CPM), customer network management (CNM), and telecommunications management networks (TMN) environments.

VI

Looking Ahead

Distributed Management and Data Integration

Even the best management platforms and their integrated applications may fail in enterprise environments because of problems in the following six areas:

1. *Event correlation*: Difficulties in correlating events generated in different domains. Most management systems cannot correlate alerts or suppress secondary alerts across the enterprise network if the source of the alert is in another management system's domain. This problem also occurs when multiple OpenViews are used in combination for enterprise management.

2. *Alert prioritization across domains*: Most management systems cannot prioritize alerts across the network because the alert may belong to another copy of the management system or a different vendor's management system. In this case, add-on expert system applications must be implemented, as described in Chap. 6.

3. *Multiuser capabilities*: Today's network management platforms often provide limited multiuser support. Users in different geographic locations find it difficult to coordinate their activities, and must resort to sending too much information manually across the network, driving up bandwidth requirements. Distributed systems with controlled handshaking can solve this problem.

4. *Displaying a networkwide map*: In large networks deploying several different management systems, or even several copies of the same management system, each system owns part of the network and is not aware of the nodes belonging to another system's domain. Map consolidation is a difficult problem. Building maps manually is not helpful because their maintenance is very complicated.

5. *Displaying networkwide events*: In large networks deploying several management systems, a system cannot display events occurring in another management system's domain. This problem is related to the preceding point. If maps can be correlated, events can drive the proper map segment, resulting in icon changes in shape, color, or size that reflect managed object status.

6. *Database integration*: A network's collective store of historical data and assets typically is scattered across multiple types of databases, both relational and flat file, residing in different management applications. Accessing this data may require use of several different database front-end tools. Of course, a physically distributed but logically integrated database would be the ideal solution. Vendors such as HP have attempted to deal with this problem, but only with superficial success.

Each of the areas listed above falls under the general heading of distributed management. In large, heterogeneous networks, distributed management capabilities are necessary for maintaining control and efficiency of management processes.

All leading management platform vendors, including HP, are conscious of customer demands for distributed management (Chap. 20), and of the current limitations of their products in this area. Each vendor's approach to this problem is slightly different; some vendors such as HP, provide distributed management through a combination of platform modifications and third-party offerings like Seagate NerveCenter; some platform vendors such as Cabletron provide distributed capabilities strictly through the platform alone. Others, including IBM, rely more on intelligent agent technology.

Distributed Capabilities in Tornado Release II (NNM 4.1)

In April 1996, HP introduced HP OpenView NNM 4.1 (Tornado Release II). The product is distributed in the sense that it addresses requirements 4 and 5 above, and partially addresses requirements 3 and 6. Requirements 1 and 2 are not addressed.

NNM 4.1 is not a radical redesign of OpenView; rather, it is an incremental yet significant release adding some forms of manager-to-manager data exchange between multiple copies of OpenView NNM. The most significant changes are:

■ The addition of the *ovrepld* processes and extensions to other processes now allows one NNM to send/receive information to another.

■ The addition of filters to control the exchange of topology and event data between multiple NNMs (these processes and filters are described in Chap. 4).

NNMs now can exchange event (SNMP trap) and topology data. All NNMs will have this capability. As a result, the architecture is not strictly hierarchical, as it may be in the case of IBM, where distributed Systems Monitor agents can send event data (not commands) to management consoles, but receive only commands (not data). In contrast, HP's Tornado II allows a hierarchial implementation, but does not impose it. Similarly, Tornado II allows peer-to-peer communications between multiple NNMs, but does not impose peer-to-peer. The capability allows all copies of NNM across the enterprise to be sychronized with respect to network maps and important status events. The various management models now supported by NNM are illustrated in Chap. 3.

With respect to events, each NNM is responsible for polling nodes and receiving SNMP traps in its own domain. Using the filters described in Chap. 4, administrators can specify which critical traps or threshold-generated events should be forwarded cross-domain to other NNMs—either a central NNM or other peers. The ability to forward events across the enterprise satisfies requirement 5 above. Because only exception conditions are shared, the need to perform active status polling over the WAN is eliminated.

With respect to topology, each NNM is responsible for discovering all nodes in its own domain at startup; as described in Chap. 4, this is accomplished by the *netmon* process. Then a large-scale synchronization of topology information occurs among all NNMs across the wide area. Once this is complete, each NNM has a complete topological picture of the entire network in its SQL database, Ingres or Oracle—satisfying requirement 4 above. However, once the initial map synchronization is complete, only changes to topology are propagated from one NNM domain to another. The administrator determines which filters to apply going forward to restrict the types of topology changes to be shared across the domains.

NNM 4.1 has several new types of filters. They include:

■ Domain filters, which allow administrators to more easily specify the objects to be discovered and polled by an individual NNM. Previously, polling objects were specified purely by IP address; with these new filters, administrators can group objects into classes such as "all routers," "all hubs," etc.

■ Interdomain filters, which dictate what information (events and topology data) should flow between NNM domains.

■ Map filters, which allow administrators to specify what portions of the network-wide map should be displayed for a given operator.

Domain filters enhance NNM's polling flexibility, making the product easier to configure and use. The interdomain filters ensure that only pertinent information is shared across domains, reducing bandwidth requirements. Because each NNM potentially can contain a large topological database describing the entire network—too much to be displayed on one screen—the map filters are important for tailoring operator views to only that portion of the network for which the operator is responsible.

Although events can be forwarded across domains from one NNM to another, there is as yet no prepackaged mechanism for setting network-wide priorities for event display. Thus, requirement 2 above is not completely met. Also, cross-domain event correlation (requirement 1) is not supported out of the box.

The ability to share topological data supports a multiuser "feeling" to some degree, but one NNM cannot just click up another NNM's screen and perform polling and other tasks. Multiuser support is provided in the local domain (requirement 3); several client GUIs can be supported from one NNM server, with some minimal degradation in performance.

The topology databases of multiple NNMs are integrated in Tornado II, partially fulfilling requirement 6. However, when an individual polls local device MIBs for the purpose of collecting asset or performance data over time, this information is stored locally in NNM's binary flat file. The ability to easily extract and manipulate end-to-end performance data is not truly supported in NNM 4.1.

Event correlation and management

In large networks with multiple management domains, it is not uncommon for a device failure in one domain to affect nodes in adjoining domains. If each domain is managed by a separate manager, it becomes difficult to suppress secondary alarms from different domains. Managing *cross-boundary nodes* that overlap into two management domains also is problematic.

Perhaps the most pressing problem that stems from using multiple copies of management platforms is the impossibility of achieving a network-wide view of real-time events. Such a view may take the form of a list that is filtered and prioritized, and clearly identifies the fault source as well as the management system reporting the fault.

IBM, HP, and SunSoft are developing new releases to correct this limitation. For example, HP and SunSoft have licensed Seagate's NerveCenter technology to enhance the polling and alert handling process. As described in Chap. 7, NerveCenter implements the concept of conditional-state diagrams to support a highly configurable polling mechanism.

Without conditional state capabilities, OpenView users are restricted to setting a threshold on a simple yes/no basis, that is, has the MIB variable exceeded a certain value? In a variety of cases, such as transient port failures and temporary spikes in Ethernet CRC errors, it is insignificant if a threshold is exceeded for a few moments, because the problem goes away. In these situations, it is more appropriate to generate an alert only if the MIB value remains above the threshold for a specified time period, or if the threshold is exceeded a given number of times within a specified time period. It may be desirable to generate an alert when the MIB value comes back down to normal.

Conditional-state alarm facilities can support this level of flexibility in event handling. One drawback to sophisticated alarm facilities such as NerveCenter is that the network administrator must think through many types of scenarios before configuring the application. Also, while the existing NerveCenter application can be used with OpenView, complete integration between the two products is not yet supported. Neither does NerveCenter work in conjunction with SunSoft Site Manager. Even future versions will support alarm handling for only one vendor's management system at a time.

To address these and other alarm handling limitations, OpenView NNM customers may use add-on applications from third parties, such as NetCool/OMNIbus from Micromuse. (Figure 18.1 depicts the OMNIbus architecture.) Netcool/OMNIbus is a configurable, client/server application that consolidates and removes duplicates of events and traps from SNMP, telephony, computer systems, and legacy element management systems (EMSs). Netcool/OMNIbus allows administrators to apply boolean correlation rules and automation to filter out extraneous and redundant information. The product has been designed to complement SNMP-based management systems such as HP OpenView Network Node Manager, Sun Solstice Domain Manager (SunNet Manager), and IBM NetView for AIX. The product also supports, out of the box, a bidirectional interface to Remedy's AR System and other trouble-ticketing systems (Huntington-Lee 1996e).

The core components of OMNIbus are software applications called *probes* that collect events; an ObjectServer for processing and storing events; and a *gateway* software module that exports processed information to other ObjectServers or management systems.

Each probe collects fault data, out of the box, from element platforms such as HP OpenView Network Node Manager, SunSoft SunNet Manager, and IBM NetView for AIX. Stratacom's management application also is supported, and support for more SNMP management applications is forthcoming.

The ObjectServer receives a continuous fault stream from many probes, unduplicating multiple occurrences of the same fault and consolidating faults from multiple probes. The information is correlated into more meaningful

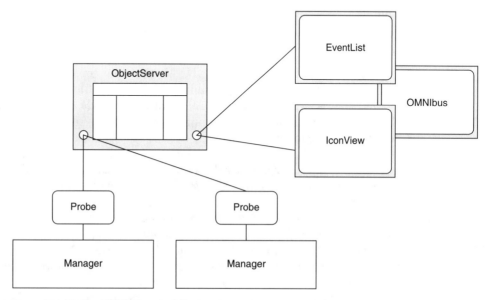

Figure 18.1 NetCool/OMNIbus Architecture

records of network or device state. The ObjectServer is a memory-resident SQL database, such as Sybase or Oracle.

Configuration of ObjectServer automation rules is done through SQL scripts and sequences which are generated when users fill in menu-based *trigger templates*.

The Desktop client provides a user-friendly GUI for Administration and Operation. The Administration function allows addition of operators, configuration of views for operators, and creation of automation rules. Correlation rules can be configured via drag-and-drop. Each ObjectServer can support multiple Desktops, allowing for multiuser support. Desktops run on Unix workstations or on Windows-based PCs.

The Operator view provides multiple filtered EventList applications and an ObjectiveView graphical topology tool. The EventList provides a real-time text listing of single and correlated faults.

NetCool/OMNIbus has several advantages over NerveCenter and other platform alarm facilities, including:

- Integrates alarms from multiple management systems into a single view.

- Requires little initial configuration to start collecting data.

- Distributes alert information from existing management systems to operators across the enterprise.

- Supports a high-performance, distributed object server.

Another more expensive alternative to OMNIbus is OSI NetExpert. NetExpert has richer capabilities than OMNIbus, including a rules-based expert system and other add-on applications. It can be used as an umbrella manager to coordinate multiple OpenView domain managers, as described in Chap. 1.

Integrating network visualization

Prior to release 4.1 of OpenView NNM, multiple copies of the product could share topology data only by sending X Window files over the network, a process that is expensive in terms of bandwidth. NNM 4.1 allows topology data sharing, but OpenView NNM cannot exchange map/topology data with other vendors' management platforms.

Similarly, sharing topology data among multiple copies of Sun Site Manager or NetView for AIX is awkward and inefficient. IBM is developing a new technology for supporting map sharing. Release dates have not been made public as of this writing.

Site Manager supports an add-on application called Cooperative Consoles that creates a single object repository among multiple copies of Site Manager. However, the product has had limited success to date. Most Site Manager customers are waiting to see how the end-user version of Solstice Enterprise Manager will handle map sharing.

Map sharing can be addressed by a third-party product called MapSynch from Bridgeway. Even when Sun's, HP's, and IBM's platforms improve their map-sharing capabilities, applications such as MapSync will be required to facilitate map sharing between different vendors' management platforms.

MapSynch is designed to sychronize object database and network topology functions across dissimilar platforms (Huntington-Lee 1995d). MapSynch concurrently supports both HP OpenView and IBM NetView for AIX. The product reads the object database and topology map of the source SNMP network manager, and then overwrites overlapping objects and attributes found in the destination SNMP manager's database and map. MapSynch also supports a second mode of operation in which only changes to the database and map are examined and compared, and any new information from the source is copied to the destination. Bridgeway recommends that customers perform the initial full synchronization weekly, with incremental changes on a daily or hourly basis.

MapSynch is useful for recopying customization onto a network map in the event of a system failure, or after complete rediscovery. It saves all X and Y coordinates of the map and paints it back when the user specifies. The product generates an audit trail of all synchronization operations. In addition to helping customers synchronize inconsistent maps, MapSynch can help dissimilar SNMP platforms act as backup topology stores for each other in the event of failure.

In less advanced cases, customers may attempt to build maps manually, a process supported by products such as GrafBase, NetWiz, and Best/Visualizer. These alternatives can be time-consuming, however, and do not lend themselves to tight integration.

Synchronization of databases

Today, management data describing the network is stored in multiple databases or files. CiscoWorks supports a Sybase relational database describing router configurations. Concord Trakker supports an Ingres database for storing traffic statistics. HP OpenView stores topology data in an Ingres database, but stores SNMP MIB data in binary flat files. IBM NetView for AIX may store data in Oracle, Sybase, Informix, Ingres, or DB2. Many applications such as Remedy AR System store data in flat files and support export to relational databases.

Occasionally, it is necessary to reach into these different databases to produce comprehensive asset or historical reports. For example, an organization may want to develop a report listing the value of all information technology assets using data from CiscoWorks, Bay Optivity, and ISICAD Command. Or there might be a need to develop a report on the maintenance history of various network devices, a task that also requires information stored in multiple relational databases. But creating reports using data from different network management databases can be cumbersome and time-consuming.

In the future, a single management repository might accept management data in standardized format from all types of applications and systems. Until then, administrators must maintain multiple management databases.

Database synchronization and integration are difficult tasks. Many client/server systems show similar weaknesses with regard to synchronization. In many cases, a sort of directory service is implemented by various applications on top of databases.

HP MetaSchema

HP OpenView customers require common management tools capable of monitoring and controlling the entire distributed, heterogeneous environment for which they have responsibility. Today, network and system management applications generally are written to manage specific objects and/or objects within a specific environment. In contrast, customers' setups consist of a large variety of differing networks, computer systems, and software. Existing tools for managing the environment typically understand a restricted set of specific objects, and have no common mechanisms for exchanging information to ensure consistency or completeness. Consequently, managing the whole environment can be cumbersome at best, and managers and administrators must resort to managing it in separate pieces while performing data integration in their minds.

Application developers have long wanted to address these problems through integration, but attempting to do so without a common approach toward integration is too costly. Because it is not feasible for each application to integrate one-on-one with potentially every other application through application-specific mechanisms, common approaches to integration must be devised. This can be done only through the efforts of standards bodies, or de facto standards delivered through the platform (rather than application) technology, since management platforms provide the common functionality and integration points that tie applications together.

Several levels of integration must be addressed if heterogeneous management through common tools is to become reality. HP believes the starting point is a common schema usage. More specifically, HP is working on plans to address data storage through specification of schema definitions in a relational database for particular types of shared management data. Mechanisms by which higher levels of integration can be achieved, such as method calls, are under development, but these are not addressed by this document.

There are several types of management data which applications need to share, and for which schema need to be specified. These types of management data include:

- Topology: Relationship information showing how the managed objects are interrelated so applications know which managed objects contain other objects and how the managed objects are connected to each other.

- Managed Object (inventory) Data: Basic information about managed objects essentially describing what is in the environment.

- Historical Trend Data: Storage of periodic samples of monitored object data used for statistical and trend analysis and, eventually, predictive management.

- Notifications: common storage of events spanning multiple protocols and sources

- Domains: Partitioning of managed objects into user-configurable subsets, to which user access and varying responsibilities can be assigned.

- Configuration Data: Object configurations, including parameter settings and dependency information, gathered into templates or historical snapshots.

Figure 18.2 shows these types of management data and their key dependencies on each other.

The next section provides a few examples of how the MetaSchema could be implemented.

Topology Schema

In the OpenView datastore, *topology* is defined as a collection of specific relationships among a selected set of Managed Objects. The relationships reveal which Managed Objects contain other Managed Objects, and how the Managed Objects are connected to each other. Strictly speaking, topology does not include the Managed Objects themselves; rather, topology data refers to the relationships among the managed objects.

There are four requirements for the Topology schema:

1. Ability to represent any collection of manageable objects, whether physical or logical in nature, and whether network-, system-, or service-oriented.

2. Allowance for the representation of completely arbitrary collections of objects; the criteria for grouping a set of objects cannot necessarily be deduced from the object attributes.

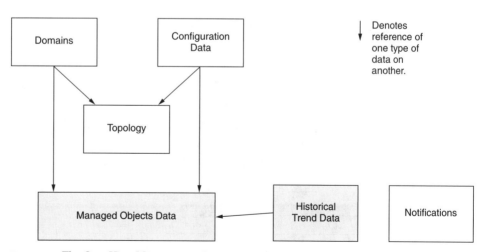

Figure 18.2 The OpenView Management Integration Data

3. Allowance for objects to belong simultaneously to multiple, possibly independent topologies.

4. Allowance for multiple types of relationships between managed objects, including Containment, Connectivity, and Dependency.

In the MetaSchema, topology is defined as a set of specific relationships applied to a set of Managed Objects. Three relationship types have been defined for OpenView topology to represent any topological form. These relationships are:

- Containment, which represents the embodiment of one object by another, such as a computer system contains particular storage devices, or a workgroup contains a given set of computers.

- Connectivity, which implys some sort of data exchange, flow, or transaction between a pair of objects; as in the way a router is connected to a network, or a print server to a client.

- Dependence, which reveals a functional dependence of one object on another. Examples include an operating system that is dependent upon the computer on which it is installed, or a networking protocol that is dependent upon a particular network interface card to which it has been assigned.

Figure 18.3 shows how topology tables are organized in the MetaSchema. Managed object data and the topology relationship data are stored independently of each other so that the topology relationships never appear within a given object definition. Rather, relationship data augments Managed Object data to describe the organization of the environment.

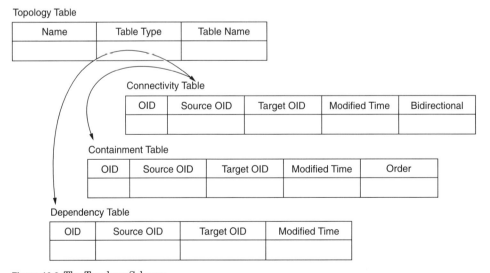

Figure 18.3 The Topology Schema

Managed Objects Schema

The Managed Objects Schema provides the structure for storing Object Class data. This encompasses the storage of general information about objects so the management system knows what is in the environment, and how object attributes or MIBs are modeled.

The primary requirements for storing Managed Object data include the following:

- Support for mapping of existing object definitions into class tables. Numerous applications will use and depend on existing MIBs, and will require corresponding tables matching those MIBs to store retrieved data. The primary MIB specification languages requiring support include the Internet Concise MIB, ISO GDMO, and CORBA IDL. Some customers require that these mappings support the scenario in which an application retrieves data for an object without knowing the actual source of the data. In other words, the application uses only an object handle and the object's class definition to specify access. This must be handled automatically and transparently to the application, whether or not access goes directly to the object or to a database.

- Access to metadata (a Data Dictionary), enabling applications to determine at runtime the object class definitions for managed objects in the environment.

- A common class integration space, i.e., a set of class tables (defined by OpenView) for storing the most commonly used object classes found in distributed environments. These class specifications are independent of protocols or MIB-specifications, thus ensuring applicability across most environments. Nevertheless, their definitions will be extrapolated from existing standard object definitions as appropriate. These common tables should form a foundation for developer-defined tables, allowing new tables to complement them.

- Extensibility of object definitions, so that developers can add to the list of attributes describing an object.

- A mechanism to ensure uniqueness of table names to eliminate unresolvable table name collisions when applications create tables in the integrated data store.

Additionally, common schema and integration guidelines must be published and available to developers. Guidelines for developing new tables must include suggested common attributes and data types to use in new class schema definitions, and a general structure into which new tables can be incorporated.

The specification for the Managed Objects Schema is divided into two parts: Structural Tables, providing the organizational framework for class tables; and Common Class Tables, defining specific "common" Object Classes used for data integration. Common Class Tables fit into the structure provided by the Structural Tables. Developers can create their own class tables that complement the common tables.

The structural schema organizes Managed Object information into two general categories: Class Definition Structural Schema and Object Instance Structural Schema. Class Definition Schema are used to store per-class information applying to all objects in a given class. Managed Object Instance Schema store per-instance object data.

Figure 18.4 shows the Object Instance Structural Tables. These tables consist of the Managed Object Table containing information about object instances, and the Object Instance Tables holding the actual attribute data.

The Managed Object Table contains at least one entry for each Managed Object. Each object is identified by an object identifier (OID). The table contains information that is common to all objects, independent of class. Accompanying each entry is its class name, so the table can be searched for all objects of a given class. The creation time and last modified time of each instance is tracked in this table.

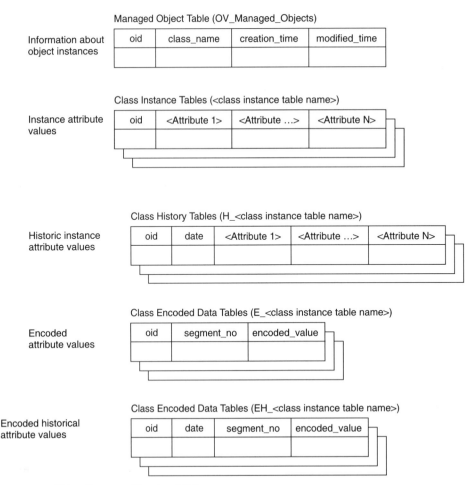

Figure 18.4 Object Instance Structural Schema

Historical Trend Schema

Trend Data Tables allow storage of data values collected from Managed Objects for analyzing network activity over an extended period. The tables provide for reduction of older data for space-saving purposes.

This schema is not well-tuned for data insertion or retrieval. This is a normalized schema meant to make the data accessible to standard applications and reporting tools. Particular collectors may require specialized schemas for their demanding data insertion rates. This is the schema that is recommended for making that data accessible to other applications.

The Trend Data Schema allows data to be collected from various sources, including SNMP, CMIS, etc. Thus, the Trend Schema is a metaschema to provide for new data sources. A collection of these tables would exist for each environment.

Additional application-specific tables not described here might hold information pertinent to the rules used by a collector for monitoring each data set, such as the currently specified polling time interval.

The trend tables are viewed as a group of four tables holding data related to a specific subset of the managed environment. One table describes each of the variables potentially being monitored, and a second table identifies each data stream or data set being monitored. Finally, there are two data tables that store individual data values for each data set.

Developments in Distributed Event Correlation: HP ECS

Distributed functionality is a key requirement for HP OpenView customers, as discussed in Chap. 20. HP made significant progress in mid-1996 with the release of OpenView NNM 4.1, which supports sharing of topology and SNMP trap data among multiple copies of NNM. In time, HP is expected to address customer requirements for distributed management in the following ways:

- Making further refinements to the topology and event sharing capabilities of NNM.
- Enhancing manager-to-manager communications, with security, via support for SNMPv2.
- Incorporating object technology.
- Incorporating new, superior event correlation technology.

The following sections describe, in greater detail, newer developments in event correlation technology from HP.

HP's Intelligent Network Computing Laboratory (INCL), based in Bristol, England, has developed a technology that appears capable of addressing the challenges of event correlation across large, distributed environments. This technology, currently known as Event Correlation Services (ECS) takes a novel approach to event correlation (Huntington-Lee 1996f).

HP has taken the complex problem of large-scale correlation and broken it down into a set of 15 simple operations. HP believes it has discovered an optimal set of data reduction/correlation primitives that can be applied at very low levels. Moreover, these simple primitives can be combined to create highly flexible, maintainable, scalable systems capable of handling situations of enormous complexity.

The ECS primitives that HP has developed are simple systems that have been proven to work; the primitives in themselves are easy to maintain, yet can be combined to accomplish highly complex correlations. ECS's new paradigm is this: Each correlation rule is implemented by a discrete decision-making element called an ECSnode.

There are 15 basic ECSnode types, each with a specific function and purpose. Each ECSnode has one or more input ports and one or more output ports. Individual ECSnodes may be linked to create an ECS (correlation) circuit. ECS's connection policy is so flexible that any single output port may be connected to any one or more input ports, and multiple output ports may feed into one input port. Groups of interconnected ECSnodes may be combined via these connections to produce reusable compound nodes. The 15 basic ECSnodes are listed in Table 18.1.

This technology is capable of doing the following:

- Processing high volumes of events by using new data reduction methods.
- Correlating events across multiple protocols.
- Concurrently handling multiple event types.
- Performing correlation based on the content of multiple events.
- Categorizing events, domains, etc., and distributing pertinent information to the relevant operators and/or management systems.
- Displaying only those events that require operator attention.

Thus, scalability, flexibility, and maintainability are supported, as is the ability to process a stream of events to identify the relationships between those events. The result is a new, smaller stream of events in which the meaningful information content is maintained or increased, producing a few significant events compared to thousands or hundreds of thousands of raw events.

This approach of filtering and correlating locally has the potential for being much more efficient than is funneling huge streams of events to a central expert system for processing. Rules can be kept simple in the ECS paradigm; maintenance of rules should be easier.

Short-term plans call for HP to incorporate ECS into an HP OpenView-DM-based offering. In the long term, HP plans to apply the ECS to other OpenView products, including NNM. Given the flexibility of the ECS architecture, the possibilities for exploiting this technology are tremendous.

Summary

Even the best management platforms and integrated applications may fall short of success due to a lack of distributed management and data integration features. In large, heterogeneous networks, distributed management capabil-

Table 18.1. Basic ECS Nodes

ECSnode	Function
Annotate	Add external information to an event
Clock	Generate period-empty events
Combine	Create event combinations from multiple input paths
Count	Count events passing through the node
Create	Make a new event
Delay	Hold events for a prespecified time
Extract	Search a stored event list and extract matching events
Filter	Pass only (forward) events meeting configured logic
Input	Point where events enter the circuit from the environment
Modify	Change the attribute values of an event
Output	Point where events are returned to the environment
Rate	Monitor the rate of events over time through this node
Rearrange	Modify the structure of a composite event
Table	Store events in a one-dimensional table
Unless	Forward events unless inhibited by another event

ities are necessary for maintaining control and efficiency of management processes and controls. HP is evolving OpenView toward greater distributed capabilities, as evidenced in Release 4.1 of NNM. The introduction of HP OpenView Event Correlation Services represents a significant advance in HP's distributed offerings.

Data integration remains a problem, as management data describing the network is stored in multiple databases or files. Occasionally, it is necessary to reach into these different databases to produce comprehensive asset or historical reports.

Ultimately, there are several levels of integration which must be addressed to make heterogeneous management via common tools a reality. HP believes the starting point is a common schema usage. More specifically, HP is working on plans to address data storage through specification of schema definitions in a relational database for particular types of shared management data.

Cost-Justifying HP OpenView

For most organizations considering the purchase of HP OpenView or a similar management system, the primary factor behind such a purchase is a desire to ensure the availability of mission-critical applications by improving the availability of the networks and systems supporting those applications. While problem-tracking and long-term performance reporting are important, the top priority for most organizations is network availability.

Consequently, the first step in justifying the cost of purchasing HP OpenView or any other network management system is to quantify the value of network availability to the organization. The following paragraphs offer a simplified formula for assigning value to network availability for a commercial enterprise. For the example that follows, the following assumptions are made:

- The network runs 24 hours a day, 365 days a year (e.g., an airline reservation system, catalog order entry facility, or a bank's automated teller machine network).

- When the network is down, revenue is lost. Customers are impatient and quickly go elsewhere to do business.

Given those assumptions, one can calculate the value of downtime based on annual revenues. Suppose that annual revenue is $10 million. The cost of one hour of downtime is:

$$10,000,000 / (24 \times 365) = \$1140 \text{ per hour (approximately)}$$

If network availability is 99 percent, then annual network downtime is 87.6 hours a year, resulting in a possible revenue loss of close to $100,000 annually. If a network management solution can improve network availability by only 0.5 percent (raising availability to 99.5 percent), the company will see a return on investment (ROI) within one year by spending $50,000 on a network management solution. The higher the organization's annual revenues, the easier it is to justify the cost of a bigger investment in network management.

While this example is oversimplified, it is a starting point for measuring the value of network availability. Factors other than estimates of revenue loss due to downtime contribute to the value of an investment in network management tools. These factors include:

- Salary cost of employees who manually identify, diagnose, fix, and track network problems.

- Value of lost employee productivity time when the network is unavailable.

- Intangible value of customer and employee irritation from dealing with an unstable network.

Over time, these intangibles can translate to lost productivity hours and lost revenue.

In client/server networks, the salary cost of network maintenance often is hidden. Departmental employees may take care of many network and systems management tasks—such as installing new software, diagnosing server problems, or adding new users to the network—in their "spare time." It takes effort to document the time spent on client/server maintenance. By interviewing employees, quantifying their time spent on network management, and multiplying by hourly salary rates, it is possible to determine the ROI gained if these tasks were to be partially or fully automated by a network or systems management system.

The next step in cost justifying the purchase of HP OpenView NNM (or any other management system) is to compare the value of anticipated improvements in network availability and automation to the actual software and hardware costs.

The True Cost of HP OpenView

The true cost of deploying a total solution based on HP OpenView Network Node Manager (NNM)—including hardware, software, and maintenance—turns out to be from 5 to 15 times the list price of the HP OpenView NNM software by itself. As mentioned, OpenView NNM is a foundation upon which customers can layer value-added or user-written applications addressing critical areas of network management. While there are close to 200 HP and third-party applications listed in HP's latest OpenView Solutions Catalog, most NNM customers select only three or four value-added applications to supplement NNM's base capability. These several applications are important, however, because they support critical network management functions that must be in place to make NNM an effective tool.

The HP value-added and third-party applications most widely used with NNM include:

- Trouble ticketing, including Remedy Action Request System, Legent Paradigm, Peregrine PNMS.

- Router configuration, including CiscoWorks, Wellfleet Site Manager.

- Hub configuration and monitoring, including SynOptics Optivity, 3Con Transcend, Cabletron Spectrum for Open Systems.

- Traffic monitoring, including HP NetMetrix and LanProbe (described in detail in Chap. 5), Network General Distributed Sniffer, Frontier NetScout, Axon LANServant, N.A.T. EtherMeter, ARMON ONSite.

- Data analysis and reporting, such as SAS CPE for Open Systems.

- Filtering and distributed management, such as Seagate NerveCenter, SNMP Research EMANATE.

Many installations run router and hub management applications on the less expensive SunNet Manager platform; the same is true for traffic monitors, including several that are not often used with NNM, such as Concord Trakker and Wandel & Goltermann IDNS. End-user organizations (and there are many) running both HP OpenView and SunNet Manager have another obstacle, the lack of interoperability between NNM and SunNet Manager. However, several new third-party applications support event integration and map sharing between NNM, SunNet Manager, and IBM NetView for AIX. Most notable are MicroMuse NetCool/OMNIbus and BridgeWay MapSync. (For more information on these products, see Chap. 18.)

Estimating Software Costs

The following examples calculate the *software* costs (based on approximate list prices) for two widely used combinations of NNM and third-party software (Morgenthal 1996).

The examples, while theoretical, are based on a collection of integration case studies implemented by Unified Systems Solutions, a Computer Horizons company (Mountain Lakes, N.J.). Unified Systems Solutions is a systems integrator with considerable Enterprise Management and HP OpenView integration experience. Product prices were accurate as of September 1996. Please contact vendors for current pricing.

Example 1. This example includes NNM, traffic monitoring for five network segments, router management, and trouble ticketing.

HP OpenView NNM	$15,975
HP LanProbe	20,000 (1 application, 5 probes)
CiscoWorks	10,000
Remedy AR System (with multiprocessing server option)	9,500 (1 server, 3 clients)
Total	$55,975

Example 2. This example includes NNM, router management, hub management, trouble ticketing, and data analysis (with only call and incident management on the Peregrine ServiceCenter).

HP OpenView NNM	$15,975
Bay Networks Optivity	14,000
CiscoWorks	10,000
Peregrine ServiceCenter	9,120 (1 server, 3 clients)
DeskTalk TrendSNMP+	12,000 (1 server, 2 clients, poller)
Total	$61,095

Example 3. A more comprehensive scheme consisting of NNM, router management, hub management for two vendors' hubs, PC LAN alert management, trouble ticketing, database monitoring, distributed management, filtering, and an additional SQL database acting as a management repository:

HP OpenView NNM	$15,975
CiscoWorks	10,000
Bay Networks Optivity	14,000
Spectrum SPMA	15,000
Seagate LANAlert	1,000
Remedy AR System	9,500 (1 server, 5 clients)
Platinum VisionDB	11,000
SNMP Research EMANATE	4,500
Seagate NerveCenter	20,000
Sybase	23,000
Total	$100,975

For Example 3, the approximate yearly maintenance costs of the software alone is as follows:

HP OpenView NNM	$2,300
CiscoWorks	1,400
Optivity	700
Spectrum SPMA	400
LANAlert	100
AR System	1,300
VisionDB	3,000
EMANATE	—
NerveCenter	4,000
Sybase	4,000
Total	$18,200

In total, the rolled-up software costs for purchasing HP OpenView NNM in Example 3 exceed $135,000.

Estimating Hardware Costs

To obtain the true cost of an HP OpenView-based solution, one also must add in hardware costs. HP recommends that the HP OpenView NNM management station *not* be used as a server for any other purpose. It is necessary, therefore, to factor in the cost of a dedicated management server. In a large environment of several thousand managed nodes, there typically will be one server and a minimum of two workstations for additional operators. Assuming a moderate configuration consisting of one HP/9000 K class server plus two HP 725/100 workstations, hardware cost will be about $115,000.

Adding in total software, maintenance, and hardware costs, the price tag exceeds $250,000. Users also must consider the "soft costs" of developing a requirements definition, outlining a network management architecture, and the time needed for installing, configuring, and customizing the solution. Outsourcing these tasks to a systems integrator would cost an additional $150,000 to $300,000 or more, given Example 3 above. Performing these tasks in-house probably will carry the same cost in terms of salaries of IT staff.

This is a very rough estimate, of course. Software and maintenance costs are fairly straightforward. Costs of requirements definition, installation, configuration, and customization may seem harder to estimate, but they are no less real. In many cases, hardware costs are grossly underestimated. More accurate methods for calculating estimated hardware resources are provided in the next section.

How to estimate hardware costs

To avoid getting caught with too many nodes to manage and not enough power or storage, it is important to estimate RAM and disk space requirements. HP provides formulas and examples for estimating resource requirements (Hewlett-Packard 1994). Unfortunately, most people buy the management workstation and install NNM without first applying the formulas, and end up on the short end of the stick. The way out of this dilemma is to buy more memory or disk after the fact—but if you run out of budgeted funds, the only answer is to "unmanage" lots of nodes, and essentially use NNM to manage only a portion of the network.

The first step in estimating hardware requirements is to determine the number of nodes to be managed, and how many (if any) redirected X display sessions may be necessary (used only if you want to support more than one operator).

Table 19.1 shows the RAM and swap space requirements for NNM 3.3 in the three supported environments (HP-UX, SunOS, and Solaris) when there is only one operator (i.e., only one OVw session).

Note: The requirements listed in Table 19.1 apply *only* to NNM version 3.3. The requirements of a given operating system, communications software, and any other applications running on the server, must be added in. As Table 19.2 shows, these requirements increase dramatically when one or more X Window displays are redirected to support multiple operators.

HP recommends that customers wishing to manage more than 1000 nodes consider purchasing high-end ons, particularly if more than one operator is to be supported. Cluster configurations are supported in the HP-UX environment only.

Tables 19.1 and 19.2 provide rule-of-thumb estimates only. For customers seeking more precise estimates of virtual memory requirements, HP provides detailed formulas (Hewlett-Packard 1994).

**Table 19.1. Resource Requirements for a Single Instance of
the HP OpenView Network Node Manager (NNM) GUI (OVw)
Running on a Management Station**

Number of managed nodes	RAM for HP 700 & 800 series, HP-UX 9.0	RAM for SPARC2, SunOS 4.1.3	RAM for SPARC10, Solaris 2.3	Swap space (all three systems)
500	40MB	38MB	54MB	100MB
1000	52MB	52MB	67MB	100MB
5000	120MB	125MB	142MB	130MB
10000	190MB	205MB	230MB	210MB

To calculate virtual memory requirements, it is necessary to consider the memory usage of all individual processes running within the HP OpenView NNM program. Table 19.3 shows the storage requirements per Global NNM process; this is actually a combination of the initial RAM used plus the amount of storage required per object. Table 19.4 lists storage requirements for each additional process that starts each time another OVw session is initiated.

HP recommends that to avoid swapping and to increase performance, customers reserve enough physical memory to accommodate all of NNM's virtual memory needs. The performance of NNM degrades noticeably when processes must be swapped.

As a result, one can estimate that a midrange workstation with 96MB RAM and 1GB storage can comfortably handle the load of NNM managing 500 nodes. However, the CPU takes a hit each time an additional third-party application is used in conjunction with NNM. Extra storage and RAM may still be required to maintain performance.

NNM 4.1 features a client/server architecture with remote distributed polling capabilities. The estimates for memory and disk usage are different than in Version 3.3, but only with respect to the local processes started up with each new session of *ovw* process. Memory and disk requirements for global processes remain approximately the same.

It is important to remember the cost of the resource requirements as well as of the software when comparing the cost of HP OpenView NNM to competing products. Generally speaking, Sunsoft Site Manager requires less memory and storage, while Cabletron Spectrum typically requires a higher-end workstation or several workstations (in the distributed configuration) to maintain good performance.

Summary

HP OpenView Network Node Manager is the most influential network management product of its kind on the market today. Many customers, however, underestimate the cost and effort involved in building a comprehensive management solution around NNM. NNM must be supplemented by third-party applications for critical areas of trouble ticketing, traffic monitoring, data analysis/reporting, and router and hub management. In addition to the cost of third-party software, organizations must consider the hardware resource requirements of NNM. At the same time, it is possible to justify the cost of a NNM-based network management solution by quantifying the value of network availability to the organization. Customers should take these factors into consideration when evaluating NNM against the competition.

Table 19.2. Resource Requirements for Multiple Instances of the HP OpenView Network Node Manager (NNM) GUI (OVw) Running on a Management Station

Number of managed nodes	Number of OVw sessions-redirected displays	RAM for HP 700 & 800 series, HP-UX 9.0	RAM for SPARC2, SunOS 4.1.3	RAM for SPARC10, Solaris 2.3	Swap space (all three systems)
500	1	40MB	38MB	54MB	100MB
500	5	138MB	135MB	170MB	200MB
500	10	265MB	255MB	315MB	300MB
1000	1	52MB	52MB	67MB	100MB
1000	5	170MB	170MB	198MB	200MB
1000	10	320MB	320MB	360MB	350MB

Table 19.3. Storage Requirements for Each Global OpenView Process (Initial Size plus Additional Storage per Object)

OpenView Global Process	HP 700s & 800s, HP-UX 9.0 (initial plus RAM per object)	SPARC2, SunOS 4.1.3 (initial plus RAM per object)	SPARC10, Solaris 2.3 (initial plus RAM per object)
netmon	1.0MB + 1.0/object	0.9MB + 1.9./object	2.6MB + 0.9/object
ovwdb	0.9MB + 3.3/object	0.6MB + 4.2/object	2.0MB + 2.5/object
ovtopmd	1.7MB + 0.7/object	1.4MB + 0.5/object	3.0MB + 1.4/object
ovspmd	0.3MB (no additional)	0.2MB (no additional)	1.4MB (no additional)
trapd	1.3MB (no additional)	1.0MB (no additional)	2.4MB (no additional)
ovactiond	1.0MB (no additional)	1.0MB (no additional)	2.1 MB (no additional)
snmpCollect	1.7MB + 1.2/collection	1.0MB + 1.0/collection	2.9MB + 1.0/collection

**Table 19.4. Storage Requirements for Each Additional
OpenView Process Started with Each OVw Session
(Initial Size Plus Additional Storage per Object)**

OpenView Global Process	HP 700s & 800s, HP-UX 9.0 (initial plus RAM per object)	SPARC2, SunOS 4.1.3 (initial plus RAM per object)	SPARC10, Solaris 2.3 (initial plus RAM per object)
ovw	4.9MB + 2.0/object	4.2MB + 3.1/object	6.6MB + 1.4/object
ipmap	1.1MB + 1.2/object	0.9MB + 0.8 object	2.8MB + 1.2/object
ovhelp	1.6MB (no additional)	1.3MB (no additional)	3.3MB (no additional)
xnmevents	3.1MB + 0.6/event	2.6MB + 0.6/event	4.5MB + 0.4/event
xnmappmon	2.2MB (no additional)	2.2MB (no additional)	3.5MB (no additional)
xnmgraph	5.0MB (max of 300/graph line)	5.0MB (max of 300/graph line)	4.2MB (max of 300/graph line)

The HP OpenView User's Forum

The HP OpenView User's Forum was formed by HP OpenView Network Node Manager customers seeking to exchange ideas both with HP and with other NNM users.

Membership is held by organizations, instead of by individuals. Each member entity must provide the name of a member of record, who will receive all membership mailings. Although there is only one member of record, all representatives of member entities are welcome to participate in OpenView Forum conferences.

To qualify for membership, organizations must hold a current runtime license for an HP OpenView platform or HP OpenView product that is dependent upon an HP OpenView platform runtime. Platforms include SNMP/NNM, DM, and OpenView for Windows. Member organizations include companies, government organizations, and other institutions. Annual membership dues are $300 per organization.

The Founding of the OpenView Forum

In April 1992, HP helped Rick Sturm at US West and Jerry Henderson at GTE organize a conference call with other interested NNM users, and the User's Forum began taking shape. Early on, founding members decided that the User's Forum should be a completely separate entity from Interex, the larger user group for general HP customers. By maintaining its own identity, the HP OpenView User's Forum has gained a platform for HP OpenView customer concerns and requirements. In addition, the User's Forum has sponsored mailing lists and annual conferences aimed at enabling OpenView customers to more easily exchange technical expertise and insights, and learn from the deployment experiences of others.

In 1994, an e-mail reflector was established to make it easier for members to share ideas, post questions, and seek advice about technical problems from other users. It is now an open mail reflector; anyone wishing to subscribe may do so by sending a message with the word "subscribe" in the subject area and to message body:

ovforum-request @ ovforum.org

Additionally, a Web server has been set up at *www.ovforum.org*.

HP OpenView Forum Conference

The annual HP OpenView User's Forum conference has become a popular, well-attended conference for both users and HP OpenView business partners. The conference features an information-rich agenda that includes technical sessions and tutorials.

The first User's Forum conference was held in 1993, with about 400 in attendance. During that conference, Forum officers collected and prioritized a list of user requirements, which were delivered to HP and HP OpenView partner vendors. The vendors reviewed and responded to these requests. About 600 people attended the 1994 conference, and 800 turned out for the 1995 conference.

Table 20.1 lists the conference sessions of the 1996 HP OpenView User's Forum conference, "Collaborating for a Manageable Environment," held in St. Louis, Mo. Conference attendence was estimated at about 2000. The conference included tutorials, birds-of-feather (BOF) meetings, hands-on lab sessions, advanced training classes, and more than 70 technical sessions. A techology showcase featuring live demonstrations of HP and HP business parter products was part of the 1996 program.

Unlike HP, IBM has not to date sponsored or encouraged a separate user group for IBM NetView for AIX customers; rather, support comes from within the larger GUIDE and SHARE user groups representing IBM systems and equipment customers at large.

Figure. 20.1 depicts the organizational structure of the Forum. Officers are elected for two-year terms, and may not run for successive terms. Voting occurs at the annual conference.

1996 HP OpenView User's Survey

In 1996, the OpenView User's Forum sponsored a survey of its members to assess the effectiveness of HP technical support services provided to NNM customers, and to identify the features and improvements most requested by NNM users. Datapro Information Services conducted telephone interviews, following the survey form drawn up by the Forum (Huntington-Lee 1996g).

Customer perceptions of technical support

Survey respondents were asked to rate the quality of remote (telephone) technical support on a scale of 1 to 4, with 1 indicating poor, 2 indicating fair, 3 indicating good, and 4 indicating excellent. Respondents also were asked to rate the quality of local (on-site) technical support on the same scale. In both

**Table 20.1. HP OpenView Forum 1996 Conference Agenda
(partial listing)**

Tutorials	Technical sessions	Lab sessions
Advanced application integration with NNM	IT/ Operations Update	Test Drive NNM 4.1
Migrating from NNM 3.31 to 4.X	NNM Update	Basic Application Integration with NNM
Tips and Techniques for NNM	Database Monitoring in a Distributed Computing Environment	Hands-On NetMetrix
OpenView Overview	Deploying IT Service Level Management in the Distributed Environment	Optivity Test Drive
NNM and SNMPv2C and SNMPv2*	Integration of CORBA with HP OpenView DM	CiscoWorks Test Drive
Extending the HP EMANATE Agent	Impact of WWW Browser Tools on the LAN	
Networked Systems Management Performance	Extending Performance Measurement to the Switched Environment	

cases, respondents were asked to give individual ratings describing adequacy, timeliness, availability of knowledgeable personnel, and value of service for the price.

Figure 20.2 illustrates the results of the survey in the area of customers' experiences with remote technical support. Figure 20.3 illustrates the results in the area of local support. Within both categories, the lowest ratings were given to *value of service for the price*. HP standard support costs $1600 per year; HP premium support, which includes phone support, costs $2400 per year; and developer assist support costs an additional $12,000 per year. An overall rating for both remote and onsite support is shown in Fig. 20.4.

Wish list of OpenView NNM enhancements

When asked "Which OpenView improvements would you like to see most," the need for distributed management, distributed scalability, and/or manager-to-manager communications was at the top of the list. Respondents also specifically mentioned "scalability" as a much-needed improvement. Taken

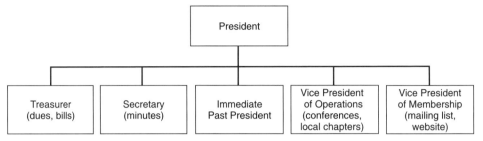

Figure 20.1 HP OpenView Forum Organizational Chart

collectively, nearly half of HP OpenView users would like to see enhanced scalability and distributed processing capabilities in future NNM releases.

HP has taken steps to enhance NNM's distributed capabilities. Tornado Release I, also known as HP OpenView NNM 4.0, shipped in October 1996, with a distributed GUI capability. NNM 4.1, which shipped in mid-1996 under the code name "Tornado Release II," provided facilities for distributed polling and distributed discovery, and had the ability to exchange topology data between multiple OpenViews.

Reporting capabilities, particularly the ability to analyze NNM-collected data and extract trends, was an enhancement request indicated by the comments of many respondents. HP has not indicated specific product plans targeting enhanced reporting capabilities.

Comments from a number of users indicated the need for more sophisticated alarm correlation and filtering. Specific comments regarding alarm handling enhancements included "the ability to limit the number of traps sent when critical pieces of the network go down," "do a better job automating event

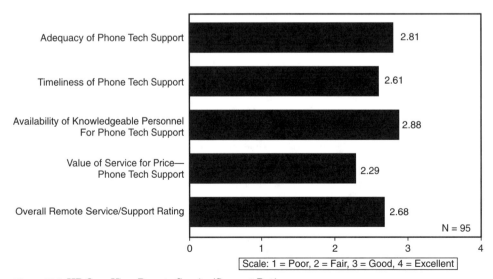

Figure 20.2 HP OpenView Remote Service/Support Ratings

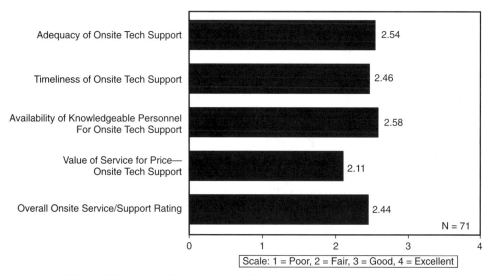

Figure 20.3 HP OpenView Onsite Service/Support Ratings

configuration—such as entering formulas," and "easier rules and automated intervention built into the product."

As of this writing, HP has not indicated product plans to add any advanced alarm handling features to NNM, although HP IT/Operations does provide event filtering. Seagate Technology provides an alarm filtering application called NerveCenter that can be integrated with HP OpenView to reduce the number of alarms displayed when nodes fail. At least one survey respondent indicated a desire to see a NerveCenter-like capability built into HP OpenView NNM.

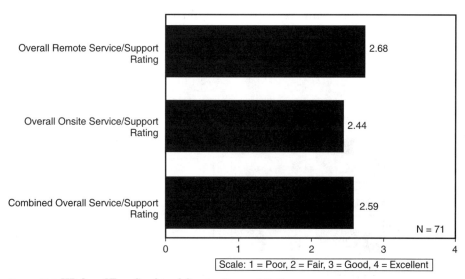

Figure 20.4 HP OpenVIew Combined Service/Support Ratings

Enhanced integration was identified by 10 survey respondents as an OpenView improvement on their wish lists. Several respondents specifically criticized the menu option for integration, while others cited a need for tighter integration with other HP products such as IT/Operations and NetMetrix. HP is, in fact, planning to market an upcoming version of IT/Operations that is preintegrated with OpenView NNM. HP also has recently enhanced its certification program for third-party business partners, providing management applications that integrate with OpenView NNM. As of 1996, approximately 20 vendors had been certified as HP OpenView Premier Solution Partners, indicating that their applications had passed tests for integration with OpenView at multiple levels.

Seven survey respondents specifically indicated a need for improvements to NNM's SNMPcollect process, the mechanism by which OpenView NNM gathers SNMP MIB values. Another 17 indicated a desire for support for other protocols besides IP. Six respondents noted problems with auto-discovery, including difficulties with using seed files. Improved maps and map configuration capabilties were listed by six respondents. Other requested improvements included better memory management, database implementations, better manipulation of utilities, and the ability to recognize bridge and hub devices as network fan-out points.

User confidence in HP

When asked to rate NNM's ability to meet their overall IP network management needs, customers responded with a somewhat positive rating of 2.74, where 1=poor, 2=fair, 3=good, and 4=excellent. Even so, customers are looking for more.

Indeed, many HP OpenView users are hopeful that NNM Release 4.1/Tornado Release II will address some of NNM's limitations. When asked, "What are your expectations of Tornado II to meet your overall IP network management needs," the collective response was a rating of 2.86 on a scale of 1 to 4, with 1 indicating poor, 2 indicating fair, 3 indicating good, and 4 indicating excellent, as shown in Fig. 20.5.

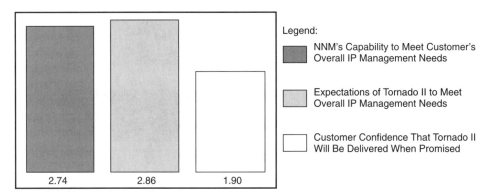

Figure 20.5 Customer Confidence in HP OpenView NNM

The survey results indicate that most users are hopeful that NNM can serve as a mid- to long-term solution for their organizations. As Fig. 20.6 shows, 89 respondents viewed NNM as part of their mid- or long-term strategy for network management.

Summary

The HP OpenView User's Forum was formed by HP OpenView Network Node Manager customers seeking to exchange ideas both with HP and with other NNM users. Since 1993, membership in the OpenView User's Forum has grown from around 100 to more than 400. While HP provides support to the group in the form of promotional mailings and other public relations assistance, to date HP has not underwritten any of the costs of the OpenView Forum.

The HP OpenView User's Forum's benefits to its members include an informative Web page, e-mail reflector, and annual conference. The Forum has surveyed its members to assess their needs and present these collective responses to Hewlett-Packard, in an attempt to influence product directions and enhancements.

In the near term, the Forum plans to work on several areas, including establishment of local chapters and special interest groups (SIGs), and a shift to a more strategic, rather than tactical, focus. In addition, the Forum is planning another survey of the membership to develop member profiles, as part of an effort to get a better idea of what members would like to derive from the organization.

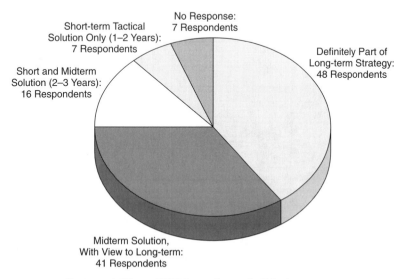

Figure 20.6 Customer's View of NNM as a Strategic Solution

An ATM Network

Planning a Network Management Strategy around HP OpenView Network Node Manager

This case study describes a large organization that currently is setting up a new TCP/IP internetwork supporting satellite-based data transmission. Collected data will be processed at two locations and distributed to 15 remote sites. The organization is designing the network to support a high volume of data transfer via an Asynchronous Transfer Mode (ATM) OC3 backbone. Aggregate data rates are expected to range from 200 to 300 mbps. Data types include time-sensitive real-time data, as well as historical data. The primary application will be file transfer; the network will not support a significant amount of interactive computing.

The data is of a mission-critical nature, and cannot be lost in the event of network failure. Because data transfer rates are high, a huge buffering capability would be required to preserve captured data in the event of even a brief instance of network downtime. As a result, one of the organization's primary goals is to avoid downtime at all costs. Accordingly, the organization is constructing the network in a highly fault-tolerant manner.

This includes provisions for redundant cabling, dual interruptible power supplies (UPSs) for all routers and hubs, as well as a completely separate emergency backup network. The transport system must have its own restore capabilities, allowing the network to take care of as many problems as possible before the network management system must step in.

In addition, the organization has decided to maintain an inventory of spare interface cards and other spare parts for its hubs and routers. This will allow technicians to swap parts quickly and perform detailed diagnostics offline. The organization has given careful consideration to equipment room design and equipment placement, ensuring such things as proper bottom-to-top airflow, and easy access to the backs of routers and other devices.

Initially, the network will comprise 40 to 60 routers supplied primary by one vendor, as well as 30 to 40 hubs, 15 T3 CSU/DSUs, and several ATM backbone switches. The network is expected to grow over the next five years.

Before selecting a network management platform, the organization tested several systems in its development lab. The systems tested included Cabletron Spectrum, SunNet Manager, HP OpenView, and NetLabs' DiMONS. The organization made its selection carefully, because its choice entails a 15-year commitment to the network management infrastructure.

The organization initially was impressed by the NetLabs product, particularly its ability to view IP data flows—including packets going into the router, and packets going out. But the organization took into consideration the company's precarious market position, and selected a larger, established player. Subsequent to the organization's decision, NetLabs was acquired by Seagate, and stopped actively marketing the DiMONS product.

The organization also decided against Cabletron Spectrum for two reasons. First was a concern about Spectrum's ability to fully manage competing vendors' hub products. Second, the organization wanted to customize Spectrum's filtering capabilities and, after extensive testing, concluded that detailed customization would be too difficult. Finally, SunNet Manager was ruled out because the organization found the user interface too archaic, and Sun's higher-end Enterprise Manager was not yet shipping.

The organization chose HP OpenView, primarily because the product offered superior flexibility for adding third-party applications, and because it appeared to pose the least risk in terms of product longevity.

The organization plans to deploy HP OpenView Network Node Manager (NNM) running on Sun SPARC 20 systems running Solaris 2.3 in a redundant configuration, as shown in Fig. C1.1.

The organization is integrating the following third-party management applications in conjunction with HP OpenView NNM:

- Remedy Action Request (AR) System, i.e., trouble ticketing
- SAS CPE, i.e., data analysis and reporting

The organization carefully considered additional types of value-added applications, but chose instead to roll out a suite consisting of the barest minimum needed to manage the network effectively.

Remedy AR System

A Remedy AR System client will be installed at each site. The AR System does the following:

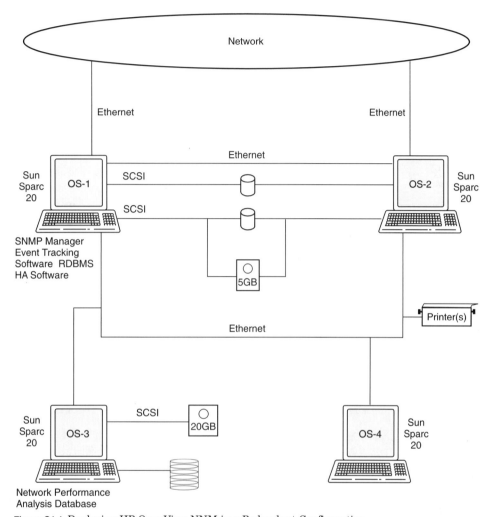

Figure C1.1 Deploying HP OpenView NNM in a Redundant Configuration

- Documents problems
- Enforces orderly repair methodology
- Supports escalation procedures
- Captures history of problem-solving experience
- Provides statistics (in part, to help justify staffing)
- Supports communications among repair personnel

The AR System will provide automatic fill-in of specified data fields once a trouble ticket is opened, although trouble tickets will be opened manually by operators. The organization decided not to integrate AR System directly into the OpenView event stream to automatically open trouble tickets. Rather, operators will use their discretion in opening tickets, thereby gaining experience in diagnosing problems. Because the scope of the network is limited to less than several hundred nodes, the organization felt that event correlation could be handled adequately by human operators.

The organization is defining three primary trouble-ticket schemas for use by the AR System. The Event Ticket schema specifies the date, time, and severity of the problem, as well as suggested problem resolution steps. The Node Contact schema provides information about repair personnel (phone number and other contact information). The Common Carrier Schema provides information about the transport circuits and carrier contact data.

To date, the organization has written about a half-dozen scripts that will integrate the AR System into the OpenView environment. The organization has developed a help desk call process model with the goal of handling the user's problem on the first call. To that end, the organization will staff the help desk with a mix of operators and operations support personnel.

SAS CPE for Open Systems

The organization wanted a direct, industry-standard SQL interface to management data collected by NNM. SAS provides such an interface to MIB data, a feature that NNM lacks. SAS interfaces to NNM by obtaining ASCII files created when the *snmpCollect* process is run; SAS handles data crunching, summarizing the data and storing it in a proprietary SAS database. SAS CPE will fulfill the following functions:

- Access configuration, accounting, and fault data from NNM

- Create/maintain SQL database

- Perform data reduction

- Perform statistical analysis

- Support configuration of custom reports

- Provide historical reporting for trend analysis (daily, weekly, monthly, yearly)

SAS CPE will continually log eight hours' worth of data. The targeted MIB variables are listed in Tables C1.1– C1.3. Values from approximately 40 different configuration variables will be collected once a day; these represent more than 1300 instances of variables, when each variable is multiplied by the number of devices in the network.

Values from approximately 20 performance variables (representing about 900 instances) will be collected once per hour; values from approximately 40 different fault variables (representing more than 1300 instances) will be collected every five minutes or less. Generally speaking, the backhaul routers will be polled more frequently than the LAN routers. Polling intervals are expected to be adjusted as time passes.

Table Case# 1.1.
Configuration Variables

Config/System

SysDescr
SysObjectID
SysUptime
SysContact
Sysname
SysLocation
ifnumber
snmpenableauthentrap
adminstatus

Config/Router Interfaces

ifindex
ifdescr
iftype
ifphyaddress
ipneettomedia
ifindex
ipnettomediaphysaddress
ipnettomedianetaddress

Config/FDDI Interfaces

ifindex
ifdescr
iftype
ifphyaddress
ipneettomedia
ifindex
ipnettomediaphysaddress
ipnettomedianetaddress

Config/T3-DSU Interfaces

ifindex
ifdescr
iftype
ifphyaddress
ipneettomedia
ifindex
ipnettomediaphysaddress
ipnettomedianetaddress

Config/T3-ORG Interfaces

ifindex
ifdescr
iftype
ifphyaddress
ipneettomedia
ifindex
ipnettomediaphysaddress
ipnettomedianetaddress

Table Case# 1.2
Performance Variables

Accounting/System

ipInreceives
ipforwdatagrams

Accounting/Router
Interfaces

ifInOctets
ifOutOctets
ifInUcastpkts
ifOutUcastpkts
locIfipInpkts
locIfipOutpkts

Accounting/FDDI
Concentrator

ifInOctets
ifOutOctets
ifInUcastpkts
ifOutUcastpkts

Accounting/ORG
Interfaces

ifInOctets
ifOutOctets
ifInUcastpkts
ifOutUcastpkts

Table Case# 1.3.
Fault Variables

Fault Variables/System

ipInhdrerrors
ipInaddresserrors
ipfragfauls
ipInunknownprotos
ipIndiscards
ipOutdiscards
snmpInbadCommnames
ipoutnoroutes
ipreasmfauls

Fault Variables Routers
Interface

ifoperstatus
ifindiscards
ifinerrors
snmpFddiSMTCFstate
ifinunknownprotos
ifoutdiscards
ifouterrors
collisions
locifinputQueueDrops
locifOutputQueueDrops
snmpfddiMACRSMTstate

Fault Variables/FDDI
Concentrator Interfaces

ifoperstatus
ifindiscards
ifinerrors
ifinunknownprotos
ifoutdiscards
ifouterrors
snmpFddiSMTCFstate
snmpfddiMACRSMTstate

Fault/ORG   Interfaces

ifinerrors
ifinunknownprotos
ifoutdiscards
ifouterrors

It is clear to see that without SAS, the overhead of storing collected MIB values would be intolerable. Analyzing and interpreting the collected data would be an administrative nightmare without SAS, because NNM creates an individual file for each MIB variable within an individual device. In other words, in polling the variables listed in Tables C1.1–1.3, NNM creates in excess of 3000 individual MIB variable files for the organization's configuration of 40–60 routers, 30–40 hubs, and 15 DSU/CSUs.

By using SAS, the organization will reduce the amount of storage needed without compromising on disaster recovery requirements; also, SAS provides the ability to more easily summarize network performance data and generate reports on circuit utilization and other metrics.

The organization anticipates a four- to six-month field test of the network. During the field test and thereafter, the network design team will take on the role of systems engineering and support.

2

A Bridged/Routed IP, AppleTalk, DECnet Network

Customizing OpenView NNM

Carnegie-Mellon University (CMU) in Pittsburgh, Pa., is a leading research university with more than 10,000 students and faculty. Management of networking at CMU is very centralized. The Computing Services department is responsible for networking to the desktop for 90 percent of the campus. This has been accomplished with a staff of five technicians, one help desk person, and a development staff of five.

CMU's network supports more than 8000 nodes, including Macintosh workstations, a variety of Unix workstations, and a growing population of PCs. The protocols in use are primarily TCP/IP, AppleTalk, IPX (growing rapidly), and DECnet (declining rapidly). Ethernet is popular at CMU, although there is a large installed base of LocalTalk due to its low cost. There are more than 1000 Token-Ring nodes, but Token-Ring use is declining, and the university is encouraging its replacement due to significantly higher life-cycle costs incurred when supporting Token-Ring.

The traffic growth rate on some network segments exceeds 100 percent per year, presenting some interesting management problems. SNMP and RMON play a huge role in managing all CMU network and system resources.

CMU's Networking Philosophy

CMU pioneered the "backbone in a box" idea by installing a Cisco AGS+ as its network backbone in 1990. CMU has discovered that the backbone in a box concept, as well as the closely related switching concept, has been a cost-effective, reliable, and manageable way of adding bandwidth. In particular, CMU does not support FDDI for the backbone due to its significantly higher life-cycle costs—exceeding those of Token-Ring. CMU instead favors 100Base-T for higher bandwidth to the desktop.

CMU is concerned about the cost of management routing, particularly when a routed network is reconfigured, potentially causing addressing problems for large numbers of hosts. As a result, CMU primarily routes only IPX and AppleTalk, and often bridges IP. IPX and AppleTalk are routed because those protocols are responsible for most of the protocol-related failures experienced at CMU. Also, the plug-and-play nature of both IPX and AppleTalk makes changes simpler, improving the cost/benefit ratio of their routing.

The lack of this same plug-and-play capability for IP has led CMU to bridge IP often; making changes to the network in a subnet-routed network is anything but simple. TCP/IP is more mature and better able to scale than IPX and AppleTalk, and CMU has experienced no problems with bridging that would drive a change to routing. Nevertheless, routing is always used in mixed-media environments and over WANs. In effect, CMU uses routing, but avoids TCP/IP subnet routing wherever possible.

CMU's Network Management Applications

To support network management of the two primary Cisco backbone routers, more than 100 critical hubs and many servers, CMU has deployed HP OpenView NNM running on a Sun SPARC 20 system with 96MB memory. Managed devices are polled every five minutes.

CMU originally evaluated SunNet Manager, but found the product could not scale well. CMU also evaluated Cabletron Spectrum, but felt that the customization effort would be too complex. CMU has customized OpenView on several levels to meet its specific needs, including map customization and the addition of CMU-created SNMP tools (applications) for data collection and analysis, and alarm correlation.

To create a customized network map, CMU's Computing Services scanned in a CMU campus map, and loaded in infrastructure nodes, file servers, and connectivity devices. The campus includes more than 50 buildings and approximately 150 wiring closets.

NNM is used primarily as an SNMP data collection tool. It is supplemented by HP LanProbes collecting RMON data. CMU has extended OpenView's alarm reporting facilities by plugging in collected RMON data to support diagnostics. The enhanced tool supports communications between operators, and a certain level of alarm correlation feeding into a trouble ticketing system. For example, if a router goes down, many devices are affected, but only one main trouble ticket describing the primary problem is generated. The CMU-developed tool provides suggested repair actions, such as disabling routing on a specific node, or shutting down a given node entirely. The tool supplies the following message for each supported event:

- Date and time of event
- Device name
- Suggested repair action

When an operator acknowledges the event, all other operators can see the acknowledgment and know that the problem is being handled.

CMU has found NNM to be a convenient "holding tank" for such custom-developed tools. By integrating the SNMP tools into the NNM menu, CMU has a visual record of where scripts and utilities are and what they accomplish. In some cases, tools have been linked to map icons.

3

A Frame Relay Network

Filtering Events Using Seagate/NerveCenter

This case study describes a network run by a global broadcasting firm that is the parent organization of more than 30 companies scattered across the world. The firm owns and operates a major cable network, as well as several large networks and entertainment production companies, and diversified news and entertainment services in the U.S. and abroad. The firm has earned a reputation as one of the fastest-growing, innovative organizations in existence today.

The firm supports more than 7000 PCs and Apple Macintosh systems throughout the world. Until recently, the wide area network (WAN) links between the various companies were typified by costly point-to-point T-1 lines that had sprung up with no central planning. As a result, the firm was maintaining a spider's web of leased lines that were, in many cases, unnecessarily redundant.

In late 1994, the firm made a corporate-level decision to define a worldwide network infrastructure for the purpose of reducing costs and maximizing network efficiency and productivity. The firm is deploying a new network that will interconnect its various sites into a common Frame Relay "cloud," eliminating many point-to-point T-1 lines and greatly expanding the network capability. The project entailed installation of all new routers and hubs, and most sites also have new wiring infrastructures. All WAN connections are TCP/IP, and many sites also run AppleTalk and Novell IPX/SPX within a campus.

The Software Services Group within the firm's Worldwide Information Technology Services (WITS) has been tasked with overseeing the management of the new network infrastructure. The new network is divided into several primary regions, including Northeast United States; Southeast United States; West Coast United States; the remaining eastern and central United States; and South America, the Far East, and Europe.

Each region has an MIS director. A separate entertainment facility is located in in Atlanta, Ga., with an internal network that is largely self-contained.

The firm's Software Services Group is responsible for providing tools for operations and management; the Network Services Group has been tasked with managing the new global network infrastructure. Several ground rules were established defining corporate policy for network management deployment. These ground rules include:

- The corporate LAN/WAN management group is responsible for all routers across the world.

- The regional site is responsible from the local router on down—including hubs, physical wiring, and client configurations.

- The regional sites are tasked with being as autonomous as possible.

- The Software Services Group is reponsible for providing tools to the regional sites; these tools must help the regions manage as autonomously as possible.

To fulfill these goals, the firm is implementing a new network management system that is a deployment of HP OpenView Network Node Manager in combination with several key third-party applications, including Seagate/NerveCenter, CiscoWorks, and Bay Networks Optivity. The first iteration of this implementation is a network management tool, used primarily for monitoring up/down status of the routers—including when they go down, and for how long. Later, the OpenView NNM portion of the system will use SNMP Get commands to pull information out of the router and produce daily performance summary reports. Future "releases" of the system will include software distribution tools and status monitoring of Oracle financials and Lotus Notes applications.

Before selecting HP OpenView Network Node Manager, the firm evaluated Sun's SunNet Manager and NetLab's now-defunct DiMONS platform. The firm felt that OpenView offered more flexibility and opportunity for plug-and-play applications implementation. The firm chose to implement OpenView NNM in conjunction with the NetLabs/NerveCenter application. All alarms fed into the OpenView NNM display first pass through the NetLabs/NerveCenter application, feeding the alarms from NerveCenter to HP OpenView's interface, and allowing the user to configure sophisticated alarms using a GUI. The firm has turned off all HP polling, and is letting NerveCenter do all the polling. In contrast, configuration of complex alarms using OpenView NNM must be done programmatically.

Setting this up through NerveCenter took a software support manager at the firm about 20 working days; in contrast, writing shell scripts through HP OpenView NNM to accomplish the same thing would have taken 200 to 300 working days. NerveCenter also provides an object database that is much easier to maintain than one that involves programmatically changing scripts to modify alarms and notifications.

NerveCenter allows users to define an alarm sequence in the form of a graphical state diagram. (For more information on NerveCenter state diagrams, see Chap 7.) NerveCenter describes the network in terms of objects, and those who are not familiar with object-oriented concepts may find that it takes some time to master the art of creating state diagrams. The software support manager estimates that he spent about a month focusing on NerveCenter before becoming proficient with the product.

There is now a copy of Network Node Manager and NerveCenter in each site, running on HP 715 model servers, each with about 100MB RAM and 2GB disk storage. The main management server runs on an HP 735 with 500MB RAM.

The Software Services Group has worked to create a reliable notification system, and is using Telamon's TelAlert paging application. The firm had been using public domain scripts for paging before using TelAlert.

The Software Services Group is working with Email Group to create customized tools for monitoring the firm's critical e-mail facilities around the world. The e-mail servers are OS/2 processors in a hub-and-spoke configuration that route mail globally. The system will be used to monitor the status of these e-mail servers initially; later, it will support detailed monitoring of network interface cards as well as the company's firewall security system.

Case Study

4

A Telecommunications Network

ALMAP Management Framework from Alcatel

The Alcatel Management Platform ALMAP 3 offers a homogeneous runtime system and a development environment. Its mission is to enable the fast and flexible development of standards-conformant management applications for distributed operations systems in a Telecommunications Management Network. These operations systems allow the uniform management of all network resources and services in terms of the user interface, regardless of the architecture of the management solution.

ALMAP aligns to all major TMN and system management standards issued by ITU-T, ETSI, and ISO, as well as NMF/OmniPoint, SPIRIT, and, to some extent, OSF. Future plans will also include OMG. Besides market products, ALMAP provides Alcatel modules and tools that fill essential gaps in the platform functionality as it is provided by the market products.

The core of ALMAP is HP OpenView DM. It provides a flexible management framework for multiple hardware platforms, transportation protocols, and network management protocols, in order to support the development of applications for network management, systems management, and application management.

HP's OpenView Communication Infrastructure has been selected by the Open System Foundation (OSF) for essential components of the Distributed

Management Environment. This makes it a de facto industry standard. Figure 10.7 in Chap. 10 shows the central role of OpenView DM in the ALMAP platform.

ALMAP is part of the Alcatel 1300 product family, which contains additionally ALMA, the Alcatel Management Applications. Together ALMAP and ALMA form a generic management system that can be used for the management of public and private networks: switching and transmissions systems, mobile networks, metropolitan area networks (MANs), broadband ISDN, virtual private networks (VPN), intelligent networks (IN), office communication systems, management systems, and networks.

Among Alcatel customers are public and private network operators, service providers, public authorities, energy providing companies, banks, and insurance companies.

ALMAP3 comes as a fine-granular open portfolio of packages. They have well-defined functionalities and a minimum of interdependencies, so that the customers have the highest degree of freedom to select and combine their particular set of packages for their specific needs.

Hardware Topologies of ALMAP

The following hardware equipment is supported by ALMAP:

- HP 9000/700 and HP 9000/800
- Sun SPARCServer or Workstation
- Sun Laptop
- X terminals
- Console
- Printer

The hardware configurations into which ALMAP-based systems can be arranged are flexible and scalable. The following three kinds of topologies are possible:

- Single main server configuration (Fig. C4.1)
- Single main server configuration with front-end workstation (Fig. C4.2)
- Distributed system with one main server and one or more dedicated servers (Fig. C4.3)

The distributed system will be the typical topology for large management systems. Dedicated servers will be used to meet specific load requirements. For instance, if a certain number of X terminals is exceeded, a separate HMI server can be set up. If a large amount of communication is expected within the management system, the communication functionality can be moved from the main server to a dedicated communication server.

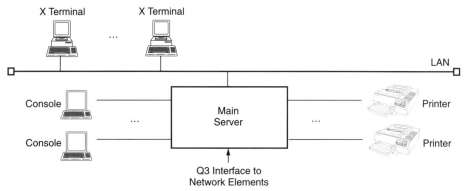

Figure C4.1. Hardware Topology of ALMAP-Based Management System: Single Main Server Configuration

ALMAP Services and Management Applications

This segment presents all ALMAP services and the packages they contain. Generally there is for each service:

- An abstract of what the whole service can do for the user
- A description of each contained package
- A figure showing the architecture of the service

Managed Objects and SMF Services

The Managed Objects and SMF Services let the user accomplish the following:

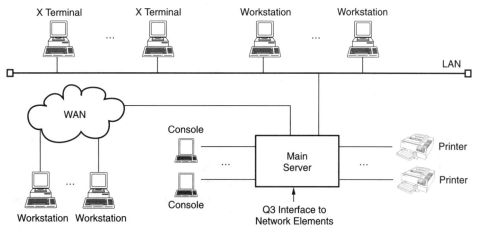

Figure C4.2. Hardware Topology of ALMAP-Based Management System: Single Main Server Configuration with Front-End Workstation

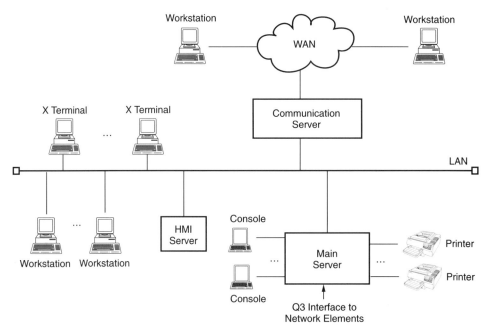

Figure C4.3. Hardware Topology of ALMAP-Based Management System: Full Distribution

- Model physical resources of the open system—the Managed Objects
- Generate stubs and headers for the XMP/XOM interface
- Use the XMP/XOM API to access CMIP services
- Manage event forwarding and logging

The Managed Objects and SMF Services rely on the following packages:

- HP OpenView DM Platform
- HP OpenView DM Developer's Tools
- HP OpenView DM System Management Functions
- RPC for TMN

Each of the packages in turn consists of several components. The HP OpenView DM Platform package consists of the following components:

- The GDMO/ASN.1 Parser, a compiler front end that parses Managed Object (MO) specifications in GDMO syntax and translates them into an intermediate presentation that becomes input for the other tools below.
- The XOM Package Generator, a complex back end that takes the intermediate representation and generates C header files, encoding/decoding definitions, and OM Package Descriptions. This output simplifies the development of software that issues OM objects to be handled by XMP APIs.

- The XOM Function Generator, a compiler back end that takes the intermediate representation and generates C data structures and functions, hiding the complexity of the XOM API from the management application and agent developer.

- The Metadata Loader is a compiler back end that takes the intermediate representation as input and populates the metadata database by sending the appropriate create, set, and delete requests to the Metadata Agent via the Postmaster.

- The Metadata Agent can retrieve GDMO/ASN.1 definitions from the Metadata Database and provide MO class information at application runtime.

- The Communication Infrastructure provides, via an XMP/XOM interface, several services to applications: Network Access using SNMP or CMIP protocol, Object Registration Service for local transparency, Event Management Service for automatic event forwarding, and Metadata Service for retrieving the definition of the object model at runtime.

The OpenView DM System Management Functions package allows management applications to control discrimination, forwarding, and logging of IS events reports and SNMP traps. This package is able to discriminate over new types of notifications and to handle multiple logs.

OpenView DM System Management Functions has the following four components:

- The Event Stack, which is attached to the Postmaster and is responsible for the discrimination of CMIS event reports and SNMP traps on the Postmaster level.

- The Event Agent, which manages the Event Fowarding Discriminators (EFDs). The Event Agent can create and delete EFDs.

- The Log Agent, which manages the logs, discriminates the potential log records, and performs storing and retrieval of the log records.

- The Metadata Cache Manager, which is responsible for extracting and caching metadata information from the metadata agent, and updating the local metadata information of the Event Stack, the Event Agent, and the Log Agent.

The HP OpenView DM Developer's Tools package consists of a GDMO Modeling tool set, which allows multiple MO designers to collaborate on the object specifications and communicate the object models to the MO programmers. It includes a central Object Dictionary for all MO specifications and several tools assessing the Object Dictionary.

The RPC for TMN package provides an algorithm and examples for mapping from ASN.1 to DCE IDL. The package is useful for projects involving migration of the internal communications from XMP/XOM to DCE IDL.

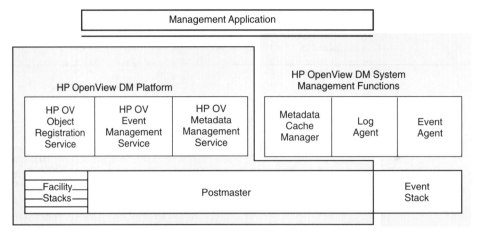

Figure C4.4 ALMAP 3 Managed Objects and SMF Services (the Runtime Part)

Figure C4.4 shows the runtime part of management objects and SMF services.

Management and communication services

The Communication Services implements the Q3 interface to network elements. In detail, Communications Services support the following APIs:

- CMIP, FTAM, ROSE, and ACSE, for the communication over X.25 or ISDN
- APPC for the communication over SNA
- The X.400-based message handling system

ALMAP Communications Services are comprised of the following packages:

- The Retix-OPI Adaptor supports access to the Retix CMIP protocol stack using the XMP/XOM API as defined by X/Open via the HP OpenView Postmaster. The Retix-OPI Adaptor realizes a mapping between the HPs Open Protocol Interface (OPI) that envelopes the HP Postmaster and the Retix CMISE/ROSE protocol stack API.
- The Retix CMISE and ROSE Protocol Stack supports the Network Management Forum definition of CMISE (Common Management Information Service Element), and ROSE (Remote Operation Service Element). This package provides a CMISE API to applications, and uses ACSE for the supervision of associations between peer application entities.
- The Retix FTAM Protocol Stack supports FTAM (File Transfer, Access, and Management). The used FTAM profile can select to be AFT11 or AFT111. The FTAM service can be accessed by either the Retix FTAM API or the MAP/TOP API. FTAM consists of a protocol machine and a responder. It con-

tains also ACSE (Application Common Service Element), the Presentation Layer, and the Session Layer. Both ACSE and the Presentation services can be accessed via the Retix Stack API, called APLI.

- The TLI Protocol Stack realizes layers 1–4 to access different networks. The following types of networks are supported: ISDN, packet-switching network in connection-oriented network service mode, packet-switching network in connectionless network service mode.

- The TLI Ethernet Protocol Stack provides access to local area networks.

- The IBM SNA Protocol Stack provides a proprietary APPC API to LU6.2. The underlying node is Physical Unit (PU) type 2.0/2.1 Cluster Controller (Peripheral Node). The communication link is Synchronous Data Link Control (SDLC).

In addition, the Message Handling System (X.400) provides access to the e-mail systems based on the ITU-T X.400 series. It has not yet been decided which product will be used for this function.

Presentation services

The presentation services let the customer build for applications an X-based user interface that may consist of maps, forms, and/or pixmap graphics. The ALMAP Presentation Services consist of the following four packages and their components:

- HP OpenView Windows: This is a runtime component that is part of the HP OpenView DM Development Kit. It displays maps showing a logical view of the network, the hierarchy of manageable network elements in the SNMP or CMIP world. The maps allow managing the elements through their symbols. It provides an API for applications that are built on top of it. It can be configured offline via Registration Files.

- Map Manager: The Map Manager allows multiple read/write access to a single map and submits all changes immediately.

- Free Graphics Support: This package is based on Vl DataViews. It extends the graphical presentation capabilities of HP OpenView Windows through bitmap-oriented symbols. DataViews is a tool that supports the development of graphical user interfaces based on geometrical objects rather than on widgets. DVdraw is a graphical editor, and DVtools (the core of DataViews) is a C library of routines that allows it to create and control graphics at runtime. DVtools provide an API for applications that are built on top of it.

- UIM/X by Visual Edge: a User Interface Management System that covers the four phases of user interface development: layout design, behavior specification, testing, and code generation. UIM/X is an offline tool. UIMIX supports also templates for user interfaces.

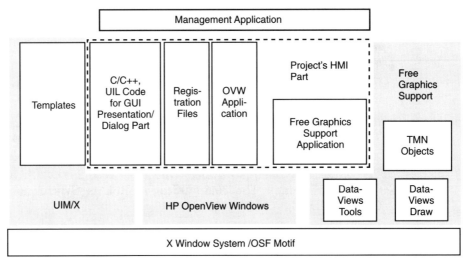

Figure C4.5 ALMAP 3 Presentation Services

Figure C4.5 summarizes the presentation services.

Distributed services

The distributed services transparently distribute applications on several hosts within a LAN by Remote Procedure Calls (RPCs), scheduling those calls, and sending messages. Small management systems can be realized by just basing them on HP OpenView.

The packages used in ALMAP distributed services have the functionality and components described in the next few paragraphs.

Distributed Computing Environment (DCE). This package provides an environment for the transparent distribution of applications over distributed computer hardware regardless of computer network size, location of processors, hardware vendor, or operating system. ALMAP 3 uses HP DCE for HP workstations, and Transarc DCE for Sun workstations. DCE contains the following closely integrated functionality: DCE Threads, the DCE Remote Procedure Call (RPC), the DCE Directory Services (CDS, GDS), the DCE Security Service, and the DCE Time Service (DTS).

Date and Time Handling. This package provides date- and time-related functions, and a basic scheduling mechanism for applications and other services. Higher-level scheduling functions such as CMIS requests or MML-Command scheduling can be implemented based on this scheduling package. This package depends on DCE RPC, DTS, and threads.

Application Message Handling. This package provides support for the definition, distribution, and formatting of messages. Messages are structured texts that originate from a management application and are routed to some output device, such as screen or printer. Message texts can be internationalized. More than one language at a time may be used in the system.

Figure C4.6 shows an overview of distributed services.

Management services

Management services are helpful to manage processes, to print and organize backups. ALMAP currently uses three packages for these services.

Distributed System Management (DSM). This package performs the management of processes and their configuration data on computing nodes, and the management of distributed applications. This service is dependent on DCE, as it requires the DCE RPC as the basic communication mechanism. DSM handles many different types of processes, such as DCE service processes, application processes, or HP OpenView processes.

Printer handling. This package consists of the HP OV OpenSpool product family (HP OV OpenSpool, HP OV OpenSpool SharedPrint, HP OV OpenSpool/Link) which provides transparent access to remote printers or plotters, and supports multivendor platforms. HP OV OpenSpool/Link provides event integration into the HP OpenView management station. HP OV OpenSpool is compatible with the OSF DME Print Services.

Backup/restore. This package consists of HP OpenView OmniBack II, which is an integral part of the HP OpenView solution portfolio. It can be integrated into HP OpenView using HP OmniBack/Link. It is a scalable, powerful backup and restore solution that is flexible enough to reflect the requirements of an individual organizational structure by defining backup domains. This policy driven, centrally scheduled, and automated backup protects data in a distributed, heterogeneous computing environment.

Figure C4.7 shows how standard HP services are used with special Alcatel services in combination.

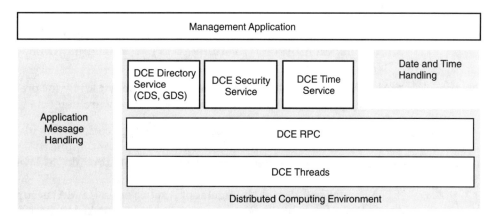

Figure C4.6 ALMAP 3 Distributed Services

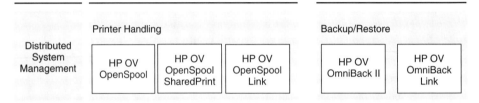

Figure C4.7 ALMAP 3 Management Services

Operating system services

The operating system services are helpful in sending faxes and receiving a radio clock time signal. Besides the underlying operating system, ALMAP uses the following packages:

- DCF-77: This package queries the DCF-77 radio clock data to determine the current time and synchronizes the system clock.

- Fax Card: This package allows the user to send faxes and view them on the screen.

Management applications

There are two groups of applications for the ALMAP platform: generic and specific management applications:

Generic management applications. Generic management applications are management applications providing a high degree of reusability, for instance generic services that are used by many management applications, and mediation services for protocol conversion, etc. The set of Alcatel generic management applications is expected to grow in the future. The generic management applications are likely to be included into the ALMAP platform. In the moment the following packages of generic management applications are available or envisioned:

- ALMA Alarm, a package providing the Alarm Management functionality for any Operation System according to ITU-T standards X.733, X.734, X.735, X.736, and Q.821.

- ALMA Trouble Ticketing, which supports the workflow for problems arising in the operations system (e.g., alarms and software defects).

Specific management applications. Specific applications provide ready-to-use TMN applications. The Alcatel specific management applications—the ALMA Portfolio—are management applications that provide a lower degree of reusability.

The Portfolio of Alcatel Management Applications (ALMA) is supported by the ALMAP platform, but it is not part of ALMAP. The ALMA Portfolio is an open set of ready-to-use TMN applications, covering management functionality for the Business Layer, the Service Layer, the Network Layer, and the Network Element Layer. The management applications of the ALMA portfolio can be arranged and configured in a building-block manner, which allows the development of scalable management systems exhibiting different combinations of functionality.

The ALMA Portfolio includes currently the following products, classified according to the above four layers:

- Business Layer: No ALMA building blocks have been identified for this layer.

- Service Layer: ALMA Administration (A 1344) and ALMA Billing (A 1343)

- Network Layer: ALMA Centrex (A 1332), ALMA CCS #7 Management (A 1333), and ALMA Trouble-Ticketing (A 1338)

- Network Element Layer: ALMA Alarm Management (A 1330), ALMA Call Routing Management (A 1331), ALMA CCS #7 Management (A 1333), ALMA Subscriber Administration (A 1334), ALMA Tariff Management (A 1335), ALMA Command Management (MML) (A 1337), ALMA Test Management (A 1339), ALMA Traffic Measurement (A 1340), ALMA Traffic Routing (A 1341), and ALMA Charging (A 1342)

Development environment. The architecture of the development environment corresponds to ECMA's "toaster" model. In the center there is a collection of tools that are used at particular instances during the software life cycle: Design/Coding Methods and Tools, Quality Assurance (testing), etc. These life cycle-related methods and tools are enveloped by tools for integration. In detail, the Development Environment of ALMAP 3 consists of the following packages: (Fig. C4.8)

- Configuration Management: The Configuration Management package manages the whole ALMAP-based software development process, and supports system integration and delivery. The configuration management system for all ALMAP packages is based on Atria ClearCase. QualTrack DDTs is used as defect tracking system.

- Design Methods and Tools: This package includes IDE Software through Pictures for hierarchical breakdown and functional design, Rational ROSE for object-oriented design with the BOOCH method.

- Coding Methods and Tools: This package includes Alcatel SSG guidelines for writing robust, readable and portable ANSI-C code, Alcatel SSG C++ coding guidelines, HP SoftBench (which provides a development environment for C or C++ for HP), error handling guideline, and QA Systems QA C and QA C++ (which supports guideline conformance checks and thus releases developers and quality assurance people from having to read code with a checklist for its syntax).

- Software Quality Assurance: This package includes graphical code structure presentation using Verilog LOGISCOPE (including Alcatel guidelines for using LOGISCOPE), test automatization using PureSoftware Purify, Alcatel

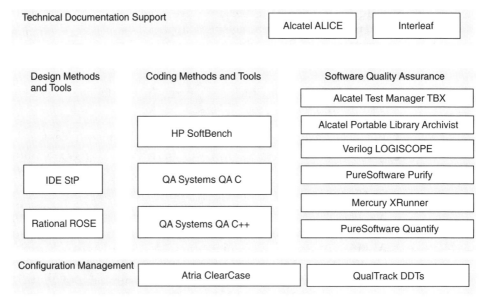

Figure C4.8 ALMAP 3 Development Environment

Test ManagerTBX, and Mercury XRunner, measurement profiling of execution times and call counts using PureSoftware Quantify, dynamic memory handling analysis using PureSoftware Purify, graphical test coverage presentation using LOGISCOPE, regression test of X applications using XRunner, plus guidelines for usage of TBX and LOGISCOPE.

■ Technical Documentation Support: Production of technical and daily-life documentation is supported by Interleaf. Additional support is provided through Alcatel ALICE by simplification of the user interface and by standardization of document layout and document administration information. The packages in the development environment can be arranged in a manner that allows for optimum flexibility with respect to the size of the project and the use of a paradigm (functional design, object-oriented design, etc.).

ALMAP is available for the Unix platforms of HP-UX and SunOS. A port to Solaris is planned for the future. It is planned that at least parts of ALMAP will also run on top of OSF/1. The usage of other platforms is under investigation and has to be decided case by case. It mainly depends on the portability of the included third-party software. The Alcatel-provided software is portable in any case.

Advantages of ALMAP and the Alcatel 1300 Product Family

The ALMAP 3 strategy offers the following advantages for organizations that buy and use management systems that were developed on the basis of ALMAP:

- Building management systems on the basis of existing market products assures that the most advanced software technologies are offered to customers.

- Use of existing market products on the basis of de facto and de jure standards assures optimal interoperability and portability, and offers the customers greatest freedom of choice for their products.

- Reduced development cost and fast provision of management functionality and services are due to the use of existing market products and the reuse of management applications.

- The building-block approach of the Alcatel 1300 product family provides for scalability of management solutions according to specific customer needs.

- Stability and smooth development, as well as long-term support, is assured.

ACD	Automated call distributor
ACSE	Association control service element
AI	Artificial Intelligence
AIX	Advanced Interactive eXecutive (IBM's Unix)
ANSI	American National Standards Institute
API	Application Programming Interface
ARPA	Advanced Research Projects Agency
ARPANET	ARPA computer network
AS	Autonomous system (connection between IGP and EGP)
ASN.1	Abstract Syntax Notation One
ATM	Asynchronous Transfer Mode
B-ISDN	Broadband ISDN
BU	Business unit
CAD	Computer-aided design
CASE	Computer Aided Software Engineering
CATV	Coaxial community antenna television
CAU	Controlled access unit
CIM	Computer Integrated Manufacturing
CCITT	Commitee Consultatif International Telegraphique et Telephonique
CLNP	Connectionless Network Protocol
CMIP	Common Management Information Protocol
CMISE	Common management information service element
CMOL	CMIP over logical link control
CMOT	CMIP over TCP/IP
CORBA	Common Object-Oriented Request Broker Architecture
CSMA/CD	Carrier Sense Multiple Access/Collision Detect
CSU	Channel service unit
DARPA	ARPA of the US Department of Defense (DoD)
DAS	Double attached station

DCE	Distributed Computing Environment (OSF)
DDE	Dynamic Data Exchange
DTE	Data circuit-terminating equipment
DES	Data Encryption Standard
DDN	Defense Data Network
DME	Distributed Management Environmnent (from OSF)
DMI	Desktop Management Interface
DMTF	Desktop Management Task Force
DNA	Digital Network Architecture (DEC)
DQDB	Dual queue dual bus
DSA	Distributed Systems Architecture (Bull)
DSU	Data service unit
DTE	Data terminal equipment
EDI	Electronic data interchange
EGP	Exterior Gateway Protocol
EMS	Element management system
FDDI	Fiber Distributed Data Interface
FDM	Frequency division multiplexing
FIFO	First in, first out
FTP	File Transfer Protocol
GB	Gigabytes
GDMO	Generic Definition of Managed Objects (OSI)
GGP	Gateway Gateway Protocol
GNMP	Government Network Management Profile
GUI	Graphical user interface
HDLC	High-level Data Link Protocol
HTML	Hypertext Markup Language
HTTP	HyperText Transfer Protocol
IAB	Internet Activities Board
ICMP	Internet Control Message Protocol
IEEE	Institute of Electrical and Electronic Engineers
IETF	Internet Engineering Task Force
IGP	Internet Gateway Routing Protocol
IIVR	Integrated interactive voice response
IMP	Interface messages processors
IP	Internet Protocol
IPX	Internet packet exchange
IS	Intermediate system (ISO for IP-router)
ISDN	Integrated Services Digital Network
ISO	International Organization for Standardization
ITU	International Telecommunications Union
IXC	Interexchange carrier
LAN	Local area network
LAT	Local Area Transport Protocol (DEC)
LED	Light-emitting device
LLC	Logical link control

LM	LAN manager
MAC	Media Access Control
MAN	Metropolitan area network
MAU	Media Attachment Unit or Multiple Access Unit
MB	Megabytes
MIF	Management information file
MIB	Management information base
MIS	Management information system
MO	Managed object
MSU	Message Service Unit (IBM)
MTA	Message transfer agent
MTBF	Mean time between failures
MTOR	Mean time of repair
MTTD	Mean time of diagnosis
MTTR	Mean time to repair
NCE	Network control engine
NCP	Network control program
NCL	Network Control Language
NE	Network element
NetBIOS	Network Basic Input-Output System
NFS	Network File System (Sun)
NIC	Network interface card
NMF	Network Management Forum
NMM	Network management module
NMP	Network Management Protocol
NMS	Network management station or network management system
NMVT	Network management vector transport
NNM	Network Node Manager
NOS	Network operating system
OEM	Original equipment manufacturer
OLE	Object Linking and Embedding
OMG	Object Management Group
OSF	Open Software Foundation
OSI	Open System Interconnection
OV	OpenView
OVW	OpenView Windows
PAD	Packet assembler-disassembler
PAW	Polycenter AssetWorks
PBX	Private branch exchange
PDU	Protocol data unit
PC	Personal computer
PCM	Pulse code modulation
PHY	Physical layer (FDDI)
PIN	Personal identification number or positive intrinsic negative
PING	Packet Internet Grouper

PLS	Physical signaling
PMD	Physical medium dependent
PSM	Product specific module
RAM	Random access memory
RFC	Request For Comments
RFS	Remote File System (AT&T)
RISC	Reduced Instruction Command Set
RMON	Remote MONitoring standard for SNMP-MIBs
RODM	Resource object data manager
ROSE	Remote operating service element
RPC	Remote Procedure Call
SDH	Synchronous digital hierarchy
SGMP	Simple Gateway Monitoring Protocol
SLIP	Serial Line Internet Protocol
SMAE	Systems Management Application Entities
SMAP	Specific Management Application Protocol
SMF	Systems Management Function
SMFA	Specific Management Functional Area
SMI	Structure of Management Information
SMDR	Station Message Detailed Recording
SMDS	Switched Multi-megabit Data Service
SMP	Station or Simple Management Protocol (FDDI)
SMTP	Simple Mail Transfer Protocol
SNA	Systems Network Architecture (IBM)
SNI	Systems Network Interconnected (IBM)
SNMP	Simple Network Management Protocol
SONET	Synchronous Optical Network
SRB	Source routing bridge
SSAP	Source service access point
STA	Spanning tree algorithms
TB	Token bus
TCP	Transmission Control Protocol
TDM	Time division multiplexing
TDR	Time domain reflectometer
TFTP	Trivial File Transfer Protocol
TME	Tivoli Management Environment
TMN	Telecommunications Management Network
TR	Token-Ring
TTRT	Target token ring rotation time
UA	User agent
UDP	User Datagram Protocol
UI	Unix Internation
ULP	Upper Layer Protocol
URL	Universal Resource Locator
UPS	Uninterruptible power supply
VAR	Value-added reseller

VNM	Virtual Network Machine
VT	Virtual Terminal
VTAM	Virtual Telecommunication Access Method (IBM)
WAN	Wide area network
WNM	Workgroup Node Manager
WWW	World Wide Web
XNS	Xerox Network Services

Addresses and phone numbers for many vendors whose products are discussed in this book are listed below.

3Com Corp.
5400 Bayfront Plaza
Santa Clara, CA 95052
(408) 764-5000

Accugraph Corp.
5822 Cromo Drive
El Paso, TX 79912
(915) 581-1171

Advanced Computer
Applications, Inc.
107 Penns Trail
Newton, PA 18940
(215) 860-0700

Answer Computer/Platinum
1263 Oakmead Pkwy.
Sunnyvale, CA 94086

Applied Expert Systems, Inc.
595 Price Ave., Suite 3
Redwood City, CA 94063
(415) 364-1222

Arcarda Software, Inc.
Lake Mary, FL
(407) 262-8000

ARMON Networking
Atidum Technological Park
Bldg. 1
P.O. Box 58030
Tel-Aviv, Israel 61580
(800) 499-RMON

Aston Brooke Division of Platinum
610 W. Germantown Pike
Suite 300
Plymouth Meeting, PA 19462
(610) 940-6020

Autotrol Technology Corp.
12500 N. Washington St.
Denver, CO 80241-2400
(303) 252-2354

Axon Networks
199 Wells Ave.
Newton, MA 02159
(617) 630-9600

Bay Networks, Inc. (Wellfleet)
15 Crosby Drive
Bedford, MA 01730

Bay Networks (SynOptics) Inc.
4401 Great America Pkwy.
Santa Clara, CA 95054
(408) 988-2400

BBN Systems and Technologies
10 Moulton St.
Cambridge, MA 02138
(617) 873-3000

BGS Systems, Inc.
128 Technology Center
Waltham, MA 02254-9111
(617) 891-0000

BMC Software, Inc.
2101 City West Blvd.
Houston, TX 77042-2827
(713) 918-8800

Boole & Babbage, Inc.
3131 Zanker Ave.
San Jose, CA 95134
(408) 526-3000

BrainTree Technology, Inc.
Norwell, MA
(617) 982-0200

Bridgeway Corp.
8585 145th Ave. NE
Redmond, WA 98052

Bull HN Information
  Systems, Inc.
Technology Park
Billerica, MA 01821
(508) 294-6000

Cabletron Systems, Inc.
35 Industrial Way
Rochester, NH 03867-5005
(603) 332-9400

Cascade Communications Corp.
5 Carlisle Road
Westford, MA 01886
(508) 692-2600

Chipcom Corp.
118 Turnpike Rd.
Southborough, MA 01772
(508) 460-8900

Cisco Systems, Inc.
170 West Tasman
San Jose, CA 95134
(408) 526-4000

CompuWare Corp.
31440 Northwestern Hwy.
Farmington Hills, MI 48334
(313) 737-7300

Concord Communications, Inc.
753 Forest St.
Marlboro, MA 01752
(508) 460-4646

CoroNet Systems
Los Altos Plaza, Suite G-22
5150 El Camino Real
Los Altos, CA 94022
(415) 960-3255

Crosscom Corp.
450 Donald Lynch Blvd.
Marlboro, MA 01752
(508) 481-4060

DeskTalk Systems, Inc.
19401 S. Vermont Ave.
Suite F-100
Torrance, CA 90502
(310) 323-5998

Diederich & Associates
625 Fair Oaks Ave., Suite 290
South Pasadena, CA 91030

Digital Equipment Corp.
146 Main St.
Maynard, MA 01754
(508) 493-5111

Epilogue Technology Corp.
919 High Point Drive
Ventura, CA 93003
(805) 650-7107

Fore Systems, Inc.
174 Thorn Hill Road
Warrendale, PA 15086-7586
(412) 772-6600

Frontier Software, Inc.
1501 Main St., Suite 40
Tewksbury MA 01876
(800) 357-RMON

Frye Computing Systems, Inc.
19 Temple Place
Boston, MA 02111
(617) 451-5400

Gensym Corp.
125 Cambridge Park Drive
Cambridge, MA 02140
(617) 547-2500

Haystack Labs, Inc.
10713 RR620 North, Suite 521
Austin, TX 78726
(512) 918-3555

Hewlett-Packard Co.
Networked Systems Group
19091 Pruneridge Ave.
Cupertino, CA 95014

Hi-Comp America, Inc.
Houston, TX 77227
(800) 323-8863

Innovative Software
 Development
Denver Technological Center
5261 S. Quebec St., Suite 250
Englewood, CO 80111
(303) 220-1500

International Network Services
650 Castro St., Suite 260
Mountain View, CA 94041
(415) 254-0800

ISICAD, Inc.
1920 W. Corporate Way
Anaheim, CA 92803
(714) 533-8910

Isotro Network Management, Inc.
440 Laurier Ave W, Suite 200
Ottawa, Ontario K1R 7X6
(613) 722-1921

Ki Networks, Inc.
6760 Alexander Bell Drive
Columbia, MD 21046
(800) 945-4454

Landmark Systems Corp.
8000 Towers Crescent Drive
Vienna, VA 22182-2700
(800) 755-4884

LANNET Data Communications
7711 Center Ave., Suite 600
Huntington Beach, CA 92647
(714) 752-6638

McAfee
2710 Walsh Ave.
Santa Clara, CA 95051-0963
(408) 988-3832

Micromuse
780 Third Ave.
New York, NY 10017
(212) 219-4450

Micropath, Inc.
40 Lake Bellevue
Suite 360
Bellevue, WA 98005
(206) 454-2676

NCR
1700 S. Patterson Blvd.
Dayton, OH 45479
(513) 445-5000

NetTech, Inc.
4040 Barrett Drive
Raleigh, NC 27609
(919) 781-7887

Network Application
 Technology, Inc.
1686 Dell Ave.
Campbell, CA 95008
(408) 370-4300

Network General Corp.
4200 Bohannon Drive
Menlo Park, CA 94025

Network Management Forum
1201 Mt. Kemble Ave.
Morristown, NJ 07960-6628

KPY Network Partners, Inc.
2290 N. First St., Suite 310
San Jose, CA 95131

Novell, Inc. (ManageWise)
2180 Fortune Drive
San Jose, CA 95131
(800) 638-9273

Objective Systems Integrators
110 Blue Ravine Road
Suite 100
Folsom, CA 95630
(916) 989-7340

OnDemand Software
1100 Fifth Avenue South
Suite 208
Naples, Fl 33940-6407
(941) 261-6678

Open Network Enterprises
Via Torricelli 34
20035 Lissone (MI) Italy

OpenVision Technologies, Inc.
7133 Koll Center Pkwy.
Pleasanton, CA 94556

Optical Data Systems, Inc.
1101 E. Arapaho Rd.
Richardson, TX 75081

Onion Peel Software
100829 W. Bridgeford Drive
Raleigh, NC 27606
(919) 233-4526

Peregrine Systems
1959 Palomar Oaks Way

Carlsbad, CA 92009
(619) 431-2400

Platinum Technology
Oakbrook Terrace, IL
(708) 620-5116

Prolin Automation
2420 Sand Hill Road
Suite 101
Menlo Park, CA 94025
(415) 854-7489

Remedy Corp.
1505 Salado Drive
Mountain View, CA 94043
(415) 903-5200

SAS Institute, Inc.
SAS Campus Drive
Cary, NC 27513
(919) 677-8000

Seagate Enterprise Management
  Software, Inc.
19925 Stevens Creek Blvd.
Cupertino, CA 95014
(408) 342-4500

SNMP Research International
3001 Kimberlin Heights Road
Knoxville, TN 37920
(423) 579-3311

StonyBrook Software
630 Johnson Ave., Suite 4
Bohemia, NY 11716
(516) 567-6060

SunSoft, Inc.
2550 Garcia Ave.
Mountain View, CA 94043
(415) 960-3200

SynOptics Communications, Inc.
4401 Great America Pkwy
Santa Clara, CA 95054
(408) 988-2400

Talarian Corp.
444 Castro St., Suite 140
Mountain View, CA 94041

Teknekron Communications
  Systems, Inc.
2121 Allston Way
Berkeley, CA 94706

Telamon
492 Ninth St., Suite 310
Oakland, CA 94607-4098
(916) 622-0630

Template Software, Inc.
13100 Worldgate Drive
Suite 340
Herndon, VA 22070

Tivoli Systems, Inc.
9442 Capital of Texas
  Highway N
Austin, TX 78759
(512) 794-9070

Tom Sawyer Software Corp.
1824B 4th St.
Berkeley, CA 94710

UB Networks
3900 Freedom Circle
Santa Clara, CA 95054
(408) 496-0111

Unison Software
5101 Patrick Henry Drive
Santa Clara, CA 95054
(408) 988-2800

Unix Integration Services
11033 Aurora Ave.
Urbandale, IA 50532
(515) 254-3074

ViaTech Division of Platinum
2459 15th St. NW
New Brighton, MN 55112

Wandel & Goltermann
  Technologies
2200 Gateway Centre Blvd.
Morrisville, NC 2756009228
(919) 460-3300

References

Listed below are the sources cited throughout the text of the book, with citations of the form: **(Bailey 1996)**.

Bailey, Angela. "Hub Management Applications." *Datapro Network Management* (May 1996). **(Bailey 1996)**

Desai, Vishal. "Integrating OpenView with Remedy's AR System." *The OpenView Advisor,* Volume 2, Number 1 (January 1996). **(Desai 1996)**

Francett, Barbara. "HP OpenView for Windows." *The OpenView Advisor* (November 1995). **(Francett 1995)**

Hewlett-Packard Company. *HP OpenView Network Node Manager Administrator's Reference, HP 9000 Series*, Part Number J2316-90005. Ft. Collins, Colo.: Hewlett-Packard Company, 1993. **(Hewlett-Packard 1993)**

———. *HP OpenView SNMP Management Platform Performance and Configuration Guide with HP Network Node Manager Examples for Release 3.3*. Ft. Collins, Colo.: Hewlett-Packard Co., 1994. **(Hewlett-Packard 1994a)**

———. *HP OpenView AdminCenter Technical Evaluation Guide Revision 1.0*. Ft. Collins, Colo.: Hewlett-Packard Co., **1994b**

———. *HP OpenView Workgroup Node Manager User's Guide*. Santa Clara, Calif.: Hewlett-Packard Company, 1994. **(Hewlett-Packard Windows 1994)**

———. *HP OpenView AdminCenter Concepts Guide*. Palo Alto, Calif.: Hewlett-Packard Company, 1995. **(Hewlett-Packard 1995)**

———. *HP OpenView: A Guide to Scalability and Distribution for Network Node Manager*, HP Part No. J1172-90002. Ft. Collins, Colo.: Hewlett-Packard Company, April 1996. **(Hewlett-Packard 1996)**

Huntington-Lee, Jill. "Baselining Is the First Step to Optimizing Networks." *Managing Distributed Systems* (April 1995). **(Huntington-Lee 1994a)**

———. "NetSys Adds Performance Tools." *Datapro Network Analyst* (March 1996). **(Huntington-Lee 1995b)**

———. "Enterprise System Administration Consoles." *Datapro Network Management* (December 1995). **(Huntington-Lee 1995c)**

———. "Bridging Management Platform Islands." *Managing Distributed Systems* (January 1995). **(Huntington-Lee 1995d)**

———. *Profiles in Automation*. San Jose, CA: Boole and Babbage, 1996. **(Huntington-Lee 1996a)**

———. "Automated Performance Reporting Tools," *Datapro Network Management* (February 1996). **(Huntington-Lee 1996b)**

———. "HP Announces Systems Management Products," *Datapro Network Analyst* (April 1996). **(Huntington-Lee 1996c)**

———. "Tivoli Announces Internet Management Strategy," *Datapro Network Analyst* (May 1996). **(Huntington-Lee 1996d)**

———. "Event Management Systems," *Datapro Network Management* (April 1996). **(Huntington-Lee 1996e)**

———. "HP OpenView Event Correlation Services (ECS)." White paper published by Datapro, May 1996. HP Part Number: 5965-1471E **(Huntington-Lee 1996f)**

———. "1996 HP OpenView User's Survey," *Datapro Network Manager* (March 1996). **(Huntington-Lee 1996g)**

International Business Machines. *NetView Association Catalog from IBM and Digital, Sixth Edition*, Document Number G325-6553-01. International Business Machines Corp., 1995. **(IBM 1995)**

Mier, Edwin. "Testing SNMP in Routers," *Network World* (July 1993).   **(Mier 1993)**

Miller, Mark A. *Managing Internetworks with SNMP*. New York: M&T Books, 1993.   **(Miller 1993)**

Morgenthal, Steve, and Huntington-Lee, Jill. "Network Management Principles." Presented at ComNet '96 (January 28, 1996), Washington, D.C.   **(Morgenthal 1996)**

Muller, Nathan J. "Using IT/Operations for Internet Management," *The OpenView Advisor*, Volume 2, Number 3 (March 1996).   **(Muller 1996)**

Nemeth, Evi. *UNIX Systems Administration Handbook, 2d Edition*. New York: Prentice-Hall PTR, 1995.   **(Nemeth 1995)**

Reeder, Ed. "Enterprise Networks and TMN," Auerbach Publications, 1994. Warren, Gorham, and Lamont—*Data Communications Management*

Schulzrinne, Henning. "World Wide Web: Whence, Whither, What Next?" *IEEE Network* (March/April 1996).   **(Schulzrinne 1996)**

Stallings, William. *TCP/IP, 2d Edition*. Reading, Mass.: Addison-Wesley, 1993.   **(Stallings 1993)**

Terplan, Kornel, and Huntington-Lee, Jill. *Applications for Distributed Systems and Network Management*. New York: Van Nostrand Reinhold, 1995.   **(Terplan 1995)**

Udupa, Divakara K. *Network Management Systems Essentials*. New York: McGraw-Hill, 1996.   **(Udupa 1996)**

Waldbusser, Steven. "Network Topology: Helping OpenView Map the Network," *The OpenView Advisor,* Volume 1, Number 2 (March 1995).   **(Waldbusser 1995)**

Waldbusser, Steven; Hoerth, Mark; and Nair, S "RMON," *Data Communications Magazine* (May 1992). **(Waldbusser 1992)**

Index

ABOUT THE AUTHORS

Jill Huntington-Lee is manager of New Business Development with SNMP Research International of Knoxville, Tennessee, and has more than 12 years of experience in the computer industry.

Kornel Terplan is author of *Effective Management of Local Area Networks* and *Benchmarking for Network Management.* He is recognized worldwide for his network management expertise.

Jeffrey A. Gibson is director of systems integration for Fiberlink Systems and has designed, implemented, and supported many network management systems using OpenView.